CAPTAIN CHARLES STUART

ANTHONY J. BARKER

Captain Charles Stuart

ANGLO-AMERICAN ABOLITIONIST

LOUISIANA STATE UNIVERSITY PRESS

BATON ROUGE AND LONDON

Copyright © 1986 by Louisiana State University Press
ALL RIGHTS RESERVED
Manufactured in the United States of America
Typeface: Linotron Aldus
Typesetter: Moran Colorgraphic
Printer: Thomson-Shore, Inc.
Binder: John H. Dekker & Sons, Inc.

LIBRARY OF CONGRESS CATALOGING IN PUBLICATION DATA

Barker, Anthony J.
   Captain Charles Stuart, Anglo-American abolitionist.
   Bibliography: p.
   Includes index.
     1. Stuart, Charles, 1781–1865. 2. Abolitionists—United States—Biography. 3. Abolitionists—Great Britain—Biography. 4. Slavery—United States—Anti-slavery movements. 5. Slavery—Great Britain—Anti-slavery movements. I. Title.
E449.S926B37   1986   973.7'114'0924 [B]   85-23703
ISBN 0-8071-1256-9

Publication of this book has been assisted by a grant from the Andrew W. Mellon Foundation.

In loving memory of my father
GEORGE PERCIVAL BARKER, 1905–1985

CONTENTS

Acknowledgments IX
Abbreviations XIII
Preface 1

1 MOST TRYING TIMES 10
2 A SACRED PURSUIT DISCOVERED 38
3 AMERICAN ISSUES IN BRITAIN 64
4 AGENT OF THE AMERICAN ANTI-SLAVERY SOCIETY 86
5 AMERICAN AFFILIATIONS 120
6 THE APOSTLE OF THE NEGRO 143
7 WEST INDIAN COMMENTARIES 159
8 WORLD CONVENTION 188
9 THE WRATH OF CAPTAIN STUART 201
10 THE SENSE OF BETRAYAL 223
11 FOR AND AGAINST BROAD STREET 236
12 ANTISLAVERY ALIENATION AND FAMINE RELIEF 259
13 RETIREMENT, MARRIAGE, AND ISOLATION 274
14 TERRIBLE ORTHODOXY 287

BIBLIOGRAPHY 311
INDEX 321

ACKNOWLEDGMENTS

I am pleased to thank formally the Trustees of the Boston Public Library for their courtesy in allowing me to quote from letters by and about Charles Stuart; the Director of the William L. Clements Library, University of Michigan, Ann Arbor, for permission to quote from letters in the Weld-Grimké Papers; the Houghton Library, Harvard University, for permission to quote from a letter by Stuart to Charles Sumner, dated Lora, June 1, 1856; and the George Arents Research Library for Special Collections at Syracuse University for giving me access to large numbers of Stuart letters in the Gerrit Smith Papers. My gratitude to all these institutions and many others goes far beyond formal acknowledgment. The staffs of the three major repositories of Stuart material mentioned above answered my questions with great courtesy and efficiency. From the Clements Library and the Arents Research Library I received photocopies and microfilm with exemplary speed. The staff of the Department of Rare Books and Manuscripts at the Boston Public Library provided superb service during my several weeks of research there. I am particularly grateful to the officials and staff of the John Rylands Library, Manchester, for making special arrangements for me to work there at a time when the building was otherwise closed by a heating failure. I also thank sincerely officials and staff of the other main British centers of my research: the India Office Library, London; Rhodes House Library, Oxford; the Mitchell Library, Glasgow; and the British Library and Goldsmiths Library, London, which were sources exclusively for printed—mainly pamphlet—material. Finally, among those institutions whose resources form the substance of this book I thank the Australian National Library, Canberra, the Library of Congress, and the Widener Library, Harvard University, from all of which I obtained useful material in microfilm collections. I also acknowledge the helpful cooperation of the Reid Library in the University of Western Australia, which has much antislavery pamphlet material on microfilm, and which obtained so many materials for me through the interlibrary loan system.

Although the institutions mentioned above collectively provided most of the source material, research also involved inquiries to many others from which the yield was relatively small but the advice received often invaluable. In this respect I am most grateful to Patricia Birkett, Archivist of Pre-Confederation Manuscripts, in the Public Archives of Canada, who answered queries and gave assistance by correspondence with remarkable thoroughness and efficiency. I also thank the Historical Society of Pennsylvania and the New-York Historical Society, both of which sent me photocopies of a few Stuart letters, which, though not reproduced in this book, helped to increase my understanding of his movements. Finally, I gratefully acknowledge the cooperation of the following institutions in sending me photocopies of printed materials by and about Charles Stuart: Cornell University Library; Hiram Walker Historical Museum, Windsor, Ontario; North American Black Historical Museum, Amherstburg, Ontario; Ontario Archives, Toronto; and Windsor Public Library, Ontario.

The process of tracking down material would have been more difficult both practically and emotionally without the help of a number of scholars who answered queries about sources and encouraged me to believe that a biography of Stuart was worthwhile: C. Duncan Rice of New York University; Richard Blackett of Indiana University; Fiona Spiers, Assistant Editor of the Black Abolitionist Papers Project and now working on the Wilberforce Papers; and Nicholas Spence, who is writing the biography of Stuart's contemporary, George Thompson.

Others have helped me even more directly in my research. Without the special knowledge of Peter Marshall of King's College, London University, it would have been impossible for me to find so quickly the large amount of manuscript material about Stuart's military service in the India Office Library, London. Even so, without the note-taking assistance of Lynne and Robert Stevenson of Perth it would have been impossible for me to make the most of that material at the end of a hectic schedule of research in Britain and the United States. Another Perth friend, Robyn

Brine, and her husband have also been immensely kind in pursuing Stuart material for me on their own visits to Britain.

In my own department at the University of Western Australia, Iain Brash has been most generous in reading a major portion of the manuscript, despite heavy pressure of teaching and administrative duties. I thank him for pointing out a number of errors in the background of British politics and of course absolve him from responsibility for errors that others may find. Dianne Hollis deserves special praise for faultless typing and endless good temper in retyping many passages when I discovered my own mistakes or changed my mind or simply lost whole pages. I also thank Pam Low, Nancy McKenzie, and Judy Charbonneau, who shared the boring business of typing late revisions.

For my wife and three daughters it was no doubt exciting but also potentially disruptive to accompany me around the world in pursuit of this research. The assistance of my English relatives in keeping disruption to a minimum was welcome but expected. What was quite unexpected was the friendly hospitality of Ron and Brenda Lyman of Lynn, Massachusetts, who had never met any of us before and yet who attended to our every need. I will never be able to thank them adequately for making the American section of our travels so happy. In the process, by enabling me to devote myself so completely to research, they made as important a contribution to the completion of this book as any of those who rendered direct assistance.

ABBREVIATIONS

ACS   American Colonization Society Papers (microfilm), Australian National Library, Canberra
AMA   American Missionary Association Archives (microfilm), Widener Library, Harvard University, Cambridge, Massachusetts
BFASS   Minute Books of the British and Foreign Anti-Slavery Society, S. 20, E2/6, Rhodes House Library, Oxford
BPL   Antislavery Papers, American Anti-Slavery Society Records and New England Anti-Slavery Society Records, Department of Rare Books and Manuscripts, Boston Public Library
GES   Glasgow Emancipation Society Records, Smeal Donation, Mitchell Library, Glasgow
JR   Raymond English Deposit, John Rylands Library, Manchester
IOL   India Office Library, London
PAC   Public Archives of Canada, Ottawa
RHL   Manuscripts of British Empire, Rhodes House Library, Oxford
SP   Gerrit Smith Papers, George Arents Research Library, Syracuse University, Syracuse, New York
WP   Weld-Grimké Papers, William L. Clements Library, University of Michigan, Ann Arbor, Michigan

CAPTAIN CHARLES STUART

PREFACE

CAPTAIN CHARLES STUART is not a totally unknown figure. Two related interests led me to him and revealed, in reference works and monographs, the bare outline of his extraordinarily varied career. After concluding in an earlier book that there were no causal connections between background racial attitudes and the relatively sudden beginnings of the British antislavery movement, I was interested in looking more directly at the people in the foreground who decided to challenge a centuries-old institution.[1] Major trends in interpretation of the downfall of British colonial slavery seemed to encourage new analysis of the motives and activities of these humanitarians. Once seen as the major cause of abolition, humanitarianism had been temporarily thrust into the background by Eric Williams' famous economic interpretation, *Capitalism and Slavery*. Although few historians remained fully satisfied with Williams' view, it was only in the 1970s that thoroughly persuasive rebuttals emerged in Seymour Drescher's *Econocide: British Slavery in the Era of Abolition* and Roger Anstey's *The Atlantic Slave Trade and British Abolition, 1760–1810*. If Drescher was correct that slavery was actually a healthy and indeed expanding economic force in the early nineteenth century, and if he and Anstey were right in their denials that the antislavery decisions were secured by the increasingly important industrial capitalist class, there seemed renewed justification for looking closely at someone who conspicuously campaigned for abolition.

The failure of abolitionism in the United States—where slavery was

1. Anthony J. Barker, *The African Link: British Attitudes to the Negro in the Era of the Atlantic Slave Trade, 1550–1807* (London, 1978).

not a distant overseas problem but woven into the socioeconomic fabric—is much easier to explain than its success in the British Empire. But the intractability of the problem did not prevent some American abolitionists from looking to Britain for inspiration and positively encouraged some of their British counterparts to turn from their own success to tackle the American institution. And as the fight against American slavery stretched through decades of frustration, abolitionists on both sides of the Atlantic argued about tactics and about the relationship between abolition and other reform goals. In these circumstances the career of an individual who worked in both British and American antislavery movements was potentially illuminating.

A few glimpses of Stuart—mainly in footnotes—in accounts of British antislavery would not on their own have convinced me that he was significant.[2] But American references to him were more intriguing. In some he was mentioned briefly as a "saintly" British abolitionist who had influenced Theodore Weld, a man often regarded as one of the greatest of all American abolitionists.[3] And Betty Fladeland, in the most detailed account of the Anglo-American antislavery community, revealed him as a colorful eccentric who had been involved in important antislavery activities on both sides of the Atlantic. The British *Dictionary of National Biography* had no entry on Stuart, but in its American and Canadian counterparts there was sufficient biographical information to suggest that Stuart might be almost uniquely representative of an Anglo-American antislavery impulse. What could be more fitting for an American abolitionist than to be born in 1783—the year independence was recognized—and to die in 1865, weeks after the end of the Civil War? As early as 1820 he had been "waging successful war with the Negro slavery of the United States" by helping black fugitives in Canada. Subsequently, like many American abolitionists, he had been involved in numerous reform activities in upstate New York, where he had been a convert of Charles Grandison Finney, one of the most famous of American religious revivalists. A decade later, after opposing the American Colonization Society in Britain, he had

---

2. For example, Lowell Joseph Ragatz, *The Fall of the Planter Class in the British Caribbean, 1763–1833* (New York, 1928), 452; Christine Bolt, *The Anti-Slavery Movement and Reconstruction: A Study in Anglo-American Co-operation, 1833–77* (London, 1969), 7. Stuart's connections with Weld and his familiarity with America are, however, indicated in footnotes in Howard Temperley, *British Antislavery, 1833–1870* (Columbia, S.C., 1972), 13, 195.

3. Alice Felt Tyler, *Freedom's Ferment: Phases of Social History from the Colonial Period to the Outbreak of the Civil War* (New York, 1962), 491; Dwight L. Dumond, *Antislavery: The Crusade for Freedom in America* (New York, 1966), 169.

been an agent of the American Anti-Slavery Society in the same New York region. Even in retirement in the 1850s he had apparently been a confidant of John Brown immediately before the notorious raid at Harpers Ferry. Yet this American abolitionist was also a British abolitionist, taking part as pamphleteer and lecturer in the campaign that in 1833 had ended slavery in the British Empire. And could there be anyone more representative of that far-flung British world than a man born in the slave society of Jamaica, educated in Belfast, who had served as a soldier in India and had twice lived for lengthy periods in Canada?[4]

Research into a single antislavery career—even one as remarkable as Stuart's—was not, I knew well, likely to revolutionize understanding of why people had turned against slavery in the late eighteenth and early nineteenth centuries. It was far more likely that I would gain insights into Stuart's behavior from the arguments of other historians about these processes. His experiences with non-Europeans—in Jamaica, in India, and on the Canadian frontier—might well have made him representative of an arrogant strain of abolitionism, recently described by Howard Temperley, in which determination to overthrow slavery was linked to a view of progress that assumed domination by Western civilization.[5] Nevertheless, despite his strenuous activities on the rim of the civilized world, Stuart was also emerging as a representative of the agonizing religious intensity which all historians would see as a major ingredient of the antislavery impulse. He was said to have had a rigorous upbringing from Presbyterian parents imbued with Calvinist principles. If this background did not conform to Bertram Wyatt-Brown's profile of young Americans who emerged from essentially evangelical backgrounds to become abolitionists or missionaries, Stuart, after all, was not quite American. But in Canada, he had undergone the "conversion experience of rich personal

---

4. Betty Fladeland, *Men and Brothers: Anglo-American Antislavery Co-operation* (Urbana, 1972), 197, 200, 212–16, 219, 221, 225–26, 276, 280; quotation from *Dictionary of Canadian Biography*, IX, 769–70. Weld's significance was first argued by Dumond, *Antislavery*, and Gilbert H. Barnes, *The Antislavery Impulse* (New York, 1933), who together published much of his correspondence: *Letters of Theodore Dwight Weld, Angelina Grimké Weld, and Sarah Grimké, 1822–1844* (2 vols.; New York, 1934). Barnes was the author of Weld's and Stuart's entries in the *Dictionary of American Biography*, XVIII, 162–63; XIX, 625–27. A later biography of Weld, which mentions Stuart's influence but contains relatively little information about the man, is Benjamin P. Thomas, *Theodore Weld: Crusader for Freedom* (New Brunswick, N.J., 1950).

5. Howard Temperley, "Anti-Slavery as a Form of Cultural Imperialism," in Christine Bolt and Seymour Drescher (eds.), *Anti-Slavery, Religion, and Reform: Essays in Memory of Roger Anstey* (Folkestone, 1980), 335–50.

meaning" also stressed by Wyatt-Brown. He had indeed become a missionary as well as an abolitionist.[6]

In one important respect, however, it seemed that exploration of Stuart's career might further illuminate the antislavery movement. In the late 1820s and early 1830s many abolitionists abruptly abandoned gradualist methods and began to insist on an immediate end to slavery. As David Brion Davis has shown, immediatism could have different meanings for different individuals, ranging from an insistence on the immediate overthrow of slavery to a belief that "slavery should be abolished without compromise, though not necessarily without honest preparation." Davis has also shown that the emergence of immediatism was the result of varied changes. These included a shift in strategy by antislavery activists who had seen the failure of gradualist methods and a more general and complex change in intellectual attitudes as many people discarded the passive eighteenth-century belief in the inevitability of progress in favor of active personal commitment to make no compromise with sin. Although Charles Stuart was only one individual who apparently underwent this transformation from gradualism to immediatism, his unique international background promised to make him particularly important to that part of Davis' argument which sees the crucial changes in antislavery thought as essentially parallel developments on either side of the Atlantic. That theme has indeed been pushed even further by Fladeland, who argues that by the 1830s American and British antislavery activity was almost inextricably intertwined.[7]

Stuart's significance in this regard, however, was by no means clear even from Fladeland's study. His influence on Weld seemed rather to support the contention of earlier historians that American immediatism was largely

6. Bertram Wyatt-Brown, "Conscience and Career: Young Abolitionists and Missionaries," in Bolt and Drescher (eds.), *Anti-Slavery* 181–203. Another recent study, analyzing the religious commitment of many abolitionists, briefly mentions Stuart but only as part of an examination of Theodore Weld's commitment without considering Stuart's background as an English emancipationist: Donald M. Scott, "Abolition as a Sacred Vocation," in Lewis Perry and Michael Fellman (eds.), *Antislavery Reconsidered: New Perspectives on the Abolitionists* (Baton Rouge, 1979), 70.

7. Davis' exhaustive treatment of the origins and development of antislavery attitudes is contained in his two books: *The Problem of Slavery in Western Culture* (Ithaca, N.Y., 1966) and *The Problem of Slavery in the Age of Revolution, 1770–1823* (Ithaca, N.Y., 1975). A succinct statement of his views, from which the quotation is taken, is his "Immediatism: A Product of American and British Antislavery Thought," in Richard O. Curry (ed.), *The Abolitionists* (Hinsdale, Ill., 1973), 64–75. See also David Brion Davis, "Slavery and Sin: The Cultural Background," in Martin Duberman (ed.), *The Antislavery Vanguard: New Essays on the Abolitionists* (Princeton, 1965), 3–31; Fladeland, *Men and Brothers*, ix.

derived from Britain.[8] So too did the assertion by Donald G. Simpson in the *Canadian Dictionary of Biography* that Stuart's "writings influenced the growth in the 1820s and 1830s of the antislavery movement in the United States." More in line with Davis' and Fladeland's views was the strong implication that Stuart's revivalist background might be as important as his British nationality. The crucial questions that were not yet clearly answered were not merely when Stuart became an immediatist—and in what sense—but when he became an abolitionist. And if, as the accounts implied, he was already an abolitionist throughout the 1820s, why did it take him more than five years to convert Weld, whom he had befriended in 1825?

There were many other uncertainties in the record, including, for instance, the question of whether in India he had been a heroic casualty in a sepoy mutiny or an enlightened critic of the way British forces had suppressed that uprising.[9] Overshadowing all these doubts was the general question: why was such an individual not better known? The vast range of his activities, with frequent movements that may have made him a perpetual outsider among antislavery leaders, hinted at one possible answer. But the records of the first great international antislavery gathering indicated to the contrary and, in the process, opened up an even more intractable research problem. "Captain Charles Stuart" appears as a tiny, nondescript face in the crowd of 136 delegates in Benjamin Robert Haydon's group portrait of the 1840 General Anti-Slavery Convention now in the National Portrait Gallery, London. The likeness is anonymous and unusable, and so, in the absence of alternatives, this is a biography without a portrait of its subject. And yet not only was a portrait painted, but Stuart was sufficiently respected for engravings from it to be advertised for sale to the antislavery faithful at the time of the convention.[10] It is hard to believe that both Edward Kilvert's original portrait and all the engravings from it are forever lost. But nothing more clearly emphasizes that Stuart was a once respected figure who drifted into obscurity than his absence from the holdings, or even records, of British galleries, libraries, and museums with collectively tens of thousands of portraits in their care.

One probable reason why Stuart remained in obscurity was that he did not marry until old age and sired no descendants to preserve his papers or write filial biographies such as had glorified the names of William Lloyd

---

8. See particularly Gilbert H. Barnes, "The Western Revival Origins," in Curry (ed.), *Abolitionists*, 12–13.

9. These alternative versions are discussed inconclusively in Fred Landon, "Captain Charles Stuart, Abolitionist," *Western Ontario History Nuggets*, No. 24 (1956), 1–19.

10. *Anti-Slavery Reporter*, I (1840), 144.

Garrison and William Wilberforce, leading figures in the American and British movements, respectively.[11] Existing biographical information derived from just two sources: the introduction by Gilbert Barnes and Dwight Dumond to their two-volume collection of the letters of Theodore Weld and his wife, Angelina Grimké; and an article by Fred Landon, discussing mainly Stuart's periods in Canada. These two references provided mixed encouragement to a would-be biographer. Although there was no collection of Stuart papers, many of his letters were in the Weld-Grimké collection—some of them published by Barnes and Dumond—and also, it appeared, a short biographical essay, apparently in Weld's hand, which was doubtless the source for the published outline of his career. Landon, writing a quarter of a century ago, relied to some extent on oral tradition and interviews with aged descendants of people who had known Stuart in his final days.[12] Any biographer would jump at the chance to interview people with even a secondhand knowledge of his subject. And any biographer would regard as important a memoir apparently written by his subject's closest friend. Unhappily, the passage of another generation ruled out the possibility of further oral research and, frustratingly, the archivists in Michigan, who helpfully and efficiently made available on microfilm the Stuart-Weld correspondence, were unable to find a short biographical essay in Weld's or any other hand.

Much later—when research was virtually completed—two new studies, each of them impressive in its main concerns, referred to Stuart without adding to the standard biographical accounts. In *Passionate Liberator: Theodore Weld and the Dilemma of Reform*, Robert H. Abzug has provided a sympathetic view of Stuart's influence on Weld though he relies wholly on Landon's account of his formative years. More surprisingly, C. Duncan Rice in his book *The Scots Abolitionists, 1833–1861* has simply described Stuart, without explanation, as a "Scottish" abolitionist.

Although Rice's comment in particular is puzzling, for the purposes of these two writers it was scarcely crucial to pursue the real Stuart. But for a would-be biographer the loss of the primary sources on which previous glimpses of the man had depended meant that research was to be, even more than had seemed likely, a question of letters and visits to numerous libraries and archives on both sides of the Atlantic. Fortunately, Stuart proved to have been as prolific a writer as he was mobile, and there grad-

11. Wendell P. Garrison and Francis J. Garrison, *William Lloyd Garrison, 1805–1879: The Story of His Life Told by His Children* (4 vols., New York, 1885–89); Robert Isaac Wilberforce and Samuel Wilberforce, *Life of William Wilberforce* (5 vols.; London, 1838).

12. Landon, "Captain Charles Stuart," 2, 18 n. 21; Barnes and Dumond (eds.), *Weld-Grimké Letters*, I, xx–xxi, 6.

ually accumulated a considerable body of manuscript material—the main items hundreds of letters to Weld and the New York abolitionist Gerrit Smith—and also of books, pamphlets, articles, and letters to editors by Stuart. All of this amounted to a full documentation of an antislavery career that proved as varied as the earliest routine inquiries had suggested. But what also gradually emerged from scrutiny of this material was that the inability to tap Canadian oral tradition or to read the missing biographical fragment was perhaps not after all a handicap. The broad outline of Stuart's career in the reference works may have been true, but many of the details—presumably emanating from these lost sources—were clearly wrong.

Scattered references to his age in his letters suggested that he was born, not in 1783, but in 1781. The Canadian census of 1851—which coincided with the start of his retirement on the shores of Georgian Bay—both confirmed this earlier birth date and resolved a doubt that had arisen in my mind about his birthplace, since many letters written during a long stay in Jamaica in 1839 and 1840 made no references to a return to the island of his birth. The census revealed that he was born in Bermuda.[13]

Research has not positively confirmed—but leaves no reason to doubt—that his father was a British army officer, who had fought in the American Revolution. His own enlistment as a cadet officer in India at the age of seventeen and the dearth of references in his later letters to boyhood haunts are consistent with a mobile military background. He evidently spent some time in his youth in New Brunswick, but he revealed no particular affection for that region, and his loyalties were always to the British Empire rather than to a specific place. In these circumstances the Bermuda birthplace was probably both fortuitous and inconsequential. Yet in its isolated Atlantic location the island is nicely symbolic of a background that was, from the circumstantial evidence, a mixture of British and American ingredients. His parents were eventually buried in the United States, three of his sisters lived there, and the fourth lived in Canada.[14] But despite these connections and his own long periods in America, he remained staunchly British in his loyalties.

His education in Belfast has also not been confirmed by research, but

13. 1851 Census: Collingwood Township, Grey County, Canada West, Personal Census, microfilm reel C-11723, PAC.
14. Charles Stuart to Theodore Weld, October 7, 1828, WP; *Liberator*, May 17, 1834, p. 79. Stuart's sisters were Mary (married name Rankin), who lived in Toronto in adult life; Harriet (del Hoyo), Charlotte (Shippey), and Anne, who all lived in or near New York City (Stuart to Weld, January 3, July 10, 1843, August 2, 1844, November 5, 1850, April 17, October 31, 1853; Stuart to Sarah Grimké, February 12, 1853, WP).

his later life revealed Irish affiliations that make this background plausible. Although such a background would be consistent with an anti-Catholicism that always conditioned his responses to Irish poverty, Stuart's letters reveal that the religious fervor, which became characteristic of the mature man, was not the result of youthful indoctrination. The biographical essays insist that his parents were "Presbyterians of an extreme Calvinistic type." Yet in his own first book, in 1820, he described himself as "by birth, and by all the tender associations of youth (to which my soul is alive) a member of the established church, and still her friend." His private letters revealed that it was after "I grew up and mixed with the world" that "extreme Calvinistic views of God, were offered to me by very dear friends." And in contrast to the suggestion in the secondary sources of a rigorous childhood religious training, it was only as an adult that he began to discover the Bible. "My early youth & manhood were entirely destitute of Scriptural instruction," he told Theodore Weld.[15]

His upbringing could well have been rigorous without being religious. But his own oblique account makes this doubtful, even as it reveals a troubled childhood burdened with a sense of guilt. His recollections were of a lonely, unguided search for values, rather than rejection of an unpalatably strict regimen. Long before he had the Bible to guide him—and when he had "nothing to do with the churches"—several things "proclaimed to me 'C. Stuart thou art a sinner.'" But these were his study of history and "the intuitions of my nature," not the discipline of his relatives, "who taught me otherwise." Through adolescence "my sense of sin & want continued & harrassed me; until . . . the pride of virtue & of reason destroyed me; and self-complacency, took in a measure the place of self-humiliation."[16]

Not only does his own emphasis on self-instruction and "self-humiliation" suggest the absence of strong parental influence. For a man whose correspondence was extravagantly emotional and frank the omission of virtually all references to his parents is striking. In a couple of public speeches he mentioned that their remains were in the United States, no doubt an effort to underline his credentials as an almost-American abolitionist.[17] But in his private letters the passing references just quoted were all that he had to say about them. Obviously any searching psychological

15. *DCB*, IX, 769; *DAB*, XVIII, 162; Landon, "Captain Charles Stuart," 2; Charles Stuart, *The Emigrant's Guide to Upper Canada or, Sketches of the Present State of That Province, Collected from a Residence Therein During the Years 1817, 1818, 1819* . . . (London, 1820), 225; Stuart to Weld, August, 1859, WP.
16. Stuart to Gerrit Smith, September 3, 1859, SP.
17. *Liberator*, May 17, 1834, p. 79; *Emancipator*, August 5, 1834.

interpretation of his personality would require much more information to establish whether this silence was the result of alienation or a childhood of separation. As the only male among five children he might have felt a certain isolation in a family situation. As the only son in a military family he may well have been consigned to the separate, distant education the reference books insist he had in Belfast.

These speculative inferences can be pushed no further. Stuart's own reticence and other deficiencies in the record make it necessary to accept his contention that his essential life began with discovery of the Bible. His generalized reminiscences do not put a date on this discovery, but his references to early manhood argue that it must have been in India. In 1798, at the age of seventeen, Charles Stuart sailed from Britain for India as a cadet officer in the Madras army of the East India Company. He became a lieutenant in 1801 in the Fifteenth Regiment, Native Infantry, and in 1806 transferred with the same rank to the newly formed Twenty-first Regiment.[18] To all appearances he was embarked on a straightforward, rather anonymous career. But the religion he had found and his own strange personality were to make his remaining years in India a crucial prelude to a much more significant later career.

---

18. *India Registers* (London, 1768–1876), 1800, p. 168; 1801, p. 120; 1806, p. 222; Register of Cadets, L/Mil./9/255, f. 140v. IOL.

1 MOST TRYING TIMES

THE OBSCURITY that envelopes Charles Stuart's formative years becomes less impenetrable after his arrival in India, for here he became "Captain Stuart" in an army that left copious records. The campaigns by Lord Wellesley, which transformed the Madras Presidency of the East India Company from a precarious outpost to the dominant power in southern India during the early years of Stuart's service, provide a plausible context for romantic notions about his military background. Here was no shortage of battles in which he might have acquired the bullet he was said by some to have carried in his body to the end of his days. Here there was indeed a notable sepoy mutiny at Vellore in 1804, which was also to find a place in oral tradition current in Canada after his death in 1865: he was said to have earned the disfavor of authority by condemning the ruthlessness with which the uprising was suppressed.[1]

Yet although the military records shed light on the man, they do not confirm these colorful rumors. Because the name "Stuart" is relatively common—and must always be checked under the alternative spellings of "Stewart" and "Steuart"—references to the right individual are not always easy to establish, and the complexity of the records makes it difficult to deny with certainty the specific details of incidents that could be recorded in numerous possible locations. The clear outline of his career, however, reveals no stage when he was incapacitated by wounds.[2] It does

---

1. Percival Spear, *A History of India*, II (Harmondsworth, Middlesex, 1971), 100–105; Landon, "Captain Charles Stuart," 3.
2. The outline of Stuart's career can be traced in the printed annual *India Registers* (1768–1876), also available on microfiche. The details have been researched in many groups of papers in the archives of the IOL, especially the Madras Military Consultations.

not rule out the possibility of action but establishes a norm of administrative rather than fighting service, which is consistent with the single recollection of Indian service in his private letters of Persian language studies rather than the battlefield.[3] And the records of the Vellore mutiny provide no evidence of Stuart's criticisms of British brutality. Instead, the archives provide less dramatic but no less revealing insights into his character and experience. Whether or not there was a bullet in his body, Stuart carried to the end of his days emotional scars from an Indian career that ended in disgrace in the aftermath of a different mutiny.

TO ANYONE familiar with the later abolitionist, the figure who emerges in the Madras military records for 1806 as Lieutenant Stuart, Hindustani instructor to the cadet officers at Cuddalore, is unmistakable. Amid the fog of cryptic references to probably several Stuarts, the instructor's memorandum to his superiors reveals an already intense, contentious individualist.

Stuart had evidently been recently commended for his work, for he began by expressing the "purest Satisfaction" at the approbation of his superiors and a firm intention to continue as "zealously as ever." These words, however, introduced an appraisal of the language program from which only Charles Stuart emerged with any credit. Although the cadets were attending compulsory classes in the mornings, most were woefully casual about their studies. They were less interested in the private instruction he had arranged outside teaching hours than in clandestine visits to Pondichery and Madras or illicit drinking bouts closer to home. By contrast, Stuart was incessantly at work instructing the cadets and, particularly, directing a team of thirty-three native "moonshees," who were compelled to share his dedication. The moonshees were meant to assist with instruction, but they also spent long periods copying manuscripts. Ten of them, who were unlucky enough to be either poor at English or very neat at writing, were, he reported, "constantly writing in my house" from 6:00 a.m. to 5:00 p.m. with an hour off for breakfast. They had produced one hundred copies of a short, simple grammar he had written when he had found himself expected to carry out his duties with an inadequate number of copies of a printed work that was also inadequate in content. There was an urgent need for the authorities either to publish a printed grammar and dictionary or to employ a separate group of writers to transcribe his manuscript. The laborious methods he had described, he

3. Stuart to Gerrit Smith, May 1, 1835, SP.

concluded in a studied understatement, "do not seem to me the most efficient that could be adopted."[4]

Despite the picture it suggests of a lone European constantly in the company of Indians, openly critical of junior officers, and cautiously sarcastic about the policies of superiors, this memorandum was in no way the work of a radical subversive. The long hours with Indian subordinates may conceivably have influenced his later sympathies for black slaves. But, more demonstrably, they conditioned or confirmed convictions about the beneficence of British imperialism, which he would never lose. He stressed the twofold potential of a properly backed language program. While British officers learned native languages so they could command, Indian instructors would improve their English, a process "which must have a very sensible influence in advancing the Enlightened views of government." In later years Stuart would many times make more explicit the belief that underlay this remark that Indian society was correspondingly benighted. In his most autobiographical publication he would reminisce about his long exposure in India to the "pre-eminence of Britain's genius," contrasting the "energetic and thriving progress of my country" with the "inert and decaying power of a native state."[5]

Yet in that same publication he revealed a distaste for his brother officers' standard "amusements of balls and plays and flattering female society" that was already foreshadowed in 1806 in his disapproval of the cadets' pursuits of worldly pleasures.[6] Although such puritanism probably isolated him from many of his compatriots, it would have taken an unduly sensitive high command to react unfavorably to the muted criticism of his memorandum. It was to be Stuart's misfortune that in the years ahead an officers' mutiny in the Madras army would induce such sensitivity and that in those circumstances his guarded criticism would be transformed into flagrant insubordination.

The mutiny of 1809 had its roots in several grievances in the army over the previous two years. Basic to the situation were the peculiar circumstances of the East India Company, with its several geographical centers of power, its dual character as trading company and territorial authority, and its ultimate dominance of the subcontinent still neither certain nor even clearly sought. The Madras officers of the company's army had for some time resented the higher allowances paid to their counterparts in Bengal—the center of British influence—and also the undue proportion

4. Madras Military Consultations, Range 255, Vol. 74, pp. 5764–69, Vol. 79, pp. 8314–22, IOL.
5. Ibid.; Stuart, *Emigrant's Guide*, 194–95.
6. Stuart, *Emigrant's Guide*, 160–61.

of commands allegedly given to officers of the royal army. More immediate grievances, emerging in 1808, concerned the sudden removal of financial perquisites, including a monthly allowance to officers for providing camp equipage and carriage for their troops. This allowance had been insufficient for its purposes during periods of active duty such as the long campaigns in southern India from 1803 to 1806. The decision to end it came in a time of peace, when officers hoped to recoup some of the expenses incurred during those years of heavy wear and tear on equipment.

Soon many officers became aware that Lieutenant-Colonel John Munro, the quartermaster general of the army, had supported the decision. He was placed under arrest, accused of justifying his support for the measure with "false and infamous insinuations" against his brother officers. His response was to appeal to the civil government, which ordered the commander in chief, Lieutenant General Hay Macdowall, to release him. Macdowall, who was on the verge of retirement, was so incensed at being overruled that, on his departure from Madras, he left for publication to the army an order severely reprimanding Munro for appealing to the civil power. The civil government responded by directing this order to be expunged from the public record and by dismissing Macdowall a day or so before his long-planned resignation became effective. At the same time it suspended all the senior officers who had supported him.[7]

A widespread mutiny of officers followed these disciplinary measures. Underlying this apparently extreme reaction was the grim financial reality that in an age of slow communication suspension meant virtual impoverishment for at least a year, pending final decision by the supreme governing body of the East India Company, the Court of Directors in London. No less important, according to the army's nineteenth-century historian, "the Madras government had shown themselves disposed to make an unsparing use of that severe, and theretofore exceptional method of punishment without trial, and without disclosing the evidence upon which they acted."[8]

The mutiny was suppressed by a combination of force and conciliation, with little bloodshed. Its significance for Charles Stuart's career lay in the way it shaped his future circumstances rather than in any immediate involvement. His name does not appear in any of the contemporary records of the mutiny. In 1808, while still language instructor at Cuddalore, he became temporary commander of the cadet company. In 1809, the year

7. William John Wilson, *History of the Madras Army* (5 vols.; London, 1882–89), III, 235–95.
8. *Ibid.*

of the mutiny, he resigned his teaching position but was promoted to lieutenant captain. And in 1811 he achieved further promotion to captain. But though Stuart's steady, unspectacular progress suggests his detachment from the upheavals of the period, the mutiny had created a tense, mistrustful atmosphere which no one could avoid. Although the authorities gave amnesty to virtually all who had mutinied, according to the published history of the Madras army, "the bad feeling, and dissension engendered by these lamentable events did not subside for many years." In 1810 several courts-martial were held on officers accused of "insulting others who had sided with the Government." And in 1812 "an officer was suspended for having refused to dine with Colonel Conran, Commanding the Hyderabad Subsidiary Force, or to make any apology for his refusal." That officer—unnamed in the published history—was Captain Charles Stuart.[9]

Stuart's suspension became a protracted case ending four years later with debate and decision by the Court of Directors in London. The accumulated mass of memorials, reports, orders, and secret letters showed that though he had not been directly involved in the mutiny, he had remained outspokenly critical of the government's arbitrary suspension of officers long after its suppression. Perhaps if he had been a convivial officer, indiscreetly blurting out his opinions over drinks in the mess, his behavior would have seemed less subversive. But, as he pointed out himself, his temperament and principles made him shun such contacts. He lived in "a more secluded manner" than most officers, refusing to drink alcohol and seeking the company of a select few who shared his apparently growing interest in religion. When his corps moved to Bellary at the end of 1810, he messed with three other officers for some weeks, but, becoming aware that his political comments had made him a marked man with the authorities, he ended this arrangement to avoid suspicion of exerting influence on them. Thereafter he messed alone and kept his "obnoxious sentiments" to himself unless asked directly to discuss his views.[10]

These maneuvers were in vain. When his company was transferred to Jalna in central India in mid-1811, secret orders preceded it from the adjutant general warning the commanding officer there, Colonel Conran, to keep a close eye on Stuart, an officer not "disposed to conduct himself with that respect for authority, and on those principles of subordination, which it is the Commander in Chief's determination to enforce throughout the

9. Madras Military Consultations, Range 256, Vol. 39, p. 10224, Vol. 53, p. 6085, IOL; *India Registers*, 1809, p. 220, 1811, p. 220; Wilson, *Madras Army*, III, 293–95.

10. Stuart to his superior officers, n.d., Madras Military Consultations, Range 257, Vol. 52, pp. 5414–16, IOL.

army." Stuart's own account, while strenuously denying any intended insubordination, made it clear why the authorities found his behavior so provocative. En route to Jalna he dined alone and associated "less with the other officers of the Corps than any other officer in it." He was the only one to refuse invitations to hospitality from officers already stationed at Jalna. Arriving on a Sunday, he spent the evening with a particular friend, who shared his belief that religion was the "Primary Duty of every Human being," and the two agreed to spend future Sunday evenings together while at Jalna. On the following Friday Conran acted on his secret orders by issuing the fateful invitation for Stuart to dine with him on the next Sunday.[11]

Stuart was busy paying his company when the invitation arrived. Without leaving his chair and without hesitation—and "regarding the Business as a matter of no importance whatsoever"—he scrawled a refusal, pointing out that he had a prior engagement that Sunday. The provocative nonchalance of his account, like the emphasis he placed on his recent solitary habits, was intended to stress that he was not part of any conspiracy to snub Conran: not until the next day, he claimed, did he hear that Conran had invited some thirteen other officers and only one had accepted. But his refusal led to a series of events that in themselves—and especially in his analysis of them—showed how easy he found it to be provocative.[12]

On the Sunday in question he was interrogated by a senior officer. Stuart pointed out that he was not convinced that this procedure was either "just or legal." But, "anxious to give as little trouble as possible," he proceeded to parry some pointed questions with formidably blunt answers. Was it by accident or design that he had refused Conran's invitation? "It was by accident, because I happened to be engaged, and design because I did intend to refuse any private invitation with which Colonel Conran might possibly honour me." Did he intend to continue to refuse? "I do intend to refuse any future invitation with which Colonel Conran may honor me."[13]

Within hours Conran told Stuart that he would be reported to the authorities in Madras as ringleader of a combination against his superior officers and that, in the meantime, he would be sent under guard to Hyderabad to await further instructions. Stuart denied the charge and

---

11. *Ibid.*; T.H.S. Conway, adjutant-general, to Colonel Conran, April 9, 1811; Madras Military Consultations, Range 257, Vol. 52, pp. 5398–5402, IOL.

12. Stuart to superiors, n.d., Madras Military Consultations, Range 257, Vol. 52, pp. 5419–20.

13. *Ibid.*, 5421–23.

demanded a trial but agreed to obey Conran's orders and expressed facetious gratitude for the "Indulgence of a Guard, so essential in that part of the Country." After safely reaching Hyderabad several weeks later, he wrote to the adjutant general of the army, insisting that he was aware of no principle—"religious, moral, political, or military"—that should have made him regard Conran's invitation as a command. With a legalistic flourish that infuriated the authorities, he reminded them that Lord Cornwallis, "one of the greatest and best men, that has ever graced the British name," had issued a regulation—"still, I believe, unrepealed"—which declared that "Officers in common with other Gentlemen, have a right to choose their private Society." Not for the first or last time he demanded the chance to defend himself at a court-martial.[14]

Although this demand was consistent with his recent criticisms of arbitrary, secretive government, he probably also knew that it placed his antagonists in a quandary. The correspondence that passed among his highest superiors and eventually between Madras and London made it plain that authority was troubled by his insubordination because it revived memories of "sentiments and . . . events, which at one period, threatened to destroy the interest of [the] Country in this quarter of the world." Yet the mutiny had ended with a general amnesty that made it awkward for authority to condemn a man for offenses it connected with the previous disturbances. "A court-martial is out of the question, I suppose," remarked Conran wistfully in his memorandum reporting Stuart's conduct to headquarters. In these circumstances, even though his superiors were writing privately of Stuart's unsuitability for military life, it is clear that he could have saved his career with a simple apology in the weeks after his brush with Conran. A full year after that event, news of his suspension was finally sent from Madras to London. The military authorities reported that after his banishment from Jalna he had been allowed time for reflection and that all possible means had been exerted by the commander in chief, Sir Samuel Auchmuty, "to induce him to correct his improper feeling; but reflection appears only to have strengthened Capt. Stuart . . . in his error; and his punishment has been courted with an obstinacy, equal to the reluctance, with which it has been inflicted."[15]

There is no denying this obstinacy. But the memorials and letters in which it was revealed also showed a relentless consistency of principle.

14. *Ibid.*, 5408–5409, 5426–40.
15. Minute of Lt.-Gen. Sir S. Auchmuty, April 21, 1812; Conran to Maj-Gen. Pater, June 16, 1811, in *ibid.*, 5387–97, 5404–5405; Auchmuty to Court of Directors, June 14, 1812; G. H. Barlow *et al.* to Court of Directors, June 20, 1812, Madras Letters Received, E/4/341, Vol. 39, IOL.

He never denied that he had been critical of arbitrary authority, on occasions in public. His obstinacy lay in his continuing and strenuous denial that he had conspired with or even attempted to influence others. To make the full apologies, which he was repeatedly urged to do as the price of reinstatement, would have been to admit such a conspiracy. And so it was integrity rather than "obstinate infatuation" which, in the words of Auchmuty, was "paving the way to his ruin" by mid-1812.[16]

He could have been in no doubt of the ruinous implications of his suspension because it was the exact form of punishment—imposed in equally secretive circumstances—that had helped provoke the mutiny and his own subsequent criticisms of government. While Auchmuty was writing confidentially to London that Stuart had "unfortunately imbibed principles that, in my opinion, must ever disqualify him for the Military Profession," Stuart himself in June, 1812, put in a caustic application to return to England at the earliest opportunity because "my residence in this Country during the period of my suspension must be perfectly useless to our Honorable Masters." Even so he could not afford to pay his passage, and it was only through the charity of a friendly ship's master that he reached London exactly a year later.[17]

The details of his case had long preceded him, yet no decision had been made about his fate nor would one be finalized for another two years. It was his misfortune that, though his misdemeanor was important enough to require adjudication by the Court of Directors, that body was concerned with far weightier matters. The company's charter had been granted for a twenty-year period in 1793. In the years of Stuart's quarrel with his superiors immediately prior to 1813, an attempt by private interests to break the company's trading monopoly had been a major issue in British political and commercial circles, marked by an extensive pamphlet war. In the background, too, was a growing demand from evangelicals for the company to abandon its laissez-faire attitudes to Indian society and take advantage of its political ascendancy to mount a frontal assault on idolatry, suttee, and other practices repugnant to Christians. All Stuart's later comments on India would show a commitment to this view of Britain's role, an attitude he had already foreshadowed in his remarks on the English language as an agency for enlightenment. But there is no evidence that in the period of his suspension he was incautious enough to become

16. Stuart to superiors, n.d.; to Conran, June 16, 1811; Minute of Auchmuty, Madras Military Consultations, Range 257, Vol. 52, pp. 5394–95, 5408–5409, 5414–40, IOL.

17. Stuart to superiors, June 19, 1812, in *ibid.*, Vol. 57, pp. 8350–51; Auchmuty to Court of Directors, June 14, 1812, Madras Letters Received, E/4/341, IOL; Stuart to Court of Directors, January 14, 1814, Madras Letters Received, E/1/127, p. 20A, IOL.

involved with this evangelical lobby. The preoccupation of the company with these varied strands of criticism was for him mainly a source of irritation when he reported his arrival in London in June, 1813, and requested the court's instructions.[18]

If the renewal of the company's charter later in 1813 raised his hopes for an early decision, he was soon disappointed. By the following January his patience had evaporated. In a long letter, which was alternately aggressive and facetious, he reminded the directors of the years that had elapsed since his suspension for conduct, which "no clause in the Articles of War, no part of your commands, no passage in the regulations of Government, nor any order of any kind that I ever received or heard of, rendered in any degree criminal." He wrote of the "destitution" that had delayed his return to Britain and of his tact in not pressing his attentions on the directors when he found them involved "in matters of great magnitude." But now he knew of no obstacles to prevent his seeking "a portion of your notice." Of course, if there were still "weighty concerns" that made such attention inconvenient, he was ready "cheerfully to await your leisure." But he reminded the directors that it was desirable and important to end his uncertainty, because he was "destitute of every other provision."[19]

At this point, although he may never have known it, Stuart was unlucky. In March, 1814, the court decided that "lenity should be extended to him" and he should be reinstated. But he was never told of that decision, for in June he wrote reminding the directors of his January letter and demanding a decision. Something—perhaps the tone of his recent letters—now prompted the court to ask its appropriate subcommittee to look more closely at the material that had accumulated on the case. Eight months later that body, the Committee of Correspondence, decided that it did not like what it had found. The language Stuart had used in his own defense confirmed "the obnoxious sentiments which had been imputed to him" and made plausible the charge that he had "most unwarrantably attacked the conduct of the Madras government." The committee believed that he ought not be allowed to return to India but recommended that he be permitted to "retire from the Company's Service upon the pay of his rank, viz. 10/- a day."[20]

18. Spear, *History of India*, 116–25; Court Minutes, East India Company, 1813, B/157, f. 233, IOL.
19. Stuart to Court of Directors, January 14, 1814, Madras Letters Received, E/1/127, p. 20A, IOL.
20. Court Minutes, 1814, B/158, ff. 1340–41; B/159, f. 243; *ibid.*, 1815, B/160, ff. 979, 998; the material on which the subcommittee made its recommendations is itemized in Personal Records, O/6/5, pp. 133–52, IOL.

Although that decision was soon endorsed by the full Court of Directors—sealing Stuart's fate—he did find one champion at that final stage of deliberation. One of the directors, Samuel Davis, submitted a long report dissenting from the court's decision. By intent an attack on the inadequacies and unfairness of the case against Stuart, Davis' defense is most interesting for the picture it gives of Stuart's character and, in particular, of the effects of his uncompromising stand on others' opinions. Davis was as puzzled as his opponents by Stuart's "real motives": "They lie perhaps to any but himself beyond the realm of human knowledge." He was no less disconcerted by the vehemence of Stuart's language, which was "neither necessary nor prudent." But he also admired the underlying integrity: "The stoic firmness with which he has endured adversity, & the freedom & acuteness with which he has endeavoured to show why he should appeal rather than submit, has been prejudicial to his cause, when meanness of spirit & the vice of dissimulation might have saved him."[21]

Yet even as it applauded Stuart, Davis' argument implicitly confirmed that he was far too individualistic to be at home in the army or properly deferential in any hierarchical system. Stuart had originally been subjected to "a species of Espionage" because he was suspected of subversion and conspiracy. No evidence had been produced to justify these suspicions, but the nature of his self-defense had convinced the directors that he was indeed "a dangerous person." His "factious disposition" had been confirmed in their eyes by the frankness with which he had admitted his dislike for the Madras government's habit of punishing without investigation or trial. It was not only the details of his arguments that were held against him but the fact that he had argued at all. One director, said Davis, had complained that Stuart's defense was written "as if he thought he was addressing himself to an Assembly of Logicians, instead of a Tribunal composed of his Sovereigns." Although Davis was impressed with the ingenuity of Stuart's arguments, he knew that the system required unquestioning obedience. The case had come to London because Stuart had refused the advice of the commander in chief in Madras to apologize and make his peace with the authorities: "It is certain that to refuse advice is not always the best way to the favour of him that offers it, but when on such an occasion superadded to the refusal, the advice itself is discussed in a manner calculated to expose the unsoundness of the principle on which it is founded, that, which might have remained as simple refusal, grows into positive offence, as it has done in the case of Captain Stuart."[22]

21. Court Minutes, 1815, B/160, ff. 1072–79, IOL.
22. Ibid.

Stuart, however, accepted his fate with only a token counterattack. He reaffirmed his innocence and insisted that he could have substantiated it if given the opportunity to confront the directors. But he bowed "with perfect submission" to the court's decision.[23] Perhaps he felt that further argument was useless. He must also have known that forced retirement was in many ways a fortunate outcome. On the one hand, it was no punishment to be denied the chance to return to India. Although he was not totally without friends in the Madras army and civil service, he had clearly been anxious to leave the subcontinent as rapidly as possible and, equally clearly, he had been a restless misfit who had goaded the authorities into punitive action.[24] On the other hand, he had avoided the disgrace of dismissal and secured a pension that would give modest independence in the future. He had also retained a military rank, which would allow him the minor prestige of remaining "Captain Stuart" throughout his life and in the near future would give him claim to a more considerable land grant than ordinary immigrants to Canada.[25]

Whether that mercenary consideration was clear in his mind during the two years of ponderous deliberation by the Court of Directors is uncertain. It is clear that he was sustained materially in this period by the hospitality of now unknown friends. But the delays were an ordeal of uncertainty from which he sought refuge in religion. He tried to secure holy orders in the Church of England but was unsuccessful, according to one account because current attitudes in the church were against the ordination of military men.[26] It may have been these new frustrations as much as the family connections he already had in North America, and the opportunities for securing land there, which prompted his emigration.

DESPITE THE relatively favorable outcome of his clash with the East India Company, it was not a relaxed and fulfilled Stuart who left Britain early in 1817 armed with a letter from Downing Street recommending him to the Canadian authorities for a grant of eight hundred acres of land appropriate to his rank. He was accompanied by John and George Rankin, brothers of his sister Mary's husband Charles. Soon the three were to make

23. Court Minutes, 1815, B/160, ff. 1033, 1046, IOL.
24. As later chapters of this book will show, an Indian civil servant friend, William Blair, was to play an important part in Stuart's antislavery career.
25. Henry Goulburn to Sir J. C. Sherbrooke, February 25, 1817, Upper Canada Land Petitions, "S" Bundle 11, 1816–19 (RG1, L3, Vol. 457), 113g, PAC.
26. Stuart to Court of Directors, January 14, 1814, Madras Letters Received, E/1/127, p. 20A, IOL; Sir J. C. Sherbrooke to Sir Francis Gore, cited in Landon, "Captain Charles Stuart," 4.

joint applications for land grants.[27] But Stuart's reminiscences, published three years later, show that he was at first in the grip of emotional and spiritual crisis.

He went alone to Montreal, "an unknown stranger, and not desiring to be known." Now even the religious faith, which had at least partly shaped his fate in India and had sustained him in London, for a time deserted him. He walked alone through a landscape of a "fatiguing sameness." Usually an admirer of the "wildness of nature," he paddled a boat on a lake and felt overwhelmed by solitude: "No voice was heard—no trace of life was seen. Death, not the destruction, but the prevention of existence—seemed to be spread along the rocks upon the matted moss." "Without Christ" for the moment, he felt as desolate as the scenery. Eventually, after weeks of misery, "the blind and raging passions" of his soul led to a renewed religious faith.[28]

Time would prove this new commitment to Christ to be permanent. Soon he was to proclaim "groundworks" of faith which he would never abandon: "the divinity of Christ, the tri-une character of the Godhead; and the Holy Scriptures, as the only ultimate test of all religious and moral truth and knowledge."[29] It would be decades before this simple orthodoxy would embitter relations with some of his closest friends. Yet even in 1817 the rediscovery of Christ did not mean a new tranquillity. Rather, the lonely weeks near Montreal proved to be a rare interlude in which Charles Stuart contended exclusively with himself rather than with every figure of authority who crossed his path.

Joining his relatives, he plunged into the life of the established church, becoming for a time a lay reader at York and once again taking up the idea of ordination. Although this ambition led to an exchange of correspondence with the lieutenant governor of Upper Canada, Sir Peregrine Maitland, on this occasion it was Stuart who rejected higher authority by abandoning the project. The local bishop, Jacob Mountain, had been criticized by others for unduly English manners and for preoccupations with questions of style, precedence, and political intrigue inappropriate to a frontier society. Stuart eventually declared that he could not accept ordination from Mountain "because I believe him to be an unchristian overseer; a secular not a spiritual character. The feelings and principles I would try to establish would be at decided variance with his principles and his life." As always, these criticisms reflected conviction as well as pugnac-

27. Upper Canada Land Petitions, "S" Bundle 11, 1816–19 (RG1, L3, Vol. 457), 113–113g, Upper Canada Land Book J, 241, PAC.
28. Stuart, *Emigrant's Guide*, 281–84.
29. Ibid., 224.

ity. He involved himself in fund-raising activities in support of new Anglican church buildings at Amherstburg and Colchester. In the process he also declared his willingness to help the local Baptists and Methodists in similar enterprises. This was a practical demonstration of his soon-to-be-published endorsement of religious toleration as the "noblest mark of political wisdom." Yet even these ecumenical exertions were accompanied by a passing lunge at those less tolerant than himself, with their "discordant and fiery principles, which are engendered by mutual ambition, intolerance, and pride."[30]

Even the task of finding land in this sparsely populated continent involved him in almost endless contention. His right to eight hundred acres as a military claimant was duly acknowledged by the colonial government in February, 1818. But he spent the next year fruitlessly attempting to take up this grant in an area of the township of Mersea already granted to an American. The authorities ultimately rejected his claim despite five separate testimonials, all written by Stuart but signed by local residents, declaring that the prior claimant had not been seen for more than a dozen years. In June, 1819, apologizing to the responsible official for being "repeatedly troublesome," he asked to locate his eight hundred acres on the Huron Indian Reserve near Amherstburg and on various islands in Lake Erie. Although acknowledging that all these various locations were probably ungrantable, he proceeded to argue a special case with notable tactlessness. Despite the "fairest claim, a claim most readily admitted"—and despite an acknowledged degree of "consideration and kindness" from officialdom—he remained "as destitute of H.M.'s bounty as if I had been an alien." He did not see how it could have been otherwise unless he had been prepared to "precipitate" himself and his relatives "literally into the Wilderness" or else be "constricted to settle on the diminutive plan of the recently formed streets of Townships." Such a plan was fine for its purposes "but utterly repulsive to every Gentleman, who is not willing at once to reduce himself to a level, with the heterogeneous mass of growing population." Because he was shortly leaving for a visit to England, he was anxious for a quick decision. The authorities obliged him by rejecting all his alternative applications within a month.[31]

30. Landon, "Captain Charles Stuart," 5 and n. 3; Upper Canada Land Petitions, "C" Bundle 12, Pt. 1, 1816–19 (RG1, L3, Vol. 101), C-12-24, 145, PAC; Stuart, *Emigrant's Guide*, 115–16, 118.

31. Upper Canada Land Book J, 295; Upper Canada Land Petitions, "S" Bundle 11, 1816–19 (RG1, L3, Vol. 457a.), 132–132g; Land Book J, 311, 511; Stuart to Major G. Hillier, June 15, 1819, Upper Canada Land Petitions, "S" Bundle 12, 1819–20 (RG1, L3, Vol. 460), 203–203c; Land Book K, p. 199, PAC.

Such rebuffs did not shake his fundamental loyalty to Britain any more than had his mauling by the East India Company. He was alarmed to return to a country disturbed by recent unrest caused by postwar social and economic problems and culminating in the Peterloo Massacre and the repressive Six Acts designed to suppress radical criticism. His reaction was a middle-of-the-road condemnation of both an authoritarian ministry and the radical leaders, William Cobbett and Henry Hunt, whom he dismissed as rabble-rousing demagogues. His main concern was that such upheavals might "mark the departure of the glory of my country." Similar patriotic effusions appeared throughout his first book, *An Emigrant's Guide to Upper Canada*.[32]

The completion and publication of this work had been the main reason for his return, along with the search for funds to further the church-building projects he had recently embraced. The book pursued its ostensible purpose honestly enough. It gave an apparently fair picture of colonial conditions, emphasizing opportunity but stressing the hardships of emigration, especially for the poor. But it was also overwritten and unbalanced with hard information swamped by passages of moralizing and almost random reminiscence. These characteristics led another advocate of Canadian emigration, Edward Talbot, to dismiss the book as less an emigrant's guide to Canada than "a Pilgrim's Guide to the Celestial Regions."[33] In fact, the work was most clearly the reader's guide to Charles Stuart.

It described his spiritual crisis in Montreal and his attitudes to the various churches, to Americans and American Indians, and even to the frivolous affectations of brother officers in India. Above all, in its reflections on the attractions of frontier society, it revealed a puritanical bachelor ill at ease with women and—given that he was already in his late thirties—likely always to be so. The frugality of the pioneering life appealed to him. Already in 1820 it was threatened by the introduction of more worldly leisure pursuits. But much more dangerous than the arrival of horse-racing and gambling was the threat to the "domestic tone" of Canadian women. Hitherto they had lacked the polish "which at once adorns and disgraces the general mass of our European ladies." But "the passion for that polish is afloat. It is tending rapidly to displace the remaining and superior charms of that simplicity."[34]

His emphasis on "domestic" virtues was literal. Women away from the

32. Stuart, *Emigrant's Guide*, 94, 100, and *passim*.
33. Edward A. Talbot, *Five Years Residence in the Canadas* (London, 1824), vi.
34. Stuart, *Emigrant's Guide*, 122–27.

home were an embarrassment. He enjoyed the rough masculine comradeship of Canadian travel: "You are served by men who look upon themselves as your equals, perhaps as your superiors." But the lack of separate accommodations was "an exceeding annoyance, and renders travelling with ladies a matter sometimes of real distress: Alone, a man may pass through profaneness, levity and noise . . . without noticing, if he cannot rectify them . . . but it is abhorrent to every tender, just, and delicate feeling, to see a woman exposed to such things, without the power of rescuing her." He was equally embarrassed by women's sexual attraction. Overtly he believed that "graciously formed" females had a spiritual effect on men: "to soften and elevate; to purify and give us strength." But clearly they "whose glance is so capable of filling us with despair" had bodies capable of filling him with lust. He implored his "future countrywomen" to "watch by all that is lovely in yourselves . . . against the delusions of the destructive vortex, which seems to slumber before you. Believe not, that because modesty is consistent with exposure, exposure can be consistent with feminine delicacy." Men were made to be women's protectors; they should be given no encouragement to betray that trust and become "villains and cowards."[35]

Although in his two years in Canada he had not found a permanent home, he had spent most time in the Amherstburg-Colchester area across the border from Detroit. According to the title page of his book, he was already a magistrate in that western district of Upper Canada, and it was to that region and office he returned after a year in England. His literary efforts had convinced him at least that he was an authority on the province, and he marked his return with a series of letters offering advice on government to Sir Peregrine Maitland. When Maitland eventually asked him to stop writing, Stuart acknowledged that "my correspondence with you has been worse than useless" and devoted his disruptive talents to his duties as magistrate. This did not mean that the authorities in Toronto had heard the last of him. He was soon involved in a dispute with the military at Fort Malden over the extent of his jurisdiction when dealing with civil offenses by members of the garrison. "Do pray endeavour," asked the local colonel, "to prevail on Sir Peregrine to cause instructions to be sent to this troublesome magistrate, not to interfere unnecessarily with matters that are purely military, as he really seems inclined to be troublesome." He believed Stuart was a "good-hearted man." He was sure the authorities had heard of his "eccentric character" but wrongly thought they might not have heard of his "strong propensity to meddle with the

35. Ibid.

affairs of other people; even, I believe, to the almost neglect of his own."[36]

The colonel was unwittingly close to detecting an important key to Stuart's behavior. He was indeed a good-hearted man, but for most of his life he had virtually no affairs of his own to engage him. This was particularly true in 1821 because, since his return, he had finally resolved the time-consuming search for suitable land by taking up his claim at Amherstburg.[37] In the long run the discovery of a great global philanthropic cause would make his lack of personal commitments a major advantage for he was able to apply his benevolence with unusual thoroughness to one objective. But for the moment some of his attempts to find an outlet for his humanitarian urges inevitably made him seem meddlesome and eccentric.

The most obvious opportunity for a Christian philanthropist on the Canadian frontier lay in missionary work among the local Indians. Stuart was interested in such activity from the time of his arrival, and his *Emigrant's Guide* contained long passages on this theme. His attitudes to the Indians were typical of humanitarian opinion in his time: "painful compassion" for their "helplessness and simplicity" and stern intolerance of the "lawless, and capricious, and horribly cruel" side of their savagery. It did not trouble him that, as a distinctive race, they were "rapidly sinking to extinction" and that within half a century there would probably be no "genuine trace" of them. But there was need for a "missionary spirit" toward them. As individuals "we require to regard them more as brethren." The hope should be that when their culture disappeared a remnant would "survive to bless, instead of cursing the day, when the Europeans arrived to settle amongst them."[38]

The records provide only glimpses of his own response to this evangelistic challenge. He expressed a wish to be a missionary in his correspondence with Maitland, and though he never carried out this ambition in a sustained way, he clearly did undertake some such activity. In late 1821 Dr. John Bigsby, who was attached to a commission surveying the boundary between Canada and the United States and who already knew Stuart, met him in the company of two American clergymen. The three were on their way to establish a mission among the Indians on the banks of the Saginaw River, which flowed into Lake Huron. Bigsby was impressed by Stuart's eccentricities: "He was handsome, frank and energetic. His iron frame was indifferent to luxuries or even comforts, any

36. Landon, "Captain Charles Stuart," 6–7.
37. Upper Canada Land Book L, 71, PAC.
38. Stuart, *Emigrant's Guide*, 240–46, 257–78.

hut was a home, and any food was nourishment, provided he could be doing good to others; for he was, and is, a working Christian."[39]

Bigsby's admiration had its origins in an encounter at Amherstburg earlier that year, when he saw another side to Stuart's philanthropy. Over recent years black fugitives from American slavery had been finding their way to Amherstburg, and Stuart had become their main benefactor. Bigsby spent an evening at the "plain but comfortable" cottage Stuart shared with his sister and her family and learned of his plans to organize a successful colony of free blacks. Later Stuart showed him around the embryonic Negro village and its adjacent farmland. Bigsby's account probably romanticized Stuart's role: "As the poor fugitives came in, friendless and breathless, though exulting, Captain Stewart [sic] offered them protection and subsistence. . . . The greater proportion of these negro refugees became his tenants." Stuart was later to make no special claims for his own contribution when he wrote of this community, though this may have been the result of a modesty that, despite his dogmatism, he always displayed about his work.[40]

In one respect Bigsby—in common with all later writers who have noticed this stage of Stuart's career—was certainly wrong. Stuart was not consciously "waging successful war with the Negro slavery of the United States." In the long run his knowledge of the fugitives—almost 150 in number—would help to consolidate his antislavery commitment, and he would recall them with affection and admiration. But this was not yet "the beginning of his antislavery labors."[41] Within a year of the meeting with Bigsby he had left the Negro community at Amherstburg and moved to the United States as a school principal at Utica, New York, but he was not yet an abolitionist.

THE REASONS for Stuart's move to upstate New York can only be guessed at. There is evidence, at least in Bigsby's account, that his work in encouraging fugitives had made him unpopular with the Amherstburg community as well as the military and civil authorities: "Being at least twenty years before his generation, and having views as much above those of the careful traffickers of Amherstburgh, as the heaven is above the earth, the excellent captain was totally misunderstood, and well abused, for

39. Landon, "Captain Charles Stuart," 7; John J. Bigsby, *The Shoe and Canoe, or Pictures of Travel in the Canadas* (2 vols., London, 1850), I, 263–66.
40. Bigsby, *Shoe and Canoe*, I, 264; Charles Stuart, *Immediate Emancipation . . .* (Newburyport, 1838), 15.
41. Fred Landon, "Captain Charles Stuart: A Figure of Importance in Struggle over Slavery," Amherstburg *Echo*, September 3, 1953; Bigsby, *Shoe and Canoe*, I, 264.

bringing them customers forsooth." It is hard to imagine his being dislodged by public opinion, and his move may have been prompted partly because the black community quickly used its land to produce tobacco. His reactions to this development are unrecorded, and his own abstinence from the weed at this stage of his life cannot be documented. But his aversion later in life was so strong that it seems probable that he was less than pleased that the Amherstburg blacks had produced their first commercial tobacco crop in 1821.[42]

The move to Utica must have had positive attractions for a man who had obviously been seeking emotional fulfillment through Christian philanthropy. Stuart's correspondence throughout his life showed an affection for children which made schoolteaching a logical choice for one without children of his own. And upstate New York, an area undergoing rapid social and economic change and with a history of volatile religious activity, must have appealed to his evangelicalism. He had written admiringly in his *Emigrant's Guide* of the American churches and defended their activities among the frontier settlers of Canada West.[43] Contacts with American clerics such as those who had shared his missionary expedition to the Saginaw Indians may well have opened up the opportunity at the Utica Academy.

The academy had been founded in 1814. Since then Utica had grown rapidly from a community of barely a thousand people to some four thousand at the time of Stuart's arrival in the summer of 1822. Since late 1819 the middle section of the Erie Canal from Utica to the Seneca River had been completed, opening up, in the words of a local historian, "new prospects, a new spirit of progress, and new resources." By 1825 the entire canal was opened, and the population of Utica had reached five thousand and would double over the next decade as the town became not only a distribution center for farm produce but a wool and cotton manufacturing center.[44]

This expansion—conspicuous even in a nation undergoing rapid change on a broad front in the 1820s—provided the context for religious activity. The region had been sensitive to religious stirrings since at least the turn of the century because its population was augmented mainly by migration from New England. The churches had increasing numbers of poten-

---

42. Bigsby, *Shoe and Canoe*, I, 264; Robin W. Winks, *The Blacks in Canada: A History* (Montreal, 1971), 144–45.

43. Stuart, *Emigrant's Guide*, 116, 229.

44. Pomroy Jones, *Annals of Oneida County* (Rome, N.Y., 1851), 545, 566; Moses Mears Bagg, *The Pioneers of Utica: Being Sketches of Its Inhabitants and Its Institutions* . . . (Utica, N.Y., 1877), 387.

tial adherents, but there were many denominations and competition was intense. The churches responded to every opportunity to increase their congregations, but the religious revivals that periodically enlivened the area were much more than simply recruiting drives. Economic adversity in the aftermath of the War of 1812 had helped to stimulate a major revival. Conversely, the economic optimism of the canal-building era had encouraged more worldly excitements. In the early 1820s campaigns were under way to counter materialism by the foundation of Sunday schools, the distribution of Bibles and religious tracts, the enforcement of Sabbath observance, and the encouragement of temperance.[45]

Stuart threw himself avidly into all these activities. It was now—rather than in his childhood, as previous writers have suggested—that he became a Presbyterian. The tolerant comments he had published about the various Protestant sects, even in the course of his fund-raising activities on behalf of the established church in Canada, suggest that the change came easily to him. Essentially he was not worried about formal denominational allegiance: the important concern was "the liberty of the Gospel, in allowing every man the undisturbed possession of his own conscience." Only Catholicism had earned his displeasure because he felt it inhibited that individual liberty. During his years in Utica he became a licensed preacher of the First Presbyterian Church, earning the title "Reverend," which in his future antislavery career would be more commonly associated with his name in America than the British "Captain." But his activities in the 1820s took him far from the pulpit. Commissioned by the Bible Society of Oneida, and at his own expense and invariably on foot, he covered the county ascertaining the number of families needing to be supplied with Bibles. In this way he became widely known as "eminently pious, actively benevolent, unsurpassedly kind, [and] rigidly austere." Contemporaries were enthralled by his piety: "It seemed," wrote one, "as if all that he did was done . . . under the Great Task Master's Eye." But they were also amused and bemused by his appearance. He wore at all times "a Scotch plaid frock, with a cape reaching nearly to his elbows." To say that he was "wildly eccentric," reminisced one acquaintance years later, "is to give after all, but a faint idea of what the man really was." As he traversed the countryside "with stalwart stride," "his quaint garb, his sun-browned face and gentle mien drew every eye."[46]

What he called his "Bible business" was only one aspect of his religious

45. Whitney R. Cross, *The Burned-over District: The Social and Intellectual History of Enthusiastic Religion in Western New York, 1800–1850* (New York, 1965), 10–13, 126–37.
46. Stuart, *Emigrant's Guide*, 115, 223–24; Bagg, *Pioneers of Utica*, 543–44.

activity. He became an assistant superintendent of his church's Sunday school, enlivening the usual scriptural lessons with accounts of the "rites of the Hindoos" to illustrate the "sad condition" of the pagan world. The children willingly contributed their cents to send these and other pagans God's word, persuaded either by his arguments or by the knowledge that, for most of them, he was their regular schoolteacher as well and capable of discarding his usual almost feminine tenderness in favor of "prompt and stern punishment." Because in both institutions his system of discipline and instruction was "eminently religious," the Sunday school and the Utica Academy became "nearly convertible terms." He was said to be the first teacher in the United States to introduce regular hymn-singing in school. However true this claim might be, the reminiscences of former pupils leave no doubt that the devotional aspects of the academy's curriculum made a lasting impression: "Ah, my comrades, can you ever forget how those walls re-echoed the grand old tune of Rochester? Do you not again hear these words '*Amazing pity! grace unknown! and love beyond degree!*' Do you not even now see the noble form of our venerated friend, with hands meekly folded on the breast, in his customary attitude of prayer? Do you not again hear those pleading tones for mercy, as with rapt irradiate gaze, he seemed to behold the mercy seat?"[47]

No less than the adults his pupils were intrigued by his eccentricities. His rooms in the academy building were as austere as "the cell of an anchorite," their only decoration freshly collected flowers. He had a pallet of straw as a bed but regularly slept outdoors in the summer months. In all seasons he began his day by deluging himself with water "externally and internally" and then walked to take a breakfast of bread and milk at a farmhouse four to five miles away. At least in retrospect, the children attributed this asceticism to the rigors of his military life in India. Many thought him fanatical, but all recognized his "thorough sincerity" and that his Spartan regimen was in some way connected to the religious zeal that dominated their school curriculum.[48]

However properly his former pupils might eventually applaud his sincerity, their reminiscences also make it plain that they hero-worshiped Stuart for his personality as much as his piety. He was a teacher who instructed and occasionally punished them, but he was also a playmate, "the willing partner of all their joys and sorrows, and of their sports as well." He would return from his distant breakfast to spend an hour of "hilarious

47. *A Memorial of the Semi-Centennial Celebration of the Founding of the Sunday School of the First Presbyterian Church, Utica, N.Y.* (Utica, N.Y., 1867), 36, 119.
48. Ibid., 117; Bagg, *Pioneers of Utica*, 544.

mirth" before morning school, "in which there was no sport too boisterous for him to engage in. . . . How they would flock around him! How they clung to him!" remembered one former pupil, who had himself gone on to be a missionary in the "pagan" East. Even on Saturday afternoons he was likely to engage in "mimic warfare" on the common, occasions on which his performances on the French horn added to the general commotion.[49]

His pupils in the academy were all boys, but he also founded and ran a society to instruct the local girls in the Scriptures and in the "duties of practical goodness." Instruction was as earnestly religious as in the academy, with emphasis on a hundred questions and answers "framed from passages of Scripture." A medal was awarded each week for the best performance and for general deportment. But the girls, too, saw Stuart's lighter side. In the holidays he would take them for country strolls, entertaining them with musical performances and regaling them with candies and nuts.[50]

The vivid recollections of his former pupils can combine with the conflicts and frustrations of the previous decade to give a misleading impression of a lonely man at last finding fulfillment. Despite the adulation he received from the children, he remained a lonely, inwardly tormented figure throughout the years from 1822 to 1825. Toward the end of his days he looked back on this period as "one of the most trying times of my life." And even those admiring former pupils remembered a man under stress, "a peculiar mixture of the severe and the playful; tremendous in his wrath, and hilarious in his relaxed moods; with a most attractive smile and a thunderous volcanic frown, in which there seemed to be a struggle to put down some violent passion."[51]

The move to Utica had not yet ended the uncertainties of the previous ten years or more. The major crisis of that period—his suspension and enforced retirement from the army—had been as much symptom as cause of the manic-depressive moods noted by his pupils. The dearth of information about his formative years makes it pointless to speculate about the origins of perhaps profound psychological problems. But from the moment in India that he emerges recognizably in the records he was clearly a man whose social behavior was shaped by religious intensity. There was the rigid puritanism that made him shun the worldly pleasures of India and inhibited his responses to women. And there was the asceticism that

49. *Memorial of the Semi-Centennial*, 36, 117; Bagg, *Pioneers of Utica*, 544.
50. *Memorial of the Semi-Centennial*, 212–13.
51. Stuart to Charles Stuart Weld, Angelina and Sarah Grimké, October 15, 1852, WP; Bagg, *Pioneers of Utica*, 543.

made his appearance and "simple-hearted and eccentric ways" a source of incredulous amusement to adults. By 1825 not even his exuberant teaching had given him satisfaction. His frustrations are revealed not only by his own and others' recollections of stress but by the intensity with which he now seized new opportunities to seek emotional and spiritual fulfillment.

The friendship he began with the youthful Theodore Weld, son of a Congregational minister at nearby Cazenovia, is the best-known aspect of his life because of Weld's subsequent fame as an abolitionist. Important though his influence on Weld was to be over the next few years, it is also clear that for Stuart the relationship with the entire Weld family was therapeutic. In later years he was to recall particularly the "parental tenderness" of Theodore's mother in this trying period. In his first surviving letter to Theodore, in May, 1825, he wrote of his wish to acquire "with all of you" the "wise & happy temper which is always pleased with what pleases God." By this date—when Theodore was fifteen years old—Stuart's friendship with the family was already well established. Absent on "Bible business," he sent "affectionate regards" to the parents and a special greeting to Theodore's sister Cornelia.[52]

Already he was strongly sympathetic to "my dearest Theodore": "Remember me in your prayers," he asked, before signing himself "your truly attached C. Stuart." It was later that year that the death of Theodore's maternal uncle, who had been financing his studies at Hamilton College, gave Stuart the chance to cement the friendship with practical help. But his offer to take over the financial responsibility was clearly designed to help himself as much as Theodore: "You have called me your friend; and reluctant as I am to attach any meaning that I could value to that word, because I find it almost universally destitute of all such meaning; yet I have not held it destitute of a meaning suited to my heart with you—and I want you to evince to me that this feeling is deeply reciprocal." Soon Weld's acceptance of the offer prompted a further revelation of Stuart's yearning for affection: "The dream of a friendship, that shall never die, nay, I wrong it—that shall grow with brightening life for ever, has risen in my soul in relation to you."[53]

Friendship for Stuart had to rest on a firm spiritual foundation. He suggested to Weld that wherever each of them might be they should make sunrise a "time of heart-meeting," a "spontaneous swell mutually of sa-

---

52. Stuart to Charles S. Weld, *et al.*, October 15, 1852; to Weld, May 10, 1825, WP.
53. Stuart to Weld, May 10, 1825, November 16, December 17, January 10, 1826, WP. Weld's uncle was Erastus Clark, his mother's brother (Landon, "Captain Charles Stuart," 9).

cred & tender feeling, seeking to bear each other & those we love to the footstool of the Glorious Majesty!"[54] Although this suggestion assumed many future separations, the opportunity now quickly arose for shared religious activity.

In the latter months of 1825 people in Utica became aware of a major religious revival gathering momentum in nearby towns such as Western and Rome. The Reverend Charles Grandison Finney, a former lawyer who had been ordained a Presbyterian minister only the previous year at the age of thirty-two, was proving to be a preacher of extraordinary power. His lucid and melodic oratory and his appeal to common sense rather than rarefied intellect were attracting large audiences and many public commitments to Christ. The way was prepared for him in Utica by this fame and by visits to his Rome meetings by several local citizens, who returned, in the words of Stuart's pastor, "weeping over the state of the church at home and anxious that something should be done."[55]

Finney reached Utica in early February. Although his revival created an emotional atmosphere, it was not attended by frenzied mass excitement. Rather, its famous "anxious meetings" were condemned by opponents as sinister manipulation, with assistant revivalists moving around silent, darkened halls, whispering such blunt questions as "Do you love God?" in the ears of individuals. The revival's spokesmen dismissed these allegations as distortions. Meetings were usually held at night but in normally illuminated rooms. In their concern to ascertain individual needs and feelings about religion, those who conducted them spoke softly to avoid distracting others before ending the sessions with a general address and joint prayer. As a result of these carefully personalized methods of persuasion, and also of Finney's own "plain and pungent and faithful preaching," his arrival in Utica led to "evident and wonderful success." Within weeks the local Presbyterian, Baptist, Methodist, and Congregational churches were welcoming an estimated total of five hundred converts, and a "fervent spirit of prayer" had revitalized the faith of many already avowed Christians.[56]

Prominent among the converts, at least in the memoirs of Finney, was Theodore Weld. His family background and the tone of his friendship with Stuart show that Weld was already a Christian. Perhaps his subsequent fame made his conversion appear more important to Finney in retrospect.

54. Stuart to Weld, January 10, 1826, WP.
55. Account of Utica Revival by Mr. Aikin, pastor of the First Presbyterian Church, in *A Narrative of the Revival of Religion in the County of Oneida, Particularly in the Bounds of the Presbytery of Oneida in the Year 1826* (Utica, N.Y., 1826), 23–25.
56. Ibid., 24, 37, 66–88.

But at least according to the recollection, he was an outspoken, even abusive, critic of Finney's revival and, with persuasive powers beyond his years, a potential threat to its success. After the two had argued publicly and privately and then Weld had undergone a solitary night of agonizing introspection, the youth stood up at Finney's next meeting and made "a very humble, earnest, broken-hearted confession." According to Finney, this transformation removed a "stumbling-block" which Weld had "cast before the whole people."[57] Whether a sixteen-year-old was really so influential, there can be no doubt that his commitment to Christ was invigorating for Charles Stuart, who soon joined his young protégé in active involvement in the Finney revival.

It is even less appropriate in Stuart's case than Weld's to call him a convert of Finney. Neither in theology nor in the connections he emphasized between religion and social conscience did Finney say anything that was not already fundamental to Stuart's belief. Rigorous theology was not part of Finney's appeal. In contrast to a contemporary Unitarian critic, who alleged that he appealed to Calvinist predestinarians, historians have suggested that Finney's main contribution was to dispel the remaining determinism from an "already thoroughly watered-down Calvinism" prevalent in his day. His emphasis on individual initiative under the guidance of the "word of God" was at one with Stuart's already published insistence on "allowing every man the undisturbed possession of his own conscience" in seeking the way to salvation through the guidance of the gospel. For Finney salvation was the "beginning of religious experience" rather than its end, as Calvinism had implied. And in arguing that converts should thereafter "aim at being useful in the highest degree possible," he was endorsing the benevolent activity to which Stuart had aspired throughout his years in North America.[58]

Nevertheless, it is easy to understand how exhilarating Stuart found Finney. The eccentric who had aroused amazement as he prayed with "rapt, irradiate gaze" now found many showing the same intensity: "Often has it been said—Christians pray as they have never prayed before," remarked the authors of a contemporary narrative. He must have seen in Finney's methods of individual and group persuasion a technique of com-

57. Charles Grandison Finney, *Memoirs of Rev. Charles Grandison Finney* (New York, 1876), 185–88.
58. Ephraim Perkins, *A "Bunker Hill" Contest, A.D. 1826 Between the "Holy Alliance" for the Establishment of Hierarchy, and Ecclesiastical Domination over the Human Mind, on the One Side, and the Asserters of Free Inquiry, Bible Religion, Christian Freedom and Civil Liberty on the Other* . . . (N.p., n.d.), 6–7; Cross, *Burned-over District*, 158–61; Stuart, *Emigrant's Guide*, 115.

munication that had eluded him in the past as he had alternately amazed and amused all except his audiences of children. This man, who had so recently been a lone misfit wandering about almost ludicrously on his Bible-distributing hikes, was now part of a successful movement as he joined Finney's loose-knit "Holy Band" of preachers, who carried the revival to the surrounding countryside while the great evangelist moved farther afield. Above all, in sharing his new commitment with Theodore Weld, he had consolidated their relationship on the spiritual foundations he had emphasized immediately before Finney's arrival in Utica. "Our friendship will be worth retaining," he had written, only if "we are careful that we don't rest it upon each other or ourselves."[59]

Over the next few years Stuart followed his own recommendations with determination. After an initial period of common activity as Finney revivalists, the two were frequently separated. Weld's attempt to combine revivalism with his studies led to a breakdown from which he was sent to recuperate on a fishing smack off the Labrador coast. On his return, Stuart was again on hand with financial assistance as Weld began studying for the ministry at Oneida Institute, Whitesboro. But soon the older man was immersed in further public activities. Involved in a failed attempt to promote "bar-less taverns," he still remained optimistic about the prospects for the temperance movement, which had been gathering strength in upstate New York since early 1826. He continued his Bible and tract-distributing walks. And on more than one occasion, he was invigorated by working directly with Finney: "With what a glorious spirit has God endowed him—and oh, what a peculiarly solemn responsibility is incurred by those alike who attend his ministry, and by those who having it within their reach, reject or oppose it."[60]

Yet even as he accepted separation from Weld and consoled them both by looking forward "to our union in that Holy Land where there is no parting & no sin," his letters are remarkable for their fervent expressions of affection for the younger man. Fully accepting their prior duty to God, he still allowed his memory to dwell on shared walks in the countryside. Although he saw Weld as the "dear brother of my soul for Eternity," he nevertheless acknowledged moments of doubt, "an unkind flurry of stupid apprehension across my heart, that you cannot continue to love me with your whole heart as you have done." Even allowing for what one historian has called the "extravagantly pious language of the day," it was

59. *Narrative of the Revival of Religion in Oneida County*, 37; Stuart to Weld, January 10, 1826, WP.
60. Stuart to Weld, April 19, May 19, July 8, 1828, April 20, July 9, 1829, WP.

a vibrantly emotional Stuart who savored their rare moments together. "Adieu, my Theodore, dearer than any ties of blood could make you," he wrote in May, 1828. "My soul pants once more to embrace you," he enthused two months later.[61]

When Stuart eventually departed for England in 1829, he added to his numerous outspoken proclamations of undying spiritual love the comment, "There are things which I would [say] but must not. But I believe you know all my heart."[62] It would be easy to conclude that his rigid puritanism was suppressing a deep homosexual affection for a youth almost thirty years younger than himself. It is, however, much more likely that the emotion-charged relationship with Weld was the outlet for a repressed heterosexuality. This repression had been strongly suggested by his prudish discomfiture at the rise of sophistication and the fall of necklines on the Canadian frontier. And through most of this first period of spiritually amorous correspondence with Theodore he conducted a fumbling, anxious courtship of the youth's younger sister, Cornelia.

Probably a man so patently attracted and yet threatened by women found it easier to attempt a relationship with someone much younger than himself. His first surviving reference to Cornelia in 1825 was to a "flighty child" on whom he had felt obliged "to intrude so much of my advice." Apart from the enclosure of a recipe for cough mixture in one letter, later references to her in his correspondence with Weld date from May, 1828, when the relationship had matured to the point that she was considering his proposal of marriage. He was pessimistic about the outcome. She was hesitant, he felt, not because of uncertain feelings—which amounted to "an affectionate tho' decided negative"—but because she wished to give the matter full "prayerful consideration." Although he tried to convince himself that he would "be enabled to rejoice in her decision whatever it may be," he clearly had a great deal at stake emotionally. Because no letters between the two survive and the relationship can be glimpsed only on the periphery of his impassioned exchanges with Weld, there is a danger of overlooking the probability that he had now reached yet another critical point in his life. He awaited Cornelia's decision once more in the grip of uncertainty about his future and of inner conflict between his emotional needs and religious convictions: "Pray for me, my beloved Theodore—I feel my soul at once strengthened & shaken. At times its baseness & feebleness rises with such giant form before me, that I abhor

61. Stuart to Weld, April 9, May 19, July 8, 1828, July 9, 1829, WP; Cross, *Burned-over District*, 219.
62. Stuart to Weld, August 8, 1828, WP.

myself, for the effort to involve another in its fortunes—but again I am persuaded, that grace would require me to prove a holy, tender, wise & faithful friend and servant, & my spirit rejoices in the pursuit, however hopeless. But why hopeless?—Or am I such at love as to have no joy in hope?"[63]

When Cornelia finally rejected his proposal, he was overtly as piously grateful as he had stated he would be. Hoping that she would be "finally freed from the pain which I have caused her," he claimed to be pleased that God had relieved his own heart of a burden "it had so stupidly fabricated for itself." Nevertheless, rejection evidently made continued residence in the region unpalatable. He departed almost at once for New Brunswick. After what he claimed to be a pleasant visit to "the scene of my earlier days," he was still "too little disposed for any company" to introduce himself to acquaintances of the Weld family on his way back to New York. It was now October, 1828, and he was planning to spend the winter in New York City and then return to the British Isles. He looked forward to his departure with an earnest postscript, which, as much as anything he would ever write, caught the essence of his relationship with Theodore Weld: "If in want of a *father's* or a *brother's* or a *friend's* assistance, won't your heart *always* tell you *in the full confidence of love,* that as God may preserve & endow me, you have a *father,* & a *brother* & a *friend* in C. Stuart."[64]

Such effusions, however, represented much more than the importance of a particular friendship. Here was the fervent voice of a man largely indifferent to the world around him. The desire for philanthropic activity that had been so conspicuous over the past fifteen years was an entirely personal quest for spiritual purity and salvation. It reflected no discernible sense of social injustice, no impulse to challenge the established order. The officer who had found military discipline in India personally intolerable had no doubt that the subcontinent's millions were well served by British domination. Content to retain his military title and the modest financial independence that went with it, he had confronted authority in Canada and flouted convention in Utica for equally personal reasons. And he had embraced Finney's revivalism apparently indifferent to the wider changes sweeping American society. The "gentleman" who had sought to distance himself from the "masses" of Canada's minuscule towns had no natural sympathy for the democratic revolution symbolized by Andrew Jackson's election to the presidency in 1828. And if, as some would

63. Stuart to Weld, May 10, 1825, April 9, May 19, 1828, WP.
64. Stuart to Weld, October 7, 1828, WP.

argue, Jackson's victory represented less the Age of the Common Man than a victory for proslavery racism, this, too, was of no interest to a man who had helped black fugitives without as yet noticing the overshadowing evil of black slavery.

During the spring of 1829 he spent three months "following the glorious Finney," but this delayed travel plans that were equally indifferent to social and political realities across the Atlantic. In August, 1829, he left New York for Ireland, expressing forebodings that had nothing to do with the perennial Irish problem of oppressive poverty or with the recent revolutionary unrest which even now Britain was attempting to soothe with Catholic emancipation. All he saw before him "frowning on the pleasant fields of the green island" were the "lures of pride, and indolence, and selfishness." The last words of his farewell letter demanded a regular report from Theodore "about yourself, your experience—your wants, your prayers, your ministry."[65] Neither of them foresaw how that planned liaison would involve them both in a great international campaign for immediate abolition of Negro slavery.

65. Stuart to Weld, April 20, July 9, August 8, 1829, WP.

2 A SACRED PURSUIT DISCOVERED

STUART'S return to the British Isles coincided with important new developments in the antislavery movement. Although the beginnings of British immediatism are conventionally traced back to Elizabeth Heyrick's pamphlet *Immediate, Not Gradual Abolition,* published in 1824, it was not until 1830 that significant changes took place in the goals and methods of abolitionists. According to most accounts, including Stuart's own short history, for six years the emphasis Heyrick had put on the need to exterminate sin by immediate action had had little impact. Abolitionists through the 1820s were concerned about extending parliamentary regulation of slavery in the colonies, but their objective was still to improve the conditions of slaves and initiate at best a gradual process of emancipation. The name of the national abolition society reflected these aims—the Society for the Mitigation and Gradual Abolition of Slavery. Usually known more simply as the Anti-Slavery Society, this body pursued cautious methods of attempting to influence government through discreet lobbying in Westminster and by articles in its own *Anti-Slavery Reporter* and in such organs of the general press that were not in the pay of the West India interest. The society had provincial auxiliaries, but their main function was to dispatch delegates to an annual meeting in London, not to undertake local agitation.[1]

Yet according to the historian James Walvin, this was an important period of preparation. A "prodigious volume" of information was being

---

1. Temperley, *British Antislavery,* 9–12; Charles Stuart, "On the Abolition of Slavery by Great Britain," *Quarterly Anti-Slavery Magazine,* I, No. 2 (January, 1836), 107–108.

published to provide a more sophisticated awareness of slavery than hitherto. As a result, he argues, the eventual flood of petitions to Parliament at the end of the decade was evidence of "a genuine and massive popular support" for abolition. The Emancipation Act of 1833 may have been the work of a reformed Parliament based on a broad middle-class franchise. But the pressure on politicians came from a much more popularly based movement. The evidence for mass involvement lies not only in huge petitions but in the large crowds regularly overflowing antislavery meetings. Walvin emphasizes how widespread the movement was, but, even while insisting on its genuinely populist base, he implies a good deal of metropolitan influence on the provinces. In the late 1820s the wide distribution of the *Reporter* gave "information, guidance, and direction to the national cause." And in the decisive years after 1830 the eventually autonomous Agency Committee of the Anti-Slavery Society divided the country into lecture circuits that "attracted large crowds and encouraged local associations and publications." The same metropolitan organization, Walvin suggests, had a major influence on the abandonment of gradualism in favor of immediatism.[2]

Walvin provides the best available brief description of the antislavery atmosphere Stuart was to find so exhilarating. At the same time his stress on the vast numbers of participants should warn against overvaluing the importance of a single individual. Nevertheless, an analysis of Stuart's role both clarifies and modifies some of the processes Walvin has described. In his writings he twice articulated arguments that marked significant advances in abolitionists' demands in relation to immediatism and to compensation. And his activities help to illuminate the organization and techniques of popular agitation. Eventually he made a major contribution to the work of the Agency Committee. But before he became one of its itinerant lecturers, and indeed before that body existed, he had performed similar functions in the provinces. To understand the circumstances in which he gained that experience is to realize that there were important networks of provincial abolitionists who were as much the creators as the servants of that radical national organization.

IT IS IRONIC that though historians have ignored Stuart's innovative role in 1830 and 1831, the few who have mentioned him have wrongly assumed that he was already an abolitionist, returning, in the words of

2. James Walvin, "The Public Campaign in England Against Slavery, 1787–1834," in David Eltis and James Walvin (eds.), *The Abolition of the Atlantic Slave Trade: Origins and Effects in Europe, Africa, and the Americas* (Madison, 1981), 63–79.

Dwight L. Dumond, "in the summer of 1829 to press for immediate emancipation." As Stuart himself was to stress in 1833, he had no knowledge of the antislavery movement in 1829. Despite his commitment to reform causes in New York, he had not heard of any American abolitionists. Despite his patronage of fugitive blacks in Canada, he was not yet even hostile to the American Colonization Society, which was implacably opposed to North American alternatives to its Liberia colony. For some months his letters from Britain to Theodore Weld made no mention of slavery, even though they touched on other social issues such as the temperance movement. It was March, 1831, before he mentioned, in apologizing for a long delay in correspondence, the pressures of his involvement in "a sacred pursuit which still absorbs me." Later in the same letter he revealed that this was the antislavery cause. He was, he told Weld, "more and more astonished" as he learned about the plight of Negro slaves.³

The first tentative steps toward immediatism had been taken in Britain even as Stuart prepared to leave the United States in mid-1829. On June 5, Otway Cave introduced a resolution in the House of Commons that it was the duty of the House to take measures to protect all British subjects henceforth born in the West Indies from violations of their natural rights as human beings. Although, to the disgust of the *Anti-Slavery Reporter,* the resolution was introduced at a time and date when full discussion was impossible, it marked the beginning of demands that were soon to become more vociferous and more radical. Those demands, however, were not emerging only in the capital. In the first half of 1829 petitions praying for the abolition of slavery had been received by Parliament from places as far apart as Ireland, York, and Norfolk. Stuart's early impressions are unrecorded, but he could easily have first read of the trends as soon as his ship reached Belfast. In late August and early September the Irish leader Daniel O'Connell—newly elected to Parliament as a result of the recent Catholic Emancipation Act—took a prominent role in antislavery meetings in Cork and Dublin demanding an early end to slavery.⁴

It is more certain that Stuart became fully aware of the abolition movement in the early months of 1830. For most of that time, with the exception of a visit to Scotland in April, he was the house guest of William and Mary Blair at Cotham Lodge, Bristol. Here almost certainly was the main

3. Dumond, *Antislavery,* 169; Landon, "Captain Charles Stuart," 11; Stuart to Arthur Tappan, August 5, 1833, in *Liberator,* October 12, 1833, p. 163; Stuart to Weld, April 17, 1830, March 26, 1831, WP.

4. *Anti-Slavery Reporter,* III (June, 1829), 14–15; *Journals of House of Commons,* LXXXIV (1829), 60, 104, 282, 292, 384; *Anti-Slavery Reporter,* III (October, 1829), 81–96.

influence on his decision to embrace abolitionism. Blair had been a civil servant in India during much of Stuart's time there. He had later spent a period in the Cape Colony, where his firsthand experiences of slavery had made him receptive to abolitionist arguments. By the time Stuart joined him he was already involved in antislavery lecturing in the West Country. His home, now in Bristol and later in Bath, would always remain Stuart's English base.[5] Meanwhile, in that same early period in 1830, the demands for an early end to slavery were being given more precision. On April 6 a meeting in Southampton passed resolutions urging that slave children under ten and those to be born henceforward in the colonies should be declared free. On April 8 a meeting in Dublin passed a resolution, sponsored by O'Connell, that Parliament should be petitioned to name a day from which all Negro children thereafter born in British colonies should be free. The same meeting resolved that all other antislavery societies should be requested to petition Parliament to the same purpose. The growing number of petitions reaching Parliament from widely scattered places through these early months of 1830 shows that such resolutions were having an effect.[6]

These purposeful provincial moves reached more directly into the capital on May 15, 1830, when the Anti-Slavery Society held its annual meeting in Freemason's Hall. The platform was dominated by the parliamentary wing of the abolition movement. William Wilberforce was in the chair, and the speakers included Henry Brougham, soon to be Lord Chancellor, and the MPs O'Connell, Thomas Denman, Dr. Stephen Lushington, and Thomas Fowell Buxton. Buxton, who had taken over the parliamentary leadership of the movement from the aging Wilberforce, revealed gradualist attitudes that lagged behind the demands of many of the provincial delegates in the two-thousand-member audience. Adult slaves, he argued, were unfit for immediate emancipation, but not so their children. If these sentiments seemed in tune with recent provincial demands, Buxton went on to present a resolution that antagonized many of those present by its vagueness. It spoke merely of leaving "no proper and practicable means unattempted for effecting, at the earliest period, its [slavery's] entire abolition throughout the British dominions." It was at this point that Henry Pownall, a well-known Middlesex magistrate, stood up in a

---

5. *Anti-Slavery Reporter*, III (1829–30), 414–16; IV (January, 1831), 58. Further biographical details of Blair may be found in Charles C. Prinsep (ed.), *Record of Services of Honourable East India Company's Civil Servants in the Madras Presidency, 1741–1858* (London, n.d.); Stuart to Weld, April 17, 1830, WP.

6. *Anti-Slavery Reporter*, III (May, 1830), 213–19; *Journals of House of Commons*, LXXXV (1830), 16, 98, 122, 135, 155, 410, 455, 495, 504, 535, 541, 547.

side gallery and made a famous intervention condemning further hesitation. After a short speech, he moved an amendment "That from and after the 1st of January, 1830, every child born within the king's dominions shall be free." According to the memoirs of the Birmingham Quaker abolitionist Joseph Sturge, "the effect was electrical." Pownall's speech was greeted with a storm of applause, which for a time left the distinguished platform group nervously struggling to retain control of the meeting. Eventually, after Brougham had pointed out practical difficulties relating to the date suggested by Pownall because of the timetable of parliamentary business, the resolution was passed in amended form, urging Parliament "to fix the day upon which all children born within the king's dominions shall be free." In Sturge's eyes these were "lowering modifications" of Pownall's original amendment. But at least one of the parliamentary leaders on the platform saw the deeper significance of the trends that had just materialized. Thomas Denman congratulated the meeting "because on all former occasions the Society had run before the public, and had in some degree been called upon to excite it—but in this instance the public had shown it would take the matter into its own hands, and had thus given the society a warning by which he was sure it would endeavour to profit."[7]

Denman's apparent enthusiasm for the new trend of greater public pressure was not shared by other members of the antislavery establishment. According to the Sturge *Memoirs*, the incident in Freemason's Hall signaled the beginnings of a breach between two parties which was too deep "to be healed by any temporary compromise." Antagonisms had emerged which eventually were institutionalized by the formation of the Agency Committee. It is tempting to look at the list of officeholders of the Anti-Slavery Society in May, 1830, and at the corresponding list of Agency Committee members a year or so later and see the division as one of conservative and prestigious vice-presidents against more radical, less eminent elements on the committee. There is some validity to this analysis. The list of vice-presidents was dominated by the nobility, headed by the dukes of Gloucester and Devonshire and by such MPs as Buxton, Brougham, Lushington, and Thomas Spring Rice. It contained no future members of the Agency Committee, whereas eight of the thirty-seven committee members were eventually Agency Committee stalwarts. But the divisions were more complex. There were outspoken immediatists among the vice-presidents, notably James Stephen, father of Sir James,

7. *Anti-Slavery Reporter*, III (June, 1830), 229–62; Henry Richard, *Memoirs of Joseph Sturge* (London, 1864), 93–94.

of Colonial Office fame. More important, the committee of the Anti-Slavery Society in June, 1830, did not reflect the provincial antislavery enthusiasm that had just made its presence felt in Freemason's Hall. Still less did that list of names foretell the significant provincial contribution to the subsequent Agency Committee, a contribution in which Charles Stuart played a key role.[8]

The most obvious evidence of rising provincial enthusiasm for abolition lies in the vast increase in the numbers of petitions to Parliament. From a relative handful in 1829 and mere dozens in the first half of 1830, the number grew into the thousands later that year. Initially in that latter period they reflected the resolutions passed at Freemason's Hall. The word "immediately" began to be used more often, but the demands still stopped short of true immediatism. A petition received from Huddersfield in June, for instance, prayed that the House of Commons take steps "for effecting the immediate abolition of slavery" but went on to qualify this demand with the familiar request "that Government will specify an early period when the children of the slaves shall be free." By the last two months of the year the tone of many of the petitions had changed to an uncompromising insistence on abolition "at once and for ever." To some extent, the demands generated their own momentum. A meeting in Edinburgh in October, for instance, achieved great publicity when its immediatist resolutions led to the withdrawal of more cautious leading citizens, including the Lord Provost himself. A second meeting attracted a larger audience and stimulated such interest that twenty-two thousand people subsequently signed the petition for immediate abolition.[9]

The reporting of such events in provincial and national newspapers must have been one reason why the same demands began to be voiced in widely separated areas. But there was also communication and a degree of coordination between at least some abolitionists. Stuart, with his unique mobility and his revivalist training in America, was well equipped to take a leading role in the activities of one significant network. These activities were responsible for some of the petitions to Parliament and for their in-

8. Richard, *Memoirs of Sturge*, 94; *Anti-Slavery Reporter*, III (June, 1830), 268; Anti-Slavery Society, *Report of the Agency Sub-Committee of the Anti-Slavery Society, Established in June 1831 for the Purpose of Disseminating Information by Lectures on Colonial Slavery* (London, 1832), title page.

9. *Journals of House of Commons*, LXXXV (1830), 547; LXXXVI (1831), 35, 38–39; *Anti-Slavery Reporter*, IV (January, 1831), 29–31; Andrew Thomson, *Substance of the Speech Delivered at the Meeting of the Edinburgh Society for the Abolition of Slavery on October 19th, 1830* (Edinburgh, 1830).

creasing radicalism. More important, they were designed to push the campaign against slavery beyond mere petitioning.

Insubstantial and circumstantial though the details of Stuart's conversion to abolitionism may be, from the time of Pownall's contentious amendment his involvement was demonstrably innovative and forceful. From his temporary base in Bristol he quickly published his first antislavery pamphlet, *Petitions Respecting Negro Slavery*, which attacked as ultracautious, not the attitudes of Buxton and his fellow gradualists but the Pownall resolutions, which had appeared so recently as the spearhead of a new radicalism. Stuart's pamphlet was not, of course, the first immediatist publication. But, injected into the new atmosphere of contention following the debate in Freemason's Hall, it was more directly relevant to the current concerns of abolitionists than, for instance, Elizabeth Heyrick's pioneering publication had been in the still complacent early 1820s. Stuart's pamphlet went straight to the heart of the issues:

> Ought the friends of lawful liberty, to petition for the complete and immediate emancipation of the oppressed Negroes, that they may at once be raised from slaves into subjects; and while they share in all the wise and wholesome restraints of law, may partake with us in its privileges and blessings—or, ought they to insert in their petitions, any subordinate clauses, such as, that the deplorably defective propositions of Mr. Canning's administration be carried into effect—and, that the children born after a certain date, shall remain free? . . . They ought to petition for *complete and immediate* emancipation of the Negroes, in the above sense.

Central to his argument was the characteristic evangelical preoccupation with sin, which had been evident even in his youth before he had discovered the Scriptures. He objected to the halfway resolution of May, 1830, "because the more we remove the filthiness and outward obnoxiousness of sin, without ceasing from sinning, the more we cloak the horrors of our guilt, and the greater is our danger of continuing at peace in its vile embraces." His case also rested on the assumption that public opinion was ready for a strong moral lead. The tactic of petitioning for the emancipation only of the children assumed that emancipation of the parents was impossible for years to come: "But this is a perfectly gratuitous assumption. All that is wanting is, the union of the nation; and what is to prevent the union of the nation? what so likely as some half-way measure, that may afford to indolence and selfishness, a convenient excuse."[10]

The "union of the nation" clearly demanded a campaign of publicity to

---

10. Charles Stuart, *Petitions Respecting Negro Slavery* (Bristol, 1830), 1–4.

arouse enthusiasm for the immediatist case. And although it was not directly foreshadowed in his pamphlet, it was such a campaign that Stuart and his associates proceeded to organize from this same period in mid-1830. Their activities—which have been overlooked by historians—meant that the eventual formation of the Agency Committee a year later was not the start of new campaigning methods but a new stage in which proven methods were to be applied on a wider scale.

In effect, two interconnected processes led to the foundation of the Agency Committee. One was a series of discussions within the London-based Anti-Slavery Society, which produced successive decisions about provincial agitation, culminating in the establishment of the agency subcommittee. The other was a process of experimentation in the provinces with the techniques of itinerant lecturing eventually characteristic of the Agency Committee. Superficially, the London deliberations might appear to be the more important of these processes because they led to a series of communications from the metropolis urging provincial action. Perhaps in some areas these communications did stimulate action. But the crucial relationship between metropolis and provinces was the reverse, with the London committee being prodded into action by Stuart's network of provincial abolitionists, who were increasingly in 1830 and early 1831 practicing what they preached about antislavery agitation.

In London, the instigator of the plan to use itinerant agents was Stuart's friend William Blair. Blair was not a member of the Anti-Slavery Society, but his offer to tour the west and south of England to organize meetings and to lecture was made in person in June, 1830, and initiated the discussion. A letter from him in July prompted the London committee to circularize provincial antislavery groups urging vigorous action. In September, Blair was the first to urge "the engaging of agents to itinerate for the purpose of holding public meetings and procuring petitions for Parliament." This demand produced a resolution by the society to contact provincial auxiliaries and ask for nominations for consideration as agents.[11]

In this same period Blair was advocating these methods in his home region of the West Country. In September he addressed an antislavery meeting at Devizes with an impassioned call for "the entire and speedy removal of this mass of misery and guilt." It was important, he went on, that hostility to slavery should not "evaporate in words, or even in petitions." If Parliament did not heed petitions, there should be boycotts of slave-grown sugar. In any case, it was essential "to establish Anti-Slavery Associations in every town and village throughout the kingdom and

11. Minute Books of Committee on Slavery, S. 20, E2/3, pp. 54, 59, 60, 61, 75, 76, RHL.

to diffuse information as extensively as possible." In October he carried the message into Cornwall, with meetings at Truro and Falmouth. Closer to home, Blair's attempts to develop his campaign in Bristol were impeded when two meetings in October were disrupted by supporters of the West India interest. But despite these personal setbacks he could have had little doubt about the efficacy of the methods he was advocating because through this same period he well knew that Charles Stuart was achieving conspicuous success with them in Ireland. Even if Stuart had not directly informed him of this activity, Blair must have learned of it in October, when he shared a platform with one Edward Baldwin, who had recently been associated with Stuart in Ireland.[12]

Although again there is no direct record of the decisions that led to Stuart's return to Ireland in the late summer of 1830, circumstantial evidence makes it clear that he went on antislavery business. The strength of his commitment to the cause—already demonstrated in his *Petitions Respecting Negro Slavery*—and the speed with which he became involved in Irish abolitionism form part of this evidence. No less important, the crucial contacts between the West Country, the Midlands, and Ireland already existed. Stuart's host in Dublin was Dr. Charles Orpen, who, like his host in the West Country, William Blair, was already active in the antislavery cause. Both Blair and Orpen were members of antislavery groups in their respective cities, which were in correspondence with Birmingham abolitionists, who, in their turn, were to employ Stuart as a lecturer immediately after his pioneering activities in Ireland and immediately before the formation of the Agency Committee. It seems probable that Stuart and Blair agreed on a division of labor in mid-1830, with Blair concentrating on lobbying the Anti-Slavery Society in London and local activity in the West Country and Stuart exploiting his great mobility and long-standing Irish connections to join the affiliated Dublin group.

The antislavery milieu in which Stuart was to operate on both sides of the Irish Sea was militantly evangelical, as his background and attitudes might lead one to expect. But it is important to emphasize that both in England and Ireland this militancy was built on an older foundation of Quaker abolitionism. From that Quaker tradition Stuart derived key elements in an antislavery philosophy which he never modified after this formative year, stretching from mid-1830 to mid-1831. In his respect for the Quaker contribution lay some of the explanation for his subsequent

12. *Anti-Slavery Reporter*, III (October, 1830), 414–16; IV (January, 1831), 41, 58, 60, 67.

connections with such important English abolitionists as James Cropper and Joseph Sturge. More immediately, he was subjected to Quaker influence as soon as he returned to Ireland.

Since the late eighteenth century Irish Quakers had opposed slavery, laying particular stress on boycotts of slave-grown produce. This commitment had been strengthened in 1824, following the visit to Dublin of Cropper, a Liverpool Quaker, whose humanitarian impulses have often been questioned because the boycotts he urged of West Indian sugar could only benefit his business interests as a major importer of East Indian sugar. Although from the same year Irish Quakers had become aware of the pioneering pamphlet of their coreligionist Elizabeth Heyrick, through the 1820s they had been as slow as other abolitionists to press for immediate emancipation. A more significant development in the mid-1820s was the appointment of a non-Quaker, Mrs. Charles Orpen of Dublin, as a district treasurer in Ireland for the Birmingham Female Society for the Relief of Negro Slaves. Two years later she became foundation secretary of the Dublin Ladies Anti-Slavery Society, which, like a similar society in Bristol, was formed "in correspondence" with the Birmingham society, whose rules and regulations it substantially adopted.[13]

Although the Dublin Ladies Anti-Slavery Society was not a Quaker organization, it continued and developed the Quaker emphasis on abstention from use of slave produce, issuing a list of grocers' shops selling only East Indian sugar. In July, 1829, men from the same Protestant middle-class circles, including Mrs. Orpen's husband, Dr. Charles Orpen, founded the Dublin Negro's Friend Society (which soon replaced "Dublin" with "Hibernian" in its title). This society, like its female counterpart, retained links with Birmingham abolitionists. It quickly adopted a more aggressive attitude to slavery than that of its Quaker forerunners. Although at its inception it did not explicitly advocate immediatism, a year later, by the time both Stuart and Blair had made their public commitments, it was doing so. Indeed, Charles Orpen was to write a few months later of the anger he and his colleagues had felt in July, 1830, when they had received, in common with other provincial groups, the circular urging greater abolitionist vigor from the London Anti-Slavery Society, which Blair's lobbying had prompted. His own society had been formed, he pointed out, because of disgust at the gradualist policies of the London

13. Douglas Cameron Riach, "Ireland and the Campaign Against American Slavery, 1830–60" (Ph.D. thesis, Edinburgh University, 1975), 18–37; Stuart, "Abolition of Slavery by Great Britain," 14, 19–20.

society and most of its provincial auxiliaries, including the one in Dublin.[14]

Even if Stuart had not crossed the Irish Sea specifically to work for the Negro's Friend Society, it is not hard to understand its attractions for him. At least four prominent members of its Board of Managers were members of the Hibernian Bible Society and, indeed, the two societies held their annual general meetings each year on successive days to facilitate attendance by a largely common membership. This membership not only was exclusively Protestant, but, with the exception of a solitary Quaker on its board, it was militantly so, with strong overtones of the anti-Catholicism that had already been publicly revealed in Stuart's book on Canadian emigration. One of its most prominent members, Major Henry Sirr, the father-in-law of Charles Orpen, was an especially unpopular figure among Dublin Catholics because of his role in the suppression of the United Irishmen at the turn of the century and his work as a police magistrate over a long subsequent period. The society's insistence that "Slavery is a Transgression of the Divine Law" accurately reflected Stuart's own intellectual convictions. In addition, from its inception it embraced policies particularly appealing to a man of Stuart's cosmopolitan experience. It was determined not to confine its efforts to opposing slavery "in the British colonies only": it stressed the necessity of "looking at Slavery as a SIN, wherever it exists, and as such, protesting and in the Lord's name, declaring war against it, *over the whole Globe.*" And it looked beyond to the "moral, and religious, and social, and political improvement of the liberated Negroes." To Stuart, with his background of philanthropy among the liberated blacks of Amherstburg, there was an obvious appeal in the society's commitment to the "improvement of the whole Negro race, whether free, enslaved, or manumitted."[15]

No less appealing was the new society's perpetuation of the traditional Quaker policy of nonconsumption of slave produce. Even without its moral overtones, abstinence from sugar must have seemed a logical extension of Stuart's austere regimen of hard exercise and frugal diet. And a boycott of cotton presented few problems to a man already celebrated for his voluminous woolen cloak and kilt and his preference for sleeping outdoors

---

14. Riach, "Ireland and American Slavery," 18–37; Charles Edward Herbert Orpen, *The Principles, Plans, and Objects of the "Hibernian Negro's Friend Society," Contrasted with Those of the Previously Existing "Anti-Slavery Societies"; Being a Circular, Addressed to all Friends of the Negro, and Advocates for the Abolition and Extinction of Slavery; in the Form of a Letter to Thomas Pringle, Esq. Secretary of the London Anti-Slavery Society* (Dublin, 1831), 1–4.

15. Riach, "Ireland and American Slavery," 37–40; Orpen, *Principles*, 2–4.

on a pallet of straw. Stuart was to adhere to these nonconsumption principles for the rest of his life, even though they led to numerous disagreements with fellow abolitionists, especially those in the United States.

But if he gained much from the Dublin abolitionists, Stuart also gave a great deal in return. His Bristol pamphlet, *Petitions Respecting Negro Slavery*, was publicly endorsed by the Negro's Friend Society as representative of its own hostility to the recent London resolutions favoring the emanicipation of children rather than all slaves. Before long the society published a new pamphlet, *On the Prospective Emancipation of Slaves' Unborn Children*, in which Stuart developed his antislavery philosophy. It was a classic statement of the evangelical preoccupation with slavery as sin, which historians have generally conceded imparted significant momentum to the shift from gradualism. Slavery, which was founded on the "principles of pirates," was inconsistent with both British and divine law. No man was at liberty to break the divine law, to choose to obey only part of it, or to choose when to begin obeying it: "He is bound to obey it immediately." Even if a man "foresaw the greatest probability of advantage, by waiving immediate obedience, in favour of some more expedient, though less equitable measure," he had no right to choose expediency: "God gives us no such liberty. Immediate duty is His holy and gracious requirement. The present moment is all, that God gives to man." Accompanying these theological imperatives was optimism that slaves were immediately capable of freedom. The examples of Negroes in Haiti, Sierra Leone, and Canada were cited along with the "broad history of man" in Colombia, Mexico, and Poland to refute the charge that men could be "so irremediably bent" by slavery "that they are no longer capable of the erect posture of freedom."[16]

In these last few months of 1830 Stuart wrote no fewer than thirteen pamphlets published by the Negro's Friend Society. In at least two of them he introduced themes he was later to develop in better-known publications. *Can West Indian Slavery Be Justified From Scripture?* was soon elaborated as *Is Slavery Defensible from Scripture?* published in Belfast the following year. Throughout his antislavery career Stuart was to return again and again to his central arguments, denying similarities between plantation slavery and various forms of servitude described in the Old Testament. In a wider sense these arguments were important for the future. They meant that he was resting his abolitionism on a rigorous and fairly narrow definition of slavery. In the long run, this position would

16. Orpen, *Principles*, 35; Charles Stuart, *On the Prospective Emancipation of Slaves' Unborn Children* (Dublin, [1830?]).

find him at odds not merely with apologists for Negro slavery but with abolitionists who would seek targets beyond the Negro plantation system in forms of servitude ingrained in Asian cultures. In the shorter term, a more important rehearsal of subsequent arguments came in the pamphlet, *Have Slave-Holders Any Right to Be Compensated on Being Deprived of Their Power to Continue to Steal Men's Personal Liberty?* In his powerfully argued negative to this question, Stuart was advancing his own position significantly from his first, Bristol antislavery pamphlet, in which he had raised but left open the question of compensation.[17] And he was introducing a theme that was to be developed fully in his most famous and influential antislavery work, *The West India Question*, first published in 1832 and subsequently reprinted several times in the United States.

The significance of Stuart's antislavery writings in this Dublin period lies principally in the early date at which he was articulating an uncompromising immediatism. Although his central arguments, rejecting anything short of complete emancipation for all slaves, seem characteristic of the attitudes that accompanied the emancipation movement, it must be remembered that at the time they were written they were, above all, trenchant criticisms of the official policies of the British antislavery "establishment." Stuart's brand of immediatism was soon to become predominant, but other aspects of his 1830 arguments—notably in relation to compensation—were never to be accepted completely by the British abolition movement. This is not to say that either Stuart or the groups of provincial abolitionists with whom he worked were alone in pushing the antislavery argument to new extremes. It is extremely likely that the same formative events, particularly the May, 1830 meeting in Freemason's Hall, were impelling many abolitionists to develop their attitudes toward the immediatist conclusion. It is even probable, as an official publication of the Agency Committee was eventually to assert, that individuals in many places "without collusion" were calling meetings that eventually influ-

17. Extract from Report of the Hibernian Negro's Friend Society for March 31, 1831, printed in *Liberator*, October 8, 1831, p. 171. This is a tribute to the devotion and talents of Stuart, "who has travelled very extensively through Ireland, and is also the author of thirteen of the Society's tracts." Not all of these have been traced, but the list probably includes, in addition to those named in the text and in note 16, the following pamphlets published by the society in the relevant period: *Appeal of the Negro's Friend Society to the People of Ireland on Behalf of the Slaves in the British Colonies; On Sophistical Arguments Against a Conscientious Disuse of Sugar Produced by Slave Labour;* and *Is West Indian Slavery Justifiable by the New Testament?* All of these were printed in Dublin by Richard D. Webb.

enced the formation of that more radical society.[18] But in this respect there can be no doubt that the work of Stuart and his associates was crucial in practicing and perfecting the methods that were to become characteristic of the Agency Committee. Stuart's prolific literary output in Ireland in 1830 is even more remarkable because, through the same period, he was involved in an extensive program of lecturing throughout southern and western Ireland, soon to be followed in the early months of 1831 by a similar tour in the north and northwest.

Stuart's tours gave him the chance to take his antislavery publications directly to the people. But he devoted most of his efforts to lecturing. Placards advertising his meetings were posted widely in advance of his arrival in every town he visited. He usually lectured in Protestant churches, chapels, and meeting halls, and everywhere he carried with him a "west-Indian slave whip . . . for every one, who doubts the cruelties of slavery, to see and examine." The only obvious difference between his lecture tours and the revivalist methods he had practiced in upstate New York was that now his earnest entreaties were not directly for a commitment to Christ but for the organization of petitions to Parliament demanding immediate abolition. The petitions that followed—sometimes from more than one congregation or group—from such places as Waterford, Cork, Clonakilty, Limerick, and Wexford were testimony to his efforts. As Charles Orpen wrote in the New Year, "The numerous meetings that he has held, and the deep interest, that has been every where excited . . . has been already proved in Parliament, by the novel fact, that petitions have been sent from very many places in Ireland, which had never before done so."[19]

This Irish outcry against colonial slavery came at a time when, from many of the same places visited by Stuart, petitions were drawing the attention of Parliament to the "deep and appalling distress with which Ireland is pervaded." Stuart was at heart too fierce a patriot ever to agree with the theme of these petitions that the lack of a domestic Parliament was a major cause of Irish distress. Despite his frequent clashes with authority on three continents, he had never challenged the British imperialism that gave him modest status, income, and independence. He was too extreme a Protestant ever to see Irish problems as wholly separate from the pernicious influence of Rome. If religion had given him a social conscience, this was confined to a belief in the power of the gospel to liberate heathens in India or Canada from ignorant depravity and white men in

18. *Report of the Agency Committee*, 2.
19. Stuart's itinerary and methods are described by Orpen, *Principles*, 10–11; for examples of Irish petitions see *Journals of House of Commons*, LXXXV (1830), 74, 86, 133, 147, 157, 163, 167.

America from enslavement to drunkenness and other sins. It was entirely consistent for him now to have declared war on an evil he had never seen in his extensive travels, while traversing a country engulfed by misery. In the longer term he would not remain totally indifferent to Irish suffering. But in the short term he had no difficulty in ignoring it to concentrate on the remoter distress of West Indian slaves.[20]

This single-mindedness combined with his American revivalist experience to make Stuart a particularly appropriate exponent of the methods that were to become characteristic of the most successful period of antislavery agitation. But he was much more agent than innovator of the policies being refined by the several loosely coordinated groups of abolitionists in Britain and Ireland. Those policies can be seen taking shape particularly in the reports of the Birmingham female abolitionists over the previous two years. In 1829 these women had announced plans for a national registry for encouraging abstinence from consumption of slave produce. This registry would consist of lists of those agreeing to boycott slave produce according to varying conditions. At that stage none of these conditions included immediate and absolute abolition. But the proposed methods of publicizing and compiling the lists foreshadowed those later used in the immediatist campaign. "Several of the largest towns" were divided into districts and itinerant "visitors" were appointed to each of them to draw attention to the connections between sugar and slavery and to solicit signatures for the registry. In the following year—and immediately before Stuart's Irish tours—the Birmingham women had explicitly outlined the procedures that would eventually become characteristic of the Agency Committee: "We have not, to this day promoted, as we might have done, the employment of a regular agency for assisting in the formation of extended associations in every accessible part of his Majesty's dominions, in order that the appalling wickedness of the colonial system might become known, if possible, to all men. That we may no longer have to reproach ourselves . . . it will be proposed . . . that we henceforth appropriate a certain portion of our funds to the support of travelling Agents."[21]

Even without any special connections, these initiatives had almost certainly been known to the Irish abolitionists for whom Stuart had been working because the Birmingham women circulated their plans so assiduously that they were soon being reprinted even in the American *Genius*

20. *Journals of House of Commons*, LXXXVI (1831), 61, 87, 133.
21. "National Registry, for Encouraging Abstinence from Sugar, the Produce of Slave Labor," *Genius of Universal Emancipation*, XII (September, 1831), 73–74; extract from *Fifth Report* of Birmingham female abolitionists in *ibid.*, XIII (August, 1833), 157.

of Universal Emancipation. But the next stage of Stuart's activities points strongly to a close liaison between the Dublin and Birmingham groups throughout this period of early grass-roots agitation. In April, 1831, after completing two separate tours that took him through most of Ireland, Stuart prepared to return to England to exploit the intense political atmosphere of an imminent general election. The Board of Managers of the Negro's Friend Society marked his departure with a public "acknowledgment of the eminent success, which, under Divine favour, has attended the disinterested and unwearied labours, Christian devotedness, and able talents of their esteemed colleague." And very soon he and Edward Baldwin appeared in the Midlands as "Agents of the Hibernian Negro's Friend Society" under the auspices of the "Ladies Negro's Friend Societies of Birmingham, West Bromwich, Wednesbury, Walsall, and their Respective Neighbourhoods." For almost a month the two men followed separate routes, lecturing virtually every day and between them covering most of the towns in Warwickshire and Staffordshire. Stuart's meetings were advertised soberly enough in the local press. He was introduced as a man "who has devoted much attention to the subject of Colonial Slavery," and his lectures were concerned with the "Evils of the System" and the "Justice and Practicality of its Immediate Abolition." With the exception of one disrupted meeting at Wolverhampton late in his tour, his lectures evidently proceeded equally soberly. The sponsoring female abolitionists, reporting their satisfaction with the experiment, made it clear that the agents were now concerned not only with organizing petitions to Parliament but with establishing a permanent network of local organizations that could carry on the work by lobbying MPs, organizing boycotts of slave-grown sugar, and raising money for use in a variety of propagandist and activist ways. Moreover, they stressed, "after their various lectures were delivered in this neighbourhood, we rejoice to state that a Committee was formed in London for propagating Christian principles, on the subject of British Slavery."[22]

The connection between the lecturing of Stuart and Baldwin and the formation of the Agency Committee was, of course, not so simply causal as the Birmingham ladies' report suggested. The discussions about lecturing agencies initiated by William Blair had proceeded intermittently in the committee of the Anti-Slavery Society in London for a year. In January Blair had again been a visitor when the London society discussed

22. *Liberator*, October 8, 1831, p. 171; Birmingham Ladies Negro's Friend Society; *Seventh Report of the Ladies Negro's Friend Society for Birmingham, West Bromwich, Wednesbury, Walsall, and Their Respective Neighbourhoods* (Birmingham, 1832), 23–25; *Aris's Birmingham Gazette*, August 22, 1831, p. 3.

plans to issue a circular urging people throughout the country to lobby their MPs in support of Buxton's parliamentary moves for abolition and also to promote antislavery meetings and organize petitions in all counties and large towns. A week later the London committee had received, in Charles Orpen's aggressive letter, details of the scope and success of Stuart's Irish antislavery tours. To bring out the contrast between London policies, which were still too gradualist, and those of his own society, he appended the two radical pamphlets by Stuart, *Petitions Respecting Negro Slavery* and *Prospective Emancipation*. But, argued Orpen, it was not only the goals of the London society that were at fault but also its tactics. The real need was to flood Parliament with petitions, to secure antislavery pledges from candidates for parliamentary elections, and to prepare for both these procedures by "interesting the public mind." The "most gratifying results" achieved by Stuart's "Deputation" through Ireland showed what could be achieved in this way.[23]

In April the Anti-Slavery Society established a small subcommittee, which included a nonmember, George Stephen, the fourth son of James, the elder, to meet daily to provide assistance for proabolition MPs. In May these outside contacts were extended when the society organized a conference "with friends from the country respecting the employment of Travelling Agents." Still engaged in the final weeks of his Midlands agency, Stuart did not attend this conference, but there were delegates from Bristol, Dublin, and Birmingham, who could not have failed to know of his activities. At this conference it was resolved "on the motion of George Stephen and with the unanimous recommendation of the Friends and Visitors from many parts of the kingdom now present that the Committee engage stipendiary Agents to travel in various parts of the country to promote the more general diffusion of correct information on the System of Slavery in our Colonies throughout every class of the population." On June 1 the London committee gave substance to this resolution by formally appointing its agency subcommittee. Although still in the provinces, Charles Stuart was named as one of the founder-members.[24]

The historian Howard Temperley has made a comment about Stuart and the innovative nature of the Agency Committee's methods which can fairly be used to represent orthodox interpretations, although its recognition that Stuart had any role is unusual:

> The Agency Committee also received the gratuitous services of a number of others, including those of that fervid but somewhat eccentric abolitionist,

23. Minute Books, S. 20, E2/3, pp. 59, 60, 61, 65, 70, 75, 77, RHL; Orpen, *Principles*, 9–11.
24. Minute Books, S. 20, E2/3, pp. 89–94, RHL.

Captain Charles Stuart, recently returned from the United States, where he had been assisting in the revivalist efforts of Charles Finney and his holy band.

The methods used by the Committee had, in fact, much in common with those used by religious revivalists. In adapting them to the needs of the antislavery cause it established a new and highly effective technique later used with even greater effect in the United States.

Temperley's account thus comes intriguingly close to recognizing the causal connection between Stuart's experience and activities and the methods adopted by the Agency Committee. But its underestimation of Stuart's role lies not only in its unawareness of his Irish and English provincial lecturing experience in 1830 and 1831. It is also misleading in its suggestion that after the formation of the Agency Committee, Stuart's was a part-time, amateurish contribution. In fact, it is doubtful whether from this time on there was any abolitionist on either side of the Atlantic who was more full time than Stuart. Taking advantage of his financial independence, his lack of close family ties, and his personal contacts in innumerable places, he was to live and breathe abolitionism for the best part of two decades.[25]

Stuart's role as a policy maker has been overlooked because his name does not appear as a member in the first published report of the Agency Committee in 1832. This omission occurred because he was by then back "in the field," lecturing throughout the Midlands and south of England. This lecturing agency has been largely ignored because, as Temperley notes, his services were "gratuitous." In fact, Stuart was one of the six original full-time agents employed by the committee, but he refused to accept any payment except his traveling expenses.[26]

From the outset there were tensions between the new subcommittee and the general committee. The parent body attempted to assert its right to scrutinize advertisements for agents and approve all circulars and publications issued by the agency subcommittee. It wanted to limit agents' remuneration to traveling expenses. And above all, it objected to the inclusion on the new subcommittee of Stuart, George Stephen, and two others who were not members of the general committee. Stuart was in London when these disputes emerged in June, 1831. He helped draft a letter of instruction to agents articulating the immediatist creed of the Agency Committee: "To uphold slavery is a crime before God, and the condition must therefore be immediately abolished." And he attended as a visitor

25. Temperley, *British Antislavery*, 13.
26. *Report of the Agency Committee*, title page, 2.

the meetings of the general committee in which the more conservative elements developed their criticisms of this new radical offshoot. At one such meeting a compromise was reached on the question of membership. The agency subcommittee was reconstituted to include only those original members who were members of the parent society but "with power to avail themselves of the co-operation of Mr. G. Stephen, Captain Stuart, Mr. J. Price, Mr. E. Cooper," the four original outsiders, "and other friends of the Society." In practice this compromise made no difference in the role of the "outsiders," for over the next year the agency subcommittee developed into a separate organization, with its own secretary, John Crisp, and with George Stephen one of its leading figures, before formally declaring its independence, aptly enough on July 4, 1832.[27]

The provincial—and especially Irish—contribution to the experiments that had preceded the Agency Committee's foundation was reflected in the choice of agents. Stuart and Edward Baldwin were two of six original full-time agents. Later, William Hume, also of the Hibernian Negro's Friend Society, was to be similarly employed. The significance of these appointments has been overshadowed by the presence in the original group of George Thompson and, among the later appointees, John Scoble.[28] These two names would loom large in the future history of British abolition; in the eventually tense relations between British and American abolitionists; and, in the process, in the increasingly contentious career of Captain Charles Stuart.

For the moment, however, all was harmony and enthusiasm in the ranks of the Agency Committee and its agents, as the immediatist message was taken into hundreds of localities. In the earliest stages, in the autumn of 1831, the focus of activities was the Midlands, the West Country, and the south of England. An important part of the agents' duties was the "formation or revival of Auxiliary Associations." As the Agency Committee's *Report* pointed out, where local associations existed auxiliary to the national Anti-Slavery Society they had often become "inert and inefficient," not least because they operated in isolation. The committee expressed confidence, after the first wave of lecturing, that these problems were substantially overcome and that local groups "are awakened to the importance of renewed zeal and increased activity, now that they have re-

27. Minute Books, S. 20, E2/3, pp. 97, 99–102, 104–106, 111, 115, 117–18, 120–21, 124, 151–54, RHL.
28. *Report of the Agency Committee*, 2; Sir George Stephen, *Anti-Slavery Recollections in a Series of Letters to Mrs. Beecher Stowe* (London, 1854), 148.

ceived decided proof that there is a central body at work, whose increasing object will be to combine the energies of all."[29]

HISTORIANS have generally acknowledged the importance of the Agency Committee in helping to bring about the Emancipation Act of 1833 by arousing public opinion and applying its pressures, not merely in Westminster but also on MPs and candidates for parliamentary elections in the constituencies. This activity is particularly important to those who stress that emancipation should be seen as a victory for a broadly based political movement rather than as the decision of a reformed Parliament now reflecting the predominance of industrial capitalism, as the once-influential thesis of Eric Williams suggested. Yet is is necessary to emphasize not only what Stuart did but also his motives, for the complex origins of the Agency Committee revealed by his activities appear to resurrect aspects of the Williams thesis.

One of the significant interests common to the various groups with which Stuart had worked was the promotion of East Indian products at the expense of the slave-grown West Indian variety. For many this was no doubt simply a logical antislavery tactic. But for key individuals the East Indian connection was more basic. Eric Williams pointed to the East India Company investments of Zachary Macaulay, an abolitionist throughout the 1820s and a prominent member of the Agency Committee. And he emphasized still more the economic convenience of antislavery activity for James Cropper, "the greatest importer of East India sugar into Liverpool." But Williams' conclusion that the "connection between East Indians and certain abolitionists has not been fully appreciated" could be turned against him. He could have reinforced his argument by emphasizing a similarly expedient commitment at a humbler level, whether among the Dublin grocers who had long promoted East Indian produce or among the Birmingham female organizers of the national registry for encouraging abstinence from slave-grown sugar. Whatever the motives of individual organizers of the registry, their scheme depended on the availability of free-grown supplies of sugar, which were to be distributed from the London warehouse of John Crisp, "dealer in tea and East-India sugar only" and soon to be secretary of the Agency Committee.[30]

Whether William Blair retained an interest in the East India Company

29. *Report of the Agency Committee*, 6, 8.
30. Eric Williams, *Capitalism and Slavery* (2d ed.; London, 1964), 186–88; Riach, "Ireland and American Slavery," 19–22; *Genius of Universal Emancipation*, XII (September, 1831), 73–74.

he had served so long has not been established. As for Charles Stuart, his correspondence reveals no evidence of any investments in company stock. Yet the same correspondence reveals that, far from being the wealthy man that at least one historian has assumed, he was almost totally dependent throughout his life on the military pension he had secured from the company.[31]

At first sight, Stuart seems to fit the Williams thesis perfectly. Along with a vested personal interest in the well-being of the East India Company, he placed a strong emphasis on the superiority of free over slave labor in his most substantial antislavery publication, *The West India Question*. As a number of recent historians have argued, there can be no doubt that such economic arguments about colonial slavery were an important part of the atmosphere of the emancipation struggle, even though Williams' central contention that the West Indian economy was in decline may have been seriously undermined. In short, what abolitionists argued about that economy was more important in this context than the probable error of those arguments suggested by Seymour Drescher's *Econocide*.[32]

Yet notwithstanding these connections and arguments, there can be little doubt that careful analysis of most abolitionists' behavior would reveal a much more complex motivation than mere expediency. Certainly to concentrate on Stuart's economic self-interest, or even the highly selective nature of his humanitarianism, would be to ignore the evidence of his earlier life and deny the force of other explanations of the antislavery impulse.

Stuart had seized on the antislavery cause with the zeal of a man at last reaching the end of a complex emotional and intellectual obstacle course. Intellectually he had reached clear ground some time before his return to Britain. If slavery seemed to many of his contemporaries to be the embodiment of sin, he himself was the embodiment of the ideology that rejected all compromise with sin. This attitude, foreshadowed by Elizabeth Heyrick's pamphlet but still dormant in British abolitionism when Stuart reached the British Isles, has been described by David Brion Davis as a "liberation for the reformer from the ideology of gradualism, from a toleration of evil within the social order, and from a deference to institutions

---

31. C. Duncan Rice, "The Anti-Slavery Mission of George Thompson to the United States, 1834–35," *Journal of American Studies*, II (1968), 15.

32. Charles Stuart, *The West Indian Question* (London, 1831); Stanley L. Engerman, "Some Implications of the Abolition of the Slave Trade," in Eltis and Walvin (eds.), *Abolition of the Atlantic Slave Trade*, 7–8.

that blocked the way to personal salvation."³³ Stuart had already been thus liberated. He had long since rejected extreme Calvinist doctrines and affirmed his belief in the individual's ability to find salvation through the Scriptures. He had also outspokenly opposed individuals, like Bishop Mountain, or institutions, like the Catholic church, that hindered such personal initiative. And his belief that men should nonetheless seek much more than personal salvation had found expression in numerous reform activities.

Immediatism was the result of emotional as much as intellectual processes—and for no one more than Stuart. He had undergone the "conversion experience of rich personal meaning," which Bertram Wyatt-Brown and others have suggested was common in the formative years of American abolitionists. But it was significant that for Stuart, whose evangelical orthodoxy was self-taught rather than the result of parental guidance, this experience had come in his mid-thirties, not adolescence. However stylized it might have been for some teenage Americans, for him its interaction with the debacle of his military career had made it a life crisis of major significance. Davis, in describing immediatism as an amalgam of "intense personal anxiety, rapturous freedom, eagerness for sacrifice, and mistrust of legalism, institutions, and slow-working agencies for salvation," could well have been describing the man who had emerged from years of conflict with the East India Company and from spiritual and emotional crisis in Canada to plunge with almost manic abandon into so many philanthropic ventures.³⁴

Yet no abolitionist's commitment can be explained simply by the neatness with which he matches a composite picture drawn from general descriptions of the immediatist impulse. In Stuart's case the commitment was also the result of personal factors that had prompted his departure from America and attended his early months in England. His rejection by Cornelia Weld had evidently driven him across the Atlantic. He had left voicing no resolutions about abstinence from marriage or the need to find emotional satisfaction in a new circle of friendships. Perhaps secretly he had still retained hopes of marrying her. But although he would briefly renew the courtship some years in the future, there can be little doubt that in late 1829, at the age of forty-eight, the failure of his one serious attempt at marriage had left him for the moment unwilling to risk another emotional rebuff. At the same time it left him with a need for warm personal relationships as great as his desire for Christian social commit-

33. Davis, "Immediatism," 73.
34. *Ibid.*; Wyatt-Brown, "Conscience and Career," 192–95.

ment. In the campaign for immediate abolition of slavery he had found a spiritually satisfying cause. And in the swelling ranks of immediate abolitionists he had found a camaraderie greater than any he had known elsewhere.

This emotional involvement was clearly revealed in his work as an Agency Committee lecturer. He was originally assigned to the Midlands region, where he had so recently worked. For three months from mid-August he visited some twenty-five towns, some of them more than once. In most places he held two or three lectures on successive evenings, frequently relying on local clergy for lecture rooms, organizational arrangements, and even hospitality. His route had been prearranged by the Agency Committee, but more than once chance encounters led him into detours when he saw the prospect of further advancing the cause. Total enthusiasm and optimism pervaded his reports of the tour. His lectures appear always to have been well attended. His usual practice of inviting questions occasionally revealed members of his audience with firsthand experience of colonial slavery, but opposition throughout his tour was minimal. There were many small incidents in his report to support his conclusion that "I have experienced kindness everywhere." There was a hotelkeeper in Wellington who "treated me like a brother, and would receive no compensation." There was the combined welcome in Stafford from the rector, his curate, "and all the dissenting ministers." And there was the unexpectedly extended meeting at Tenbury, "the most interesting which I have had," when the audience remained discussing slavery until late at night, "and there seemed no weariness."[35]

His effectiveness as an agent was very much defined by this emotional warmth. It is clear that he was far from being a great orator in the sense that another Agency Committee lecturer, George Thompson, clearly was. Thompson was an even more recent antislavery convert than Stuart, but he rapidly laid the foundations of a reputation which, within a few years, made him the most celebrated and, indeed, notorious abolitionist speaker to operate on both sides of the Atlantic.[36] In contrast to the careful organization, fluency, and composure of Thompson's lectures, Stuart was frequently criticized for allowing religious enthusiasm and emotional excitability to mar his performances. According to George Stephen, he became widely known as the "Anti-Slavery Quixote," a man "too apt to

35. *Report of the Agency Committee*, 6, 13–14.
36. Rice, "Anti-Slavery Mission of George Thompson," 13–31; Stephen, *Anti-Slavery Recollections*, 150–51; *Report of the Agency Committee*, 16–19; Thompson's own accounts of his Agency Committee tours are contained in twenty-three letters to his wife, September, 1831–August, 1832, in JR.

sermonize on all occasions." Edward Cropper, a member of the Liverpool Quaker family, attended Stuart's lectures at Leamington and Norwich and reported: "I think his lectures would be improved if he attended a little more to the arrangement of his subjects." But it is also clear that Stuart's effectiveness as a campaigner was considerable despite these criticisms because of a personality that inspired far more affection than did Thompson's. Whereas Thompson, away from the public platform, frequently aroused guarded suspicion among casual acquaintances, who regarded him as essentially a mercenary and even, despite the physical danger he was often to face, questioned his moral courage on contentious issues, Stuart invariably impressed people with his enthusiasm, affectionate warmth, and stubborn moral consistency.[37]

In the long run, when antislavery goals were less clear-cut, these qualities, in combination with his outlandish dress, would enable critics and later historians to dismiss him as an eccentric. But this eccentricity did not, in this dramatic stage of activism, alienate people; indeed, it impressed enormously those who were potentially sympathetic to abolition. George Stephen, after condemning Stuart's "sermonizing," went on: "There was an affectionateness in his manner so truly Christian, and an earnestness so simple and sincere, that people loved to hear him, and if he seldom convinced by his argument, he was so obviously a good man, that to have enlisted him in the cause, of itself implied that the cause was good. I believe that his example induced many pious men to think of it who had never bestowed a thought on it before." In the same way, Edward Cropper, after criticizing Stuart's lecturing technique, continued: "Yet the fearless manner in which he advocates the cause and the sound principles on which his arguments are founded seemed to be very convincing to those who had neither read nor heard much upon the subject, and were peculiarly suited to the religious portion of the middle and lower classes."[38]

Stuart's activities and personality thus serve to emphasize the importance of aspects of the antislavery impulse which Eric Williams' economic interpretation once threatened to obscure. Yet the popular enthusiasm for

37. Stephen, *Anti-Slavery Recollections*, 144; Edward Cropper to Thomas Pringle, September 1, 1831, S. 18, C1/15, RHL. Examples of the various reactions to Thompson are Stephen, *Anti-Slavery Recollections*, 151; "Journal of Henry C. Wright," Garrison Papers, BPL. A reminiscence critical of Thompson but containing an affectionate portrait of Stuart is by Maria Waring in Alfred Webb, "Copies of Letters by Sarah Poole," Garrison Papers, BPL.

38. Stephen, *Anti-Slavery Recollections*, 144; Cropper to Pringle, September 1, 1831, S. 18, C1/15, RHL.

slave emancipation they reveal is a reminder of the persistence of another interpretive problem. Williams' contention that emancipation was the work of a reformed Parliament reflecting the new ascendancy of industrial capitalism may be too simplistic. But agitation for parliamentary reform mingled with the threat of more radical upheaval to form the atmosphere in which the demands for immediate emancipation were being voiced. In the autumn of 1831, as Stuart pursued his Midlands agency, the rejection of the Reform Bill by the House of Lords left Britain on the edge of political chaos. In the West Country Bristol was in the hands of rioters for three days. In the Midlands Nottingham Castle was burned; the jail at Derby was sacked; and Thomas Attwood's Political Union in Birmingham threatened revolution. And in London revolutionary placards appeared, rioters thronged the streets, and the king's carriage was attacked. Eventually this instability was exploited by middle-class reformers insisting that only democratic reform could avert revolution. Even then there was a succession of ministerial crises before the threat to create many new peers forced the House of Lords to abandon attempts to emasculate the bill.[39] Historians who have plausibly argued that the antislavery campaign must be seen as a mass political movement have not yet explained why a distant colonial evil should have had popular appeal in a time of such immediate political turmoil.

For Stuart himself there was no problem. The tense atmosphere, he felt, encouraged a more general political sensitivity beneficial to the antislavery cause:

> I have found no reason to believe that the agitation of the public mind in other questions, interferes at all materially with attention to this. I rather am persuaded that the commotion is useful. I mean, of course, only as is consistent with good order and the public peace. The present appears to me just such a juncture (excepting always the outrages on the public safety which have so disgraced one or two places) as we could desire, and it seems given to us for the very purpose of using every sinew of our diligence in informing the public mind.[40]

This assessment may well have been valid for the "religious portion" who formed a significant part of his audiences. People with reforming instincts, who nevertheless felt threatened by the prospects of domestic upheaval, may have found comfort in this worthy but less disruptive cause.

39. G.D.H. Cole and Raymond Postgate, *The Common People, 1746–1946* (London, 1964), 254; Williams, *Capitalism and Slavery*, 133–34.
40. *Report of the Agency Committee*, 6, 13–14.

But the comment clearly leaves much of the popular support for emancipation still unexplained and is much more important as further evidence of the personal detachment from immediate social problems which Stuart had so recently displayed in Ireland.

The detachment was equally evident in the climax of the emancipation struggle as he worked to focus British attention not only on the West Indies but politically even farther afield to the United States. It was typical of his enthusiasm, and of the high esteem he enjoyed with the Agency Committee as "a well known, persevering, and uncompromising friend of the cause," that he should step into the breach when one of the original lecturers, Edward Clarkson, quickly withdrew from his agency. Immediately after his Midlands tour, he embarked on a second agency in the south of England. The *Report* of the Agency Committee contains little detail of this tour along the coast. The American abolitionist newspaper the *Liberator*, however, gave a glimpse of the more sensational side of Stuart's expository technique by reporting a series of lectures he had given at Brighton on the "horrors of slavery" with a wealth of quotation about floggings of females and stretching of male slaves by block-and-tackle.[41]

These transatlantic reports did not mean that Stuart had discovered new information about the barbaric extremes of slavery nor that he had developed new skills as an orator. They showed that already by early 1832, he was in the process of becoming a celebrity in American antislavery circles. Important though his contribution had been to the foundation of the Agency Committee; dedicated though he was to his work as an agent; a no less significant part of his abolitionism in the two years before the Emancipation Act of 1833 was in introducing an American antislavery issue to Britain at a time when one might have assumed all abolitionist attention would be focused on the issue of British colonial slavery.

41. *Ibid.*, 2, 7; *Liberator*, April 30, 1832, p. 50.

3 AMERICAN ISSUES IN BRITAIN

IN THE United States as well as Britain the early 1830s saw a shift from gradualist to immediatist antislavery policies. There is interpretive debate about many aspects of this change of emphasis, but certain broad trends seem indisputable. First, however dubious the ultimate importance of transatlantic links between abolitionists, there is no doubt that Americans at first looked for encouragement and inspiration to the British, who were moving rapidly against colonial slavery. Second, whatever debate there might be about the long-term significance of William Lloyd Garrison in the American abolition movement, it is generally accepted that his visit to Britain in 1833 gave him sufficient prestige to make him at least for the next few years the most prominent of American abolitionists. Finally, if Garrison's New England has a rival as the key area of American abolitionism, it is the revivalist belt of western New York and Ohio under the inspiring influence of Theodore Weld.[1] In all these trends Charles Stuart had a role that has either been ignored or seriously underrated by historians but that made him a key figure in Anglo-American abolitionism from mid-1830 to mid-1834. He was the main contempo-

1. A study that examines the fluctuations from "virtually a single trans-Atlantic antislavery community in the 1780s" to "more tenuous" ties in the early nineteenth century and stresses the very different circumstances in which abolitionists operated in the two countries thereafter is Howard Temperley, "British and American Abolitionists Compared," in Duberman (ed.), *Antislavery Vanguard*, 343–61. The controversies over Garrison and the competing claims of the West and New England as formative regions are most accessibly set out in the editor's Introduction and in essays by Barnes, Dumond, and John L. Thomas, in Curry (ed.), *Abolitionists*, 1–38.

rary British abolitionist hero promoted by the American antislavery press, especially Garrison's *Liberator*. He paved the way for Garrison's visit to Britain with his campaigns against the American Colonization Society throughout the British Isles. He brought his protégé, Weld, into the movement, made contact with other western abolitionists, and in early 1834 prepared to join the burgeoning movement in America. Before he left—and at his instigation—the Agency Committee transformed itself into a society devoted to global abolitionism, with American slavery as its first target.

THE COMPARATIVELY long break in Stuart's letters to Weld in 1830 may be attributable to the emotional reorientation he was undergoing as he shifted his attention from American friendships to almost total involvement in the antislavery cause. Certainly it is possible from a historical perspective to realize that the two men were never to be so close again as they had been in the first few years of their relationship. But the tone of Stuart's renewed correspondence was as warmly effusive as ever, suggesting that he was as yet unconscious of any fundamental change of feeling: "Altho' the same land has not held us—altho' the ocean rolls between us—Altho' pursuits beyond our energy to fulfil as we would wish, have engaged our attention . . . yet unalterably dear art thou to me, my Theodore, and still my 'untravelled' heart trusts in thine."[2]

It was in this letter that he revealed his involvement in the "sacred pursuit" of antislavery. And at once he began the process of converting his younger friend. He begged Weld to study some enclosed "articles of information" on the subject "because they involve a cause of deep and peculiar interest, and because I want to have my Theodore's soul engaged in a work to me the most interesting, with which I have ever met." Another letter also reflected the same fervency of commitment both to the cause and the old friendship: "I send you ten copies of a pamphlet—read one—and make the best use that you can of the rest. I long to hear of your being engaged in the sacred cause of Negro emancipation. My soul thirsts after you beloved Theodore."[3]

Weld was soon associating with other reform-minded individuals in New York City, including Arthur and Lewis Tappan, George Bourne, and William Goodell. The letters and antislavery literature he was receiving from Stuart almost certainly would have been discussed by this group at meetings that are often seen as the seeds from which the American Anti-

2. Stuart to Weld, March 26, June, 1831, WP.
3. *Ibid.*

Slavery Society was to flower two years later. The link between Weld and his new associates was Charles Grandison Finney, who had now moved to a ministry in New York City under the patronage of the Tappan brothers.[4] It seems probable that Weld would have embraced abolitionism sooner or later in such circumstances, for one could hardly claim that, without Stuart, so many men already committed to religious revival and social reform would have forever been indifferent to the evils of slavery. Even so, in view of their close relationship and the tone of his letters, Stuart's influence must be seen as primary. And it was to be formative for years to come, as he supplied Weld with a constant stream of British abolition material.

In many ways, however, the most intriguing aspect of the Stuart-Weld correspondence at this period is not Stuart's conversion of his protégé. That contribution has been generally acknowledged by a number of historians.[5] What has not been generally realized is that the same transatlantic correspondence marked an injection of American issues into the British antislavery atmosphere. Stuart's conversion to abolitionism had sharpened his interest in social and racial questions in the United States, which he already knew something about. His letters to Weld consequently demanded as well as imparted information. He asked about American slavery, about the free blacks of the United States, about the Cherokee Indians, and especially about the American Colonization Society (ACS).[6]

It is doubtful whether Weld's replies to these questions would have been of more than private interest to Stuart, if the ACS had not sent its agent Elliot Cresson to England on a fund-raising mission in mid-1831. For American abolitionists in general, and for William Lloyd Garrison in particular, the ACS policy of shipping former slaves to Liberia provided the great issue, equivalent to the British attack on colonial slavery, which marked the shift from gradualism to immediatism. The ACS had been founded in 1816 with policies that seemed at the time to many to offer the best hope for abolition and a chance of avoiding sectional bitterness by offering the South a method of at once freeing its Negroes and removing them as a social threat. By the 1830s the paltry numbers actually freed and sent to Liberia had shattered this hope, and the policy was being increasingly regarded by radicals as a sinful compromise with the slave-

4. Dumond, *Antislavery*, 175–76.
5. For example, Dumond, *Antislavery*, 169; Temperley, *British Antislavery*, 13 n. 28; Tyler, *Freedom's Ferment*, 491; Landon, "Captain Charles Stuart," 1.
6. Stuart to Weld, June, 1831, WP.

holding South and an implicit support of its racist attitudes. Garrison came to the fore in 1831 with vigorous denunciation in the *Liberator* of the ACS as a proslavery organization.

In June, 1831, when Elliott Cresson arrived in England, none of these American developments was known to Stuart, but he had recently become suspicious of the ACS on his own. As he was to explain two years later, when he returned to the United Kingdom in 1829 he had thought favorably of the ACS, though his knowledge of it was vague. Even the hostility to it which he had encountered among colored American friends had not yet made him inquire further. But now that he had embraced "the sacred cause of immediate emancipation in our own Colonies," he was less complacent about the far from immediatist policies of the ACS. An ACS pamphlet he had seen during his recent antislavery tour in Ireland had made him anxious for further information, which is no doubt why he asked Weld for intelligence about the organization. It was certainly the reason why he jumped at an invitation to meet Cresson and discuss colonization over tea at the home of Thomas Pringle, secretary of the Anti-Slavery Society.[7]

According to the accounts of both men, the meeting was stormy. Stuart came to the conclusion that "the principles and system of the society, upon the whole, were so decidedly criminal and cruel, that it ought to be strenuously reprobated and opposed. This I stated upon the spot to Mr. Cresson without reserve." Cresson was taken aback not only by this bluntness but by the radicalism of a man who "goes the whole length of intermarriage, amalgamations &c &c and sets down our prejudices against the blacks as highly criminal—with such men, reason is thrown away and argument pointless." He was soon to find, however, that argument was necessary and that Stuart could not be ignored. Within three days he had another "cautious skirmish with the Quixotte Stewart [sic]." Within a month he was enraged to find himself confronted by Stuart's *Letter on the American Colonization Society*. "Stuart," he complained bitterly to ACS headquarters, "has never applied to me for facts, or intimated his intention until it was sent me *printed*." His initial reaction was to make "ceaseless efforts" among influential friends to suppress the pamphlet. When this failed he rushed into print himself with a short rebuttal and then had a wild confrontation with Stuart at Pringle's home, where he

---

7. Stuart to Arthur Tappan, August 5, 1833, reprinted in *Liberator*, October 12, 1833, p. 163.

came to the conclusion that his "canting, hypocritical and abusive" adversary was "a second Garrison."[8]

Even before he met Stuart, Cresson had been dismayed at the militancy of many British abolitionists. They were as "thorough-paced" as Garrison. He believed that in their unconditional immediatism they had been "indoctrinated by the pamphlets sent over by our abolitionists."[9] This comment, made within a week of Cresson's arrival at Liverpool on May 26, 1831, can be seen as a striking illustration of the parallel lines British and American abolitionists were following to reach the immediatist position. But the suggestion that Americans were significantly influencing British immediate abolitionists is wrong. And in the near future the relationship would be the reverse of that imagined by Cresson, with Garrison drawing inspiration from British pamphlets. If his meetings with Stuart confirmed for Cresson the extremism of many British abolitionists, for American abolitionists the news of those meetings was an unexpected inspiration. To their jubilation they discovered that they had a champion in Britain, who, even as he fought for West Indian emancipation, was taking up the American immediatist cause against the ACS.

Through the early months of 1831 the newly founded *Liberator* had gleefully reported every snippet of news and comment that could discredit the ACS. Issue number 40 of October 1 offered its readers not a snippet but Charles Stuart's pamphlet *A Letter on the American Colonization Society*, reprinted in its entirety and spread across two-thirds of the front page, instead of in the usual columns, and under an unprecedentedly bold headline, proclaiming "A VOICE FROM ENGLAND!" Editorial comment followed on an inside page: "An anti-colonization voice greets us from across the Atlantic!—We refer our readers to the preceding page, for a Circular put forth in England, by a distinguished friend of the abolition cause. It is drawn up in a wonderfully comprehensive and cogent manner, and must produce an electrifying effect in this country. May the blessing of those who are ready to perish rest upon its benevolent author!" The article went on to quote a covering letter from an unnamed Englishman who had forwarded Stuart's pamphlet and who wrote of Cresson's rage at the "determined opposition" being organized in Britain by Stuart. Not only did Garrison reprint Stuart's *Letter*, but the same

---

8. *Ibid.*; Cresson's letters are in Series 1, Domestic Letters/Incoming correspondence, microfilm reels 10–19, ACS. For accounts of his early dealings with Stuart see Cresson to R. R. Gurley, corresponding secretary of the ACS, June 20, 1831, reel 14 (letter filed out of order), July 22, 1831, reel 11, ACS. Charles Stuart, *A Letter on the American Colonization Society Addressed to the Editor of the "Herald of Peace"* (Birmingham, 1832).

9. Cresson to Gurley, May 31, 1831, reel 11, ACS.

number of the *Liberator* referred to his intention to print copies for sale, "with a few introductory remarks of our own": "Many thousand copies ought to be sold wherever the colonization influence is felt."[10]

This publication marked the effective start of cooperation between militant British and American abolitionists. In November the *Liberator* printed Stuart's first direct communication with Garrison and made it plain that the initiative for the developing international exchanges had come entirely from Britain. It acknowledged a "munificent gift" of abolition literature from the London Anti-Slavery Society and apologized that "we have sent none of our papers to England. . . . We blame our negligence in this matter." Stuart was not alone responsible for the new contacts. Over the next few months the most frequently acknowledged sources of British material sent to the *Liberator* were James Cropper and Joseph Phillips, two prominent members of what Cresson was privately referring to as the "Stuart faction" in British antislavery circles."[11] No doubt one of these two had first sent over Stuart's *Letter*. But it was Stuart whose arguments and activities made British abolitionism seem relevant to the Americans.

The *Letter on the American Colonization Society* began with a summary of the numbers of free and slave blacks in the United States and a comment on both their degradation and rapid increase in numbers. The duty of the United States to its blacks, wrote Stuart, was exactly the same as the duty of Britain to its colonial slaves, "viz. to obey God, by letting them go free, by placing them beneath wise and equitable laws, and by loving them all, and treating them like brethren." In arguing that ACS policies were a rejection of these duties Stuart put forward points which Americans such as Garrison had been making for some time and also developed the theme of similarity between American and British antislavery preoccupations. "Great Britain and the United States," he concluded, "the two most favoured, and the two most guilty nations upon earth, both need rebuke. They ought to be brethren, mutually dear and honourable to each other, in all that is true and kind. But never, never, let them support one another in guilt. People of Great Britain, it is your business—it is your duty—to give Negro slavery no rest, but to put it down."[12]

In the following year Garrison again reproduced most of this pamphlet in his own *Thoughts on Colonization*, which has come to be regarded as the standard anticolonization publication. The same work included lau-

10. *Liberator*, October 1, 1831, pp. 158–59.
11. *Ibid.*, November 19, 1831, p. 185; November 24, 1832, p. 187; December 15, 1832, pp. 197–98; February 16, 1833, p. 26; Cresson to Gurley, November 10, 1831, reel 12, ACS.
12. *Liberator*, October 1, 1831, p. 158.

datory references to the Hibernian Negro's Friend Society and quoted extensively from another Stuart pamphlet. And Stuart himself—although clearly unknown to Garrison, who described him as a captain "of the English Royal Navy"—was quoted more than any other abolitionist. Indeed, after his dramatic debut in the columns of the *Liberator* Stuart was important enough for even his minor interests and activities to be seen as newsworthy by Garrison, who commented on the series of lectures on West Indian slavery he gave in Brighton and reproduced his own account of his friendship with a rescued slave resident in Britain who converted to Christianity. But what justified the attention given to these otherwise parochially British concerns and won for Stuart the *Liberator's* accolade as "one of the most distinguished and indefatigable philanthropists in Great Britain" was his continuing role as a spokesman of essentially American antislavery attitudes in British circles.[13]

At the end of 1832 a new Stuart pamphlet, *Remarks on the Colony of Liberia and the American Colonization Society*, was reprinted in full in the *Liberator* as "one of the most eloquent and powerful productions which the anti-slavery controversy has elicited in this country or England." It was easy to see why Garrison went on to declare that Stuart, "this indefatigable, generous and efficient champion deserves the thanks of the free colored people for his vindication of their rights." Garrison himself was always notable for the closeness of his contacts with free blacks, and now here was Stuart mixing effective polemical use of the ACS's own publications with quotations from the anticolonization resolutions of a "public meeting of the Free Coloured People of New York" held in January, 1831. The pamphlet was evidence of the growing transatlantic links among abolitionists. Whereas Stuart's first pamphlet had revealed his general familiarity with the United States, this one showed a new knowledge of American abolitionist activity. It cited as references all the significant American abolitionist journals and such pamphlets as Garrison's own address to the colored community, which had gone through several editions in 1831. It also put forward as an alternative to Liberia the Wilberforce settlement of free blacks in Canada and mentioned that a black cleric, Nathaniel Paul, was currently in Britain soliciting support for that venture. Stuart was as scathing in his condemnation of American slavery and American race prejudice as Garrison: the Wilberforce settlement

13. William Lloyd Garrison, *Thoughts on African Colonization: Or, an Impartial Exhibition of the Doctrines, Principles, and Purposes of the American Colonization Society. Together with the Resolutions, Addresses and Remonstrances of the Free People of Color* (Boston, 1832), 41–42, 77, 87, 151–54; *Liberator*, April 30, 1832, p. 50; October 27, 1832, p. 171; October 22, 1831, p. 171.

would be necessary only if "the prejudice in the United States against a colored skin is invincible." Such comments might have been resented as foreign interference by Americans who agreed with them if Stuart had not once again linked them to a theme of joint Anglo-American guilt. Great Britain boasted that Britons never shall be slaves—"yet she is a *slave-mistress*! Still she keeps 800,000 *guiltless Britons* in the most brutal bondage."[14]

Stuart's next major broadside against the ACS was reprinted in the *Liberator* in March, 1833. This was *Prejudice Vincible: Or the Practicality of Conquering Prejudice by Better Means Than by Slavery and Exile, in Relation to the American Colonization Society*. To Garrison it was "an unanswerable and soul-thrilling pamphlet": "For clearness of moral vision, energy of expression, eloquence of language, and ardour of piety, Captain Stuart has no superior among the philanthropists of the age."[15]

The main reason for this hyperbole was that Stuart was again articulating arguments well known to American abolitionists and displaying, in a publication aimed at British readers, an unusually detailed knowledge of the American scene. It was no doubt mainly because of the reputation he had thus acquired but also because of a similar grasp of American realities that his *West India Question* from this era became accepted as the most important British abolitionist work in the United States. In arguing the economic superiority of a free over a slave system Stuart in that tract had used predominantly American illustrations. His references to differences between northern and southern Maryland and between Pennsylvania and Virginia or Kentucky and Ohio had probably meant little to his British readership.[16] But they must have helped enliven a polemic about British colonial slavery for American audiences. Regularly advertised in the antislavery press, *The West India Question* quickly became an abolitionist best seller in the United States. Eventually it was endorsed by the American Anti-Slavery Society not only as the standard work on British abolitionist demands but, at least until 1835, as the virtually definitive statement, English or American, of immediatism. The society was to distribute thousands of copies of its several American editions and commend

14. *Liberator*, November 24, 1832, pp. 185–87; Charles Stuart, *Remarks on the Colony of Liberia and the American Colonization Society: With Some Account of the Settlement of Coloured People at Wilberforce, Upper Canada* (London, 1832).

15. *Liberator*, March 30, 1833, p. 51. For an example of the impact of the pamphlet see the request for copies by George W. Benson to Isaac Knapp, May 27, 1833, BPL.

16. Nevertheless, its influence was considerable. See, for instance, the laudatory editorial references to it in the Leeds *Mercury*'s announcement of its conversion to immediatism, October 13, 1832, p. 4.

it to its itinerant agents as the most important available antislavery document.[17]

If these developments still lay some way in the future at the beginning of 1833, Stuart's publications were already playing a part in the spread of American abolitionism in areas other than Garrison's New England. In November, 1832, Beriah Green and Elizur Wright, Jr., two professors at Western Reserve College, wrote of the conversion of themselves and many fellow instructors and students to immediate abolitionism. In asking for "facts, *facts*, FACTS" from the newly formed New England Anti-Slavery Society, they cited Stuart's *West India Question* and Garrison's *Thoughts on Colonization* as their main existing abolitionist sources. Three months later the two men wrote to Theodore Weld thanking him for copies of anti-ACS pamphlets by Stuart and Cropper, the latter in the form of a letter to the venerable Thomas Clarkson urging him to read Stuart's attacks on the ACS. These, wrote Green, were most acceptable, as was a copy of *The West India Question*, "for a copy of the same, which I received from Mr. Garrison sometime since, has quite worn out with hard service." As they embarked on distinguished antislavery careers, both Wright and Green continued publicly to give prominence to Stuart's name and views. The former wrote a long and spirited defense of *Prejudice Vincible* against a hostile procolonizationist review in the *Christian Spectator*. The latter attacked the failure of the orthodox American press to discuss abolition responsibly and especially to give any real news of the moves against slavery in England by asking, "Why have we heard nothing of Charles Stuart's pamphlets?" These signs of awakening western abolitionism were eagerly reported by the *Liberator*, which could find no higher praise for the "unanswerable" antislavery essays of Elizur Wright than to dub him "the Charles Stuart of the West."[18]

17. Stuart, *West India Question*; an abridged version was published in the *British Quarterly Magazine and Review* (April, 1832). The first American edition was published at New Haven in 1833, later republished as *Immediate Emancipation* . . . (Newburyport, 1838). For examples of its promotion in the antislavery press see *Liberator*, April 14, 1835, p. 55; January 9, 1836, p. 7; December 24, 1836, p. 208; *Emancipator*, April 23, 1836, March 23, 1837. Its use by American antislavery groups is discussed by Barnes and Dumond (eds.), *Weld-Grimké Letters*, I, 74 n. 1, 102 n. 4.

18. Extract of letter, Beriah Green to Rev. S. Jocelyn, *Liberator*, January 5, 1833, p. 2; Green and Wright to Weld, February 1, 1833, Barnes and Dumond (eds.), *Weld-Grimké Letters*, I, 102–103. For Wright's acknowledgments to Stuart in his own published writing see "The Sin of Slavery," *Genius of Universal Emancipation*, XIII (October, 1833), 186–88. Cropper's letter commending Stuart's writings to Clarkson is reproduced in the *Emancipator*, June 22, 1833, p. 1; *Liberator*, February 16, 1833; *American Anti-Slavery Reporter*, I (June, 1833); and *Abolitionist* I (March, 1833), 39–40. A letter from Cropper to

Stuart also had letters published in Benjamin Lundy's *Genius of Universal Emancipation*, which gave only slightly less prominence than the *Liberator* to extracts from his anti-ACS publications. And through Weld he was drawn into correspondence with the Tappan brothers in New York. In a long letter to Arthur Tappan Stuart explained in detail how he had independently come to question and oppose the ACS before he had ever heard of Garrison and his fellow New England activists.[19]

In 1833, with West Indian emancipation imminent, there would inevitably have been keen American interest in the deeds of their British abolitionist counterparts. But it seems inconceivable that without the especially American-oriented activities of Stuart this interest would have produced contacts so warm. Americans no doubt would have found some alternative representation of British immediatism if Stuart's *West India Question* had not been written. But without Stuart it is extremely unlikely that Garrison would have been publishing a book called *British Opinions of the American Colonization Society*. Not only was Stuart's *Prejudice Vincible* the core of this anthology, but its other components, including Cropper's *Letter* to Clarkson and a series of extracts from the Liverpool *Mercury*, were a direct result of the controversy Stuart had provoked and sustained with Elliott Cresson for the previous two years. Garrison might well have gone to England in any case in 1833 to celebrate the triumph of West Indian emancipation and to solicit financial support for a proposed school for colored youth. But the contacts he had developed with Stuart and his fellow activists assured his welcome. And in particular the existence in England of that live American issue meant that, thanks to Stuart, he need not be merely a spectator and suppliant but could find an active role in pressing home the attack against Cresson. Considering that Garrison's visit to England was to enhance his American reputation and help to confirm him as the de facto leader of American abolitionism, he owed no small debt to Stuart.[20]

Arnold Buffum commending Stuart's anti-ACS campaign was reproduced in *ibid.*, I (January, 1833), 8. The final quotations are from *Liberator*, January 5, 1833, p. 3; April 6, 1833, p. 51; June 8, 1833, p. 90.

19. *Genius of Universal Emancipation*, XII (February, 1832), 142–43; XIII (January, 1833), 34–35; XIII (September, 1833), 165–66; this last consisted of extensive extracts from Stuart's *Petitions Respecting Negro Slavery*. Stuart's letter to Tappan was printed in the *Liberator*, August 5, 1833, p. 163.

20. Details of Garrison's publication were first announced in the *Liberator*, June 22, 1833, p. 99, and in the *Abolitionist*, I (July, 1833), 106. It was regularly advertised in the *Liberator* and—for sale at the American Anti-Slavery Society office in New York—in the *Emancipator*, throughout 1834–36. For Garrison's trip to England see Louis Filler, *The Crusade Against Slavery, 1830–1860* (New York, 1963), 62; Tyler, *Freedom's Ferment*, 492–93.

The two men quickly established contact in London. Later evidence suggests that Garrison was somewhat disconcerted by Stuart's "exceedingly eccentric appearance" and began to "wish he had more taste and neatness about his person, for it is worthy of some regard." But, seeing him regularly for some four weeks, he had no reason to regret the praise he had bestowed so liberally in the *Liberator*. And he had new reason to be grateful for Stuart's American interests, even at a time when the Agency Committee was desperately exerting pressure to prevent the parliamentary abolitionists from conceding too much to the West India interests by accepting a twelve-year apprenticeship for slaves and generous compensation for the slaveowners. Although these concerns were precious to Stuart, the author of the most famous anticompensation tract, and although he became involved in a local antislavery issue, he showed himself willing not only to continue the anti-ACS campaign but also to raise money for Garrison's colored school project.[21]

Stuart was in the background at the anti-ACS meetings held after Garrison's arrival. At a meeting on July 27 in Exeter Hall he did win applause with his characteristic demand that the assembly should denounce not only slavery but racial prejudice in general. But usually the speakers who attracted attention were Garrison, the black American Nathaniel Paul, and such distinguished British orators as George Thompson and Daniel O'Connell.[22] Garrison, however, in writing home to the Board of Managers of the New England Anti-Slavery Society, made it clear who deserved the credit for the hard work that had preceded the almost ritual victory represented by these celebrity-adorned public meetings: "Cresson may succeed a little longer in deceiving a few lords and dukes; but his career has ended among the friends of abolition and the religious com-

21. Garrison to Helen E. Benson, June 25, 1834, in Walter M. Merrill and Louis Ruchames (eds.), *The Letters of William Lloyd Garrison* (5 vols.; Cambridge, Mass., 1971–79) I, 372; New England Anti-Slavery Society, *Annual Convention 1834: Proceedings* (Boston, 1834), 42; *Liberator*, July 19, 1834, p. 113; Stuart to Garrison, October 16, 1833, *Abolitionist*, I (December, 1833), 191. The local antislavery issue was an intervention by Stuart and Joseph Phillips to secure the liberation of a slave, William Williams, who had escaped from the West Indies to London. At the end of June, 1833, the two abolitionists took legal and police action to prevent the forcible return of Williams to the West Indies by the master of a vessel in the Port of London (London *Times*, June 24, 1833, p. 7).

22. *Liberator*, November 23, 1833, p. 186; August 31, p. 9; November 16, p. 181; November 23, 1833, pp. 185–86; Leeds *Mercury*, July 27, 1833, p. 6; James Cropper, *Speeches Delivered at the Anticolonization Meeting in Exeter Hall, London, July 13, 1833* (London, 1833), 40, lists the names of the antislavery leaders, including William Wilberforce, T. F. Buxton, Lord Suffield, and O'Connell, who signed a document to "utterly repudiate the principles" of the ACS.

munity. Charles Stuart, Esq. has done much to obstruct his progress; and we cannot be too thankful to this eminently pious and indefatigable philanthropist for his labours of love."[23]

Stuart well deserved Garrison's thanks for he had done much more to obstruct the progress of Cresson than publish the pamphlets that had been so warmly welcomed by Americans. Moreover, his task had been much more difficult than was implied by the laudatory references to his writings which regularly appeared in the *Liberator*.[24] Cresson had been brought to the brink of defeat by the time of Garrison's arrival, not primarily by brilliant debating points in a pamphlet press that probably preached mainly to the converted but by two years of sustained harassment by a determined lobbyist, exploiting the connections and goodwill he had established with antislavery workers in many parts of Britain.

CRESSON was from the start a formidable opponent. As a Quaker he had an entrée into one of the most respected circles of British philanthropy. Not only was he able through this affiliation to gain introductions to important individuals in politics and the press in London, but on his tours through the provinces Friends' meeting houses were regularly available to him as forums for disseminating his views. He assiduously cultivated numerous editors and as a result was able, at various times, to have favorable essays on Liberia inserted in such respected monthly journals as the *Westminster Review*, *Gentleman's Magazine*, *Eclectic Review*, and *English Magazine*; in religious journals headed by the *Evangelical Magazine* and the *Herald of Peace*; in the *Times* and other London newspapers; and in such major provincial organs as the Liverpool *Mercury* and the Leeds *Mercury*.[25]

To acquire such influence Cresson must doubtless have been an articulate and plausible conversationalist at ease not merely among his fellow Quakers. The introduction he secured to the duke of Sussex and the latter's willing patronage of the ACS smoothed his path in many areas: the

---

23. *Liberator*, August 31, 1833, p. 139.

24. For further examples of such praise see *ibid.*, October 12, 1833, p. 163; November 9, 1833, p. 177; November 23, 1833, p. 187; December 23, 1833, p. 205; January 4, 1834, p. 1.

25. For Cresson's accounts of his meetings with editors and the insertion of articles see his letters to Gurley, July 22, September 6, 1831, reel 11; December 5, 10, reel 12; December 28, 1831, January 6, 1832, reel 13, ACS. For examples of pro-ACS articles see *Gentleman's Magazine*, CI (December, 1831), 546–48, CII (January, 1832), 634–35; *Westminster Review*, XV (1831), 506–22; Leeds *Mercury*, January 21, March 10, 17, 24, 31, April 4, July 21, 1832; London *Times*, June 27, 1832; Glasgow *Chronicle*, March 12, April 4, July 13, 1832.

duke's name, he wrote, "gives much currency among the higher classes." But Cresson also owed much of his early success with editors and aristocrats, and even many members of the antislavery "establishment," to the fact that immediatist abolition was a new and far from widely popular phenomenon. The *Times*, for instance, condemned the effrontery of the Agency Committee in seeking to examine the antislavery credentials of parliamentary candidates. And on at least one occasion it lost no opportunity to mobilize the support of the parliamentary leader of the abolitionist movement, Thomas Fowell Buxton, against the Agency Committee's insistence on radical proposals to pay no compensation to the slaveowners, which had appeared in Stuart's *West India Question*.[26]

Cresson was probably right when he claimed that the British were too preoccupied with impending West Indian emancipation to contribute lavishly to the ACS. But the same preoccupation did mean a widespread British willingness to look sympathetically at any humanitarian endeavor concerned with the Negro. Moreover, in portraying the founding of Liberia as a civilizing mission toward Africa, Cresson appealed to aspirations that, at least since the 1780s, had been much more strongly felt in Britain than in the United States. It was significant that the two veteran champions of that earlier campaign against the slave trade, Thomas Clarkson and William Wilberforce, were prominent among a roll call of English critics of slavery who initially welcomed his mission. Other famous names included Harriet Martineau, whose descriptions of American slavery were widely read; George Thompson, Stuart's fellow Agency Committee lecturer; and T. F. Buxton himself, who welcomed Cresson as a house guest and whose children promptly decided to raise the seven pounds needed to free an American slave.[27]

Welcomed so warmly by the political, press, and antislavery establishments, Cresson had every reason to feel confident about the prospects of a successful visit to Britain in June, 1831. That confidence was shaken but not shattered by his early encounters with Stuart. Stuart's attacks—in person and in print—did not prevent Cresson's receiving an invitation to address the committee of the Anti-Slavery Society in August. Stuart, characteristically, also attended that meeting as a visitor and must have expressed his opposition to Cresson's mission. But this was the period when the composition and role of the agency subcommittee was a sensi-

26. Cresson to Gurley, December 5, 1831, reel 12; September 6, 1832, reel 15, ACS; London *Times*, June 14, 1833, p. 5; June 15, 1833, p. 3.
27. Cresson to Gurley, July 22, 1831, reel 11; June 9, 1832, reel 14; January 29, 1833, reel 16; June 23, September 6, October 6, 1831, reel 11; November 10, 1831, reel 12; July 25, 1832, reel 15, ACS.

tive issue, and Stuart's credentials, because he was a provincial "outsider," were in question. Although the society's minute books contain no details, it is extremely likely that his opposition to Cresson was coolly received by the more conservative elements on the general committee.[28] Certainly there was no speedy official repudiation of the ACS, and Cresson continued to enjoy warm relations with many leading abolitionists for months to come.

In the autumn of 1831 Cresson set off on a provincial tour, piqued by Stuart's attacks but with high hopes that "by patient labour" he could establish a pro-ACS party. In September his contacts with the press enabled him to "counter the poison of Stuart" with an article in the *English Magazine*. In Ipswich he had an encouraging first interview with Clarkson, and in Bath in the following month he stayed for a week with Wilberforce. But already perhaps he sensed that his difficulties were only beginning. In his letters back to America, while reporting the warm friendship extended by the two great men, he also prepared his defenses. Clarkson was virtually blind, so "we cannot hope for any testimonials of his regard in written form." Wilberforce's feeble health "and his wife's superintendence of it prevented him writing strong testimonials on behalf of A.C.S."[29] The reality was that while Cresson was devoting his attention to these illustrious relics of a bygone age of abolition, Stuart was assiduously mobilizing the support of the new generation of unknown but already well-organized provincial radicals.

The war between the two men was to last for more than two years with skirmishes in virtually every region of the British Isles. Some of the most conspicuous battles were fought in the columns of monthly periodicals and provincial newspapers. But the most informative record of the underlying realities lies in the unpublished letters Cresson sent back to the ACS in America. These reports were often optimistic. Cresson regularly claimed to have made Stuart's supporters question their allegiance and to have reduced hostile questioners to silence with his calm lucidity. In early 1833 he claimed a significant triumph when Stuart attended one of his meetings in Belfast. His own speech had produced "a powerful effect," whereas Stuart's attempted reply was "*hissed* down." A few weeks later one of his supporters sent him news of a subsequent Belfast meeting addressed ineffectually for three and a half hours by Stuart, who had praised Garrison and dismissed the still vaguely pro-ACS Thomas Clarkson "as

28. Cresson to Gurley, July 22, 1831, reel 11, ACS; S. 20, E2/3, 104, 105, RHL.
29. Cresson to Gurley, August 6, September 6, October 6, 1831, reel 11; November 10, 1831, reel 12, ACS.

far advanced in years and failing in intellect!" If these claims have a certain plausibility in view of the faint praise that had damned sympathetic accounts of Stuart's platform appearances, the incidents described did not indicate a general trend. The truth, as Cresson's letters also implicitly reveal, was that Stuart's effectiveness was grounded on so much more than isolated public speeches that the American had clearly failed comprehensively by the time of these exchanges in Belfast. In a mission designed to raise £100,000 he had raised at the most a few hundreds.[30] In his task of swinging British public and antislavery opinion behind the ACS, notwithstanding a sprinkling of genteel auxiliaries around the country, he had failed equally decisively.

Other sources, in addition to Cresson's letters, indicate how completely he saw Stuart as his main British enemy; how completely his ultimate failure in Britain was the result of Stuart's relentless opposition; and how important Stuart's intervention was to subsequent relations between British and American abolitionists. Much of this evidence lies in various accounts by Stuart's fellow Agency Committee lecturer, George Thompson, who was eventually to become the most celebrated British abolitionist in America. Thompson was originally deceived by Cresson into believing that the ACS was concerned primarily with abolition. In the early stages of his British tour Cresson had also been at pains to convince people that Garrison was a dishonest "pest to society" and Stuart "a raving madman" and "artful calumniator." Thompson had first come to realize, through personal acquaintance, that Stuart was an "excellent" man and, through him, that the ACS "plan is bad; that the means used to carry it into operation are dishonest; and the supporters of the society, in this country at least, have been deceived." Cresson had also been making the most of the period Garrison had spent in jail in Baltimore after being unable to pay the fine imposed for a libel conviction. Once he had gained Thompson's respect, Stuart began the process that was to lead to enduring and significant friendship between Thompson and Garrison. He had obtained from America "all the documents revealing the cause of the imprisonment of Mr. Garrison, as well as illustrative of his early history, and the share he had taken in the emancipation cause." As Thompson eventually revealed in a speech at Exeter Hall, in these ways he had come to see as "foul slander" Cresson's allegations against both Stuart and Garrison.[31]

30. Cresson to Gurley, n.d., reel 17; March 24, 1833, reel 17; Gerrit Smith to Gurley, April 3, 1832, reel 13; Cresson to Gurley, June 28, 1833, reel 16 (filed out of order), ACS.
31. *Liberator*, August 10, 1833, pp. 126–27; January 11, 1834, p. 7; September 10, 1841, p. 145. Stuart's influence was also acknowledged in the same period by the British *Anti-*

Because of his own mobility Thompson was able to do a good deal to counter Cresson's allegations, particularly in Scotland, where he was laying the foundations of his main antislavery constituency. When he addressed the ladies' committee of the Edinburgh Anti-Slavery Society, he mentioned Garrison and Stuart and was asked, "Are not these men blackguards and villains?":

> I rose and emphatically exclaimed, "They are not. The one is the intrepid and noble-minded champion of the negro's rights in a country disgraced by its prejudice and despotism—the other is an enlightened, benevolent Christian-minded and holy man. If I were asked to select, from among men, the one I conceived to be most truly and disinterestedly devoted to the service of God and of mankind, I should answer Captain CHARLES STUART—a man whom I am proud to be permitted to call my friend."

Stuart himself was soon on the scene in Edinburgh to reinforce Thompson's argument. He arrived to find an atmosphere still poisoned by Cresson's slanders, but, reported Thompson, he "won the heart of every person to whom he was introduced."[32]

Thompson's support was useful. But he was a relatively late convert to Stuart's views, and although Cresson was bitter about his defection, a more basic cause of the American Quaker's problems was that, from the start, Stuart commanded similar loyalty among numerous less well-known antislavery workers. To some extent Cresson was unlucky in choosing to begin his campaign in the western and Midlands areas, where Stuart was particularly well known. His public meetings were likely to be interrupted, as happened at Worcester, when a "Stuartite rose to oppose us" and demanded immediate, unconditional emancipation. Often the presence of Stuart supporters made him refuse to risk such encounters, particularly in the Midlands, "the H.Q. of ultraism and where Stuart is almost deified." In these areas of early conflict Stuart had established warm relations with the female abolitionists who had sponsored his earlier lecturing agency and with their friends. There is evidence from many periods of his life that, when there was no question of a purely personal re-

---

Slavery Reporter, when it reviewed favorably Garrison's *Thoughts on Colonization* but stressed that similar "strong, and as they appear to us, conclusive statements of Mr. Stuart" in *Prejudice Vincible* had already helped to "dissipate the mist which enveloped the Colonization scheme" (V [1832–33], 296–300).

32. *Liberator*, January 11, 1834, p. 7. Stuart's activity in Scotland is also indicated by yet another anti-ACS pamphlet, *Liberia: Or, the American Colonization Scheme Examined and Exposed. A Full and Authentic Report of a Lecture Delivered by C. Stuart, Esq. at a Public Meeting in Rev. M. Anderson's Chapel, Glasgow, 15th April 1833* (Glasgow, 1833).

lationship developing, he was at ease with women and they, in their turn, were charmed by his eccentricities. Describing this period a few years later, he was to write admiringly of the work of such female friends as Lucy Townsend in West Bromwich, Sarah Wedgwood in Staffordshire, Maria Schimmelpenning in Bristol, and Rebecca Yerbury in Cheltenham. Although in his letters Cresson rarely named specific women, he did attempt to cultivate a constituency of female support and was frequently taken aback at the evidence of Stuart's prior influence. Indeed, a fruitless encounter with the female abolitionists of Birmingham led him quickly to conclude that his task there was hopeless among "a most prejudiced and unbelieving people, where Capt. Stuart is idolized—we despised."[33]

At various times Cresson was also to refer to Bristol, Bath, and Belfast as particular Stuart strongholds, where no rapid progress could be expected. But even where Stuart was less directly known, his influence was considerable through the loyalty he commanded within the Agency Committee. It took a long time for Cresson to realize that the eminent figures he was attempting to cultivate, and even those who, like Buxton, were leading the moves for abolition inside Parliament, were not in command of a monolithic national antislavery movement. At the outset he was surprised and annoyed that the Anti-Slavery Society would not circulate his own pamphlet defense of the ACS to the provinces. For several months he tended to attribute such obstruction to the work of an extremist splinter group, the "Stuart faction." In September, 1832, he indignantly reported that although some Anti-Slavery Society members had opposed Stuart, the Agency Committee had been distributing Stuart's "tirades" "as the agent of that body." Only now was he beginning to realize that it was the Agency Committee, which Stuart had helped to found, and not the Anti-Slavery Society, which had strong influence in the provinces. Cresson's subsequent letters consistently revealed how effective this organization was. Stuart's "lies," he wrote in November, 1832, had spread like wildfire—"so much so that by the malignity of the Agency Committee they now precede me wherever I go." An otherwise pleasant visit to Scotland in January was marred by the "constant libels" circulated in advance of his "every step."[34]

33. Cresson to Gurley, March 15, 1833, reel 17; February 20, 1832, reel 13, ACS; Stuart, "On the Abolition of Slavery by Great Britain," *Quarterly Anti-Slavery Magazine*, I (January, 1836), 108; Cresson to Gurley, February 20, 1832, March 17, 1832, reel 13, ACS.

34. Cresson to Gurley, November 10, 1831. Cresson believed that the Dublin Negro's Friend Society had actually been founded by Stuart "for the purpose of asserting a higher standard of principle than the A.S.S. [sic]" (to Gurley, April 26, 1832, reel 14, ACS). Cresson to Gurley, August 6, September 6, 1831, reel 11, ACS. On his attribution of obstruction

Stuart was not content to rely simply on his personal influence and on the Agency Committee's network of communication. The energy and mobility that had given him these advantages through his previous antislavery tours were again in evidence. Even Cresson's more optimistic letters give strong evidence of a difficult path obstructed at every turn by a relentlessly mobile adversary. Stuart was in Cheltenham, ready to give a series of lectures, when Cresson arrived at his very first provincial speaking appointment. He had already visited and influenced a woman in Tewkesbury to whom the American had been given an introduction. And in Cirencester Cresson's warm welcome by fellow Quakers was marred by the evidence of Stuart's recent activity in the form of opposition from the "Secy. of the A.S.S. whose esprit d'corps [sic] would not allow him to dissent from the Stuart creed." On a second visit in 1832 to the same West Country region Cresson found that little had changed. From Cheltenham he wrote: "I shall try during the few days I am here, to leave a proper impression on the minds of some of the most influential residents, so as to counteract the projected course of lectures by the new 'Pretender'—(Stuart) who is daily expected."[35]

Stuart was eventually to pursue Cresson as far as Ireland and Scotland. But in the north of England, where he was less well known, he pressed the attack with the pen rather than in person. Cresson could initially report considerable success. His private accounts of the formation of committees, of large public meetings, and of fruitful contacts with local editors in 1832 are corroborated by the public evidence of local newspapers. The Leeds *Mercury* reported the success of his meetings and printed a series of articles accompanied by an editorial expressing the expectation that the Anti-Slavery Society "would be among the foremost to aid Mr. Cresson in his truly Christian mission." But without immediately abandoning its editorial posture, some time after Cresson's visit it also printed a series of anti-ACS resolutions by free Negroes in Baltimore, which it had "had sent for insertion," presumably by Stuart. Certainly Cresson blamed "Stuart's letters" for a less favorable reception across the Pennines. They had induced his "good friend," J. J. Gurney, to refuse to take part in a public meeting on his behalf in Manchester. Here indeed the atmosphere was so hostile that Cresson was accosted and abused for his views by a man who stopped and got out of his carriage. If this incident cannot be

---

see Cresson to Gurley, November 10, December 5, 10, 1831, reel 12; January 28, 1832, reel 13. For the final quotations see Cresson to Gurley, September 2, 1832, reel 15; November 10, 1832, January 28, 1833, reel 16, ACS.

35. Cresson to Gurley, November 10, 1831, reel 12 (last portion of letter is misfiled in reel 10); January 28, 1832, reel 13, ACS.

surely linked to Stuart's activities, there is no doubt who had prepared the unfavorable welcome Cresson received in Liverpool, where he arrived expecting to establish cordial relations with James Cropper, to whose care early in the year he had asked the ACS to direct all his mail from the United States: "No sooner had I arrived here than at every place I visited, I found a copy of Stuart's letter . . . had been sent around, with a cautionary note attached to each, and their great oracle James Cropper so prejudiced by the Liberator, Genius of U. En. & Stuart, that it would be most prudent not to call upon him."[36]

Cresson was also confronted by an anti-ACS article in the Liverpool *Albion*, which was "a servile copy of an attack made upon the society by C. Stuart." At this stage, in April, 1832, he was consoled by the way Egerton Smith, editor of the Liverpool *Mercury*, "nobly" sprang to his defense. Yet later the same year he was writing bitterly of the "guile" with which Stuart had won over Smith, a change of allegiance that was reflected in the *Mercury*'s public endorsement of Stuart's pamphlets and acknowledgment of its early error in supporting the ACS.[37]

Prophetically, Cresson himself had earlier written that Egerton Smith's continued support was assured provided that the ACS supplied him with the necessary intelligence and arguments. This support was not provided. Without doubt Cresson attributed his overall failure in Britain to such negligence. His letters to R. R. Gurley, corresponding secretary of the ACS, complained even more bitterly about this treatment than about the activities of Stuart. But again it was Stuart who exploited a virtual breakdown in communication, which deprived Cresson of necessary information and left unheeded his pleas for more discreet editing of the society's publications. In June, 1832, he complained that Stuart was exploiting his isolation to raise doubts about his credentials as an official ACS representative. In August he warned Gurley to be cautious not to publish "all I write for your private use, else the A.S.S. zeal will be kindled yet more against us—Stuart being yet busy denouncing us." Repeatedly he warned that virtually proslavery statements published in the ACS's *African Repository* were providing some of the main ammunition for Stuart's attacks. Stuart's extracts "from our own pages" were doing "immense harm," he wrote in November. They formed the substance of the attacks

---

36. Cresson to Gurley, March 17, 1832, reel 13, ACS; Leeds *Mercury*, January 21, March 10, 17, 24, 31, April 14, July 21, 1832, May 4, 11, 27, 1833.

37. Cresson to Gurley, April 16, 20 (enclosing copy of Cresson's printed reply to *Albion* article), 1832, reel 14; November 10, 1832, reel 16, ACS; extracts from the *Mercury* article reprinted in *Liberator*, March 30, 1833, p. 50.

that were being circulated in advance of his movements around the country.[38]

It is easy to sympathize with Cresson's mounting frustration with his American colleagues, for his lengthy and informative letters and requests for American news and publications were consistently ignored. In contrast, by mid-1832 the enthusiastic reception accorded Stuart's pamphlets by the *Liberator* had led to such warm transatlantic relations among abolitionists that Cresson was far less well informed about events and trends in the United States than were his British adversaries. Again Cresson's letters show this difficulty only too well, when he urgently demanded information abut the Reverend Nathaniel Paul, whom Stuart was acclaiming "as a man of God"; about the New England Anti-Slavery Society, "which seems to have just sprung into existence"; about Stuart's "story of 1100 being exiled from Ohio into Canada"; and about the claim that a college for colored youth was being organized by American abolitionists.[39]

The isolation that had prompted these largely fruitless requests for information had made Cresson's mission a hopeless cause by mid-1833. But this was so only because he had found in Stuart an adversary willing to fight with a single-mindedness that almost justified Cresson's allegations of fanaticism. This quality was still in evidence even after Garrison left England. Stuart continued to hound Cresson as long as the American remained in Britain refusing to acknowledge publicly a defeat he was bitterly admitting in private. And when one of Cresson's English converts, Dr. Thomas Hodgkin, published a pro-ACS pamphlet, Stuart responded with *The American Colonization Society Further Unravelled* with a speed and facility that amazed Nathaniel Paul, who was still in Britain and preparing his own rejoinder. Interspersed among the standard anticolonization points in the new pamphlet was implicit evidence of Stuart's unique qualities. Few contemporaries would have pressed arguments about colonization and racial prejudice with well-informed comments both about American treatment of free Negroes and Cherokee Indians and about missionary activities in the Sandwich and Society Islands, New Zealand, and Africa. And fewer still could have illustrated such arguments with anecdotes of personal experiences among the Huron and Wyandot Indians and fugitive blacks of Upper Canada and the Mahrattas of India. At the same time, references to Garrison, Elizur Wright, John Greenleaf

38. Cresson to Gurley, April 16, June 9, 16, 1832, reel 14; July 6, 25, August 25, September 2, 7, 1832, reel 15; November 10, 1832, reel 16, ACS.
39. Cresson to Gurley, September 2, 7, 1832, reel 15, ACS.

Whittier, Arthur Tappan, and the major American abolitionist publications reflected the new transatlantic friendships formed in the last two years of campaigning in the British Isles.[40]

By the end of 1833 Stuart was indeed in a uniquely favorable position in the antislavery world. While many abolitionists in Britain were groping for a new role in the aftermath of the Emancipation Act, he had achieved merely one goal in a much more ambitious antislavery program. Emotionally conditioned by his years of travel and intellectually prepared by the specific programs for global abolition of the Hibernian Negro's Friend Society, he had never confined his abolitionism to British colonial slavery. He had already enrolled in the New England Anti-Slavery Society as a life member and taken a close interest in the moves to form a national antislavery society in the United States. Those moves, in a sense, had begun with the New York meetings of Weld, the Tappans, and their associates, to which he had made a proxy contribution, in 1831. They had broadened with the activities of Garrison and reached fulfillment in a convention held in Philadelphia on December 4, 1833. Even before the American Anti-Slavery Society was born on that day, Stuart had sent out circulars in Britain about American slavery and the work of American abolitionists, and he had organized fund-raising appeals to help the cause across the Atlantic.[41] Most important, he had seen the Agency Committee transformed into the British and Foreign Society for the Universal Abolition of Slavery and the Slave Trade, with American slavery proclaimed as its main concern. And he enthusiastically supported the plan of the new society, in conjunction with the organized abolitionists of Glasgow and Edinburgh, to send George Thompson, who had greatly impressed the visiting Garrison, to lecture in the United States.

Perhaps because his mission was the first task undertaken by the new society, Thompson tended to regard himself as its founder, although he did concede to Stuart the leading role as a fund-raiser. Joseph Phillips, however, wrote to Garrison late in February, 1834, that the transforma-

---

40. Cresson to Gurley, August 3, 1833, reel 18, ACS; Thomas Hodgkin, *An Inquiry into the Merits of the American Colonization Society: And a Reply to the Charges Brought Against It. With an Account of the British African Colonization Society* (London, 1833); Charles Stuart, *The American Colonization Scheme Further Unravelled* (Bath, ca. 1833), reprinted in *Liberator*, April 19, 1834, pp. 61–62; Nathaniel Paul to Garrison, January 22, 1834, reprinted in *Liberator*, April 12, 1834, p. 58.

41. Records of the New England Anti-Slavery Society, Vol. 1, 1831–33, Minutes, November 5, 1832, BPL; Stuart to Garrison in *Liberator*, January 4, 1834, p. 1; Dumond, *Antislavery*, 175–76. Stuart's pamphlet *To the Friends of Religion and Humanity* (Bath, 1833) contained details of his fund-raising attempts. See also George Thompson to Glasgow Emancipation Society, February 18, 1834, GES.

tion had been "effected through the perseverance of our most valuable friend, Captain C. Stuart, who has been in London for that purpose for the past five weeks." Even if Phillips' assertion overstated Stuart's role, this was the version that Garrison published in the *Liberator*, thus confirming Stuart's importance in American abolitionists' minds.[42] And this in its turn was significant because, all the while, Stuart had been making plans to return to the United States and participate directly in the American struggle. His reasons are implicit in the first broadsheet put out by the new Agency Society for the Universal Abolition of Negro Slavery and the Slave Trade Throughout the World. The society introduced itself to the public with the reassurance that the "essentially expensive" recent methods of agitation were "no longer the tactics necessary to follow."[43] Although Stuart probably accepted the logic of this decision, such tactics were central to the mixture of emotional and intellectual ingredients that formed his abolitionist creed. His contacts with America made him well aware of the emerging transatlantic opportunities for continued agitation.

He left in May, 1834, some months before Thompson. In anticipation, the *Liberator* reprinted in full *The American Colonization Society Further Unravelled*, welcoming it as "cogent, solemn, thrilling, irresistible—a ponderous mass of pure gold": "the Negro and his champions in America" were more deeply indebted to Stuart "than to any man in Great Britain. We are looking daily for his arrival in the United States. He shall have a noble reception."[44]

---

42. Copy of letter, Thompson to Glasgow Emancipation Society, April 17, 1834, Minute Book I, GES; Phillips to Garrison, February 21, 1834, cited in *Liberator*, April 12, 1834. Stuart modestly claimed no credit for himself in his subsequent historical survey but was probably more accurately describing Thompson's role when he referred to him as "an agent" of the new society ("On the Abolition of Slavery by Great Britain," 115).

43. Agency Society for the Universal Abolition of Negro Slavery and the Slave Trade Throughout the World, [Broadsheet] 18, Aldermanbury, October 14, 1834.

44. *Liberator*, April 19, 1834, pp. 61–63.

4 AGENT OF THE AMERICAN ANTI-SLAVERY SOCIETY

Despite the parallels and connections between the two national movements, there were fundamental differences between the antislavery atmosphere Stuart was leaving and the one he was approaching as he crossed the Atlantic. The British shift to immediatism and its institutional expression in the work of the Agency Committee preceded similar trends in the United States. The recent formation of the American Anti-Slavery Society had not yet led to organized agitation, and Stuart was arriving in time to play a significant role in the development of lecturing agencies. Even now some of the eventually most celebrated names in American abolitionism were still outside the movement or hesitantly clinging to gradualist attitudes. Yet American abolitionists were already embroiled in more heated controversies than any that had accompanied even the climax of British emancipation. The bitter disputes between Stuart and Cresson had been entirely verbal, and even the occasional disruptions of antislavery meetings by the West India interest had been rowdy and unruly rather than physically violent. That this small group of absentee planters and their associates were those most directly affected was symptomatic of the remoteness of slavery from the British experience. In contrast, American slavery was a domestic problem embedded in the formal political structure of the nation and sustained by its underlying realities. Sectional compromise over slavery in the late eighteenth century had influenced the drafting of the Constitution and been imperative to its ratification. And although the system of government then adopted had been seen by many as an assault on states' rights, in practice the federal Constitution had made slavery a national problem while denying abolitionists any national means of assailing it. Except in the minuscule District of Columbia the national government had no constitutional power to abolish slavery, even had the representation of the southern states in Congress not made such intervention politically improbable.

In the early 1830s criticisms of slavery had become increasingly a matter of polemics hurled across the Mason-Dixon line, as southern abolitionism, never strong, disappeared completely. But the debate involved far more than sectional confrontation. Abolitionists were on the defensive in the North. Their assault on slavery was seen as economically disruptive by businessmen with southern links and as more generally divisive by those caught up in an incipient American nationalism. In particular, proposals to abolish slavery in the South threatened to bring still more black immigration into northern states, which had already demonstrated their Negrophobia in racist social and political legislation.[1]

The tensions so far had been most apparent in New England. Garrison's *Liberator* had been inflaming opinions in and beyond the Boston area since 1831. But it was in Canterbury, Connecticut, that the most extreme events had occurred. Prudence Crandall's attempts to teach black children had been subjected to public harassment, ranging from the withdrawal of medical and other community services to outright violence against person and property. Eventually, despite, or perhaps because of, the intervention of such leading abolitionists as Samuel J. May and George Bourne, extralegal hostility had been followed by legal coercion. In the early months of 1834 an appeal was pending in the supreme court of Connecticut against a lower court decision to close the Crandall school. That decision, as much as the intimidation that preceded it, was strong evidence of the depth of feeling against northern blacks and their abolitionist friends. Legal proceedings had been possible only because Crandall's opponents were able to secure hasty passage of a state law against the teaching of black children.[2]

Stuart had learned from Garrison something about the atmosphere of New England abolitionism and the details of Prudence Crandall's ordeal.[3] But in more important ways he was uniquely equipped to make the transition from British to American abolitionism. It is more than a minor curiosity that in crossing the Atlantic "Captain Charles Stuart" was trans-

1. The pioneer and still most complete general account of northern racism is Leon F. Litwack, *North of Slavery: The Negro in the Free States, 1790–1860* (Chicago, 1961).
2. Dumond, *Antislavery*, 211–17.
3. Stuart to Crandall, cited in *Liberator*, January 4, 1834, p. 1.

formed into "the Reverend Charles Stuart." The titles were mainly bestowed by others rather than insisted upon by the man himself. But the change symbolizes the relative ease with which he was able to shed a potentially embarrassing British imperial identity and assume a clerical status typical of so many American abolitionists. There was, of course, no sham or deception about the transition. If anything, his British title was more suspect than his American one, although no one had so far made any recorded reference to the scandalous circumstances of his departure from the East India Company army. In the tougher world of American abolition there would be few scruples about challenging his clerical title, but, in truth, it was a status he had not only acquired through his license in the Presbyterian church but earned through years of preaching in Utica and far beyond. Those years of Christian commitment, his friendship with Theodore Weld, and his attachment to Cornelia, all in different ways had prepared him for abolitionism. The cause he had discovered in Britain had channeled his emotions more purposefully than any previous enthusiasm he had embraced. Now, in the spring of 1834—in a sense that was important to his effectiveness—he was returning to an area he knew as well as any part of Britain.

STUART ARRIVED in New York in time to take an active part in the first convention of the American Anti-Slavery Society early in May. Welcomed as a representative of the admired and successful British abolition movement, he responded with appropriately ambassadorial words about the "flight of the American Eagle and the Dove of Peace" and with a gift of an "Anti-Slavery Album" in which the American society could record its constitution and membership. But he quickly made it clear that he had come to offer much more than symbolic gestures. He drew the convention's attention to the transformation of the Agency Committee into an organization committed to making the overthrow of U.S. slavery its main priority. The convention responded by including him on a new committee appointed to cooperate with the British society. Such cooperation was always dear to Stuart's heart, and his major speech at the convention included a firm rebuttal of charges in the American press that Garrison had slandered his country while in Britain and that Wilberforce had signed an anti-ACS resolution while deranged by sickness. But in the same speech Stuart stressed that he did not want primarily to be a spokesman of British abolition or a respected outsider lending temporary support to the fledgling American movement. He was not "a stranger and a foreigner" in North America. The ashes of his parents were there; his sisters lived there; and he was a returning "friend and brother." Before the convention ended, his wish had been given substance by his formal appointment as an agent of the society.[4]

Soon his agency was to involve him in spreading the antislavery gospel in the western regions he knew so well from his days as a Finney revivalist. But immediately after the New York convention his destination was the New England Anti-Slavery Convention, to which he had been appointed a delegate of the national society along with the Reverend John Frost. On his way to that convention Stuart had a dramatic initiation into the tense atmosphere of American abolition at Middletown, Connecticut. He was accompanied by Frost and Charles W. Denison, previously editor of the American Anti-Slavery Society's paper, the *Emancipator*, but now a field agent of the society. It was perhaps Denison's presence that particularly inflamed local feelings for he was known in the area as the main instigator of antislavery activity the previous winter. Pointed references were made to Stuart's nationality, however, and colonizationists were identified among his opponents, so Stuart's reputation, so carefully cultivated by the *Liberator*, may have been the main provocation. Whatever the cause, after an incident-free afternoon meeting, Stuart quickly found that colonizationist opposition in the United States was much more tangible than the genteel skirmishes he had experienced with Cresson's supporters in Britain. After he had opened the evening meeting with a prayer, a mob took possession of the room, shouting down Frost's attempt to begin a speech and laying siege to Denison and Stuart on the rostrum. Among many who heaped abuse on Stuart, a retired naval officer from Georgia took the lead in questioning him about his British and military background before challenging him to a duel. Stuart's calm refusal of the challenge and his further assurance that he had no intention of returning a threatened slap on the cheek ended this exchange. Others, however, were more enraged than mollified by the "smiling countenance" with which Stuart announced that "he desired no other protection than that which God and the laws afforded." A broadside of rotten eggs and redoubled shouting led to an abolitionist withdrawal with the mob in pursuit. Stuart and Frost managed to escape unscathed, but others were caught and manhandled in the street, including Denison, whose coat was torn from his back, head severely bruised, and face deeply cut. The following evening, at nightfall, the mob closed in again, surrounding the house in which Stuart and his friends were staying, threatening to tar and feather them. Eventually sufficient friends of the cause were mustered to form a pro-

---

4. American Anti-Slavery Society, Reports of Meetings, 1–6, 1833–39, pp. 4–5, 7, 9, 10, 37, 52–53, BPL; *Liberator*, May 17, 1834, pp. 78–79; May 24, 1834, p. 83.

tective phalanx around the doorway, and the mob was repulsed "after chafing and rolling like a stormy sea."[5]

If these scenes were a far cry from anything he had experienced in Britain, over the next few weeks Stuart was to see mainly the positive side of the intense antislavery agitation now building in New England. At the convention at the end of May he reiterated the themes of his major speech to the national convention defending the reputations of Garrison and Wilberforce. And again he involved himself actively in the work of the convention, serving on subcommittees concerned with fostering cooperation among abolitionists and with drafting the convention's *Address to the People of New England*. His new American colleagues were not disappointed by the presence of a man who had been so extravagantly praised in his absence over the previous three years. John Greenleaf Whittier confessed: "I can think of him only with admiration and love. His peculiar and solemn eloquence—his fervent zeal—his steadfast faith—his humble reliance upon the great Pattern of Philanthropy—all unite to render his presence among us the occasion of gratitude to God."[6]

Stuart was sufficiently excited by the new friendships he was forging with American abolitionists to delay writing to Theodore Weld for nearly a month after his return to the United States. But his eventual letter of apology from Concord, New Hampshire, early in June revealed another source of distraction: his love for Cornelia had been reawakened by an unexpected meeting with her in Hartford, Connecticut: "I found her sweet and kind; and a new tide of suppressed but not extinguished feeling poured at her presence over my heart." The next sentences in the letter, uniquely in the Stuart-Weld correspondence, have been heavily crossed out with Theodore's characteristically thick, black pen strokes. Cornelia's name is one of the few words still decipherable in the obliterated passage, which was obviously of a very personal nature because Stuart continued: "I tell you, my dearly beloved Theodore, of these things, in that sacred confidence of love by which God has united us I am persuaded for ever. Let them not perplex you. They do not perplex me. They rather give new vigor and sweetness to my life, and help I believe to prostrate my will the more cordially and perfectly to that blessed will of God our Father, which alone without defect is ever wise and kind."[7] Events two months later were to make it clear that Stuart's recent meeting with Cornelia had rekindled his hopes of marrying her.

5. *Liberator*, May 31, 1834, p. 87; *Emancipator*, June 3, 1834, p. 3.
6. New England Anti-Slavery Society, *Annual Convention 1834*, 15; *Liberator*, May 31, 1834, pp. 86–87, July 19, 1834, p. 113; *Emancipator*, June 10, 1834, p. 3.
7. Stuart to Weld, June 3, 1834, WP.

In the meantime, however, his "renewed vigor and sweetness" was expressed entirely in the public arena of antislavery campaigning. He embarked on a demanding program of lecturing and preaching, initially in the Boston area, at Lowell, Salem, Danvers, South Weymouth, and Beverley, but then on into Rhode Island and Connecticut. At every stage his efforts attracted admiration and praise. Indeed, in contrast to some of the British criticism of his emotionalism, Americans, perhaps accustomed to impassioned sermonizing, found Stuart an impressively restrained performer in the pulpit and on the rostrum.

At Lowell, according to the local newspaper, he "enchained the attention of his audience to a late hour." His delivery was "lucid and convincing," and his "startling facts and arguments" made a "deep and salutary" impression: "The cause of abolition came home to the feelings of the people in a manner it had never done before." The Hartford *Chronicle* referred to his "usual tender, persuasive, and inoffensive manner" and expressed the hope that he would soon return for further lectures. And the Brooklyn *Unionist* agreed that "Mr. Stuart's manner, though far from being showy and oratorical, is peculiarly solemn and impressive, and for that reason, well adapted to so solemn and important a subject." The paper went on: "We are highly pleased with the evident Christian kindness which without in the least relaxing his rigid principles of Christian morality, dictated every sentence, and breathed in every word he uttered. While he hesitated not to pronounce slavery an atrocious crime—a daring transgression of the divine law . . . his reproofs were administered in the spirit of love—in the temper of one who would much rather have occasion to forgive the reformed, than to punish the incorrigible offender."[8]

Stuart was equally impressed by his reception in this month of June. He found "hearts and houses open" almost everywhere and forged many new friendships. He wrote privately of a "most pleasing" general impression he had gained from the tour, "and I trust that I am not guilty of presumption in believing it gratifying and beneficial to others." But he was realistic enough to know that the obstacles in the path of abolition in America were infinitely greater than in Britain. Probably the main reason he was moved to report that Reading, Connecticut, "seemed to me like a truly English anti-slavery population" was that the previous day he had had the very American experience of visiting Prudence Crandall's school in Canterbury to offer moral and financial support from the female abo-

8. Lowell *Observer* cited in *Liberator*, June 14, 1834, p. 91, and *Emancipator*, June 17, 1834; Hartford *Chronicle* and Brooklyn *Unionist* quoted in *Emancipator*, July 7, 1834.

litionists of Britain, particularly Scotland. Although still open, the school had been subjected to mob attack only a few days before, evidence of the continuing hostility that within two months was to drive the newly married Crandall into exile in Illinois. Shortly afterward Stuart himself was given a further mild taste of the mob violence he had experienced on his first visit to Connecticut a few weeks previously. At Plainfield his lecture was interrupted by what he described as "a set of boys and young men." An antiabolition newspaper claimed that he was put to flight, after indulging "in the usual style of exaggeration and falsehood," by an audience of farmers cracking cart-whips around his ears. Stuart contended that the mass of his audience had been sympathetic and attentive and had "effectually curbed" the hostility of the small rowdy faction. At all events, the incident was relatively minor and did not seriously mar his New England tour, which was rounded off with a series of Fourth of July meetings in Providence, Rhode Island, in which he took a prominent part, along with Garrison, Samuel J. May, and others.[9]

Overall, his initial American efforts had been a success. But although the hope was frequently expressed that he would return to many of the towns he had visited, there were good reasons why these two months of 1834 were to be his only extended antislavery campaign in New England. Beneath the surface goodwill lay the faint beginnings of estrangement from Garrison. Despite the warmth of their earlier relationship, the praise heaped on Garrison in Stuart's early American speeches and the continuing eulogies of Stuart in the Liberator, and their shared platforms on many occasions, the two men were clearly drawing apart. Stuart made no mention of Garrison in his surviving correspondence of this period, but Garrison's letters to his future wife began to express his lurking distaste for the Briton's outlandish appearance even as he continued to stress his admiration for his piety and dedication.[10]

Garrison had a more important reason for being impatient with Stuart. After the American had left England the previous year, Stuart had informed him that he personally would continue to raise funds for the projected colored school that had been the ostensible main reason for Garrison's transatlantic journey. He had written in October, 1833, that he had already raised some five hundred dollars and had decided to remain in England that winter to try to double that sum. In April, on the eve of

9. Stuart to Elizur Wright, Jr., *Emancipator*, July 1, 1834; letter from Stuart and extract from the antiabolition New York *Commercial Advertiser*, in *Emancipator*, August 5, 1834; see also *Liberator*, July 12, 1834, p. 110.
10. *Liberator*, July 5, 12, 19, August 16, 1834; Garrison to Helen E. Benson, June 24, 1834, in Merrill and Ruchames (eds.), *Letters of Garrison*, I, 372.

his departure from England, the *Liberator* had announced that he would be bringing a thousand dollars "for the establishment of the Manual Labor School for Colored Youth in New England." Stuart had duly arrived in New York with the money and then, amid the euphoria of his hero's welcome by the assembled delegates at the American Anti-Slavery Society Convention, he promptly handed it over to the national society. Within a few weeks he tried to retrieve his mistake by asking that at least a share of the funds be given to the New England society. The national committee thought it "rather singular that they ask any at all." The members voted "to take a little time to consider" the matter and then, only ten days later, Elizur Wright, the corresponding secretary, wrote on their behalf to Garrison, apologizing that the money had been accepted "without a thought of the claims the New England Society might have upon it—& it is spent."[11]

Garrison did not publicly complain of Stuart's action, and even privately he continued to regard him as a man of the deepest integrity.[12] But Stuart's impulsive action must have hastened the process by which George Thompson displaced him as Garrison's main British ally. Within two months Thompson had followed Stuart to the United States and immediately began an antislavery tour marked by almost daily violence such as Stuart had encountered at Middletown. From this point on—and long after Thompson was driven from America, after a period in hiding, to escape the very real possibility of being lynched—references to Stuart in the *Liberator* were comparatively rare, and George Thompson became the new heroic representative of international abolitionism.

The Thompson-Garrison friendship had begun the previous year in England, and there can be little doubt that the two men, who were much the same age, were more at ease with one another than Garrison could ever be with the older and more eccentric Stuart. Inasmuch as the threats to Thompson's life in New England strengthened the relationship, Stuart's relatively easy passage in the same region must be regarded as a further reason why his relationship with Garrison cooled from mid-1834 on. There can be no doubt that Garrison was at times genuinely fearful for Thompson's safety. But, equally, the dramatic turbulence of his tour—the mob activities and the published threats to murder a presumptuous foreign intruder—all provided excellent material for Garrison's contentious jour-

11. Letters from Stuart to Garrison, *Liberator*, January 4, 1834, p. 1, April 12, 1834, p. 59; editorial, *ibid.*, April 19, 1834, p. 63; Wright to Amos Phelps, June 20, 1834, and to Garrison, June 30, 1834, BPL.

12. Garrison to Samuel J. May, January 17, 1836, Merrill and Ruchames (eds.), *Letters of Garrison*, II, 14.

nalism. Thompson's superb oratory in the face of almost constant disruption made much better copy than reports of Stuart's "solemn," "impressive," and "loving" speeches. It was true that at Middletown Stuart had faced danger with duly reported sangfroid. And in the more ambiguous incident at Plainfield there was heard the epithet "foreign incendiary and emissary," which was to be regularly directed at Thompson. He argued in response to the Plainfield incident, "I *am* a foreigner. But I AM NOT an emissary. My nearest relations are here—many of my dearest friends are here. I have often before been in these states. I have experienced some of the richest blessings of my life here."[13] A hostile mob, of course, would be unlikely to be silenced by such reasoning. But it does seem likely that Stuart's familiarity with American conditions and his experience as a preacher in America enabled him intelligently to adapt his material and techniques to the American situation and, in the process, avoid provoking the extreme hostility which Thompson aroused by oratory that appeared the more inflammatory because it smacked of British intrusion.

As in Britain, the insistent theme both of Stuart's speeches to the converted, at the great antislavery conventions, and his lectures to the uncommitted, in a score of New England towns, was the *"one great object, immediate emancipation, under law."* He also added the necessary American requirement that this emancipation should be "at home." But now, unless questions from the audience left him no alternative, he deliberately ignored the ACS, which had so often been central to his lectures in Britain. This omission was not because he feared the wrath the colonizationists had displayed at Middletown but because he felt that the ACS was "crumbling into nothingness." And as it crumbled, he perceptively argued against "offending the prepossessions of the many excellent persons who still support it." The wisdom of these tactics was to be shown within the next few months when he began what were to be lifelong friendships with two of the most notable colonizationists, James G. Birney, recently transformed into an abolitionist, and Gerrit Smith, who was even then agonizing over the decision to throw in his lot with the American Anti-Slavery Society.[14]

Those friendships were to flourish well away from Garrison's New England, in the near-frontier regions of western New York and Ohio. And

13. *Liberator*, September 27, October 4, 11, 18, 25, 1834, and thereafter in every edition of the paper until the end of 1835 and in numerous later editions after Thompson's return to Britain. Quotation is from *Emancipator*, August 5, 1834.

14. Stuart to Wright, *Emancipator*, July 7, 1834; Betty Fladeland, *James Gillespie Birney: Slaveholder to Abolitionist* (New York, 1955), 75–89.

in a sense the most important reason of all for the withering of Stuart's friendship with Garrison—some five years before a real enmity developed—lay in his rapid involvement in the emerging western center of abolitionism. If he had felt as much American as foreign in New England, in upstate New York and beyond he was once again in the region where he had unwittingly prepared himself for abolitionism by his work as a Finney revivalist.

MOMENTOUS EVENTS were under way in the West even as Stuart crossed the Atlantic and began his career as an American abolitionist. He had already made a considerable proxy contribution in the encouragement he had given Weld to join the antislavery struggle. In that period Weld had been preparing for the ministry, along with a number of other Finney converts, at the Oneida Institute. He had already achieved a considerable reputation as a lecturer on temperance and moral reform. That reputation and the connections he had through Finney with the Tappan brothers explained his presence at the meeting in New York City early in 1831, which laid the foundations on which the American Anti-Slavery Society was eventually constructed. In the short term, however, that meeting had led to Weld's appointment as general agent for the Society for Promoting Manual Labor in Literary Institutions, another Tappan project. On an extensive tour through Ohio, Indiana, Illinois, Missouri, Kentucky, Tennessee, and Alabama, Weld lectured on temperance but prepared himself ever more thoroughly for his abolitionist role. He became exceptionally well-informed about slavery and formed vital friendships with future stalwarts of the antislavery movement. Among these were Beriah Green, professor of sacred literature at Western Reserve College, and Birney, a lawyer and planter from Alabama, who was at that time about to become an ACS agent in the South. Weld was also commissioned by the Tappans to find on this tour a suitable site for a theological seminary they intended to finance. The foundation of Lane Seminary in Cincinnati, with Lyman Beecher as president, was the result of this quest.[15]

Weld persuaded many of his fellow students at Oneida to transfer to the new seminary, which opened in late 1833. The site could not have been better chosen to force the antislavery issue. Cincinnati was a growing industrial center on the border between slave and free territory. There was strong white prejudice toward its significant and growing population of free blacks. The Lane students, most of whom were mature men in their late twenties and thirties, quickly involved themselves in missionary and

15. Dumond, *Antislavery*, 158–65.

social work among this black community. And almost as quickly they began to discuss the questions of colonization and immediate emancipation. These discussions became a formal debate in January, 1834. Weld introduced the question of immediate abolition and was followed by Henry B. Stanton, soon to be another leading abolitionist. Subsequent speakers included William T. Allan and James A. Thome, who had been born and educated in the South. After days of discussion the debate ended with an almost unanimous vote in favor of immediate emancipation and the formation of a student antislavery society with Allan its elected president.[16]

It was to be some months before the authorities' attempts to dissolve this society and suppress all discussion of slavery were to lead to the famous withdrawal from the seminary of fifty-one students, many of whom were to work actively in the spread of abolitionism as official agents of the American Anti-Slavery Society or as antislavery ministers. In the months when Stuart was lecturing in New England the Lane debate was still boiling within the seminary, in the city of Cincinnati, and in educational circles well beyond Ohio. Stuart's correspondence with Weld must have made him aware of what was happening in Cincinnati. But although his letters showed an eagerness to be reunited with Theodore, he was initially drawn out of New England by other personal ties.[17] He had his sister in Canada to visit and, above all, his relationship with Cornelia to resolve.

It took only a few days at the Weld family home in Apulia for his romantic interest in Cornelia to be dispelled forever. In a letter to Theodore in early August, he made it clear that his brief reunion with her two months before had indeed made him anxious to renew his courtship. But now, he was able to report with finality after further meetings, "she is not to be mine." He had not renewed his marriage proposal. It was simply, as he told Weld, that "the magic is broken": "I have said nothing to her about it. I love her still as a sister . . . there is altogether too great a discordancy of temper & of mind between us—I see the fact now glaringly, and wonder that I did not formerly perceive it; and I cannot be sufficiently thankful for the integrity which she then displayed, and which dissipated the foolish & romantic affection with which I had entangled myself and for the prevention this time of a similar entanglement, for which I was prepared."[18]

And so, once again without entanglements, Stuart was ready to play his part in one of the great surges of abolitionist activity in the United

16. *Ibid.*
17. Stuart to Weld, June 3, 1834, WP.
18. Stuart to Weld, August 5, 1834, WP.

States. His role in this western movement was to be less significantly innovative than had been his influence on the Agency Committee in Britain. But it was more important than historians have hitherto recognized. Most writers have seen Stuart's significance largely in the influence he had already exerted on Theodore Weld in his correspondence from Britain over the previous few years. Dwight L. Dumond, one of the great historians of western abolitionism, has added, without much elaboration, that "Stuart remained in the United States and rendered great additional service to the cause, but not as a public speaker," apparently because, like George Thompson, he "encountered the usual public antipathy for British men and measures."[19]

It would be absurd to claim that Stuart's activities in the western movement were comparable to those of Weld. His greatest contribution may have been the indirect one of enabling Weld to function so effectively. It is evident that once again, as in the early years of their friendship, he gave financial assistance to the younger man.[20] He took a lively interest in the developing crisis at Lane Seminary, offering Weld intellectual and emotional encouragement in the stand against Lyman Beecher. And even before they were reunited he was sending Weld copious information and arguments from the British abolition movement. Early in August, Weld, who was helping to plan the first abolition campaign of James G. Birney, wrote to the former colonizationist that he had just received from Stuart, "the distinguished English Abolitionist," all numbers of the English *Anti-Slavery Reporter*, bound in five volumes, and all the tracts and pamphlets, some thirty or forty in number, published by the British Anti-Slavery Society. He hoped it would be possible to get this valuable material to Birney to help him prepare his forthcoming antislavery addresses, for it contained "everything you need in preparing your essays."[21]

Stuart's influence on Weld, Birney, and others, notably Gerrit Smith, continued through the next three climactic years of the early immediatist campaign. But it would be misleading to suggest that his role was confined to this indirect influence. According to Dumond, the decisive stage in the western campaign was about to begin in the fall of 1834. The limitations of campaigning through newspapers and pamphlets had been re-

19. Dumond, *Antislavery*, 182.
20. "God has bountifully preserved me to receive again my half yearly income, and the sweetest use to which I can apply a portion of it, is to offer you fifty dollars—for *your own personal* service, if you please, my dearest Theodore" (Stuart to Weld, January 20, 1835, WP).
21. Stuart to Weld, August 5, 1834, WP; Weld to Birney, August 7, 1834, in Dwight L. Dumond (ed.), *Letters of James Gillespie Birney* (New York, 1938), 129.

vealed. Such methods were essential to provide inspiration and education, "but at least a few people in any given community had to be aroused and enlisted in the cause before this literature could come into the community and through these people be passed on to others. Agents, more specifically lecturers, had to awaken the community and do it effectively enough to establish a local anti-slavery society." It would be unthinkable to deny Dumond's contention that Theodore Weld and, to a lesser extent, Henry B. Stanton, were the men who most triumphantly fulfilled this need.[22] But Charles Stuart, who had pioneered these very methods two and three years before throughout the British Isles, was a wholehearted and effective field agent in New York and Ohio. Even as he was supplying Weld and others with necessary pamphlet and newspaper ammunition—some two months before the climax of the Lane Seminary revolt—he was beginning his own work. There is ample evidence that, judged by Dumond's essential criteria of arousing the community and founding local antislavery societies, Stuart was successful.

STUART HIMSELF was to look back from an embittered retirement twenty years later and recall these months of promise, crisis, and achievement as a golden era: "How gloriously did the anti-slavery cause arise. . . . With what holy vigor did it proceed and ramify itself, with rich fruits of glorious promise, amidst slander and persecutions, and mobbings, at the risque and sometimes at the sacrifice of property or life." His reminiscences were designed to underline the decline into acrimony and confusion of a movement that had lost its pioneering enthusiasm. But his argument was in no way a distortion, least of all of his own sense of elation in the fall of 1834. The day after reporting to Weld of the end of his infatuation with Cornelia, he was writing to Elizur Wright back in New York City: "I seem to be in a different world. I am in the midst of a republican and enlightened yeomanry." He had just preached once and lectured twice in Apulia and in the next few days had engagements in four nearby communities. Although these appointments delayed his journey to Canada, he had been unable to refuse them: "Oh, what a privilege to be employed in so sacred a cause!"[23]

Before making his visit to Canada he also lectured at Cazenovia, a township he knew well from his earliest contacts with the Weld family. Here, in dealing with a hostile intervention from a colonizationist, he

22. Dumond, *Antislavery*, 183–85.
23. Stuart to Frederick Douglass, *Frederick Douglass' Paper*, January 26, 1855; Stuart to Wright, August 6, 1834, *Emancipator*, September 2, 1834.

showed that for all his firmness of principle, he was capable of a tactical flexibility in adapting his arguments to the American situation. When his opponent challenged him on the question of interracial amalgamation, he was aware that this issue was emotive enough to be causing heated controversy and even riots in New York City. And so, the man whose English writings had excoriated race prejudice above all else—a man whom Elliott Cresson had described privately as an out-and-out amalgamationist—now in upstate New York replied judiciously that it was slavery not freedom which encouraged miscegenation. He clung loyally to the official American Anti-Slavery Society line that abolitionists did not favor such liaisons and that freedom of choice would mean each race showing a preference for its own color. He may deliberately but subtly have introduced his own views when he rounded off the exchange by saying that should his adversary "fall in love with a coloured woman" he would have Stuart's "hearty" blessing to marry her. Although it was Stuart's own report which insisted that the audience was on his side and that "a loud cheer filled the house" at his repartee, there was soon to be independent corroboration that his lecture had had some impact. A month later William Goodell, touring the region as editor of the *Emancipator*, visited Cazenovia and reported that "Charles Stuart had lectured there, some time previous and several converts had been made."[24]

Soon Goodell's tour revealed evidence of a less successful appearance by Stuart in Buffalo. Stuart was returning in late September from a brief visit to his relatives in Canada when he took advantage of an invitation to address the Erie County Bible Society by using a discussion about proselytizing the "heathen nations" to introduce the question of immediate emancipation, "on the ground that slavery was shutting out the Word of God from two millions of our innocent . . . fellow-beings." The following Sunday he preached at both the Baptist and Second Presbyterian churches. But then he found a projected antislavery meeting for the next evening in the Baptist church had been canceled because the church trustees feared mob activity. According to Goodell's later intelligence, the obstruction came from one or two "aristocratic lordlings," who had used the rumored mob as an excuse to close the church against Stuart "even though multitudes desired to hear him speak." Goodell's account implied that the reasons lay at least partly in long-standing tensions between the trustees and "an entire church or congregation of humbler fellow-worshippers." Stuart's account, in a letter to the local newspaper, suggested a more spe-

24. *Emancipator*, July 15, 22, 29, August 5, 1834; Stuart to Wright, *ibid.*, August 5, 1834; "Tour of the Editor," *ibid.*, January 27, 1835.

cific hostility to the antislavery cause or even to him personally as a foreigner. He had refused to accept the forecasts of mob activity but had found the church closed at the appointed hour: "Why," he asked, "should the people of Buffalo reject the lawful, and peaceful discussion of slavery? Are they told that I am a foreigner? Well; why should a foreigner's information be rejected by a country which is the progeny and asylum of foreigners?"[25]

Although the reaction in Buffalo appears to support the notion that Stuart was rendered ineffectual in the United States because he was regarded as an interfering outsider, this particular incident cannot be taken to indicate a general trend. There is ample evidence that Stuart was able to work effectively in the future with only occasional objections to his nationality. And it is plausible that the reasons for this general acceptance lay in the facts he went on to mention in his letter to the Buffalo press about his long familiarity with North America in general and upstate New York in particular. These facts included not only the references he had already made in his New England speeches to resident friends and relatives but also his reminder that "I am a licensed minister of the Oneida Presbytery of this state; and am a life member of several of the most important of its benevolent institutions." It was not so much that such arguments would convince a hostile audience but rather that the affiliations he was describing must frequently have made him well known in the circles into which, in the coming months, he was to carry the antislavery message. The colorful Utica schoolmaster, Sunday school teacher, preacher, itinerant distributor of Bibles, and Finney revivalist of a few years before might conceivably have been dismissed as an eccentric. But his claim that "God has given me a little independence; and it is my soul's delight to spend it in the service of the poor, the suffering, and the oppressed" must have rung sufficiently true to enough people for his nationality hardly to be a serious problem. Indeed, even before his return to the region, Goodell's extensive tour was revealing evidence of Stuart's former affiliations to the readers of the *Emancipator*. In Elyria he had met a clergyman with whose family Stuart had stayed some years previously: "It was truly delightful to hear the commendations passed on our distinguished co-worker. His private intercourse appears to have been as distinguished for humble piety, and gentlemanly politeness, as his public . . . enlarged benevolence, and sagacious argument."[26]

25. *Emancipator*, October 14, 1834, February 10, 1835; Stuart's letter to the editor of the Rochester *Literary Enquirer*, reprinted in *Liberator*, October 18, 1834, p. 166.
26. *Liberator*, October 18, 1834, p. 166; "Tour of the Editor," *Emancipator*, May 25, 1833.

It seems equally likely that where Stuart was not personally known his intimate connections with Weld would have prepared the way for his acceptance in many of the pious religious circles that were poised to receive the antislavery argument. It is scarcely conceivable that Weld would make no verbal mention of a man to whom he owed so much and whom he had praised so highly in his recent letter to Birney in the weeks before Stuart's campaign began.

Stuart's activities in August and September, 1834, in Apulia, Cazenovia, and Buffalo were not directly related to his agency with the American Anti-Slavery Society. They were voluntary contributions squeezed between his personal visits to the Weld family and to his sister in Canada. The terms of his agency were defined on October 1 at the same meeting when the committee of the national society appointed Weld and Birney as agents. Stuart was to "labor in the State of New York" and "be requested to devote special efforts to the raising of funds for the Society." Exactly six months later the committee minutes recorded a decision that he "be requested . . . to keep us advised of his movements more frequently."[27] From these two entries and the superficial record of Stuart's movements in that six-month period one could conclude that his work in the field had been far from satisfactory. He had spent the first six weeks in Ohio, rather than New York, and the subsequent months almost entirely in the Utica region, rather than in any extensive fund-raising exercise. But a closer scrutiny of his activities reveals an intensive involvement in the awakening antislavery campaign. Perhaps more important than his considerable direct contribution was the way he had prepared himself for later effectiveness by familiarizing himself more thoroughly than ever with the issues and many of the personnel of the movement.

Stuart was probably already committed to an extensive tour of key Ohio centers before he learned of the national committee's request that he concentrate on New York. Immediately after his controversial visit to Buffalo, he went to Cleveland, where he gave two lectures in the Presbyterian church and preached once. After he delivered two lectures at Elyria, an antislavery association was formed. The atmosphere was much more contentious at Western Reserve College, where the local synod of the Presbyterian church was held in early October. This area had a recent history of controversy, despite, or perhaps because of, the existence of an antislavery society. In the previous year there had been bitter disputes over the question of expatriation of free blacks from the region. Now the

27. American Anti-Slavery Society, Committee on Agencies, Minute Book, October 1, 1834, March 31, 1835, BPL.

committee that decided the business of the synod refused requests to put antislavery resolutions on the agenda. Stuart was chosen by the antislavery faction to present an appeal against this decision. His advocacy led to the appeal being sustained. But subsequent debate produced an eventual decision by the synod to postpone indefinitely a firm resolution about slavery. According to F. W. Upson, secretary of the college antislavery society, many who felt slavery was sinful were reluctant to be identified as abolitionists. In spite of this reluctance, Upson forecast that similar antislavery resolutions would be passed "by an overwhelming majority" at the next synod. And in his report to Elizur Wright and the American Anti-Slavery Society, he made it plain that Stuart had made an important contribution to this improving trend: he was "an excellent man, an unassuming and warm-hearted philanthropist." He had left for Cincinnati, but it was hoped that he would return in the future to help form a county antislavery society.[28]

In Cincinnati Stuart found fortification both emotionally and professionally for the months ahead. His long-awaited reunion with Weld lasted three weeks, "and much did I find, as I have always found in his company to instruct and delight me." The pleasure the visit gave him is most clearly indicated by the pain he was to express a few weeks after their parting: "I have felt the want of you my beloved Theodore ever since I left you. . . . Will you remember that we are brethren by dearer ties than those of blood. . . . I know you pray for me; & you know that I am for ever with all my heart your faithful C. Stuart." But for the two men this great friendship was now subservient to the moral crusade which both were on the threshold of pressing home with redoubled energy.[29]

The passions of the Lane Seminary revolt were about to be channeled into the antislavery campaign. Stuart arrived in Cincinnati as the famous withdrawal was just taking effect. Some of the students had already dispersed from what he described as the "degraded institution." But he met some twenty of the rebels and was inspired by the "holy vigor of simple truth and love." During his three-week stay the *Declaration* of the fifty-one seceding students was being prepared, and it was almost ready for publication when he left. One of the students who most impressed him was James Bradley, an emancipated slave, from whom, as well as from Weld, he learned much about the South which he could use in forthcoming lectures. And during his stay in Cincinnati he also reinforced his long-

28. F. W. Upson to Wright, October 14, 1834, *Emancipator*, October 28, 1834; Stuart to Wright, December 11, 1834, *ibid.*, December 23, 1834.
29. Stuart to Weld, November 24, 1834, WP.

expressed sympathy for the free black population of the United States by visiting colored schools and families.[30]

After leaving Cincinnati Stuart made his way back across Ohio, lecturing at Talmadge and Middlebury and helping to form a county antislavery society at Portage before undertaking further lectures at Hudson College and Cleveland. At Ashtabula, Ohio, during a brief break in his journey, he sought out a fugitive Negro, about whom he had recently heard, and completed his research for a communication he was soon to have published in the *Emancipator* entitled "THE PURSUER CONVICTED! THE FUGITIVE RELEASED! Being a practical answer to the question, 'What is the use of Anti-Slavery Societies at the north?'"[31] By the time this article appeared in January, 1835, Stuart was doing his utmost directly to promote the spread of antislavery societies in the familiar surroundings of Utica. With winter closing in, extensive traveling would be difficult, and, in any case, he knew that in and around Utica there were both apathy and outright opposition to be overcome, as well as a major task of converting to immediatism some genuine opponents of slavery, who were either gradualists or supporters of colonization.

Prominent in this last category was Gerrit Smith, a wealthy businessman and landowner, who was a major supporter of many reform causes and a key figure in the ACS. By early 1835 Smith's support for colonization had been vigorously challenged, particularly by James G. Birney, who, soon after his own conversion to immediatism, wrote a famous public letter to Smith attacking the futility of gradualism and labeling colonization a positive bulwark of slavery. Smith's commitment to colonization was almost certainly severely shaken by Birney, who accused him of being, thanks to his wealth, influence, and reputation, the single most important upholder of slavery. But Smith did not follow Birney into open support of the immediatist cause for some months.[32] Through most of 1835 he agonized over the decision, and in this period Charles Stuart was active among the abolitionists who urged him to take the final step.

The two men met for the first time in mid-January at an antislavery meeting at Peterboro, where Smith had a vast estate. Stuart felt he had "found a brother's home and a brother's heart with Gerrit Smith," and this meeting was the start of a friendship that was to persist until Stuart's death. That the still nominally colonizationist Smith should so warmly welcome the most prolific and trenchant of anticolonization pamphleteers

30. Stuart to Wright, *Emancipator*, December 23, 1834.
31. *Ibid.*, January 13, 1835.
32. Fladeland, *Birney*, 102.

was a sign of how far his attitudes had changed since the day, four years before, when he had greeted the departure of "my friend Cresson" with the expectation that he would achieve "great things for our cause" in England. Stuart found that now Smith was in principle in favor of immediatism but was "yet somewhat perplexed about the mode of procedure." And although he wrote soon afterward to Weld that Smith "is all but with us," he also worked hard to make the conversion complete. Less than a week after staying at Peterboro he was sending Smith antislavery pamphlets and affectionately remonstrating: "The difficulty with you, dear & honored brother, appears to me to be, substituting your own ideas of what the Society *ought to be,* for what it is!"[33]

The relationship was clearly so friendly, with Stuart a regular visitor to Peterboro and an enthusiastic admirer of the school for colored children which Smith had established there, that there must have been a great deal of unrecorded debate about Smith's attitudes. But for the moment Smith remained a sympathetic bystander rather than an active supporter. Stuart's immediate concern was to carry the antislavery message directly to numerous less eminent Americans in dozens of rural and urban meetings in the counties around Utica. For the time being, opposition was muted, and the early months of 1835 saw him complete a first year of American campaigning notable for its industry and symptomatic more of the exhilarating progress of immediatism than of the violence and xenophobia that surrounded George Thompson in the East over the same months.

From the time of his first public meeting in late December, 1834, when he lectured in the familiar surroundings of the Second Presbyterian Church in Utica, all the evidence indicates that Stuart was a diligent, impressive advocate with the knowledge and intelligence to adapt his immediatist arguments to American conditions. A full report in the Utica *Baptist Register*, for instance, showed that in his second lecture on January 3 he used scriptural and global evidence to illustrate the universal sin of slavery but that he brought his arguments closer to home with references to the American system and emphasis on abolition in the District of Columbia as a priority. In these two meetings he persuaded his audience to organize a petition to Congress in favor of action in this one area in which abolition was directly attainable by federal intervention. Throughout January he pursued this theme in a series of public meetings of the Utica Anti-Slav-

33. Stuart to Wright, *Emancipator*, March 17, 1835; Smith to Gurley, April 27, 1831, reel 11, ACS; Stuart to Weld, January 20, 1835, WP; Stuart to Smith, January 20, 1835, SP.

ery Society and was able to report that the petition had been completed and that there had been "an accession of names to the anti-slavery cause."[34]

No doubt Stuart's long previous residence in Utica partly explains the absence of any recorded hostility to his nationality in this period. But there were other factors as well that probably helped to disarm criticism. No American abolitionist could have been better informed about American slavery. In his three weeks with Weld in Cincinnati he had learned much about the institution. Something of the thoroughness of his preparation, as well as the content of his lectures, is suggested by a letter he wrote to Birney in early February demanding both detailed information and colorful illustration. He requested the names of the states where slave labor was probably more productive than free, and vice versa, and those in which "emancipation without expatriation is prohibited by law." And he requested anecdotes, "with names and dates," about twelve different facets of southern slavery, including the insecurity of marriage, the "destitution of parental authority," and slaveowning clergy.[35] But this was the thoroughness of a total enthusiast, who, as in Britain, was likely to impress audiences as much by his personality as by the information he imparted.

Something of that personality was shown in the naive enthusiasm of his request to Birney for a description of a bloodhound—"its genus, size, temper, education, how kept, how used, whether common or frequent"—and for a list of "*all* the epithets which are applied to the domestic [slave] dealers." His main visual aid was now no longer the West Indian slave-whip he had brandished in Ireland but a miniature edition of the United States Constitution. But his lectures were no less naive for he invited audiences to show him where the document sanctioned slavery.[36]

His public insistence that the Constitution, properly interpreted, was "worthy of the noblest nation on earth" was, of course, not without an element of calculation. And he was speaking for local consumption when he declared himself "by natural character and by religion, a republican, that is a lover of holy and impartial liberty." For although his private correspondence contained references to the solid virtues of a still predominantly rural America, he was also intensely critical. Yet even his criticism was expressed with the fervor that was his most conspicuous characteristic. A republic that sanctioned slavery, he told Gerrit Smith, "is not a

34. Stuart to Wright, *Emancipator,* March 17, 1835; Utica *Baptist Register* report reprinted in *ibid.,* January 27, 1835.
35. Stuart to Birney, February 16, 1835, WP.
36. *Ibid.*; Stuart to Frederick Douglass, *Frederick Douglass' Paper,* January 20, 1854.

republic—it is a many-headed despotism more really contemptible and hateful, in these respects, than the Czarship of Russia. The lie which is concealed under the Star Spangled banner, must be repented of—the Eagle must be unchained—or this nation must perish, God being God!"[37]

Later in his life such sentiments would harden into a comprehensive cynicism about the American system. But for the moment his public advocacy was more optimistic and his sincerity and passion for the cause were as appealing as they had been in his Agency Committee days.

The newspaper account of his second meeting in Utica reported: "He spoke for about an hour, on the evils and remedy of slavery in our country, with a clearness and force which could not fail to carry conviction to every unprejudiced mind. He exhibited throughout, as he is wont to do on all occasions, that spirit of candor and Christian kindness which is so peculiarly characteristic of the man." Thanks to the circulation of such published reports and also of private communications among his friends, Stuart's efforts in these early months of 1835 were widely appreciated. Early in February Weld wrote to Birney expressing pleasure that Stuart was "doing great good in New York." The following month Birney commented to Gerrit Smith: "I am delighted to hear of the success of our brother C. Stuart. He is a dear brother. The pure truth seems more precious to him, than to almost any other man with whom it has been my happy lot to become acquainted." In March also semiofficial congratulations appeared in the columns of the *Emancipator*. In a review of the recent striking progress of the cause, the paper claimed 7,500 members affiliated with the American Anti-Slavery Society through more than 150 "thorough-going anti-slavery societies." Thanks to "the labors of four agents employed by the society, and the two noble champions of humanity, Stuart and Thompson from England, and those of the devoted Mr. Birney of Kentucky, the number of abolitionists is daily and most rapidly increasing." Among the praise given to each individual agent was the comment that "Mr. Stuart has produced the happiest impression in Ohio and New York."[38]

In view of all this recognition, public and private, the national committee's vote on March 31 to request more information from Stuart about his movements is puzzling. He had written regularly to Elizur Wright over

---

37. Letter from Stuart refused publication in New York *Commercial Advertiser* and printed in *Emancipator*, August 5, 1834. For reference to rural virtues see Stuart to Wright, *Emancipator*, September 2, 1834; Stuart to Birney, February 16, 1835, WP. The final quotation is from Stuart to Smith, May 1[?], 1835, SP.

38. *Emancipator*, January 27, March 10, 1835; Weld to Birney, February 16, 1835, Dumond (ed.), *Letters of Birney*, 180; Birney to Smith, *ibid.*, 191.

the previous few months and much of his activity had been reported in the *Emancipator*. It is ironic that on the very day on which the committee recorded its vote—and before he could possibly know of its implied criticism—he had dispatched to that body a long, detailed letter about his most recent activities and his immediate plans. If Stuart had made no other contribution to the antislavery cause, these activities alone could serve as a testimonial to his dedication. Their revelation of the purely physical demands of itinerant lecturing is a useful reminder of the conditions faced by many in this pioneering stage of abolitionist activity. But it is worth stressing that Stuart, now fifty-three, was some twenty years older than most of those engaged in similar activity. In general, it was only much younger men who were both fit enough physically and free enough from domestic ties to work so relentlessly "in the field."[39]

In his letter he reported that he was nearly at the end of a walk around Oneida County "hunting up anti-slavery men" for the formation of a county antislavery society. Oneida County had twenty-five towns, he reported, and he would shortly have visited eighteen of them; "want of time" prevented his visiting the other seven. He had managed to form two antislavery associations in Herkimer County and was confident that the Oneida association would materialize. Just returned to Utica "after a fatiguing walk this morning of 14 miles," he expected to start before dawn the following day for Sherburne in Chenango County "and thence to G. Smith's at Peterboro." In a letter to Smith the same day he outlined his plans to lecture in Chenango County and asked for help in arranging a full program in the Peterboro-Cazenovia area.[40]

His program proved very full indeed. He lectured three times at Sherburne on the way to Peterboro. In his letter to Smith he had looked forward to the "delights of again being with your dear family." But the delights must have been severely rationed by the demands of a hectic schedule of preaching in the local Presbyterian church, attending the quarterly meeting of the Peterboro Anti-Slavery Society, and visiting nearby Morrisville to arrange forthcoming lectures. Before giving those lectures he spent a long weekend in Cazenovia, where several "ardent friends" were longing for an antislavery society. After lectures on three successive evenings the society was formed. In Morrisville the subject was new, but he found some "brave yeomen" who were sympathetic, and after three evening lectures in the Baptist church, another antislavery so-

---

39. Stuart to Wright, *Emancipator*, April 14, 1835.
40. *Ibid.*; Stuart to Smith, March 31, 1835, SP. Stuart also referred in a letter to Edwin C. Clark to a pressure of engagements which left him exhausted and without leisure (March 16, 1835, Clark Papers, New-York Historical Society, New York City).

ciety was formed. Returning to Utica on April 16, he attended a meeting of the Juvenile Anti-Slavery Society, which, along with its female counterpart, he had helped form as auxiliaries to the Utica Anti-Slavery Society.[41]

On April 22 Stuart figured prominently at a meeting at Hampton, which established the Oneida County Anti-Slavery Association. Because he had done so much to stimulate the formation of local groups in this county, it was logical that, along with Beriah Green, he should be a principal speaker in support of the motion to form the association. His contribution, however, reflected his role as a national and international as well as local figure. He read aloud extracts from letters recently sent him by Weld, Birney, and George Thompson. After serving on the committee that organized the business of the meeting, he was chosen as one of five delegates to attend the imminent annual convention of the American Anti-Slavery Society.[42]

And so Stuart's second year as an American abolitionist was to begin, as the first one had, at the great national gathering in New York City. The year he had just completed had been a significant one for the American movement, with accentuated violent controversy in the East and a vast proliferation of immediatist societies in the West. Stuart had experienced violence but not been paralyzed by it, mainly because his role had been as a grass-roots agent of the western movement rather than a visiting foreign celebrity as George Thompson was in the East. Around Utica he had walked with a new sense of purpose the same countryside he had covered so extensively in his teaching and preaching days nearly a decade earlier. In the same region he had developed a significant new friendship with Gerrit Smith. And although Smith still demurred from immediatist commitment, his hospitality had sustained Stuart physically and spiritually and his influence had smoothed his path with many introductions. These experiences, as well as the success of numerous meetings and conventions, filled his letters with optimism. Apathy, he reported, was everywhere beginning to "thaw." The "finest minds" were adopting immediatism, "either stung to inquiry" by abolitionist activity or "already satisfied."[43]

In the long term Stuart's familiarity with the region would prove less important in his abolitionism than the lack of roots, which also facilitated his activities in this period. Already his enthusiasm hinted at an idealism

41. Stuart to Wright, *Emancipator*, May 12, 1835.
42. *Ibid.*, May 5, 1835.
43. Stuart to Wright, *Emancipator*, March 17, 1835; Stuart to Birney, February 16, 1835, WP.

that would not bend to the changing realities of American society. The admiration he expressed for America's "yeomen farmers" and his frequent quotation of Oliver Goldsmith's words about "a bold and generous peasantry their country's pride" betrayed essentially an outsider's view of the area.[44]

For the moment, however, he was realistic enough to recognize that formidable obstacles still lay ahead. Although it was true that the agricultural population "seem only to need information to be with us—the difficulty exists in the pride and selfishness and slave-holding and slave-dealing connexions of the towns." In Utica, when he had begun his advocacy, "almost death was creeping upon our sacred cause." Some progress had been made: although the Dutch Reform Church "still fraternates with its brethren, the boors [sic] of the Cape," and although the Episcopalians were "too polite for our Servant work," the ministers of other denominations—Presbyterian, Baptist, and Methodist—were "all with us." But all except the Methodists were "hampered variously by their people."[45]

This analysis was to prove accurate. In the coming months those pro-slavery urban "connexions" were to organize an opposition to abolition that was to explode spectacularly at the time of Utica's greatest antislavery gathering. And in those same months Charles Stuart was to look forward almost eagerly to such violence as a means of forcing the issue and making more difficult the neutrality of men such as Gerrit Smith.

AT THE SECOND annual convention of the American Anti-Slavery Society in May, Stuart renewed acquaintance not only with many leading American abolitionists but also with George Thompson. The two had corresponded occasionally in the months they had been in America, and their mutual admiration was still unqualified. But at the convention they served somewhat different functions. Thompson commanded some of the attention Stuart had attracted a year before as an eminent representative of British abolitionism. The younger man's major speech showed a preoccupation with this role in its criticisms of a recent visit to America by two prominent Baptists, the Reverends Cox and Hoby, who had refused to condemn American slavery, even though they were known as abolitionists in Britain. Stuart, on the other hand, acted very much as a local American abolitionist. While his fellow delegate from Oneida County,

---

44. Stuart to Wright, *Emancipator*, May 12, 1835; Stuart to Birney, February 16, 1835, WP.

45. Stuart to Wright, *Emancipator*, April 14, 1835; Stuart to Birney, February 16, 1835, WP.

Beriah Green, took the chair, he opened proceedings on May 15 with a prayer and subsequently moved resolutions urging a day of fasting and prayer in June and commending the conduct of colored Americans "in the face of the most irritating provocations, and in some cases of the most lawless outrages." Behind the scenes he devoted some of his energy to the problem of Gerrit Smith's continuing hesitations. He wrote to Smith reiterating his previous insistence that the society should be accepted on its existing principles rather than changed to facilitate Smith's membership. In fairness to Smith, he had discussed the matter of modifying the society's published principles with the "brethren" in New York. They had agreed that there should be no compromise, and Stuart's main concern was to balance regret and conciliation with firmness in communicating this decision to Smith.[46]

But despite such activities Stuart was not allowed to forget that he still had a no less important role as a spokesman and interpreter of British abolition. The society's annual report bracketed him with Thompson in expressing thanks to the "noble philanthropists of Great Britain. . . . For the mission to our aid of two of their noblest advocates in the cause of the oppressed, thousands will rise up and call them blessed."[47]

Thousands of other Americans, of course, were inclined to rise in anger at what they deemed foreign intrusion. Although by now Thompson's performances had aroused far more antagonism, Stuart was reminded in the weeks he was in New York City that he, too, was not immune to xenophobia. He provoked controversy at the General Assembly of the Presbyterian Church by submitting a memorial that characteristically attacked in scathing terms the support given to slavery by many ministers. One of those present, a Dr. Miller, asked if this was "the same Charles Stuart the *foreigner*, that he had heard of as lecturing and raising an excitement in different parts of the country." Another delegate, the Reverend J. Breckenridge, said it was doubtless the same individual, "who was often, he presumed by way of contempt, called the *Reverend* CAPTAIN Stuart." Insulting though these attacks were, Stuart's relative invulnerability compared with Thompson was revealed once again when other delegates sprang to his defense. As one pointed out, "Mr. Stuart was a Christian brother of unblemished character, and a regular licenciate of Oneida presbytery." Eventually the original critic, Miller, though with-

46. American Anti-Slavery Society, *Second Annual Report, with the Speeches Delivered at the Anniversary Meeting of the American Anti-Slavery Society in the City of New York, 12th May 1835* (New York, 1835), 16–22, 24, 31–33, 53; Stuart to Smith, May 1 [?], 1835, SP.

47. American Anti-Slavery Society, *Second Annual Report*, 53.

drawing none of his contempt for the "offensive" nature of Stuart's memorial, was moved to concede that "he has received a sort of ecclesiastical naturalization by being licensed by one of our presbyteries."[48] Here was further evidence of Stuart's acceptance, at least in the Oneida area, where he had undertaken his most sustained American antislavery activity.

Underlying the criticism he received on this occasion there may have been a degree of confusion in some people's minds between him and Thompson. Miller's references to "raising an excitement in different parts of the country" seems more consistent with Thompson's controversial tours than with all but a few incidents involving Stuart. A few months later, virtually on the eve of Thompson's forced departure, Stuart was condemned in a local New England newspaper in a clear confusion of his background with Thompson's. The American abolitionists had imported a "brazen-faced Englishman named Stuart": "It was thought among a certain class, that even the stoutest hearts could not withstand such mighty arguments—such bewitching eloquence as he could command. And when to these rare qualifications were added the virtues of an 'humble Christian', it was thought that to listen to him, was to become a convert to his doctrine! However, Stuart's arrival in America was not much in advance of the reception of information which proved him to be a fellow of at least doubtful reputation and withal a hyprocrite." These allegations could only be the result of the way Thompson's opponents were by then exploiting the revelation that in his youth he had been guilty of embezzlement from an employer, though never legally charged with the offense.[49]

Thompson was eventually forced out of the United States, not primarily because of rumors of a disreputable past but because of his eloquence and attractiveness as a platform speaker. Over the same latter months of 1835, Stuart was far less controversial. This was not least because he was for the time publicly less active than Thompson. At the end of May he was recommissioned by the national society as an agent for another year. In June he made an antislavery tour of Long Island. But over the next three months he was out of the public eye—in a period when Thompson was becoming ever more controversial—as he devoted most of his time to writing a series of articles eventually published in the abolitionist press.[50]

48. *Liberator*, June 13, 1835, p. 93.
49. Reprinted from the Norwich *Courier* in *Liberator*, November 21, 1835, p. 185; Rice, "Anti-Slavery Mission of George Thompson," 13–31.
50. American Anti-Slavery Society, Committee on Agencies, Minute Book, May 29, July 10, 1835, BPL. Stuart's articles were "On the Abolition of Slavery by Great Britain," *Quarterly Anti-Slavery Magazine*, I, No. 1 (October, 1835), 3–21, I, No. 2 (January, 1836), 107–17; "On the Colored People of the United States," *ibid.*, II, No. I (October, 1836), 11–22; "On the Use of Slave Produce," *ibid.*, II, No. 2 (January, 1837), 153–72.

Stuart's literary activities show that his contribution, particularly to Anglo-American antislavery cooperation, was more varied than Thompson's. As such—and because it included diverse strands—it cannot be readily related to a strict chronology of events and will receive separate analysis in the next chapter. But it has to be emphasized that Stuart's temporary withdrawal from day-to-day abolition campaigning did not reflect fear of the violent opposition that was threatening his compatriot. He eventually took his place with almost provocative nonchalance in a series of turbulent events in western New York. That he welcomed such opposition both intellectually and emotionally through the second half of 1835 is made clear by the letter he wrote in May from New York to Gerrit Smith. After regretting that Smith could still not take the final step into membership of the national society, he had expressed confidence "that the time is at hand, when you will wave [sic] the scruples which restrain you; and join us with all your heart in the great principles which already are as much yours as ours." And he had clearly seen violence as a catalyst that might hasten this process: "If, in pursuing this righteous, manly & republican course, we should indeed meet with embittered opposition, the call of duty only becomes the more solemn & more loud, to be found at our posts—*each* man open, doing *his* duty & none *waiting* for his neighbour."[51]

Violent crisis, he evidently felt, had a wider value than simply forcing decisions for individual commitment. It promised to loosen some of the shackles fastened on abolitionism by the checks and balances of the American system. To an extent that belied his public enthusiasm for American institutions his private letter to Smith revealed impatience with the political impregnability of slavery: "The idolatry of this people for their political institutions, is full of guilt and pregnant with danger—For the present case it is completely insane and suicidal. Free men, so fond of freedom, that they crush the main spring of all freedom, *free inquiry*—so fond of liberty, that they not only keep slaves, but insist on depriving their *fellow free men* of some of the dearest of their rights, viz. their rights at the elections and in petitioning." He looked to the day when "*liberty, republicanism,* and *Protestant Christianity*, may no longer be made a stink in the nostrils of every upright and unprejudiced mind, by thus continuing, as they now are, the efficient shield of the most atrocious system of legalized tyranny which disgraces the world."[52]

51. Stuart to Smith, May 1 [?], 1835, SP.
52. *Ibid.*

Stuart's longing for a crisis was emotional in more than its language. Recalling a Persian aphorism he had encountered in his language studies in India—"it is glorious to die with one's friends"—he went on: "But how much more sweet and glorious, if called to die—to die in the cause of God and impartial humanity." In a postscript to the same letter he revealed as clearly as anywhere the intense satisfaction he had found in the camaraderie of the antislavery movement. He expressed amazement at Smith's assumption that the rebels at Lane Seminary were mere boys:

> Boys!—and in the flower of manhood, nearly thirty years old, upon an average!! Boys—and glowing with heaven's fire, matured and prayerful!!— Boys—and masters completely in moral grandeur and wisdom. . . . Boys & standing like Christian martyrs, invincibly yet meekly in the gap for God & man—for liberty and law—for republicanism and truth—for love and righteousness—Oh, what a glory of the world would these States be, were all our men and women boys like them—Birney whom you love, & most worthily love, delighted to be instructed & edified by those boys—Perhaps you may some day experience the glorious grasp of their intellect & rejoice in the holy fire of their hearts—You ought to be knit together—you are made, to love one another.[53]

The violence Stuart had looked for almost eagerly in May took place in the following months not only everywhere George Thompson spoke in the East but sporadically at many western centers as well. But for western abolitionists the first climax came at Utica on October 21 and 22 when more than six hundred abolitionists met to form the New York State Anti-Slavery Society. In his lecturing in the first half of the year Stuart had been responsible for the formation of many of the local societies that sent delegates to the convention. But other prophets had been at work as well. Beriah Green, now president of Oneida Institute, had ironically lost his best students to Lane Seminary before turning his own institution into an antislavery center. He had also lectured in the wider western New York community. The biggest contribution from outside lecturers came from Amos A. Phelps, who had been one of the first permanent appointees to an agency of the American Anti-Slavery Society. He drew a salary of one thousand dollars a year plus traveling expenses, in contrast to Stuart, who, as in Britain, continued to accept only expenses. Phelps's agency was principally in New England, but in the months before the Utica conven-

53. *Ibid.*

tion he embarked on an extensive tour in western New York.[54] His letters to his wife provide some of the best evidence of the tensions building up between abolitionists and their opponents.

After early letters mainly preoccupied with the discomfort and fatigue of travel even in a region now penetrated by canal and railroad, Phelps wrote in August to his wife from Le Roy, "far West, almost to Buffalo," with a mixture of optimism and foreboding. The country was "really a splendid one." Its resources were "inexhaustible—& its population good material to make radicals of." The cause was in its infancy, "but it has laid hold of the right kind of materials &, by the blessing of God, will speedily grow up to the maturity & strength of manhood." If this estimate tallied with Stuart's reports from the Utica region a few months before, Phelps went on to describe even more pessimistically than Stuart the unfavorable aspects of the situation: "There is the same negro hatred here, the same political influences, the same love of Colonization, the same Corruption in the Priesthood . . . the same shutting of the eyes to light, the same stopping of the ears to the cry of the suffering and oppressed—in one word, the same every thing that is wicked & hateful to God to contend with here as at the east."[55]

Like Stuart, Phelps foresaw violence. Unlike Stuart, he prepared for it with resignation rather than near-enthusiasm: "I am more and more persuaded that some of us will have to fall as martyrs. . . . The spirit of slavery is so desperate—so relentless—so cruel—that I do not believe we shall escape its wrath." He referred to the rumors of a group of killers leaving the South to seek out Arthur Tappan, one of the main financial backers of the American Anti-Slavery Society: "Very possibly it is all a hoax & still I should not be surprised to hear at any moment that Arthur Tappan has been assassinated."[56]

In a letter of August 31 Phelps revealed that, if Stuart had been relatively inactive on the platform in recent months, he was now playing his part in confronting the opponents of abolition. The two men met in Rochester, where, Phelps reported, "the enemy is raging on all sides, & foaming out his wrath and shame." He reiterated his belief that "this cause will never triumph without the shedding of martyr blood." He had not

54. Dumond, *Antislavery*, 159–60, 182; American Anti-Slavery Society, *Third Annual Report, with the Speeches Delivered at the Anniversary Meeting of the American Anti-Slavery Society in the City of New York, 10th May 1836* (New York, 1836), 37, commends Stuart, who "has during the year given his time, and more than his time, gratuitously to this cause."
55. Phelps to Mrs. Phelps, August 11, 22, 1835, BPL.
56. Phelps to Mrs. Phelps, August 22, 1835, BPL.

intended proceeding beyond Rochester, but some two weeks later he was writing to his wife from Buffalo, explaining that Stuart had insisted that he should not fail to visit Erie County. On the way to Buffalo Phelps had been mobbed on a return visit to Le Roy and then found Buffalo itself closed to the abolitionist message: "His Excellency King Mob governs the city & holds the friends of God and man, if indeed there are any there, in awe, so that they dare not move, or mutter, or peep, except by his permission."[57]

It was against this background of violence that the antislavery delegates converged on Utica a month later and the reluctance of Gerrit Smith to embrace the immediatist cause seemed more and more intolerable. On October 2 Amos Phelps, perhaps influenced by his recent conversations with Stuart, added his support to the demands Stuart had been making in person and by letter for the past nine months. "Although not personally acquainted" with Smith, he knew of his great interest in philanthropy among the black population and urged him finally to cast his lot with the immediate abolitionists in the forthcoming convention. He had learned "from personal conversation with many individuals" of Smith's great influence in New York, "to say nothing of other sections of the country." In every cause there was a crisis point when failure to make a commitment was tantamount to opposition. The antislavery cause had reached such a crisis: "The influence of Central and Western New York on the country at large, on any such moral question, is incalculable. The public mind in this section is now in a plastic state. If the friends of God & human rights would come out boldly on the subject in question, the public mind could be gained to the cause of Immediate Emancipation with perfect ease. And I know of no one man whose influence would do more to bring them out than yours."[58]

Once it was learned that a major antislavery convention was to be held in Utica, opposition was organized and several attempts were made to deny the abolitionists a forum. The opposition was neither simply the young, rowdy element eventually conspicuous in the mob nor all of the many leading citizens who were opposed to abolition. A meeting in the Utica courthouse some days before the convention was to begin passed hostile but, according to an abolitionist report, "temperate and dignified resolutions." Indeed, although this meeting was strongly antiabolitionist, there was only minority support for the proposal to ban the convention. In the same way, shortly afterward, the Utica Common Council concluded a long

57. Phelps to Mrs. Phelps, August 31, September 18, 22, 1835, BPL.
58. Phelps to Smith, October 2, 1835, BPL.

debate by deciding that it was more important to uphold the right of free speech than to suppress abolitionist arguments which probably a majority of councillors opposed: the convention should be allowed to proceed. At this point, the moves to organize mob opposition began: an inflammatory handbill "in flaming colours" was posted in the streets calling a public meeting for the evening of October 17.[59]

According to abolitionist accounts, the organizers of the mob were respectable, substantial citizens. Certainly the most conspicuous antiabolition spokesman fell into that category. Samuel Beardsley, a lawyer and judge, a state senator in the early 1820s, and since 1830 a national congressman, was one of the most significant Democratic politicians in New York State. An ardent Jacksonian, he was virtual state leader of the slave-owning southern president's party. At the original meeting in the courthouse he had justified and defended some of the nationally most controversial recent antiabolition measures, including the seizure of mail at Charleston and the burning of antislavery papers by a mob. And now at the October 17 meeting he delivered "violent invectives against the Common Council" and insisted that if the abolitionists persisted in convening, they would be "responsible for all the consequences."[60]

Beardsley still did not command a majority. On Tuesday, October 20, a meeting of conservative antiabolitionists, in passing resolutions in favor of free speech, ensured that the convention could be frustrated only by extralegal means. When some six hundred abolitionists met early the following day at the Second Presbyterian Church in Bleecker Street, their opponents met in the courthouse to form a Committee of Twenty-Five. The convention had time to complete the formalities of establishing a state antislavery society before being interrupted by some three hundred supporters of the newly formed committee massed at the church doors. A city elder, attempting to bar their entry, was overpowered "and his coat rent from his back." Beardsley and his committee, backed by the mob, poured down the central aisle and took charge of the rostrum. Beardsley made an inflammatory speech, calling the abolitionists "incendiaries and

---

59. "Defensor," *The Enemies of the Constitution Discovered; Or, an Inquiry into the Origin and Tendency of Popular Violence. Containing a Complete and Circumstantial Account of the Unlawful Proceedings at the City of Utica, October 21st, 1835; the Dispersion of the State Anti-Slavery Convention by the Agitators, the Destruction of a Democratic Press, and of the Causes Which Led Thereto. Together with a Concise Treatment on the Practice of the Court of His Honour Judge Lynch* (Utica, N.Y., 1835), 57–58, 63–64.

60. *Ibid.*, 64–82; *Emancipator*, November 1, 1835; Samuel J. May, *Some Recollections of Our Anti-Slavery Conflict*, Boston, 1869 (Facsimile reprint, Miami, 1969), 162–68. These allegations are sustained by Leonard L. Richards, *"Gentlemen of Property and Standing": Anti-Abolition Mobs in Jacksonian America* (New York, 1970), 85–92.

fanatics." He encouraged violence while affecting to condemn it. He hoped that there would be none, but if there were, the "deluded" abolitionists would be responsible. In the same manner he silenced the mob, insisting that the abolitionists had a right to be heard. It was right that their apology for their "insulting" presence be heard. It was right that they should say whether they would forthwith adjourn their convention. Even these dubious rights were not recognized, as another committee member insisted that the convention should adjourn and not meet again in Utica. Beardsley then declared the convention adjourned, and the mob proceeded to force the abolitionists out of the building amid "a scene of terrible disorder."[61]

Charles Stuart was among the hundreds of ejected delegates, though not one of the main targets of the mob. Almost certainly it was not he but Alvan Stewart, a venerable local cleric and abolitionist, who was in demand when the cry arose: "Beardsley, say the word, and we will tear old Stewart to pieces in an instant! give us old Stewart! give us Tappan! hustle them out of the house! clear out! clear out! disperse the fanatics!" According to Theodore Weld, however, when Stuart was asked by one of the mob to say where Tappan was he replied bluntly: "I shan't tell you!"[62] This was apparently a minor incident, and most subsequent attention has focused on Stuart's friend Gerrit Smith and on the decisive influence of the mob on his commitment to the cause. Smith's immediate response to the violence was to invite the delegates to reconvene at his home at Peterboro and accept his hospitality.

The mob was still on the rampage, although proabolition forces were rallied in sufficient numbers to prevent the threatened destruction of Alvan Stewart's house and other sympathizers' property. But with delegates being forcibly ejected from their lodgings and jostled and abused in the streets, the convention obviously had no future in Utica. Some 350 to 400 delegates accepted Smith's invitation and climbed into carriages for the twenty-five-mile journey to Peterboro.[63]

Charles Stuart, characteristically, decided to walk. According to the reminiscences years later of one of his old Utica friends, "in accordance with his early habits, [he] trudged on afoot through mud and rain," catching up with many fellow delegates for an overnight rest at Vernon, some seventeen miles from Utica. Mob activity was still not at an end. A large crowd appeared that night at Vernon, damaging delegates' carriages

61. "Defensor," *Enemies of the Constitution*, 68–69, 77–87.
62. *Ibid.*, 82–84; Weld to Lewis Tappan, March 9, 1836, Merrill and Ruchames (eds.), *Weld-Grimké Letters*, I, 274.
63. "Defensor," *Enemies of the Constitution*, 87, 94.

and injuring some of them. The hotel was besieged by rioters threatening violence to the antislavery guests. At the height of this crisis Stuart was aroused from his sleep by the landlord, Captain Hand, and told of the threats of the mob. He responded by sending a message to the rioters "that if they would wait until the morning he would meet them without fail; and then he composed himself again to sleep." Whether this provocative reply was conveyed to the mob is not recorded. The reports make it clear only that it was the resourceful Captain Hand, rather than the sleeping Stuart, who managed to keep the mob at bay.[64]

If Stuart did indeed sleep as soundly as his admiring Utica friend suggested, the reason no doubt was not only fatigue after his seventeen-mile hike but also intense satisfaction that, as he had foreseen months before, violence had finally forced Gerrit Smith into open support of immediate abolition. The official *Proceedings* of the convention, reconvened at Peterboro the next day, noted the presence of Stuart, "long known as a tried and trusted friend of abolition." Along with the other delegates he heard Smith formally embrace the movement in an often-reproduced speech variously described as "powerful and eloquent" and "of surpassing power."[65]

Smith's adherence was important for the vast influence and wealth it promised to place at the disposal of abolitionism. It could not, of course, dispel the antiabolition violence that had by now become almost commonplace throughout the North. On the very day of the Utica riot a mob in Boston had assembled at the news that George Thompson was to address the Massachusetts Female Anti-Slavery Society. Forewarned, Thompson had stayed away, and Garrison had become the mob's victim, dragged through the streets with a rope around his body. He was eventually rescued by the mayor and held in jail overnight for his own safety. In the following months there were numerous less famous mobbings. It is perhaps because there were so many that it has been impossible to locate precisely the details about Charles Stuart's most violent experience, when he was felled momentarily by a mob in western New York. But also relevant is the more general neglect of Stuart's antislavery reputation, not least because of the fragmentation of the American movement after 1840. Had he remained the Garrisonian hero he had been hitherto, the incident would doubtless have been rescued from the obscurity of Garrison's pri-

64. Baggs, *Pioneers of Utica*, 545; "Defensor," *Enemies of the Constitution*, 87 n; May, *Recollections*, 169.

65. *Proceedings of the New York Anti-Slavery Convention Held at Utica, October 21, and the New York State Anti-Slavery Society Held at Peterboro, October 22, 1835* (Utica, N.Y., 1835), 15; May, *Recollections*, 169 and Appendix III, 400–403.

vate letters. On December 28, 1835, the Boston editor wrote to his wife: "Charles Stuart has been mobbed in the western part of the state of New York. A brick bat struck him on the head, which made him senseless for a time—but as soon as he recovered, he began to plead for the suffering and dumb, until he was persuaded by a clergyman to desist." Typical of this neglect was the Garrisonian Samuel J. May's *Some Recollections of Our Anti-Slavery Conflict*, published in 1869, which contained accounts of numerous mobbings but made no mention of Stuart. In 1834 Garrison had told his future wife of the impending visit of his "dear friends May and Stuart," who were traveling together with news of the recent national convention. And in early 1835 May had expressed concern at the "rough usage" Stuart had suffered at the hands of the New England mobs.[66]

These tumultuous final months of 1835 marked the end of Stuart's most intensive phase of American campaigning. Although he was to give many lectures and even undertake short antislavery tours in the next year and a half, his work as a full-time agent of the national society was at an end. This did not mean, however, that he had been frightened into silence or that his commitment was diminished. The months ahead were to confirm his significance as an abolitionist and also consolidate attitudes and friendships in ways important for the future when abolitionism was to be convulsed by those internal dissensions.

---

66. Filler, *Crusade Against Slavery*, 76–77; May, *Recollections*, 126–211; May to Phelps, January 1, 1835; Garrison to Helen E. Benson, June 14, 1834, to the same (now Mrs. Garrison), December 28, 1835, BPL.

5 AMERICAN AFFILIATIONS

STUART REMAINED in the United States until mid-1837. These final eighteen months saw the climax of abolition campaigning. The national society expanded its activities significantly with the plan to appoint seventy full-time agents. Although fewer than seventy actually went into the field, this was still a major enterprise that could never be repeated. In later years strained financial resources restricted such methods,[1] but a more important problem was internal dissension, with William Lloyd Garrison the central figure of controversy. The crucial disagreements over tactical priorities and more fundamental questions of social and political philosophy had not significantly emerged before Stuart's temporary return to Britain. But already Garrison was becoming controversial, well aware that he was suspect in the eyes of many abolitionists.

Stuart's contribution in this period was less public than in 1834 or 1835. Even in the important regions of upstate New York his role was now secondary to that of Weld. But behind the scenes he remained an important figure. And reduced public speaking gave him more opportunity for writing, thereby consolidating his position both as an American abolitionist and as a diligent promoter of Anglo-American antislavery cooperation. Probably the major significance of the period, however, can be seen only in the light of the future controversies in which he was to be a crucial figure. In this early period, when the eventual issues were submerged or embryonic, he had moved still further from Garrison. More important, he had developed strong friendships with some of Garrison's most sig-

1. Dumond, *Antislavery*, 185.

nificant future opponents. For all these reasons it is more fruitful to analyze themes and trends during these eighteen months rather than to give a strict chronological progression.

STUART'S PUBLIC activities are the easiest to summarize. He attended numerous antislavery conventions: the Rhode Island state convention in February, 1836; a special convention at Utica in April; and, also in Utica, the first anniversary convention of the New York State Anti-Slavery Society, meeting in much more tranquil circumstances a year after the great riot. He was also active at the national level, attending the third and fourth annual conventions of the American Anti-Slavery Society in May, 1836 and 1837. On all these occasions he played a conspicuous though not dominating role. He moved resolutions, led the delegates in prayer, and, on at least one occasion, became involved in controversy. He again acted as a delegate from the national society to the New England Anti-Slavery Convention in 1836, and he took part in many other public antislavery meetings. He did his share of lecturing in support of others, but he undertook only one independent lecturing tour—to Washington County, north of Albany, New York. When his second year as an agent of the American Anti-Slavery Society expired there was a recommendation that he be recommissioned to work in New England, but he did not accept this agency, and the last year of his stay he remained independent of institutional ties.[2]

One reason for Stuart's relatively peaceful life in these eighteen months was that the center of extreme antiabolition violence seemed to have shifted farther west. Over the previous year, Theodore Weld had campaigned in Ohio, with massive effect if measured by the proliferation of antislavery societies. But although he had turned Ohio into numerically the most significant antislavery state, opposition to abolition had not been obliterated, least of all in Cincinnati. There James G. Birney had established a base from which to send the antislavery message into the nearby slave states through a newspaper, the *Philanthropist*. In July, 1836, after debate and threats, the press was destroyed by a mob, and Birney was forced to stay away from the city for some weeks. Farther west still Elijah P. Lovejoy was attempting to publish antislavery views in the St. Louis *Observer*. In 1836, his office and press were smashed, and he was forced to

2. Stuart to Birney, March 7, 1836, WP; *Voice of Freedom* (new monthly version of *Emancipator*), May, 1836; *Liberator*, November 5, 1836, p. 179; *Third Annual Report of the American Anti-Slavery Society*, 3, 23, 27, 30; *Fourth Annual Report . . . of the American Anti-Slavery Society* (New York, 1837), 18, 23; American Anti-Slavery Society, Committee on Agencies, Minute Book, June 15, 1836, BPL.

move to nearby Alton, Illinois. There he quickly faced opposition, which, in late 1837, was to make him the first martyr of the abolition movement.³

Lovejoy was a convert of the Reverend David Nelson, a former southern colonizationist, who had freed his slaves and sent them to Liberia before opening a theological school in Missouri in 1830. In that exposed position he had developed dangerously radical antislavery views and had eventually become an agent of the American Anti-Slavery Society and also one of its vice-presidents. Nelson visited Utica in January, 1836, and became sufficiently friendly with Stuart for the latter to write enthusiastically about him to Gerrit Smith. Within months, however, he was back in Missouri and facing violent opposition that was soon to produce at least one incidental death and force him to seek refuge in Illinois.⁴

In contrast to these trends and to its own recent history, western New York was relatively peaceful. A symptom and probably a cause of the improved atmosphere was a successful six-month lecturing agency by Weld. In January and February, 1836, he labored in and around Utica, where Stuart had done the spadework a year before but where memories of the October mob were fresh. There was no repetition of violence, and Weld is said to have made six hundred new converts in Utica alone.⁵ In subsequent months he was equally successful in Rochester and Troy.

Stuart accompanied Weld to Troy and presumably attended many of his meetings in the Utica area. Their closeness meant a break in their correspondence, which, ironically, makes it harder to chart their relationship than in periods when they were apart. But there are sufficient references to "our beloved Theodore" in Stuart's letters to Birney to make it clear that he shared in some and rejoiced in all of his old protégé's missionary successes. There is also evidence that he regarded the relative absence of opposition not as the end of a storm but as "the lull, which often divides its fury. It has had a fearful sweep—and how soon it may recommence we know not!—I regard its present calm, not as its cessation, but as its mustering for a deadlier blast."⁶

Again, it was not fear of this expected violence that explained Stuart's relative withdrawal from public campaigning in the months ahead. He had written those words of foreboding immediately after completing his antislavery tour of Washington County, a commission he had willingly accepted in the knowledge that the area had been the scene of mob activity,

3. Dumond, *Antislavery*, 183–84, 221–27.
4. Ibid., 223–24; Stuart to Smith, January 25, 1836, SP.
5. *Emancipator* (monthly), March, 1836.
6. Stuart to Birney, March 7, September 30, 1836, WP.

encouraged by an antiabolition press, only two months earlier. His letters to Birney revealed the same excitement about the mounting turbulence in Cincinnati as he had shown a year earlier when writing to Gerrit Smith of possible violence. He was indeed tempted to join Birney "& to share all your dangers." But he concluded that his presence "would only further madden the madness, which raves and rages against impartial liberty, & holy law, & brotherly love, around you."[7]

Stuart may have thought his nationality would be unduly provocative if he moved into contentious situations away from the New York region, where he was well known. But his conclusion that to go to Cincinnati would be "like rushing upon a lion at bay with a straw" suggests also a growing sense of physical frailty after years of almost constant antislavery lecturing. These words were written in September, 1836, some two months after Theodore Weld had delivered his last antislavery lecture. Weld had performed prodigiously since the Lane Seminary revolt, yet he retired because of physical and nervous exhaustion after only two years of campaigning. Stuart, almost thirty years older than his friend, had been lecturing and preaching with the same intensity for five years on both sides of the Atlantic and had also been a prolific writer, whereas Weld's great literary contributions were yet to come. Stuart suffered no dramatic physical breakdown comparable to Weld's almost complete loss of vocal power, nor is there evidence that he was in serious ill-health. But eighteen months later, writing to Weld from England, he was to mention that relative lack of vigor made him hesitate to commit himself to a further campaign in the United States: "Were I with you I could be of little or no service to you, as was the case for the last year before I left you."[8]

These trends did not mean that either man had diminished his commitment to the cause. For Weld retirement from lecturing was the prelude to equally influential contributions as an author and administrator. He began the research that in 1839 was to produce one of the masterpieces of antislavery literature, *American Slavery As It Is: Testimony of a Thousand Witnesses*. And taking charge of the central office of the American Anti-Slavery Society, he began to organize the famous "seventy," many of whom he had personally recruited, who were to consolidate and extend the work of the first two years of grass-roots activity. In both these spheres Stuart gave important support. He greeted Weld's antislavery researches by bombarding him with questions and suggestions and also wrote

7. *Liberator*, January 2, 1836, p. 3; Stuart to Birney, September 30, 1836, WP.
8. Stuart to Birney, September 30, 1836; Dumond, *Antislavery*, 184; Stuart to Weld, February 23, 1838, WP.

independently for the antislavery press. And he made a significant contribution to Weld's training program for the "seventy," in the process demonstrating that his credentials as an American abolitionist were widely respected.[9]

Many whom Weld had known personally at Lane Seminary and recruited directly were sent straight into the field, but some thirty agents were assembled in New York between November 8 and 27, 1836. There they were confronted by relentless questioning to prepare them to cope in the field: "What is slavery? What is immediate emancipation? Why don't you go to the South? The slaves, if emancipated would overrun the north. The consequences of emancipation to the south. Hebrew servitude. Compensation. Colonization. Prejudice . . . all the prominent objections to our cause were ingeniously raised and as conclusively shown to be futile." This description was by Garrison, who was one of many famous abolitionists present. The gathering was designed partly to draw on the experience of such men and partly to introduce to the new agents figures such as Garrison, Phelps, Henry B. Stanton, Arthur and Lewis Tappan, and the Grimké sisters, Angelina and Sarah—individuals who had already achieved a notoriety with which future abolitionist campaigns would have to contend.[10]

Garrison felt that with the exception of the foundation meetings of the New England and national antislavery societies, this convention was "of higher importance than any meeting which has been held to advance the anti-slavery cause." Weld, he wrote, was "the central luminary, around which they all revolved." But, he noted, Charles Stuart was one of the three principal speakers, along with Weld and Beriah Green, at the intensive three sessions a day, which—"scarcely allowing ourselves time to eat"—were held over three weeks.[11]

Garrison's account also makes it clear that the convention succeeded in developing the camaraderie which for Stuart was a vital psychological ingredient in his commitment to the cause: "It was a nice stroke of policy bringing the Agents together, that they might see and hear each other, understand each other's feelings and sentiments, cheer each other's heart, and form a personal friendship with each other." He was particularly pleased that the agents should get to know him personally because his reputation made him, he conceded, "a great stumbling-block." He was referring not only to his notoriety in the eyes of the enemies of abolition

9. Dumond, *Antislavery*, 184–85; Stuart to Weld, February 4, March [?], 1837, WP.
10. Garrison to Henry E. Benson, December 3, 1836, BPL; *Liberator*, December 5, 1836, p. 195.
11. *Liberator*, December 5, 1836, p. 195.

but also to his increasingly controversial position within the movement. Despite the success of the convention, he wrote of the "wide difference of opinion between us on some religious points." Even at the end of long religious discussions with Lewis Tappan "we harmoniously agreed to differ."[12]

Such harmony was to be increasingly difficult to maintain in the years ahead with many others as well as Tappan. The issues that were to split the American movement irrevocably—and carry dissension across the Atlantic—were emerging in embryo in 1836 and 1837.

THE AMERICAN movement eventually split because Garrison and his supporters were seen to be retarding the momentum of antislavery activity by advocating women's rights, nonresistance, abstention from the polls and related political activities, and a series of unorthodox religious views, including repudiation of the Sabbath and rejection of a regular church ministry. Real conflict on these issues still lay in the future, and it is only with hindsight that the issues and enmities can be traced back to 1836.

This qualification is as relevant to Stuart's personal relationship with Garrison as it is to the wider split. Although the two men had not restored their earliest warm friendship, there is evidence of Garrison's continuing regard for Stuart. It had been revealed in the private solicitude of his comments on Stuart's mobbing in western New York. It was revealed more publicly on more than one occasion when he insisted that American supporters of George Thompson must not forget Stuart's contribution. Thompson, he wrote to Samuel J. May in early 1836, would be gratified if a resolution could be passed at a forthcoming meeting "in kind remembrance of him and those who sustained his mission." But he added: "I think our brother Stuart ought also to be remembered, inasmuch as he is laboring with all his might most nobly, successfully, and disinterestedly in our sacred cause."[13]

Garrison's name is conspicuous by its absence from Stuart's writings, public and private, in this period. But in his continuing solicitude for the free black population of the United States he shared one of Garrison's deepest concerns. In private letters, in resolutions moved at the great public conventions, and in one extensive published article, Stuart continued to display the distaste for racial prejudice that had been born when he was among the fugitive blacks of Canada and articulated so clearly in all his anticolonization publications. He spoke extensively on this theme at the

12. *Ibid.*
13. Garrison to May, January 17, 1836, BPL.

New England Anti-Slavery Convention in May, 1836, with a detailed anecdote to illustrate the nobility of character of one of the chief ogres of proslavery propaganda, Toussaint L'Ouverture.[14]

At this same convention the man whom Garrison's *Liberator* still termed "our beloved C. Stuart" delivered a major speech attacking the role of the churches in upholding slavery. He inquired "what were the American churches but the apologists of wrong and despotism: what were they but slave-holding churches, in deed and precept?" It was necessary to purify the church, and he moved a resolution that "it becomes those who love and reverence the gospel, to associate themselves anew, for the support of its fundamental principles; and that such associations are the true and only Church of God." He envisaged not rejection of all church organization, but a purification, "as was done by the reformers, and again by the puritans."[15] It was thus entirely consistent for him in the future to recoil in anger from Garrison's rejection of any regular church ministry. But in mid-1836 his pungent criticism of existing churches could only have seemed complementary to a Garrisonian position that had not yet moved to the radical extreme.

On another religious issue—the Sabbath question—there is evidence, at least from Stuart's subsequent reminiscences, of incipient dispute with Garrison in these years. A man who had invited court-martial in India, at least partly by insisting on the sanctity of the Sabbath, almost inevitably would object as Garrison's views moved toward total repudiation of the concept. But this was an argument Garrison was having with many people in 1836 without provoking real enmity. Even later Stuart was to admit that the disputes had been far from explosive.[16]

In contrast to the private arguments on that issue, one conspicuous public disagreement occurred over the question of boycotts of slave produce. Stuart attempted to make the abstention he had practiced since 1830 a formal policy of the national society at the 1837 annual convention. Garrison's intervention led to the abandonment of his motion. The Boston man was successful, however, only because he expressed the opinion of a majority of American abolitionists. Stuart had already conducted a

14. Stuart to Weld, November 5, 1835; to Birney, March 7, 1836, WP; *Second Annual Report of the American Anti-Slavery Society*, 33; *Third Annual Report of the American Anti-Slavery Society*, 29; Stuart "On the Colored People of the United States," 11–22; *Liberator*, June 2, 1837, p. 90; New England Anti-Slavery Society, *Proceedings of the New England Anti-Slavery Convention Held in Boston: May 24, 25, 26, 1836* (Boston, 1836), 33–34, 74.

15. *Proceedings of New England Anti-Slavery Convention, 1836*, 74.

16. Stuart's comments cited by John Murray to J. A. Collins, December 23, 1840, BPL.

public argument on the issue with his friend Elizur Wright, corresponding secretary of the national society and editor of its *Quarterly Anti-Slavery Magazine*. His impassioned advocacy of the policy in that journal had been accompanied by an editorial rebuttal acknowledging that he "sheds light as well as heat on his subject; albeit, the former seems to us more refracted than the latter." At the national convention Stuart's drastic policy of total boycott was replaced by an innocuous resolution moved by Gerrit Smith, in which members were invited to examine the question "whether they can innocently make an *ordinary* use, or be concerned in the traffic of the productions of slave labor." Smith later wrote, with admiration, that this resolution was carried "with but one dissenting voice— that of Charles Stuart, a man, who never consents to sacrifice a hair's breadth of moral principle."[17]

With Stuart a lonely protagonist, opposed by both Garrison and his closer antislavery friends, this issue had no direct relevance to the eventual divisions within the movement. But the dispute was to have an indirect influence on Stuart's attitudes. He was later to make much of the claim that, faced with this evidence of the unpopularity of the policy, he had at once ceased to advocate it publicly, while continuing his own abstemious practice. He was to contrast his own forbearance with Garrison's alleged determination to pursue extraneous reform issues under the antislavery banner. His recollection was more than a convenient rationalization. In the course of his published debate with Elizur Wright he had written:

> My dear brother is unwilling that the *Anti-Slavery Society* should also become an *anti-slave produce* society. So am I—but on grounds different from his. I am unwilling on the same grounds, on which I am unwilling, that the *Sunday School Society*, or the *Temperance Society*, &c &c should become also, an *Anti-Slavery Society*. Those societies *sin*, I think grievously by rejecting Anti-Slavery facts and Anti-Slavery principles, so much as they do. . . . But yet I would by no means have them become anti-slavery societies. Their appropriate course is already marked out and it is a glorious one. No

---

17. A short reference to the dispute at the 1837 convention is in *Fourth Annual Report of the American Anti-Slavery Society*, 23, which merely says that Stuart's motion was "laid upon the table" and "indefinitely postponed" after "considerable discussion." Much more detail about the issue and Garrison's opposition is in the manuscript Minutes of the American Anti-Slavery Society Convention, 83, BPL. Stuart, "On the Use of Slave Produce," 153–72; Wright's comment, *ibid.*, 172–74. Smith, in praising Stuart, claimed that he (Smith) had introduced the more innocuous motion to promote harmony. At the same time he expressed the wish that Garrison would speak out against the use of slave products, which he had never done (*Liberator*, July 2, 1836, p. 106).

important work can be accomplished efficiently without a wise division of labour.[18]

Apart from this question of reform priorities, there were eventually three key issues in Stuart's antagonism to Garrison: the "woman question," nonresistance, and acceptance of government and the Constitution. On all these issues his opposition was to be consistent with views he held in 1836 and 1837. But in that early period the issues were so embryonic that subsequent Garrisonian allegations of betrayal by Stuart are understandable.

Stuart's position on the woman question was later to seem erratic because, throughout his years in the United States up to 1837, he had been particularly associated with women in the movement. His account of British emancipation, written for American audiences, stressed the contribution of women. On his arrival in the United States after that successful campaign, he had been prominent in advocating female abolitionism. His visit to Prudence Crandall had been symbolic of that advocacy. In the same period he had made a fervent plea to the assembled Salem Ladies Anti-Slavery Society: "My dear Sisters!—we need all your tender and holy sympathies in this cause. In our struggle with the proud of heart and the mighty of this world, we ask your aid."[19] He frequently returned to this theme in his addresses to both male and female antislavery societies, and he pressed it nationally at successive conventions of the American Anti-Slavery Society. He did not protest the emergence of the two first famous women abolitionists, Angelina and Sarah Grimké, in 1836, even when Angelina was accepted by her future husband, Theodore Weld, as one of the seventy antislavery agents.

Although this record makes Garrisonian bewilderment at Stuart's subsequent hostility almost inevitable, his attitudes both in 1836–37 and in the 1840s were consistent with a long-cherished belief that in all fields men and women had complementary but separate roles. This, after all, was an attitude he had already revealed years before he became an abolitionist in published comments about the need to uphold the civilizing influence of women on frontier society in Canada. His advocacy of female abolitionism similarly stressed unique female capacities and roles. As he told the women of Brooklyn, Connecticut, there were "peculiarities in the character and circumstances of woman, which enable her to be an important instrument in all moral reforms." His particular concern then and

18. Stuart, "On the Use of Slave Produce," 167.
19. Stuart, "On the Abolition of Slavery by Great Britain," 108; Stuart's remarks at Salem recalled in *Liberator*, July 20, 1838, p. 113.

on many occasions was to encourage a sense of affinity among white women for their black sisters. The annual convention of the national society in 1836 carried his resolution that "we earnestly invite every lady in the land, who feels for female honor, for human happiness, and virtue and for God's holy law, to join her prayers and efforts with ours in behalf of the suffering and the dumb." But his resolution to the next annual convention made it clear he was not advocating that women should join men in a formal, corporate sense. He regarded "as one of the most cheering signs of the times, the assembling of the convention of American women, now in session in this city, to adopt measures, and mingle their prayers and sympathies with ours, for the redemption of our suffering brethren and sisters from slavery."[20] His commitment to separate male and female roles within the same general movement was not made more explicit because, until the events of the late 1830s, there was no reason for it to be so.

Although Stuart's role among female abolitionists in the 1830s could be easily misinterpreted, his attitudes to the other central issue in the split—political action—could never have been in doubt. The Garrisonians might well have been ignorant of the orthodox reforming political attitudes he had published in 1820, condemning alike "the career of such demagogues as Cobbett and Hunt" and the ministry of Liverpool, "absolute in the suppression of every direct and decided, though lawful and duteous attempt at reformation." But they could scarcely be unaware that the hallmark of his work as an abolitionist in the early 1830s had been political agitation within the framework of the reformed parliamentary system. His campaign against Elliott Cresson and the American Colonization Society, which had made Stuart a hero in their eyes, had been successful only because of his preceding and parallel work in Ireland and then for the Agency Committee in England. Although he would have recoiled from the term, Stuart was essentially throughout his career a political agitator whose one aim was to arouse public opinion and guide it into channels where the maximum pressure in favor of abolition could be exerted on the institutions of government. The methods he had helped to perfect in Britain of arousing electorates, lobbying MPs, and forcing parliamentary candidates to declare their allegiances in relation to slavery could not, he well knew, be so swiftly successful in the United States, where the federal system meant that there was no single central target for political pressure. But this did not mean that he was so conservative that he would

20. *Liberator*, August 16, 1838, p. 132; *Third Annual Report of the American Anti-Slavery Society*, 28; *Fourth Annual Report of the American Anti-Slavery Society*, 27.

accept the status quo in regard to slavery or so radical that he saw the need to repudiate the political system. Government in the United States, he had written even before his return there in 1834, is "not of the few, but of the *many*. For the people to blame the Government is to blame themselves. . . . The abolition and the government are both perfectly in their power, it is therefore their duty to abolish slavery, and to discard prejudice, immediately and totally." It was the business of abolitionists to convince the people of this power and duty. And to this end it was useless to rely on "private, earnest, and affectionate remonstrance. . . . No, it needs all the terrors of punishment, human and divine, to awaken them from their infatuation, and one of the most powerful of all terrors is public opinion. But how is public opinion to be revolutionized?, how, but by proclaiming the truth *everywhere*!, how, but by lifting up our voices like a trumpet, and showing our people their sins."[21]

His American antislavery career had been true to these principles. He emphasized the sin of slavery and also its incompatibility with the principles of the Declaration of Independence and the Constitution. He lifted his voice like a trumpet and also organized petitions to Congress urging abolition in the District of Columbia.

Closely connected with these attitudes was his position on nonresistance, the other central issue in his breach with Garrison. Again, in the mid-1830s the principles of his eventual opposition were clear in his own mind even though expressed only in private correspondence. He may have been known for his unmilitary career in a military force. He may have responded to mob violence with "a smiling countenance" in Connecticut and by going back to sleep in western New York. But the rationale for such behavior was not an unqualified pacifism. In September, 1836, in the aftermath of the Cincinnati mob, he urged James Birney to exercise the same restraint he had himself shown in the face of violence, even while articulating a theory of justifiable force by responsible government:

> You ask me, dearest brother for my sentiments about *Peace*. . . . In the Bible, I find no limit to the principles of *Peace, suffering without retaliation* or *violent resistance*, between Individuals, or Nations. I do not find that God has any where, given authority of violence, to individual, over individual, or to nation, over nation—and if He have not, His general law of Peace, conquering by suffering & love *only*, remains in all its force—But I do find, that God invests civil governments, with corrective powers, without limit, for the support of good, & for the punishment of evil doers—Roms. 13. 1–4. What-

21. Stuart, *Emigrant's Guide*, 100; Charles Stuart, *Letter Addressed to Elisha Bates, Esq. Minister of the Society of Friends by Captain Stuart* (Bath, n.d. [ca. 1833?]), 1–3.

ever degree of violence therefore may be requisite for these sacred purposes; for *sustaining* right, & *punishing* wrong, by the civil power, must be exercised—In *your* soul-trying case, dearly beloved and most honored brother, I should say, *in your individual and domestic capacity, lean on the Lord & trust in Him only*—Let every man know, that as to arms & violence, you are *defenceless*; and I am persuaded, that, if you do this, of *your own heart*, in faith & love, in prayer and obedience, you will be safer, than the terrors of earth and hell clustered round you, could make you.[22]

Largely through such correspondence Stuart developed with Birney an enduring relationship. The two had met and corresponded from early 1835, but it was during Birney's difficult days in Cincinnati that Stuart's letters grew in effusiveness. In March, 1836, he sent via Weld a subscription to Birney's *Philanthropist* with the assurance that "my dearly beloved and honored brother, my soul is with you." Even so, he regretted that "I can but feebly realize your condition." He implored Birney to send him "some details—some of those familiar details which embody common life before you." He wanted to know "the amount of physical security & or physical danger around you. The comparative strength in your neighbourhood of friends and enemies. The security & insecurity as you deem it of your press" and numerous other details about "the state of Cincinnati in regard to abolition . . . but particularly, all about youself, that you can afford to say."[23]

In August, after the crisis in Cincinnati had broken, Stuart wrote a letter to Birney beginning with a page of biblical quotations on the theme "Blessed are they which are persecuted for righteousness sake, for theirs is the kingdom of heaven." And he proceeded with a series of urgent questions infused with the same breathless enthusiasm revealed in his correspondence with Weld:

> I write not to instruct thee. Thou art instructed! I write not to comfort thee. God is comforting & will comfort thee—I write not to tell thee of my poor sympathy. Thou knowest it, & thy kind heart forgives its paucity. But I write to thee, to ask thee . . . to tell me how it has been with thee, since Satan outwitted himself, and God took him in his own craftiness & rage on the night of 30th Ultimo; to tell me how the family are . . . how our dear Coloured people are—how the Schools are—how the more than ever blessed

22. Stuart to Birney, September 30, 1836, WP. Although Birney had gone much further than Stuart advised by providing himself with arms and ammunition, he was eventually to articulate peace principles very similar to Stuart's (Fladeland, *Birney*, 132–46, 231–32).

23. Stuart to Birney, March 7, 1836, WP.

Anti-Slavery Spirits are about you—how the Anti-Slavery Society stands
. . . whether Right & Law & Liberty are entirely prostrate.

Birney's response was a "kind and deeply affecting letter," which prompted a renewed flood of quotation and question from Stuart in September.[24]

Birney was eventually to embrace political abolitionism to the extent of becoming the Liberty party's candidate for the presidency. And in conjunction with Stuart and Henry B. Stanton, he was to be important in introducing the American dissensions into Britain in 1840. Because Stuart was to be absent from the United States in the years before 1840, when those dissensions developed from minor irritants to a complete rupture, it was most important that his antislavery friendships had all developed on the anti-Garrisonian side, with the exception of his continuing ties with the eventually neutral Weld. No doubt, as with Birney, those friendships had grown from compatible attitudes that would have predisposed him to anti-Garrisonian allegiance. But it was to be of some importance that when the split occurred his sources of intelligence were virtually all to be on the one side.

He had, for instance, met Stanton on several occasions in 1834 and 1835, even though the former Lane Seminary man had applied his major antislavery effort in New England. At the Rhode Island State Convention in February, 1836, he was able to renew the acquaintance at the height of Stanton's great campaign to organize that state. Another anti-Garrisonian with whom Stuart was to collaborate in Britain in the 1840s was Amos Phelps, whose friendship he had cemented in the difficult days in western New York in late 1835. During his tour of Washington County a few months later, Stuart had recommended the appointment as an agent of the American Anti-Slavery Society of Nathaniel Colver, whom the Garrisonians eventually saw as a particularly virulent antagonist.[25] Another was Lewis Tappan, whom Stuart met and corresponded with on numerous occasions over a long period.

But apart from Weld, his major American abolitionist friendships were with Gerrit Smith and Beriah Green. Smith was less explicitly anti-Garrisonian than many, but, like Birney, he sought the political path to abolition, which was anathema to Garrison's principles. Stuart built on the relationship established with Smith in early 1835 to reach a familiarity

24. Stuart to Birney, August 31, September 30, 1836, WP.
25. Stanton to editor, *Emancipator*, February, 1836; American Anti-Slavery Society, Committee on Agencies, Minute Book, March 15, 1836, BPL.

second only to that he shared with Weld. The relationship was exemplified by the boldness with which he solicited a large contribution from Smith to the funds of the American Anti-Slavery Society, the impatience with which he demanded that Smith forget self-pity at the death of a child and attend the anniversary convention at Utica of the New York society, and the solicitude with which he sent his friend patent remedies for the relief of constipation and piles. He continued to enjoy Smith's hospitality from time to time, writing, in his absences, of his longing "to pay home a visit—the *sweet home* which God has given me in your house." That this was more than a figure of speech was shown in a letter he wrote in September, 1836, which also provides a revealing glimpse of the physical regimen that had always accompanied his more regularly recorded spiritual exertions:

> I may mention that I anticipate being able to spend from four to six weeks with you, that I shall need a room to myself with fire, so that I may retire whenever I feel inclined, & especially, that I may be at liberty to withdraw early in the evenings, say eight o'clock ordinarily at latest. You must let me saw and split my own wood—and if your village has a friendly Cabinetmaker's shop, to which I could resort for exercise, without reserve, it would much gratify me,—I need not tell you that I should feel under your roof, completely as with a brother.[26]

His more permanent base in this eighteen-month period was with Beriah Green at his Oneida Institute. There he enjoyed similar facilities to those he had requested of Smith. As he wrote some years later, the college had attached to it "a workshop for carpentering and cabinet-making, a farm for roots, vegetable and grain, and cows to supply milk for the fine market at Utica, some four miles distant." This was his base while he wrote extensively to his friends in the cause and also for the press. He departed from time to time on short antislavery engagements after his official agency had ended to such places as Schenectady and Troy. Above all, he enjoyed the company of Green and the kindred antislavery spirits who had joined his institution. The enjoyment was evidently mutual. In common with all other abolitionists, Green was particularly impressed by Stuart's fervent religious sincerity. This general reaction is well summed up by an entry in Lewis Tappan's journal in May, 1836. Stuart had led prayers in a New York City church: "He prays like a saint. Beriah Green

26. Stuart to Smith, January 25, March 3, June 15, September 29, October 1, 1836, SP.

told me he did not know a man who seemed to take hold on God in prayer as C.S. did."[27]

The relationship between Green and Stuart had been consolidated in the months immediately before that encounter in New York City, when Oneida became an embattled institution early in 1836. The threat was political and economic rather than a repetition of the physical coercion of a few months earlier. It showed that the hostile elements in Utica were using alternative techniques of opposition in the months that Theodore Weld was advancing the cause so conspicuously. A state senator from Utica, David Wager, successfully moved a resolution in the upper house cutting off the Oneida Institute from the benefits of the "Literature Fund," a government subsidy to further literature in educational and other institutions. As Stuart wrote after the event:

> The only *real grounds* of the restriction were, that, both among officers and students, there was freedom of thought, speech, and action, agreeably to the laws of the state, on the subject of Slavery and Abolition; the only *pretended* grounds, "that the Institution was the hot-bed of sedition,"—"that it was exerting a political influence,"—and that its President, Beriah Green, had been active in propagating the doctrines of Abolition &c. That is, dauntlessly declaring the Truth of God, against Slavery and Hypocrisy; exerting a moral and religious influence in favour of Liberty, Law, and Justice, and propagating the eternal principles of righteousness and love.[28]

Stuart was one of the leading figures, along with Gerrit Smith, Alvan Stewart, and Henry B. Stanton, speaking and leading his fellow abolitionists in prayer at a special convention held in Utica in April to protest the decision. The protest was in vain, but the episode reinforced Stuart's admiration for the "heroic faithfulness of Beriah Green."[29] It was an admiration that was eventually to lead him, at the height of the controversy with the Garrisonians in the 1840s, twice to lend his pen to public pleas in Britain for financial support for Green's institution.

WHILE HE WAS unwittingly preparing himself for a future role as an extreme partisan, Stuart's conscious endeavors in the period before 1837 were

---

27. Charles Stuart, *Oneida and Oberlin; Or, a Call Addressed to British Christians and Philanthropists, Affectionately Inviting Their Sympathies, Their Prayers, and Their Assistance, in Favour of the Christians and Philanthropists of the United States . . .* (Bristol, 1841), 12; Stuart to Smith, March 3, September 29, 1836, SP; Stuart to "My dear brother & friend," April 26, 1837, Historical Society of Pennsylvania, Philadelphia; Journal of Lewis Tappan, May 22, 1836, Lewis Tappan Papers, Library of Congress, Washington, D.C.

28. Stuart, *Oneida and Oberlin*, 13–14.

29. Ibid.; *Voice of Freedom*, May, 1836; *Emancipator*, April 23, 1836.

to promote harmony, not simply within the American movement but particularly between American and British abolitionists. His eventual significance as an opponent of Garrison was a result of his having consolidated his position as a leading spokesman of international abolitionism.

Superficially, Stuart's international significance may appear much more questionable than in the years when he had opposed Elliott Cresson in Britain and been lauded in the American antislavery press. It is all too easy to assume from the controversies that had surrounded George Thompson that Stuart had been displaced as an intermediary between American and British abolitionists. But the vast publicity achieved by Thompson was inextricably associated with violent opposition. His oratory may have warmed Garrisonian affections for Britain, but it seemed only to confirm the anti-British feelings of the hostile and uncommitted. And even within abolition circles, there had been some uneasiness about Thompson's character even before the allegations of dishonesty emerged. Unlike Stuart, Thompson had no claim to the title "Reverend," which was often bestowed on him. And at least one eminent Garrison supporter, Henry C. Wright, was seriously disturbed by the news that Thompson had worn clerical robes in some of his public appearances. In contrast, every report, public and private, affirmed Stuart's burning sincerity. One local newspaper, which had commented somewhat critically on the lack of organization in some of his speeches, had gone on to affirm that "he is always solemn—impressive—and at times exceedingly eloquent. . . . For zeal for the truth and devotion to the cause of humanity, we have never seen his equal." Perhaps even more revealing of his reputation was a passing reference in the Vermont *Telegraph*, eventually reprinted in the *Liberator*. Insisting that abolitionism would eventually prevail despite current opposition, a correspondent could find no higher praise for the leaders of the American movement than to proclaim: "They will go down to posterity along with Wilberforce, and Clarkson, and Stuart, and be registered in the archives of future generations as benefactors of the world."[30]

Stuart's continuing importance as an ambassador of British abolitionism rested on far more than the impact of his personality. It was during this period that his *West India Question* became an abolitionist best seller, extensively advertised in the antislavery press, including the *Liberator* as

30. Journal of Henry C. Wright, 39–43, 88, 89, 90, Garrison Papers, BPL; extracts from Vermont *Telegraph* and Pennsylvania *Freeman* quoted in *Liberator*, January 2, 1836, p. 3, July 28, 1838, p. 113.

well as the national society's organs. Until 1837 the same journals continued to advertise the Stuart-dominated anthology, *British Opinions of the American Colonization Society*.[31] And in 1836 and 1837 the American Anti-Slavery Society also published two editions of Stuart's *Memoir of Granville Sharp*, which had first appeared in England and had already been extensively quoted in the American *Anti-Slavery Record*. This work was as much a polemic against American proslavery forces as it was an appreciation of Britain's first abolitionist hero. Sharp's patronage of Sierra Leone "as a place of refuge, not for Englishmen, but for poor strangers most of whom were Africans," was contrasted with the ACS's provision of Liberia "for people almost all of whom were born and bred in the United States." Colonization and other proslavery policies were based on a "color phobia," which was a "distinguishing characteristic of the United States, from which *all other civilized people* are free."[32]

At the same time Stuart was persuaded by Elizur Wright to become the historian of British emancipation for American audiences by writing two long articles for the *Quarterly Anti-Slavery Magazine*, which were titled "On the Abolition of Slavery by Great Britain." The *Quarterly* was presumably read mainly by the converted. Stuart's articles were an attempt to convince American abolitionists and their sympathizers of the relevance of the British emancipation experience to their own situation. For this reason the remoter parts of the story were notable more for their claims about the political ethos of the empire than for their description of the well-known landmarks of the late eighteenth-century campaign against the slave trade. Well aware that popular Anglophobia was at least dimly reflected even in abolitionist circles, he was at pains to confront some of the more common American prejudices. Britain still had an aristocracy, but the once "mighty barriers" between "nobles and vassals" had long since been beaten down so that the people now enjoyed the "protection of equal laws, the inalienable rights of mankind, 'Life, liberty, and the pursuit of happiness.'" Britain was now in effect a "republican kingdom." In the same manner he presented Britain's morally vulnerable presence in India as an evangelistic enterprise offering freedom along with Christianity to benighted, subjugated multitudes.[33]

The core of his story, however, was the recent rapid success of the immediatist campaign. As such his account was as much an affirmation of

31. For these advertisements see Chapter 3, nn. 17 and 20.
32. Charles Stuart, *A Memoir of Granville Sharp, To Which Is Added Sharp's "Law of Passive Obedience" and an Extract from His "Law of Retribution"* (New York, 1836, rpt. 1837), 66–84; *Anti-Slavery Record*, I (1835), 128.
33. Stuart, "On the Abolition of Slavery by Great Britain," 3–21, 107–17.

the current methods of the American Anti-Slavery Society as a historical record of British achievement. While modestly omitting any mention of his own role, he put major emphasis on the provincial agitation by itinerant lecturers before and after the foundation of the Agency Committee. He ignored the tensions within the British movement and acknowledged a greater contribution from the parliamentary leadership than he had conceded while in Britain. But he made it clear that the decisive work had been that of the Agency Committee and that this body was now primarily committed to American abolition. To allay any emerging uneasiness about Thompson's credentials, he represented him as the Agency Committee's major asset: among its lecturers "George Thompson had the widest sphere and eminently distinguished himself. Ten times ten thousand hearts in Britain were awakened and confirmed by his powers and blessed God for his invaluable services." And Thompson, "grossly slandered by ignorance and falsehood in the United States, honored and beloved by those who have long known and tried him," was the agent of the committee in its new concern with international abolition.[34]

Stuart also did his best to ensure that British abolitionists continued to be informed about the progress of the cause in America. He sent packets of American antislavery literature across the Atlantic and also, from time to time, his own commentaries on American trends. Something of the flavor of these activities is conveyed by a letter he wrote to Weld in March, 1837, enclosing "one of my periodical circulars to our British friends" and asking that Weld send it off along with the following papers: "A. & S. Grimké's Appeals. The Address of the Kentucky Presbyterians against Slavery—Papers containing General Jackson's parting address, & Mr. V. Buren's inaugural, on slavery—The Texan question Govr. Ritner's message—6 Reports of the N.Y. Vigilance Committee—together with any other papers or documents, which you think would throw light upon the present posture of the subject in this country."[35]

Stuart also enclosed six copies of the *Friend of Man*, which he asked Weld to forward in the same parcel. Although his letter does not indicate which issue of this Utica journal he was sending, it seems more than likely that it was one published late the previous year, containing his rebuttal of a recent letter by the Reverend J. Breckenridge.[36] Certainly that particular Stuart letter must be seen as crucial, not merely to assessments of

---

34. Ibid.
35. Stuart to Weld, March [?], 1837; cf. Stuart to Weld, February [?], 1837, WP.
36. Rev. J. Breckenridge, "Letter to Dr. Wardlaw" (August 26, 1836), and C. Stuart, "Remarks on the Above Letter" (reprinted from the Whitesboro *Friend of Man*, October 24, 1836), in *Liberator*, November 26, 1836, pp. 190–91.

his role as an intermediary between abolitionists on both sides of the Atlantic but also to analysis of his principles and attitudes. No document from any stage of his career better illustrates the range of his experience and the mixture of influences that made his attitudes both consistent over a long period and fundamentally conservative despite his sometimes radical pronouncements on race and slavery.

Breckenridge's published letter—first sent in August, 1836, to Ralph Wardlaw, a key figure in the Glasgow Emancipation Society—had been an attack on the intrusion of British abolitionists into the United States. Antiabolitionist without being overtly proslavery, it had mainly condemned the activities of George Thompson. Stuart responded "as a personal friend of Dr. Wardlaw and of Mr. Thompson." But although he reiterated the praise he had already publicly accorded Thompson, he was evidently stirred mainly by Breckenridge's central theme that British abolitionists should not interfere in America when so many evils remained within the British Empire. In the process of countering that argument, Stuart implicitly showed the inaccuracy of Breckenridge's secondary theme that British abolitionists were ignorant of American conditions.[37]

His method was not to defend Britain unconditionally. He argued that some of the evils attributed to British imperialism had close counterparts within the United States and that others should be understood not in terms of Breckenridge's crude generalizations but by more precise analysis of underlying circumstances. Britain had indeed much to answer for: "I deeply feel, and fully acknowledge, that the *crimes* of my country are her deadliest foes." It was inexcusable that slavery still lingered on in the British West Indies and the Cape of Good Hope, "and he [Breckenridge] might have added in the Mauritius." But while agreeing that the system "miscalled apprenticeship" was still slavery, he pointed out, in detailed references to moral and legal criteria, the numerous ways in which it was a mitigation of both the previous British and current American institutions. In the same way, he would not deny that British "slaughter of the . . . Bushmen, Caffres. &c, in South Africa, is, beyond expression, infamous and criminal." But it "bears a strict resemblance to the conduct of the United States in Georgia, Alabama, Florida, &c. towards the Indian nations."[38]

These were more than debating points, and his argument revealed "deep feeling" as well as detailed knowledge about moral crimes on both sides of the Atlantic. He had already spent more of his life in the United States

37. *Ibid.*
38. *Ibid.*

than in the British Isles—far more in North America as a whole. The years he had spent in the wider British Empire had been confused and unhappy compared with those he had enjoyed in and around western New York. And yet he still considered himself British with a secondary loyalty to the United States. The crimes he was prepared to concede in Breckenridge's indictment made him "blush and hang my head to think myself an Englishman." But the real iniquity of Breckenridge's attack was that, by denying the British any moral authority to comment on America, he was in effect using British crimes to "sanctify the crimes of the United States." British guilt was great: "But Oh, that Grace may forbid, that another people, less dear to me only than my own, should sooth itself to destruction by my country's crimes."[39]

There can be no questioning his sincerity in identifying slavery and racial prejudice as the worst of these crimes. It was true, he conceded, that many British people were ignorant of American slavery. But in the case of the "anti-reform aristocracy of England," it was a willful ignorance deliberately closing its eyes to available truth. This, he went on, was not the ignorance referred to by Breckenridge: "And what does he refer to? Why, the blindness and prejudice, as he deems them, of the enlightened reform and anti-slavery spirit of Great Britain—blind, because it will not see through the medium of an apologist for oppression! prejudiced, because it cannot think *white* a more honorable color than black or brown, or yellow or red; and the lineage of the wrongdoers, a more virtuous parentage than the lineage of the sufferers of wrong!" This had been a consistent theme of his advocacy since his anti-Cresson campaign had prompted the scathing denunciation in *Prejudice Vincible*. In the same way, when he wrote of the "purifying of the American churches, from the guilt and curse of slavery," he was repeating what he had so often said in public speeches in America. His concern about the removal of the Cherokees and other southern tribes had been expressed in his private correspondence since the issue first arose long before his return to the United States. Equally well established in the same correspondence was his concern at the emergence of an independent slaveowning Texas.[40]

Yet his sincere concerns also revealed once again the biases of his background. Despite his passing sneer at the antireform aristocrats, he was no more interested than they were in domestic British social reform. And when he looked overseas he had no wish to challenge any other aspect of

39. *Ibid.*
40. *Ibid.* On the Cherokees see Stuart to Weld, June, 1831; on Texas see Stuart to Weld, March [?], 1837, WP.

British imperialism than Negro slavery. Drawing on his intimate knowledge of India, he foreshadowed bitter arguments he was to have with both British and American abolitionists a decade later by pointing out the total dissimilarity between East Indian domestic slavery and the Negro plantation systems of the New World. White men in India were forbidden to hold slaves; British courts there made no distinction between master and slave. His comments on India, however, betrayed the intolerance of indigenous religions that, despite his own troubled career there, had always made him a defender of British rule. And his strictures on the "horrid system of Hindoo idolatry" were matched by no less typical comments about British rule in Ireland. Not for the first or the last time he attributed much of the blame for Irish poverty to "the existence of the Catholic Church."[41]

Nevertheless, despite this conservatism, the passion of his antislavery commitment was still a powerful force. Without doubt the continuing "crime" of virtual slavery in the West Indies, rather than patriotic loyalty, impelled his return to Britain. In his rejoinder to Breckenridge he attacked the apprenticeship system as a breach of the Divine Law, which made immediatism the only defensible antislavery policy. He also pointed out that the apprenticeship phase had given the lie to proslavery predictions of economic and interracial chaos.[42] By late 1836 his contacts with such men as William Blair, to whose house he was soon to return, must have made him aware that many British abolitionists, after a period of mingled self-congratulation and uncertainty, were becoming convinced of the need for one final campaign on behalf of the West Indian slave. The apprenticeship scheme, which they had reluctantly accepted, should no longer be allowed to run its projected course till 1840.

The most significant advocate of the renewed campaign was Joseph Sturge, the Birmingham Quaker abolitionist, who was well known to Stuart from the agitation of 1832 and 1833. Stuart had decided to return to Britain in early 1837, but in May that year his plans must have been given more precision when he met Sturge in New York at the time of the American Anti-Slavery Society's annual convention. Sturge was on his way back to Britain after an extensive fact-finding tour of the West Indies. Before the end of May he was confronting London abolitionists, as he had those in New York, with an "almost inconceivably large mass of evidence" about the "horrid character of apprenticeship." These were the words of George Thompson, writing from London to Elizabeth Pease, a

41. *Liberator*, November 26, 1836, p. 190.
42. *Ibid.*

member of a well-known Quaker family in Darlington. Sturge and another abolitionist, Dr. A. L. Palmer, were, Thompson reported, about to appear before a parliamentary committee of inquiry. They would "deluge the Committee, and through the Committee, the country, with evidence of a most awakening kind."[43] In conjunction with many abolitionists, especially Sturge, Thompson, Elizabeth Pease, and Palmer, Stuart would play an important role over the ensuing year in arousing opinion against apprenticeship in every part of the British Isles.

As he planned his return in the early months of 1837, Stuart's divided loyalties to Britain and the United States presented no problems for him. Theodore Weld originally intended to accompany him, evidently more for the sake of his health than to take an active part in the British movement. But in late April Stuart heard from Weld that this arrangement was in doubt. And in early May, at the national convention in New York, he heard from mutual friends that Weld would not come but would instead recuperate from the strains of his antislavery work at his parents' home. Stuart's overtly equable response to the news almost certainly masked deep disappointment. He blamed neither Weld nor those who advised him, "nor," he went on with a hint of self-pity, "is disappointment so new a thing to me, as to produce much heartbreaking."[44]

In June he visited Weld and his parents and then his sister in Canada.[45] In July he crossed the Atlantic alone—as always. No doubt he was looking forward to reunions and renewed activity among his British abolitionist friends.

DESPITE HIS loneliness, it would be wrong to see the end of Stuart's three years in America as a sad anticlimax. His constant public activities were emotional compensation for the setbacks and frustrations of his private life. Nor was this a completely unconscious psychological process. In late 1836 he had implicitly described the therapeutic nature of abolitionism for him as he urged Gerrit Smith to fight the grief he felt after his child's death: "Nothing relieves the heart overburthened with its own cares, so much or so wholesomely, as generous exertions for the rescue or relief of others—the self sacrifice gives the tone & the buoyancy & the vigor, to

---

43. *Fourth Annual Report of The American Anti-Slavery Society*, 18, 23; Stuart to Rev. Hawkes, May 15, 1837, Stuart Correspondence, New-York Historical Society Manuscripts, New York City; Thompson to Elizabeth Pease, May 25, 1837, JR.

44. Stuart to Weld, May 8, 15, 1837, WP.

45. Unless his firm plans for this itinerary were changed (Stuart to Weld, May 15, 1837, WP).

the heart which it wants instead of leaving it the prey of its own enfeebling & corroding cares."[46] In pursuing such a course himself, Stuart had experienced more specific fulfillment as well. He had established friendships with American abolitionists, notably Smith and Birney, which were to endure to the end of his life. He had seen less of Weld than their earlier relationship and their mutual commitment to abolitionism might have implied. Yet Weld's failure to accompany him to Britain did not at that stage imply any weakening of the emotional bond between them.

Writing at the end of 1837, Weld explained something of the nature of that bond in discussing an issue of disagreement with the Grimké sisters. In his youth he had been intolerant of contrary opinions, "but our dear Charles Stuart has entirely cured me of that and made me ashamed of it. While yet a boy I became acquainted with him, and from that time till now our intimacy has been that of *an indivisible existence*; and yet our creeds and speculative opinions, doctrinal views and philosophical belief are as wide asunder as the poles. We are always discussing when together and always disagreeing in opinion." In the long run, despite these sentiments, the two men were to be estranged by such disagreements. But in 1837 that rift was still inconceivable. The lack of surviving letters from Weld to Stuart can combine with the fervid language of Stuart's own correspondence to make the relationship seem one-sided in its affections. In common with many others, Stuart was inspired by the force of Weld's personality and his powers of explication and persuasion. But even in 1837, Weld was the first to admit the priority of his own debt to the older man. As he grew closer to his future wife, Angelina Grimké, he was particularly disappointed that she barely knew Stuart:

> I can hardly trust myself to speak or write of him: so is my whole being seized with love and admiration of his most unearthly character that whatever I say of him seems to others like the extravagance of *enthusiasm*. I feel humbled and shrink with a sense of conscious and sometimes almost overpowering unworthiness when I look upward to the pure heights of his heavenly character. *I have never known such a character*! Like the eagle he flies alone! His absence almost seems like the subtraction of a portion of my being; and I daily render thanks to my Lord and master and "elder brother" that he has stooped so low as to take a man of earth and clothe him so richly with the beauty and purity and majesty of his own spirit.[47]

---

46. Stuart to Smith, October 16, 1836, SP.
47. Weld to Angelina Grimké, December 28, 1837, Barnes and Dumond (eds.), *Weld-Grimké Letters*, I, 507, 509.

6 THE APOSTLE OF THE NEGRO

EVEN BEFORE Charles Stuart had gone to the United States in 1834 there had been disagreements within the British abolition movement. At first largely hidden from public view, the tensions had become conspicuous when the Agency Committee—influenced as much by Stuart as anyone—had transformed itself into the British and Foreign Society for the Universal Abolition of Slavery and the Slave Trade. The parent Anti-Slavery Society had not accepted the goals of worldwide, and especially American, abolition adopted by the new society. During Stuart's three-year absence in pursuit of those goals, the divisions had widened. In particular, fundamental differences in method became obvious, paradoxically as the two societies again found a common objective.[1]

Though not abandoning the interest in American abolition which Stuart's letters and Thompson's activities had kept alive, the Universal Abolition Society found its attention drawn more and more to disturbing reports about the functioning of the apprenticeship scheme in the former slave colonies. In the process its members quickly became disillusioned with the more cautious method of attack of the Anti-Slavery Society. After agreeing to press for a parliamentary committee of inquiry, they were enraged when T. F. Buxton allowed his demands for the inquiry to be brushed aside in the House of Commons by government assurances that abuses of the apprenticeship system were minor and already being remedied.[2]

1. Temperley, *British Antislavery*, 24–41.
2. Ibid.

For a time the most public issue between the two antislavery groups concerned Mauritius. The absence of reliable statistics about slave numbers, compounded by the continuation of illegal slave trading, had made it difficult for the government to compute the proportion of compensation funds due to the island out of the £20 million that had been awarded in toto to the former slave colonies. Buxton provoked a published denial from the Universal Abolition Society when he claimed to represent all abolitionists in offering to support the claims of the Mauritian planters if they would agree to end apprenticeship.[3]

Soon, however, the Mauritius issue was overshadowed by continuing reports of major problems in the West Indies. The end of slavery appeared to have done nothing to abate the cruelty of the labor system. Floggings of both sexes continued and, on the major island of Jamaica, a previously unknown form of punishment—the treadmill—had been introduced to render conditions apparently more barbaric than ever. Reports, many of them from missionaries, suggested that a background factor of major importance was that most of the special magistrates, who had been introduced with the apprenticeship system, had thrown in their lot with the planters rather than the former slaves.[4]

In short, abolitionists could feel that although the apprenticeship period had justified their confidence that there would be no violent upheaval after emancipation, it had also confirmed their suspicions that the planters would do all in their power to retain virtual slavery. In particular, plantocratic policies were seen as an abuse of the generous compensation that had been granted despite the bitter opposition of more radical abolitionists.

But the more insistently the reports from the West Indies demanded action against slavery, the more marked became the differences in approach between the two wings of the movement. According to the leading historian of British antislavery in this period, Howard Temperley, the options were to work through Parliament—as Buxton and the Anti-Slavery Society preferred—or to take the more radical course of a nationwide campaign to bring popular pressure to bear on the government. As Temperley points out, the situation was thus strikingly similar to that which had existed in 1832–33, except that on that earlier occasion the Anti-Slavery Society had not entirely neglected wider public support, as it did in the struggle against apprenticeship. In fact, because of the special cir-

3. *Ibid.*
4. *Ibid.*; William A. Green, *British Slave Emancipation: The Sugar Colonies and the Great Experiment* (Oxford, 1976), 129–61.

cumstances, discussed in a previous chapter, that led to the formation of the Agency Committee, the parallels between the two periods are even closer than Temperley suggests. He points out that in late 1835, just as the issues and policy alternatives were becoming clear-cut, the radical Universal Abolition Society disappeared. Its disappearance is puzzling, and the almost complete lack of records offers little hope of a solution. But that provincial abolitionists took the lead in organizing the national campaign represents a striking repetition of the trends that had preceded the foundation of the Agency Committee. Despite its metropolitan location and its initial phase as an offshoot of the national society, that body had resulted very largely from provincial experimentation and pressure: it rationalized and coordinated, rather than initiated, provincial action. In the same way, in the campaign against apprenticeship, provincial agitation led to a national convention in London. The resultant Central Negro Emancipation Committee was again a metropolitan coordinating body serving the interests of the numerous provincial abolitionists who had brought it into being. There was one other parallel between the two periods. The campaign against apprenticeship, as Temperley points out, drew heavily on the services of George Thompson, John Scoble, and Joseph Sturge, all of whom had been activists in the Agency Committee era. But it also drew once again on the energies and commitment of Charles Stuart, now, after his years in America, as experienced an abolition campaigner as any in the world.[5]

DESPITE THE eventual similarities between the two periods, Stuart did not play the same innovative role in the campaign against apprenticeship that he had in the agitation leading to the Emancipation Act. Unquestionably, the foremost instigator of the opposition to apprenticeship was Joseph Sturge, secretary of the Birmingham Anti-Slavery Society. In October, 1835—at the time Stuart was experiencing the extreme violence of American antislavery controversy in and around Utica—Sturge was launching the new British campaign with a mass meeting in Birmingham Town Hall, followed by other demonstrations. To spread the agitation more widely, however, he badly needed more detailed information about the situation in the West Indies. Current sources were both unreliable and incapable of full exploitation because of the danger of exposing informants resident in the islands to reprisals. A parliamentary committee of inquiry was finally introduced the following March. But four months of investigating conflicting witnesses produced a report that played down

5. Temperley, *British Antislavery*, 24–41.

plantocratic abuses without producing hard evidence in support of its predictions of improvements.

It was in these circumstances that Sturge decided to undertake his fact-finding mission to the West Indies along with two other Birmingham Quakers, Thomas Harvey and William Lloyd, and the former Agency Committee lecturer and secretary of the Universal Abolition Society, John Scoble. At the end of this tour, Sturge met Stuart in New York in May, 1837. There are no records of their discussions, but there can be little doubt that the meeting confirmed for Stuart the probability that he would again be involved in a campaign of itinerant lecturing and organizing on the now familiar pattern. Certainly it is clear from George Thompson's comments later that month that such a campaign was foreseen even before Sturge reported to a new parliamentary committee of inquiry. If the "deluge" of evidence marshaled by Sturge and A. L. Palmer failed to stir the committee, wrote Thompson, "they will with all possible despatch attempt to arouse the country by printing, public meetings, &c &c. The apprenticeship must be annihilated."[6]

During June, July, and August, 1837, while Stuart was winding up his affairs in America and Canada and then recrossing the Atlantic for a reunion with William and Mary Blair in Bath, the foundations of the new campaign were being laid. It was essentially to be run by men who were already his close associates and would draw its major strength from the provincial centers where he had become so well known between 1830 and 1834. Although the record is deficient, his association with Sturge almost certainly dated from the days of his lecturing agency in the Birmingham area immediately before the formation of the Agency Committee. The antislavery circle in Birmingham was, as elsewhere, small and close-knit. Sturge, as the leading Quaker in a heavily Quaker antislavery network, must have become aware early in 1831 of the eccentric lecturer who was soon to be described by his enemy, Cresson, as an idol of Birmingham abolitionists. Certainly the two men were associated in the foundation of the Agency Committee. So, too, was Sturge's father-in-law, James Cropper, who became one of Stuart's major allies in the war against Cresson. Stuart and Sturge, sometimes accompanied by William Blair, had attended several meetings of the Anti-Slavery Society in the summer of 1833 to press the opposition of radicals to the compromises that produced compensation and apprenticeship. In the same period, Stuart, Sturge, and Cropper had combined to give hospitality to William Lloyd Garrison in London. Later that year the two Quakers had lent their support to a fund-

6. *Ibid.*, 36–37; Thompson to Elizabeth Pease, May 25, 1837, JR.

raising appeal organized by Stuart and Blair on behalf of the emerging antislavery societies of the United States. Stuart had gone on to serve with Sturge on the foundation committee of the Universal Abolition Society, and the latter's letter to Garrison had appeared in the *Liberator* as part of the publicity preceding the transatlantic missions of Stuart and Thompson.[7]

Stuart's association with Thompson over the same period and beyond requires no further elaboration. But it is necessary to point out that the sponsorship of Thompson's mission by the abolitionists of Glasgow and Edinburgh, the publicity that had accompanied his eventful stay in America, and the public meetings he had held on his return had combined to keep abolitionism vigorously alive, particularly in Glasgow, in the years after the Emancipation Act. This had not been the case in Stuart's original stronghold, Ireland. Despite the indignation that had greeted the award of compensation and the acceptance of apprenticeship, the two most prominent Irish antislavery societies—in Dublin and Belfast—had disintegrated after the achievement of the Emancipation Act.[8]

Accordingly, Scotland rather than Ireland responded most speedily to the campaign launched by Sturge. In June, at a large public meeting organized by the Glasgow Emancipation Society, numerous resolutions were passed in favor of the immediate end of apprenticeship. But soon, thanks to Thompson and the old Agency Committee network, antislavery was being revived in Ireland. In July and early August, Thompson wrote letters to another former Agency Committee lecturer, Edward Baldwin, discussing the need to combat apprenticeship. Later that month Thompson went to Ireland and lectured in Belfast and Dublin. On September 18 the Hibernian Anti-Slavery Society was formed in Dublin to succeed the defunct Negro's Friend Society. Many of its members had belonged to its predecessor, but the new society had a larger Quaker component, and people relatively junior in the earlier 1830s had achieved prominence. Stuart's old friend Charles Orpen, for instance, now shared the secretaryship with a Quaker, Richard Allen. Another Quaker was Richard Webb, whose earlier contribution had been mainly as printer and pub-

---

7. Minute Books, S. 20, E2/3, May 25, June 1, 15, 1831, July 8, 9, 11, 12, 16, 17, 1833, RHL; Cropper to Garrison, July 5, 1833; Phillips to Garrison, August 30, 1833; Clare Taylor, *British and American Abolitionists: An Episode in Transatlantic Understanding* (Edinburgh, 1974), 19, 25; Stuart, *To the Friends of Religion and Humanity*, 2: Sturge and Cropper were listed as men who could vouch for Stuart and who would accept donations for the project. *London. Agency Society for the Universal Abolition of Slavery and the Slave Trade* [Broadsheet] 18, Aldermanbury, March 14, 1834; *Liberator*, April 12, 1834, p. 58.

8. Riach, "Ireland and American Slavery," 49.

lisher of the Negro's Friend Society's pamphlets, including many by Stuart.[9]

Thompson's success was to prove important to Stuart's subsequent activities in two contrasting ways. In the short term Stuart was to follow up his work in both Scotland and Ireland in the agitation against apprenticeship. But Thompson had unwittingly prepared his strongholds of support for future controversies in which he and Stuart would be leading opponents. His influence with the Glasgow Emancipation Society was already well established; he had been employed as its agent for the past year. But his visit to Ireland had enabled him to form new friendships in antislavery circles in which Stuart had been a pioneering influence. Equally important to both the immediate and longer-term future was the close liaison by correspondence between the Glasgow and Dublin societies fostered by Thompson's work.[10]

Stuart made his first appearance in the new campaign in Scotland, soon after Thompson's return from Ireland. The two men met in Edinburgh on October 26 at a committee meeting of the Edinburgh Anti-Slavery Society, which chose Thompson as its delegate for an antiapprenticeship convention to be held in London the following month. Thompson wrote to Baldwin in Ireland that he was keen to accept the commission because it would bring him together with the most uncompromising elements in the antislavery movement. There were many of these in Edinburgh but also too many who were "inclined to listen to the (so-called) dictates of prudence and expediency." In this context, he went on, "I was delighted to see Captain Stuart. He did our Committee here good by his noble adherence to principle and his fearless denunciation of timid measures."[11]

Stuart left Scotland for the north of England immediately after this Edinburgh meeting, but a similar meeting of the committee of the Glasgow Emancipation Society five days later revealed the significant role he was playing in the new agitation. When the committee met to consider the appointment of delegates to the London convention, it was informed in detail of the resolutions passed and the delegates chosen at a recent meeting of Sturge's Birmingham society. It was also told of similar resolutions passed in the Blair-Stuart stronghold of Bath and of the recent events in Edinburgh. Moreover, the Glasgow society's minutes went on, "the meeting was also informed that Captain Stuart, who had for four

9. Minute Book II, June 19, 1837, GES; Thompson to Baldwin, July 26, August 4, October 20, 26, 1837, BPL; Riach, "Ireland and American Slavery," 56–60.
10. Riach, "Ireland and American Slavery," 56; Minute Book II, April 6, 1836, October 31, 1837, GES.
11. Thompson to Baldwin, October 16, 1837, BPL.

years past been engaged as an Anti-Slavery Agent in the United States, had lately returned . . . and has for some time been engaged in conjunction with Joseph Sturge, Esq. in furthering the success of the proposed convention of Delegates in London."[12]

In pursuing these activities, Stuart was as active as ever in cooperating with female abolitionists to an extent that was to confuse and anger his opponents when the woman question became a divisive issue. He contributed two "Anecdotes of American Slavery" illustrating cruelty to female slaves to the pamphlet *Three Years Female Anti-Slavery Effort*, published in Glasgow late in 1837. After leaving Scotland, he made quick visits to Newcastle, Darlington, Sheffield, Manchester, Liverpool, and Birmingham to urge active support of the coming convention. Although the eventual presence of delegates from these centers may have reflected his influence, the only detailed description of his activities on this latter tour comes from the subsequent accusations of his most bitter Garrisonian opponent, John A. Collins. When he met the antislavery committee in Darlington, according to Collins, writing some four years later and citing the authority of Elizabeth Pease, "Captain Stuart again and again begged the Committee to send up a *female* delegate. 'If there be a lady,' he continued, 'who has the *head* and *heart to represent you*, I am sure she will be joyfully received, and they will *thank heaven* for sending her.'"[13]

As a result of the itinerant activities over the previous few months of such men as Sturge, Thompson, and Stuart and of more local activity by scores of other abolitionists, hundreds of delegates arrived in London in November, 1837. With a general election due, the time seemed ripe for a full revival of the Agency Committee's methods of sensitizing public and parliamentary opinion. The convention accordingly formed the new coordinating body, the Central Negro Emancipation Committee, and agreed to publish a newspaper, the *British Emancipator*, to publicize the new cause.[14]

Any hopes that matters might be brought swiftly to a conclusion were soon dashed when a delegation from the convention took its memorial against apprenticeship to the prime minister, Lord Melbourne, in Downing Street. According to the Irish abolitionist Edward Baldwin, "His Lordship received us in the most uncourteous and ungracious manner

12. Minute Book II, June 19, 1837, GES.
13. *Three Years Female Anti-Slavery Effort* (Glasgow, 1837), 60–61; Stuart's itinerary described by Thompson to Baldwin, October 26, 1837, BPL; Collins' comments in *Liberator*, May 21, 1841, p. 82.
14. Temperley, *British Antislavery*, 39.

possible. . . . 'You call yourselves Delegates, (said he, abruptly on entering) who sent you here and what do you represent?'" Baldwin attributed much of the hostility of Melbourne to insinuations by the "Buxton party" that the provincial delegates were "a radical off-shoot who were marring the cause by extreme opinions and unreasonable agitation."[15]

Regardless of the truth of Baldwin's precise allegation, the old divisions between the two branches of the antislavery movement were from this period more marked than ever. The Minute Books of the Anti-Slavery Society through these November weeks reveal a policy of standing aloof from the growing movement for nationwide agitation. On November 13 the society's committee considered a letter from Sturge which gave news of recent provincial moves and invited cooperation with the convention due to assemble in Exeter Hall the following day. On November 15 it considered the resolutions passed at that meeting but then, a day later, rejected an invitation from the convention to coordinate activities. The committee decided that it would do more good for the antislavery cause "by continuing for the present to act independently."[16] In fact, independent action was to mean inertia. And with Buxton's surprise loss of his parliamentary seat, antiapprenticeship activity fell firmly under the control of the more radical abolitionists.

The Central Negro Emancipation Committee, agreed to in principle at the November 14 meeting, was formally brought into being at a second convention in Exeter Hall on November 23. According to Edward Baldwin, it was a "cheering, glorious Meeting!" But although he also referred to "a good array of M.P.s in attendance," the list of speakers suggests that, in keeping with the recent resolutions of the Anti-Slavery Society, these were not people closely associated with the establishment parliamentary antislavery lobby but rather such men as Daniel O'Connell, long associated with Irish abolitionism, and Joseph Pease, a member of the well-known Darlington Quaker family. The majority of speakers were not MPs: prominent among them were several who had not only been active in recent months but were veterans of the earlier Agency Committee agitation—Sturge, Thompson, Blair, and Baldwin. Seven other former members of the Agency Committee took places on the new emancipation committee.[17]

15. Edward Baldwin to Richard Allen, November 18, 1837, S. 18, C154/185, RHL.
16. Minute Books, S. 20, E2/5, November 13, 15, 16, 1837, RHL.
17. Central Negro Emancipation Committee, *Report of the Proceedings of the Public Meeting Held at Exeter Hall, on Thursday the 23rd of November, 1837, to Take into Consideration the Present Condition of the Negro Apprentices in the British Colonies* (London, 1837), 1–52, committee listed 45–46; Baldwin to Allen, November 23, 1837 (postmark), S. 18, C155/73, RHL.

Charles Stuart's absence from the new committee does not indicate his role was insignificant. Because the committee was a metropolitan coordinating body, none of the other important figures, such as Sturge and Thompson, whose work had brought it into being, were members either. Stuart's prestige in the movement had been recognized at the November 14 meeting when he and Dr. A. L. Palmer were made joint secretaries of the convention.[18] He was absent from the subsequent permanent committee because, like Sturge and Thompson, he saw his main task in the months ahead as continued provincial agitation. True to his temperament and experience, he would abandon these activities and take his place as a metropolitan administrator only some seven months in the future, when the campaign had been successfully concluded. His attitudes were made clear in a letter to Theodore Weld two months after the formation of the new organization. The "glorious work" was progressing. In contrast to his American experiences, "no physical opposition molests us." But still success was far from inevitable: "The English people are prepared for the extirpation of colonial slavery—but they are prepared, as fertile earth, yet unploughed, is prepared for the plough. But our *ploughing* equipments are miserably defective! We have but a fraction of the force in the field, which the work demands. God indeed is working mightily by that fraction, and doing wonders by it—and should the object be obtained, it will be eminently his work." The same letter showed that there were also personal reasons why he expected the work to be difficult. Both his financial and physical resources were feeling the strain. The greatest problem was "the extreme narrowness of my means in the light of the call." But he also lacked his "former vigor." It was in this letter that he referred to his relative ineffectiveness during his last year in the United States. It pained him that "whatever I do, I do with a blighted effort—and many things which my soul would exult in doing, I cannot even attempt."[19]

Despite this sense of inadequacy, there was never any question that Stuart would participate in the new campaign to the limits of his ability. Indeed, even in this same letter he consoled himself with the thought that financial and physical frailties were "properly considered . . . not my concern—and that my proper business is, to occupy my talent, without being disheartened because it is not ten." The determination of his commitment stands out clearly because the same correspondence reveals that duty to the cause was pursued at the expense of a devotion to Weld as intense as ever. Apologizing to the younger man for being "so hatefully

18. Baldwin to Allen, November 18, 1837, C154/185, RHL.
19. Stuart to Weld, February 23, 1838, WP.

and contemptibly defective in my correspondence," he went on: "Why do you, or anybody, love me? I sometimes almost wish that you did not, so vividly do I feel the painful evidences of my own unworthiness—but oh, what a loss were mine, could you cease to love me! But this is out of the question. I know that we are united, one with each other & with our Lord, for ever, unless I apostasize; and then I would not have you with me for worlds." In this letter he wrote almost wistfully of mutual hopes for a reunion later that year but doubted whether his new antislavery commitments would permit it "before the ensuing Spring." All he could say was that it was his "one hope . . . that as far as diverging duties may permit, you and I shall be companions."[20]

Even as he wrote, a letter was on its way to him from Weld offering an even stronger personal challenge to his antislavery dedication. Weld and Angelina Grimké were to marry and wanted to delay the wedding until Stuart could be with them. Moreover, they were inviting him to share their new home. His response was typically emotional: "Yes, Theodore, you are mine—and I am yours—God made us one from the beginning. . . . And Angelina is my Sister—she always was my Sister—now she is doubly so—I know not a more sacred joy that God could have given me on earth, than by your union. My soul would not have leaped more with gratitude and love, had He given me an equal blessing!" But they must not delay the wedding for his return: "The principle is wrong—the feeling is idolatrous, most generous & pure & tender tho' it be—Theodore your heart's own Charles, says, *you must not delay!*"[21]

He was no less moved by the offer of a home: "Had I let loose my imagination to fabricate *a castle in the clouds*, I could not have desired a sweeter and a nobler one, than the share to which you invite me, in your new abode." But he could not be sure of his ability to acccept for some time—late 1838 at the earliest, more probably not until May or June of the following year. When it came their reunion would be all the more sweet because it had been delayed "by the claims of love": "Ah, what claims are those! how they ring through the heart, in the cry of our brother's blood—in the ceaseless wail of his stricken heart—in the leer & the sneer & the scoff & the curse of his oppressor!"[22]

Already the public campaign that monopolized his sense of duty was under way. On February 20 Lord Brougham had startled the House of Lords with an attack on the planters and a demand for the end of appren-

20. *Ibid.*
21. Stuart to Weld, March 8, 1838, WP.
22. *Ibid.*

ticeship. Although easily outvoted, the demand was an embarrassment to the government, not least to the colonial secretary, Lord Glenelg, who, as recently as the previous November, had congratulated the colonial governors on how well apprenticeship was operating. He responded to Brougham's attack by promising remedy of specific abuses but held firm to the announced timetable for apprenticeship in the belief that premature abolition would introduce racial and social confusion into colonial society.[23]

Although these parliamentary exchanges prodded the government out of its complacency, the nationwide agitation organized by the Central Negro Emancipation Committee was to maintain the pressure for real concessions. Already, between its formation in November, 1837, and Brougham's speech in February, there had been an impressive public response to the issue in most parts of the British Isles. The *British Emancipator* reported twenty-four public meetings in December, fifty-eight in January, and a further fifty in February and the first two weeks of March.[24]

There were several reasons for this accelerating trend, not least the determination of those who had attended the November convention to make the issue the major priority for local antislavery committees. George Thompson, for instance, persuaded the committee of the Glasgow Emancipation Society to postpone the society's annual meeting till August pending an all-out assault aimed at making August 1 the day on which apprenticeship would end for all former slaves rather than only the nonpraedials categorized in the existing legislation.[25] If few had the advantages of Thompson's eloquence and reputation, many other advocates of the new cause were morally encouraged and intellectually equipped for the campaign by the publication in January of *The West Indies in 1837*, the detailed indictment of apprenticeship by Joseph Sturge and Thomas Harvey. At the same time the weekly publication of the *British Emancipator* was supplying campaigners with the basic arguments and also with the invigorating news of public activity on a broad front.

As Howard Temperley has written, not only was the campaign "a repeat performance of that of 1832–33," with petitions and remonstrances pouring into Parliament from public meetings and antislavery societies old and new, but "even the performers were the same." While Thompson aroused Scotland by addressing meetings and organizing committees, "Sturge, Scoble, and their associates did the same in England."[26] It was

23. Temperley, *British Antislavery*, 40; Green, *British Slave Emancipation*, 154–57.
24. *British Emancipator*, March 14, 1838, p. 36.
25. Minute Book II, February 14, 1838, p. 121, GES.
26. Temperley, *British Antislavery*, 39.

at this period that Charles Stuart's activities make the parallel even stronger than Temperley suggests. Just as Stuart had perfected the lecturing methods of the Agency Committee by his extensive Irish tour in 1830 and 1831, so he now did for Ireland what Thompson, Sturge, and others were doing in Scotland and England.

Stuart's characteristic modesty combines with the lack of Irish antislavery society records to make the details of his work elusive. He later wrote merely that he had spent the spring "running over Ireland." Almost certainly many of the petitions that again came in from the same places he had canvassed in 1830–31 were prompted by his efforts.[27] No less probable is that his activities confirmed his reputation among some of the newer Irish abolitionists such as Richard Allen, who were soon to join him for the climax of the crusade in London.

His Irish tour kept Stuart away from another abolitionist confrontation with government which came before that climax. Some four hundred delegates assembled in mass meetings at Exeter Hall on March 22 and 27. Their presence and the continuing arrival of petitions were making the government further modify its commitment to apprenticeship. Lord Glenelg was preparing a bill to meet some of the most obvious antislavery criticisms by regulating working hours, outlawing flogging, and giving stipendiary magistrates the right to free apprentices who received brutal treatment. But these proposals did not satisfy campaigners who wanted nothing short of immediate abolition. It is likely that Stuart heard quickly of the new impasse that was reached by the contending parties on March 28, for the same day a long, informative letter passed between two of his Irish friends, Edward Baldwin in London and Richard Allen in Dublin.[28]

Although there was evidence of sympathy from some cabinet members, wrote Baldwin, the government "has resolved to oppose us." The four hundred delegates had just had an unsatisfactory interview with Melbourne, Glenelg, and Lord John Russell: "Lord Glenelg stood stupid, motionless, and mute. Not *one* word did he utter; but seemed to feel deeply; but he feels for himself, not the suffering Negro." Baldwin felt confident that "the Delegates are resolved to do their Duty," that the "insulted, long-suffering country" would not allow the government to pursue its policies with impunity, and that Melbourne would be "taught what (under Divine Providence) men engaged in the cause of mercy and justice can do."[29]

27. Stuart to editor, *British Emancipator*, June 27, 1838, p. 126; *Journals of House of Commons*, XCIII (1837–38), 247, 338, 413, 499, 509, 540, 541.
28. Baldwin to Allen, March 28, 1838 (postmark), S. 18, C154/186, RHL.
29. *Ibid.*

Baldwin's confidence proved fully justified. Pressed by continuing remonstrance and petition, parliamentary votes swung steadily toward the abolitionist demands. In contrast to the crushing defeat of Lord Brougham's motion in the House of Lords in February, by late March a Commons vote was only narrowly lost. The turning point was to come on May 22, when a resolution by Sir Eardley Wilmot, calling for the end of apprenticeship on August 1, was narrowly passed by the House of Commons. Although, as Temperley writes, this was "a snap division in a thinly attended House," it was also the result of careful planning by the radical campaigners. On May 17, for instance, the committee of the Glasgow Emancipation Society appointed George Thompson and William Smeal in response to a letter from the Central Negro Emancipation Committee urging that delegates be dispatched to London on the nineteenth "preparatory to the bringing on of Sir E. Wilmot's motion on the 22nd." The same committee was confronted with a similar request from Joseph Sturge. Committees from many other parts of the country responded to the call. No doubt those in Ireland received the same explanation as the Glasgow committee that "the principal business of the Delegates, during the few days they might remain in Town, [was] to canvass as extensively as possible the Irish and Scotch members."[30]

Stuart was by now back in London. Among the many friends and acquaintances who joined him and the other organizers of the campaign was Richard Allen, who sailed with his wife from Dublin to Liverpool and "proceeded post-haste to London." Years later Mrs. Allen provided a vivid description of "that memorable reunion in London which did not separate until the voice of the people, through their representatives in Parliament assembled, declared that the fetters should be knocked off the limbs of the miscalled apprentices on the 1st August."[31]

It was, she recalled, "a spirit-stirring time." Despite the careful planning, the actual moment of the division in Parliament came with unexpected speed. Many delegates' wives were quietly dining, not expecting to see their husbands before morning, when a sudden clamor of shouting and bell-ringing aroused them. For a time all was a confusion of clapping, cheering, and shouting. At length the words "A glorious majority of three; we have gained our cause!" were distinguishable. At the same time there was seen amid the entering crowd "the negro's champion—George Thompson." His appearance was the cue for redoubled enthusiasm among

30. Temperley, *British Antislavery*, 40; Minute Book II, May 17, 1838, p. 131, GES.
31. Mrs. Allen's account is reprinted in Hannah Maria Wigham, *A Christian Philanthropist of Dublin: A Memoir of Richard Allen* (London, 1886), 22–24.

both men and women "scarcely able to believe the work indeed achieved." And then, wrote Mrs. Allen, "while our spirits were thus elated, and we were as noisy and uproarious and as confused as Babel, in glided one who may well be called the apostle of the negro, Captain Charles Stuart." Amid the uproar, he "calmly said, 'Let us kneel down and return thanks to God for having thus inclined the hearts of our representatives to the side of mercy'. All was hushed in a moment. The Christian knelt and prayed; he prayed for the oppressor and the oppressed fervently and impressively. Soon we all retired."[32]

Despite the abolitionist jubilation, the government could still have resisted. It did indeed have the decision of May 22 overturned by another Commons vote within a week. But the agitation was having its effect on the colonies. The planters, seeing the erosion of parliamentary support, felt increasingly suspicious of the permanence of any commitments emanating from London. The agitation in Britain, they felt, was unsettling the black population of the West Indies, and this was likely to be exacerbated to dangerous levels on August 1, when nonpraedial apprentices would gain their freedom. Indeed, even before May 22 more than half the colonial legislatures had unilaterally abandoned apprenticeship. Over the next two months the remainder—including the crucial island of Jamaica—followed suit.[33]

Over those same two months Stuart at last felt free to pause in his travels and assume the significant administrative position in London which his prestige commanded. For some weeks he became acting secretary of the Central Negro Emancipation Committee and editor of the *British Emancipator*. With the great national campaign effectively won, this was consciously only a temporary job—almost a holiday activity. For the British antislavery movement the final victory over colonial slavery was to be followed by a period of reorganization and redefinition of objectives. The Central Emancipation Committee was about to be replaced by the British and Foreign Anti-Slavery Society, which has survived with several changes of name to the present day. Stuart was sufficiently respected to be named the first honorary life member of the new society, and he would eventually be for a period one of its most diligent organizers.[34] But in 1838 he had no intention of taking on a permanent administrative role.

Nor did the climax of the campaign mean that he would join some fellow abolitionists in turning to domestic reform. As in 1832–33 the agi-

32. Ibid.
33. Temperley, *British Antislavery*, 40–41.
34. *British Emancipator*, June 27, 1838, p. 124; Barnes and Dumond (eds.), *Weld-Grimké Letters*, II, 701 n. 3.

tation against overseas injustice had proceeded in an atmosphere of domestic social and political unrest. But, again, for Stuart this was only a relatively unimportant backdrop to the middle-class agitation against apprenticeship. As he wrote to Weld about the imminent success of that agitation, he indulged only a passing comment on the emerging Chartist campaign of 1837 and 1838. Any sympathy he had for the Chartists was because they had a common enemy in the proslavery ministry. He had no sympathy for the "extravagances" of their demands.[35] In these circumstances the resolution of the apprenticeship problem meant that he was ready to travel again.

If American abolitionists had had their way he might well have gone straight back to the United States. The *Friend of Man* greeted the news of British antislavery's triumph by referring to the "glorious results of West Indian Emancipation, which everybody knows to have been secured by the labors of such men as Charles Stuart and George Thompson." It was now time to issue the "long-suppressed call" for the two men: "England can spare them now. Jamaica can spare them." This was more than a parochial plea from the Utica journal. The demand was reprinted by the *Liberator* with the hope that "it will be responded to by every anti-slavery society and press from Canada line to the dark borders of the patriarchal institution, in a voice which will be heard across the wide Atlantic." More specifically, suggested Garrison's organ, the Executive Committee of the American Anti-Slavery Society should invite the two men to return, a proposal soon endorsed in the paper's columns by an anonymous correspondent who suggested that Joseph Sturge should be included in the invitation.[36]

Stuart, of course, was far from indifferent to American trends, and he was additionally influenced by the pull of personal attachments. On July 18 he wrote with his usual passionate enthusiasm to Theodore and Angelina Weld. He wanted to hear about them personally and also about the prospects of the cause in America, in particular about a women's antislavery convention in Philadelphia attended by Angelina and disrupted by a mob while Garrison had been addressing the audience of three thousand. But despite this interest and despite his detailed explanation of the imminent triumph of the British campaign, he made no mention of a possible early reunion. Although he said nothing specific about his next venture, he gave a clue in his warning that, despite the end of apprenticeship, "much & horrible abuse, will still be perpetrated & for years will call for

35. Stuart to Weld, July 18, 1838, WP.
36. *Liberator*, July 27, 1838, p. 119; August 17, 1838, p. 130.

the prayers & supervision & efforts of all who love God & their neighbours."³⁷ Whether or not he had yet made definite plans, it was almost inevitable that he would choose to take a close personal interest in that supervision: the next stage in his endless travels would be to the West Indies.

37. Stuart to Weld, July 18, 1838, WP.

7 WEST INDIAN COMMENTARIES

CONDITIONS in the West Indies were tense and unstable in late 1838. Although the island legislatures had ended apprenticeship, most had done so reluctantly in response to the campaign of the Central Negro Emancipation Committee. The speed of this plantocratic surrender had exacerbated the problems of the sugar islands. Ever since the Emancipation Act it had been obvious that the end of slavery would demand fundamental social, political, and economic reform. The apprenticeship phase had offered an opportunity for planning and consultation between the Colonial Office and island governments and for inquiry into some of the more intractable problems. The unexpected end of apprenticeship—two years ahead of schedule—meant that reform became a matter of hurried, uncoordinated decisions made in the Caribbean and in London. Although both local and metropolitan authorities shared a desire to maintain the plantation economy, they differed fundamentally in their attitudes to the black labor force. The determination of the Colonial Office to protect the liberties of the emancipated slaves led to a wholesale disallowance of colonial legislation, which, in the autumn of 1838, replaced the old slave codes with measures designed to preserve planter control over the labor force.[1]

Conditions varied from island to island, but in every case, except the three directly ruled crown colonies of St. Lucia, Trinidad, and British Guiana, tensions between planters and British policy makers related both to the general principle of British interference and to specific measures.

1. Green, *British Slave Emancipation*, 164–75.

During the seventeen months which Charles Stuart spent in the West Indies from November, 1838, these tensions emerged in the form of a handful of crucial issues. On the central question of control of the freedmen, the planters were sufficiently alarmed by the real or threatened evaporation of their labor force to flirt with the idea of seeking alternatives in European or Indian immigration. For their part, the critics' forebodings about a continuing virtual slavery led them to challenge planter control of rents and access to freedmen's living quarters by encouraging the establishment of new free villages. But above all, one particular British measure, the West India Prisons Act, led from mutual suspicion to a constitutional crisis in Jamaica, which was to force the British ministry of Lord Melbourne momentarily out of office.[2]

It would be difficult to find a better account of West Indian conditions during this eventful period than that provided by Stuart in installments to his friends in both Britain and the United States. He visited all fourteen of the British islands. Sometimes his stays were brief, but, in many cases, he traveled extensively within a colony, and he remained ten months in Jamaica through a period of smoldering crisis. If the extent of this itinerary was a tribute to his thoroughness, his commentaries were enhanced by other personal qualities; notably an ability to command the respect of diverse elements in the island societies. Arriving at a time of intense suspicion of British interference—and at the end of decades of planter hostility to abolitionists in particular—he was consistently fair-minded without sacrificing any of his ardent commitment to racial equality.

Despite their thoroughness and relative objectivity, Stuart's observations had little subsequent impact. Partly this is because they were not published in a comprehensive form but were contained in a series of letters only some of which were published and those in the fairly ephemeral form of articles in the abolitionist press while he was still in the West Indies. But two other factors combined to leave his reports buried in obscurity. First, although he provided a detailed, often compelling account of West Indian problems, he retained an overall optimism which events were soon to discredit as the islands slid into economic decay and racial strife by midcentury. Second, this period marks the beginning of Stuart's own drift into obscurity: posterity has seen no reason to focus attention on the descriptions and attitudes of a man who was thereafter to seem only a minor, idiosyncratic figure in the movement.

Yet to rescue him from that obscurity is to do more than recall the unusual religious fervor, physical stamina, and emotional commitment of

2. Ibid.

one somewhat eccentric abolitionist. He had been one of the most outspoken exponents of the argument that slavery was economically less efficient than free labor. The doggedness with which he now clung to his views is a further reminder that such economic assumptions were important in the period of emancipation even though later research has shown they were probably wrong. Additionally, although friends and colleagues hesitated to question his optimism on this issue, in other ways his rigid consistency was already separating him from the antislavery mainstream and in the process demonstrating how much abolitionism itself was changing. In the West Indies and especially Jamaica he remained the activist of old, convinced that the time-honored methods of grass-roots agitation and organization were needed to keep governments active in support of moral rectitude. While his friends in the new British and Foreign Anti-Slavery Society were only cautiously beginning to organize provincial auxiliaries in Britain—and firmly rejecting the idea of resurrecting the old system of stipendiary agents—Stuart was improbably tramping and riding through Jamaica, not merely to observe local conditions but to organize a Jamaican antislavery movement concerned with the global problem of slavery. For him that global problem still meant exclusively Negro slavery, whereas many of his British friends were about to embrace new causes, particularly in India. His distancing from erstwhile American friends was to be even more clearly the result of changes within the movement. During his months in Jamaica the crisis over the woman question and other issues was preoccupying American abolitionists to the exclusion of any sustained interest in West Indian events.

STUART SAILED for the West Indies on October 17, 1838, with two other stalwarts of the Central Negro Emancipation Committee, John Scoble and Dr. A. L. Palmer. Their brief, according to the committee's organ, the *British Emancipator*, was "to acquire full, accurate, and authentic information, upon all points affecting the permanent welfare of the coloured classes; and, secondly, to facilitate and encourage the adoption of such practical measures, as may seem conducive to the security and growth of their nascent liberties." Stuart, in particular, was to pursue these aims with a thoroughness that was to make a mockery of the protestations of waning vigor which had crept into his recent correspondence. But he left Britain with a sense of trepidation as well as elation, taking the trouble to write to Theodore and Angelina Weld, asking them to care for his elder sister and nieces in Canada should he fail to survive the arduous journeys ahead.[3]

   3. *British Emancipator*, October 17, 1838, p. 171; Stuart to Weld, October 15, 1838, WP.

He arrived in Barbados on November 15 to hear of a past summer of extreme heat and more recent epidemics of fever, with a fatality only three days earlier. But now conditions were tempered by frequent tropical storms, and the three visitors were quickly and totally preoccupied with social rather than meteorological conditions. Within hours of their arrival they were given a reminder of recent racial tensions when a steamer arrived carrying troops who had been stationed at the other end of the island for the past three and a half months in readiness for the violence the authorities had expected to accompany the end of apprenticeship on August 1. Stuart was delighted to discover that although the whites had overreacted, "the emancipated labourers, as they themselves pleasantly expressed it, were 'making 'em 'shamed of it', by behaving with a propriety so remarkable as to exert applause even from their enemies, and to equal the best hopes of their friends." Within a week he was able to write a comprehensive report to Joseph Sturge in which optimism was qualified by emphasis on the continuing need for vigilance.[4]

He had found that liberty was "more effectually recognized" than he had expected: "The emancipated labourer, I am induced to believe, is generally safe in his person and has largely a free control of his time. His wages are small, but moderately competent: he is sensibly beginning to assume the stature of a man, and generally with great gentleness and kindness." Improved cottages were being constructed all over the island, and he was confident that the excessive work of females in the fields would "gradually be corrected." The reason for these improvements was the Colonial Office's disallowance of local contract and other laws rather than the goodwill of the masters. "Grave evils" remained because the representative government of the island was an oligarchy, whose "prejudices against colour are inferior in intensity only to those of the United States." In particular, the laborers held their cottages under a tenure "woefully subject to the caprice of their masters." The "happy disallowance of the island acts" had created an opportunity to substitute an "efficient dominion of laws really wise, and as actually impartial as possible." But the interregnum must not be too long or the traditional rulers would take the opportunity to reassert themselves. As so often in the past in both Britain and the United States, Stuart's hopes rested on the pressures of an informed and concerned public opinion: "If the nation will do its duty, I believe that the colonial office will, in good measure, fulfil theirs. And if the colonial office do its duty with the manly energy which the case demands, I see the fairest prospects before the island." Insisting that the

---

4. Stuart to Sturge, November 22, 1838, *British Emancipator*, January 9, 1839, p. 199.

victory of emancipation could still be undone "if we leave the colonies to themselves, as though the work were done," Stuart saw as the first priority the appointment of a *"suitable* special magistracy, made independent of the gentry of the islands."[5]

Underlying this detailed appraisal was Stuart's usual physical energy. He and his companions had already attended a session of the court of appeal, finding the proceedings essentially fair but its size inadequate to offset the need for special magistrates. And they had visited two of the island's seven police districts, finding evidence of extensive jail reconstruction and conditions generally greatly improved since a visit by Scoble in 1836. They had also interviewed a penal gang working, Stuart noted approvingly, without fetters. But his personal observations were clearly supplemented by local informants. Stuart wrote of "some intercourse with the whites" and of "much intercourse with the free coloured and black people." In particular, he singled out the colored editors of the Barbados *Liberal*, Samuel Prescod and Thomas Harris, "two exceedingly interesting men." That journal gave detailed accounts of the visiting abolitionists' activities, including their efforts to interview former slaves as well as educated whites and free coloreds. On one estate, it reported, black reaction to the visitors initially had been confused by the misconception that they were friends of their absentee master in England. On discovering their true identity, the laborers had reacted with a mixture of voluble enthusiasm and deferential respect. The philanthropists were suitably gratified when "one old woman . . . wound up her thanks and blessing, with the exclamation: 'Massa, freedom too sweet!'"[6]

Such activities and attitudes inevitably earned the disapproval of the white community. Scoble was particularly singled out by a rival Barbados paper, the *Globe*, because his comments on improved prison facilities were held to contain distortions about the conditions he had observed on his earlier visit. But although Scoble was a notoriously abrasive character even within antislavery circles, it was impossible for any visitor to be acceptable to both sides in this deeply divided society. Scoble responded to the *Globe*'s criticisms with his own article in the *Liberal*, but Stuart confined his published criticisms to the *British Emancipator* in England.[7] But both men made their commitment to the black community conspicuous when they attended, as guests of honor, an "Emancipation Dinner" on Novem-

5. *Ibid.*

6. Barbados *Liberal* quoted in *ibid.*, 195. See also "Letter from Mr. Scoble . . . ," *ibid.*, 198; and "Dr. Palmer's Journal," *ibid.*, March 20, 1839.

7. The *Globe*'s attack on Scoble, his reply, and Stuart's critique all reprinted in *ibid.*, January 9, 1839, p. 199.

ber 27 (Palmer having departed from the island to tour independently a few days earlier).

According to the *Liberal*, the dinner was "the greatest social party that Barbados ever witnessed." The organizers had planned for two hundred guests; twice that number crammed into the Boys' School Room and many more were unable to gain entry. But nobody had come simply for dinner: "to be there was the aim and end of desire," and there was "not a symptom of disorder" when the time came to sit down: "There they stood, in double and treble ranks, many of them men who were three months ago degraded slaves, beaming satisfaction and enthusiasm from their countenances, and here and there, politely declining the offers made by their friends who had obtained seats to vacate those seats for their accommodation!"[8]

Scoble rather than Stuart made the major speech of the evening. Its themes were the same that had dominated Stuart's report to Sturge: the excellent bearing of the freedmen, the virulence of racial prejudice on the island, and the need for continuing vigilance by Britain to consolidate the victory of emancipation. Two days later, in a long letter to England, Scoble elaborated his arguments with new illustrations about white exploitation of black wages and rents, balanced by anecdotal and statistical evidence of a buoyant colonial economy. This letter was given a wider impact by Stuart, who sent on most of it verbatim to Weld, adding some comments of his own. This embellished letter was in turn published in the New York *Journal of Commerce* and in both the *Liberator* and the American *Emancipator*.[9]

If anything, Stuart's added comments showed him to be slightly less optimistic than Scoble about prospects for Barbados. Whereas Scoble had generalized comfortably that abuses "cannot long continue," Stuart saw the "Planter Government" as a serious obstacle to the happiness of the island. As long as planters were "in all ordinary cases, Judge, Jury and Executioner, there can be no such thing generally speaking as fair play in law or practice." He cited the case of a black woman arbitrarily evicted from her cottage "in a most petulant and perfectly inequitable manner" and unable to seek legal redress. Such injustices would continue until sti-

8. "Remarks on the Emancipation Dinner," reprinted from the Barbados *Liberal* in ibid., January 9, 1839, p. 198.

9. "Reception of Mr. Scoble and Captain Stuart in Barbados," ibid., January 23, 1839, title page; "Letter from Mr. Scoble to Messrs. George Stacey and Josiah Forster," ibid., January 9, 1839, p. 198; Stuart to Weld, December 11, 1838, WP; extract from *Journal of Commerce* reprinted in *Liberator*, March 15, 1838, p. 44; *Emancipator*, March 7, 1839, p. 180.

pendiary magistrates were appointed who were independent of the "Planter Government."[10]

A private, unpublished section of this letter made it clear that he was driven as relentlessly as ever by an almost masochistic sense of duty to the cause. He had just heard with alarm of the insurrection in Upper Canada and was concerned for the safety of his sister and her family in Toronto. He asked again for Weld's intervention and, if necessary, Gerrit Smith's, to inquire after and aid his relatives because his own engagements "bind me imperiously for the next six or eight months and the climates which I have to traverse are in some cases climates of the borders of death."[11]

He began those engagements that same day by embarking on a trip which, over the next month, was to take him south to Tobago and back to Barbados via St. Vincent. He felt that Tobago was particularly in need of attention because it was very much out of "national and commercial observation" with hardly any ships calling there except the mail packet. Here, as in many other places later on, he not only observed and inquired but also lectured to masters and former slaves. His emphasis was on conciliation rather than recrimination. He urged the masters to "look not so much to your cane fields as to the happiness of your labourers." Such an attitude, he conceded, would not instantly command complete loyalty among the former slaves "for there are evil minds amongst them." But if the majority could be convinced "that you regard their honour and happiness as much as you regard your own," they would go "beyond their mere hiring *to please and serve you*, as I know that some of them are doing where they are so dealt with." To the laborers he acknowledged that exemplary behavior would not win the affections of all masters "for there are bad minds amongst them too"; but it would favorably influence most of them.[12]

Underlying these reassurances was an obvious concern that the postslavery stability he and other abolitionists had predicted was in jeopardy. The "blameless conduct" of the former slaves on August 1 had confounded proslavery fears of bloodshed. But it was also necessary to vindicate the oft-expressed abolitionist faith in the economic superiority of free labor: "Show all," he urged the blacks, "that liberty makes better labourers than slavery, and the honourable and happy motives of freedom produce better industry than all the powers of slavery can do." The

---

10. *British Emancipator*, January 9, 1839, p. 198; *Liberator*, March 15, 1838, p. 44.
11. Stuart to Weld, December 11, 1838, WP.
12. *Anti-Slavery Reporter*, I (1840), 222; "Address of Capt. Stuart at Tobago," December 26, 1838, reprinted in *British Emancipator*, March 20, 1830, title page.

freedmen should be law-abiding, so that no one had reason to blame them "as idle, or disorderly, or troublesome." They should avoid getting into debt, and they should not be tempted to improve themselves by leaving the island.[13]

If such homilies were conciliatory and reassuring to the planters, he also made it clear that his aims were not to provide them with a captive, submissive labor force. The preservation of the plantation economy was essential, but the fundamentals of slavery must be obliterated. The freedmen were urged to marry because "society is every where wretched and vicious where woman is degraded; and it is always happy in proportion as women are honoured and improved." They were urged to educate themselves and their children. And above all they were urged to insist on wages in money and on legal, written leases for their houses.[14]

Inevitably he placed great emphasis on religion. Marriage was extolled as "an appointment of God." The Sabbath must be kept as "a day of sweet and sacred communion with God," and the freedmen should obtain Bibles as soon as they could do so by honest means. They should "remember God continually, and try, above all things, in all things to please." All of this was, of course, consistent with the religion that had always been fundamental to his abolitionism. But what emerged strongly for the first time in this lecture was that his concern for racial equality was accompanied by ethnocentric contempt for African barbarism. In upholding the sanctity of marriage he was well aware that slavery had encouraged the proliferation of "adulterers and whoremongers," who would earn God's wrath. But he also recoiled puritanically from imported profanities "such as your bellie dance." The freedmen, he "earnestly advised," should "give up all such amusement, immediately and for ever": "Cultivate a better taste that you and your children may have better pleasures. One chief reason why Africa has been so long plundered of her children is, that the people of Africa still keep themselves in ignorance and vice by such practices."[15]

Here was revealed an underlying reason for his opposition to Liberia, which had not been conspicuous during his campaigns against the American Colonization Society. It was an attitude that was not unusual in the period, but it made logical his subsequent support for the African Civilization Society, an organization that was about to emerge as T. F. Bux-

13. "Address of Capt. Stuart," *ibid.*
14. *Ibid.*
15. *Ibid.*

ton's solution to the problem of redirecting abolitionist energies and was to be suspected by many abolitionists as a colonizationist Trojan horse.[16]

That later commitment was never to make him an intimate of Buxton or to alienate him completely from those abolitionists with whom he had recently been closely associated and who, even now, were in the process of forming the British and Foreign Anti-Slavery Society. Throughout his West Indian tour he was to remain in contact with Joseph Sturge in particular. He had already written to him twice in early December from Barbados; he wrote again on Christmas Day from Tobago and on January 5 from St. Vincent.[17]

After a brief return to Barbados in January, 1839, Stuart departed with John Scoble on a two-month visit to British Guiana. For a time he was well received even by the master class, unlike Scoble, who seemed to go out of his way to provoke controversy. Both men addressed public meetings attended by masters and former slaves. With Stuart a silent spectator, Scoble was constantly heckled by planters in a meeting at Charlestown, Demerara. The controversy was ostensibly about incidents that had allegedly occurred during Scoble's antiapprenticeship campaign in Cornwall the previous year. But Scoble had antagonized his audience by remarking disparagingly on the unexpected presence of the "most wealthy and influential." By contrast, at a meeting at New Amsterdam, Berbice, Stuart seemed determined to uphold the plantation economy by scolding the freedmen for symptoms of idleness. Such behavior would "strengthen the fetters of the slave in other lands" by making credible proslavery claims that blacks would work only if coerced. Privately, as a letter to Weld a few months later indicated, and as he was to make clear in a still later public speech, Stuart was impressed by the bearing of the blacks in Berbice and not nearly as critical of their indolence as his lecture suggested.[18] For the moment, however, he had made himself a popular figure among the master class.

That popularity could not last for long, and he was soon to be as outspoken as Scoble in condemning what appeared to be a sinister attempt to

16. Temperley, *British Antislavery*, 42–61.
17. Stuart listed the dates and places of origin of ten letters he had sent to Sturge between December 5, 1838, and May 15, 1839, in a letter he sent to both Sturge and Weld from Basseterre, St. Kitts, June 8, 1839, WP.
18. *British Emancipator*, May 15, 1839, title page; Green, *British Slave Emancipation*, 191 n. 2; Stuart to Weld, June 8, 1839, WP; British and Foreign Anti-Slavery Society, *Proceedings of the General Anti-Slavery Convention Called by the Committee of the British and Foreign Anti-Slavery Society and Held in London from Fri. June 12 to Tues. June 23, 1840* (London, 1841), 532–33.

introduce a new form of slavery into British Guiana. A group of planters led by Sir John Gladstone had transported some four hundred Indian coolies to Guiana on five-year contracts, promising eventual return passages to those who desired them. The two abolitionists soon heard rumors of floggings and other cruelties and of coolies fleeing into the bush. Attempting to investigate, Stuart was refused entry to one of Gladstone's estates, Vriedenhoop. Later he managed to visit another estate, Highbury in Berbice, and, taking advantage of his Indian linguistic training, interview the coolies. Exactly what took place is impossible to substantiate because the only detailed account was provided by a certain William Hilhouse, who wrote an indignant letter to the press denouncing Stuart and Scoble as "prying inquisitors, who have no business in Demerara, or any where else." According to Hilhouse, Stuart had told the coolies "they would never get back to India, but that as fast as their period of service expired with one employer they would be made over to another, esto perpetua." This "harangue" had the effect of "disorganizing" the coolies "and inducing an immediate strike."[19]

Stuart made no detailed reply to this version of events but flatly denied that he was "poisoning the minds of the agricultural labourers of this province" and ridiculed the "insanely slanderous abuse" by Hilhouse. The editor of the *Colonial Reformer* implicitly endorsed Stuart's criticisms by inserting in brackets through the published version of Hilhouse's letter a running tally of his "fictions" about Stuart. In effect, the editor was saying, little credence could be given to a man who alleged that Stuart ("a rigid *water* drinker") was addicted to pineapple punch and who believed that the title "Captain" had been earned aboard "an East Indian Tea Ship."[20]

Eventually it was to be Scoble who did most to press home the criticisms of Indian coolie exploitation. Recovering from a severe bout of yellow fever, which had given substance to Stuart's recent misgivings about "climates of the borders of death," Scoble succeeded in persuading the governor to order a commission of inquiry into the alleged cruelties on Vriedenhoop estate, and he also pressed charges in a criminal court against the manager of another plantation. Although Scoble was less than satisfied with the punishments eventually meted out at the end of these judicial processes, he had at least ensured that the worst abuses of Indian labor were publicized and checked. And he had incidentally given the lie

19. "Inquiry Obstructed: or 'A Great Stir in Demerara,'" and "A Feather in the Cap of Capt. Stuart," *British Emancipator*, June 26, 1839, 258.
20. Ibid.

to a further allegation by Hilhouse that he was "lamentably deficient" in the courage that had induced Stuart to enter the controversy.[21]

By the time Scoble had thus forced the issue nearly to a climax in April, 1839, Stuart had left the colony. The two men had decided that he must continue the tour of investigation alone, in the hope that Scoble's health would permit a reunion later in Antigua, St. Kitts, or Nevis. By late March Stuart was in Trinidad in the midst of what the local newspaper was soon to describe as "an extensive, although rapid, examination of the Colony." His reactions were extremely favorable, judging from a lecture he gave in Port of Spain on April 11 to an audience in which masters heavily outnumbered laborers. And once again his main criterion of assessment was the survival of the plantation economy under the new conditions of free labor:

> I adore the gracious Providence which enables me to say, that the state of this island disappoints my fears, and vastly exceeds my expectations. The general condition of your labouring classes, at this moment, is happy almost beyond compare. I am perfectly satisfied, that it is now the universal effort of the masters to hire labour at fair and liberal rates; and I am equally convinced, that, as generally as can be reasonably expected, it is the desire of the labourers to find employment at the same, especially on their former plantation.

Naturally his audience was delighted. According to the Trinidad *Standard*, "the lecture was received not only with marked respect, but with many demonstrations of approbation. It evinced an extensive inquiry, an anxiety for attaining the truth, and a greater degree of impartiality than we could have anticipated."[22]

From Trinidad Stuart sailed north in late April to spend two months in the Windward and Leeward Islands, visiting in turn Grenada, St. Vincent, St. Lucia, Dominica, Antigua, Montserrat, St. Kitts, Nevis, and Tortola. To judge from the long lithographed letter in which he reported his experiences to both British and American abolitionists, this proved to be the most satisfying part of his West Indian tour. His crowded itinerary left him with little opportunity to lecture as frequently as he had done hitherto. But as in Trinidad, his enthusiasm seems to have impressed (and possibly relieved) the local white establishments. Certainly his usual mode of procedure involved close liaison with leading officials and planters. For

---

21. "Mr. Scoble's Lecture at Demerara," *ibid.*, May 15, 1839, pp. 245–46; Scoble to Sturge, May 22, 1839, *ibid.*, July 24, 1839, title page.

22. Stuart to Weld and Sturge, June 8, 1839, WP; *British Emancipator*, June 12, 1839, p. 255, June 26, 1839, p. 260.

instance, in St. Lucia he pursued his tour of investigation in company with the chief justice, Reddie, and impressed the editor of the local newspaper with "the justice he rendered our fellow inhabitants." He interviewed the governor, chief justice, and attorney general in Dominica and the stipendiary magistrates in virtually every colony. His optimism seemed to grow as he moved from island to island. At the end of a week he concluded that Dominica was one of the happiest colonies he had visited. But almost at once he found Antigua "still happier" and then Montserrat, in some respects, "the happiest island which I have yet seen." Soon he was "delighted with St. Kitts—not on account of its surface, for it has a great quantity of parched and barren land, but on account of its moral and social condition."[23]

Subsequent trends in the West Indies can make his mounting euphoria seem almost naive. Almost certainly there was an element of wishful thinking in the way his investigations seemed to discover all the proper ingredients previously prescribed for the postslavery situation by abolitionist theorists, including himself. Thus in Antigua education was being organized, free villages had been founded and were expanding, and a happy labor force was continuing to work the sugar plantations, with the result that "the last crop had been an exceedingly fine one" and there were good prospects for the immediate future. Similarly, St. Kitts had flourishing churches and schools, "beautiful" mutual benefit societies, and, despite its physical disadvantages, very promising agrarian prospects. Perhaps he was too willing to draw conclusions from exceptional situations without sufficient consideration as to what might be typical. In this category can be placed his praise for one Louis Bellot in Dominica, who, "having a sugar estate and 80 labourers under him, has commuted their allowance of rum into an equivalent in money or molasses, at their discretion." And the same doubts are prompted by his visit to an Antigua estate, where he was shown "cottages of remarkable commodiousness and comfort and I saw the people happy."[24]

But notwithstanding these criticisms it would be unfair to see Stuart as either the dupe of plantocratic interests or culpably superficial in his analysis of island conditions. Despite his close contacts with the white establishment, his overriding concern continued to be the welfare of the black populace, and his highest praise was reserved for their general conduct in

---

23. Stuart to Weld and Sturge, June 8, 1839, WP; *British Emancipator*, July 10, 1839, p. 266.
24. Stuart to Weld and Sturge, June 8, 1839, WP.

situations that still needed much improvement. As he wrote to Theodore Weld,

> Had I time and strength, I could write you things that would cheer your soul in relation to the population of these islands. Generally speaking, they are a noble race of men; with grievous faults indeed; but with eminently admirable qualities. Of the *three* great charges brought against them, that if freed at once in a body they would be: 1. *revengeful*, 2. vagabond and 3. idle; the two first are acknowledged by every body to be totally disproved, and a fair enquiry into every fact is all that is requisite as abundantly to disprove the latter. Their intelligence, whether cultivated or not, their peacefulness, their docility, and their sobriety, are amongst their prominent characteristics.[25]

And despite his regard for numerous whites—including the "charming" Bellot, the "noble" governor of Antigua, Sir William Colebrook, and his "bright and generous" secretaries[26]—Stuart's warmest anecdotes concerned the black response to emancipation.

In St. Lucia he had met a refugee slave from Martinique who had swiftly made himself indispensable to the proprietor of a sugar estate in the northern part of the island. The estate had virtually ceased production when apprenticeship came to an end and its labor force evaporated. But the refugee "found no difficulty in hiring twenty-five labourers, and in conducting the manufacture to advantage," and he went on to use a further fifteen hired laborers to dig a canal. Well aware that St. Kitts had experienced some of the worst racial tensions at the time of the 1834 Emancipation Act, when apprenticeship was ushered in under martial law, Stuart took delight in reporting an encounter with a black named Conrad, who had been emancipated only the previous August. Now head laborer on a sugar plantation, Conrad boarded and lodged in his own cottage "an intelligent poor white man," whom he paid to instruct him in reading, writing, and arithmetic.[27]

But Stuart knew that such men were unusual and also that the planters' attitudes had not changed so abruptly that even exceptional blacks would automatically be given opportunities to advance themselves and excel. At every stage of his progress through the Windward and Leeward Islands his optimism was based on the existence of the impartial stipendiary magistracy which he had found crucially lacking in Barbados. In St. Kitts the stipendiaries had been the "great healers of the deep wounds inflicted upon

---

25. Stuart to Weld, June 8, 1839, WP.
26. Stuart to Weld and Sturge, June 8, 1839, WP.
27. *Proceedings of the General Anti-Slavery Convention, 1840*, 532–33; Stuart to Weld and Sturge, June 8, 1839, WP; Green, *British Slave Emancipation*, 131 n.

the labouring population by the atrocities of August 1834," when militiamen had enforced martial law and driven runaways back to the plantations. Montserrat surpassed all colonies "in the security enjoyed by its people, in their houses, on the plantations, and in the fruits of their provision grounds" because of the "happy, just and powerful influence there of the stipendiary, Warren." In Dominica he was delighted to discover that one stipendiary magistrate was Joseph Phillips, his staunch ally during the campaign against Elliott Cresson some seven years before. His job made Phillips "one of the most importantly useful men in the island." Stuart's conclusion that the stipendiaries here exercised "a very benign and powerful influence" rested, however, on more than loyalty to an old friend. He recounted in detail how a conflict between an estate manager and his labor force over wages and conditions had been resolved by the intelligent conciliation of another stipendiary, Lynch. In keeping with these anecdotes he ended his report to Weld and Sturge from Basseterre, St. Kitts, on June 8 with a quotation allegedly from a local stipendiary whose words seemed conspicuously like Stuart's: " 'Let England continue to watch and support us. I feel that I need such supervision, both to animate me to duty, and to encourage and sustain me in its performance. These Colonies need the controlling and purifying influences of the British and the Christian heart, as much to evolve with real benefit to all the glorious law of liberty, as they did, the same, to extirpate the slave system, so nefarious and hateful.' "[28]

Stuart needed his unique resources of enthusiasm and optimism, for his two months since leaving Trinidad had been particularly arduous and, despite the many passing encounters with kindred spirits such as Phillips, he had been traveling alone as well as traveling hard. The expected rendezvous with Scoble had not materialized because of the latter's continuing ill-health. Something of his loneliness was conveyed by the enthusiasm with which he looked for news from his friends. His heart, he wrote early in June, had been "panting for intelligence from Britain and America." He had been excited to receive in St. Kitts letters from Sturge, Theodore and Angelina, and "one from my dearly beloved William and Mary Blair": "My soul is refreshed. I bless the Lord. Oh how sweet and magnanimous, and rich and unwearied is His love to us. . . . Oh how excellent beyond compare, how perfect is God! Our God! unchangeably ours! bound to us by His own blood, poured out in love!"[29] He felt he needed such refreshment for, as he reminded Angelina Weld, he was now "verg-

28. Stuart to Weld and Sturge, June 8, 1839, WP.
29. *Ibid.*

ing upon 60 . . . weary and worn and only half a man." This comment prefaced an apology for not writing more extensively and should not be taken at face value as an indication of either imminent physical collapse or of self-pity. Stuart's letters at this and every period were as notable for their lack of concern about personal physical privation as they were replete with spiritual introspection. It was far more typical that in the same letter he condemned his own "indolence and selfishness" in momentarily considering curtailing his arduous journey. That temptation was swiftly rejected, but there was a further revealing reference to the strains of his travels when he again apologized to Weld and Sturge for the inadequacies of his report: "This disorder you will readily and kindly account for when you remember the constant urgency of getting onward which is upon me, that I am overwhelmed with occupation during my stay, that nausea at sea unfits me for every thing, and that the utmost which I have energy to do, beyond the imperative and ceaseless urgency of daily and local occupation, is to scrawl, rather [than] to write the few letters, which I have written." Although the idea of returning directly to England from St. Kitts in June had been swiftly discarded, Stuart's firm intention, as he sailed via Nevis, Tortola, and Cap Haitien to Jamaica, was to spend only a brief time there before proceeding to New York "and thence, without undue delay, to England." Apart from the rigors of travel, he was finding the expense of his tour very heavy.[30] But the situation in Jamaica was to prove altogether too complex and challenging to allow a short visit.

RESENTMENT AT the premature end of apprenticeship had been most bitter in Britain's largest and most populous Caribbean colony. Receiving no compensation for the loss of two years' expected compulsory labor and with the colony abruptly losing the revenue from a poll tax on apprentices, the Jamaica planter oligarchy faced considerable economic problems. But their objections were most vocal against the wider political and constitutional implications of British control. Much of the assembly's legislation for the postapprenticeship period had already been disallowed before August 1, 1838. And then in that month the British Parliament had passed the West India Prisons Act, which seemed even further to emphasize the subordinate status of the colonial legislature. The act followed an inquiry into British West Indian prisons, which had revealed grossly unsanitary and insecure conditions. The West Indian oligarchies tended to accept the need for reforms, pointing out that public prisons had assumed a new importance because most discipline had previously been ad-

30. Stuart to Weld, June 8, 1839; Stuart to Weld and Sturge, June 8, 1839, WP.

ministered privately on the plantations. Indeed, reform had already been initiated in Barbados—in ways noted by Stuart and Scoble—and the Jamaica assembly resented having reform imposed from outside rather than being allowed the independence to devise its own measures. In response, it announced a moratorium on all public business until the act was withdrawn.[31]

The governor of Jamaica, Sir Lionel Smith, dissolved the assembly in November, 1838. New elections returned an assembly even more vocal in its repudiation of British interference. Smith may have overreacted to the opposition in his conjectures about future violence, which foresaw a planter-led militia tyrannizing the black population. But he was well aware that the principles of freedom and legislative independence were being invoked by a body elected by fewer than 2,000 voters out of a population of 350,000. His recommendation that the assembly be removed received some support at the Colonial Office, where one school of thought considered that a uniform system of crown colony government would best protect the interests of the emancipated West Indian blacks. The powerful permanent undersecretary, James Stephen, however, was committed to representative government, even though he was a firm supporter of Negro freedom. Responding to his advice, the cabinet of Lord Melbourne adopted the compromise measure of suspending the Jamaican constitution for five years rather than permanently abolishing the assembly.[32]

But even this course was politically controversial, not least because the suspension of the constitution of Lower Canada a year before gave it a wider relevance. The leader of the opposition, Robert Peel, stressed the demoralizing effects of such suspensions on colonial opinion throughout the empire, and he was joined in his denunciation by a disparate group from across the political spectrum. There were radical supporters of the government, who were prepared to withdraw their support because of the issue of colonial liberty. There was Lord Brougham, normally a staunch supporter of the blacks but nursing a grudge against Melbourne for excluding him from his second ministry. And there were arch-conservatives such as the duke of Wellington and the traditional supporters of the West India interest. Even with the defection of ten Radicals from the government the opposition was not strong enough to defeat the measure when it was put to the vote in the House of Commons on May 6. But Mel-

31. *British Emancipator*, January 9, 1839, pp. 195, 198, 199; Green, *British Slave Emancipation*, pp. 164–65.
32. Green, *British Slave Emancipation*, pp. 164–65.

bourne interpreted the narrow, five-vote victory as a rebuff and resigned.[33]

The fall of the government was only temporary. But although Melbourne swiftly returned to power when Queen Victoria refused to relinquish her ladies-in-waiting and Peel declined to form a government, the effects of the crisis on Caribbean policy were profound. When a new Jamaican measure received scarcely stronger support, the government decided to abandon its attempts to coerce the planters. In June, 1839, as Stuart headed toward Jamaica, Sir Lionel Smith was replaced as governor by Sir Charles Metcalfe, who was encouraged to pursue new policies of conciliation. The burning problem in Jamaica, as elsewhere in the Caribbean, was maintaining the plantation system now that freedmen had the opportunity to support themselves either by squatting on vacant land or by purchasing freeholds through savings from wages. In effect the new policies were to involve an attempt to save the plantation system by reinforcing the authority of the planters rather than by attempting to improve conditions for labor.[34]

At the time of Stuart's arrival in Jamaica these new policies had yet to be introduced, but already the *volte-face* by the imperial government was deeply suspect in antislavery circles. Stuart's associates in the Central Negro Emancipation Committee had strongly supported the suspension of the Jamaican constitution. On June 12 the committee's organ, the *British Emancipator*, reported its recent strong resolutions against the rumored decision to recall Sir Lionel Smith, gave strong editorial support to Smith, and berated the "Jamaica tyrants." With the Jamaican question so much in the news, Stuart at this stage was the source of slightly puzzled concern to his abolitionist friends as reports of his optimistic reactions to conditions in other colonies filtered through. The same page of the *British Emancipator* carried news of his April lecture in Trinidad in which, "if we are to believe the Trinidad *Standard*," he had expressed confidence in the future of a plantation economy based on free and equitable master-servant relations. On June 26 the paper's editorial page informed its readers that "the spirit of oppression . . . rages dreadfully" in Jamaica and reported the "deepest regret and dismay" at Smith's recall expressed by Birmingham abolitionists in a memorial to the colonial secretary. The same editorial commented on Stuart's reception in Trinidad with obvious caution. Noting that "the Trinidadians of course exalt him to the skies," the paper remarked that Stuart's favorable view was a source of "unfeigned

33. Ibid.
34. Ibid.

pleasure," which would be even greater "if information from other sources shall altogether corroborate it." Perhaps to reassure themselves as well as their readers, the editors recalled the "very different honours heaped upon him in Demerara" by William Hilhouse.[35]

But if British abolitionists had momentary fears that Stuart might have unwittingly become the mouthpiece of the planter class, these were allayed when he dispatched detailed descriptions of the Jamaican scene soon after his arrival in July. These reports began to reach England in August and September in time to be read and discussed at the first meetings of the British and Foreign Anti-Slavery Society. And soon publication of copious extracts from these letters in the *British Emancipator* revealed that Stuart had in no way changed his fundamental beliefs: his desire to see the plantation economy maintained was still subordinate to the priority of racial and social justice. The introductory paragraphs to these extracts summed up the antislavery case against Jamaican trends with typical Stuart vigor:

> Jamaica is mourning the expected departure of Sir Lionel Smith—Jamaica is astounded at the ignorance, the feebleness, or the corruption of the government, which removes him, at this time especially. A faction in Jamaica, probably not numbering more than 2000, worshipping still their great idols, sugar and rum, and insanely dreaming that fraud and force are better ways of getting sugar and rum than equity and kindness, is triumphing in the suicidal success of its machinations; but the Lord reigneth, and bids the earth rejoice.
>
> The difficulties of this island consist fundamentally in the desire of the proprietors, or their agents, to get as much sugar and rum as possible, with the smallest possible remuneration to the labourers employed; so that instances have abounded in which the labourers, after working well and hard for the week, at the end of it have been brought in, sometimes debtors, sometimes with a fraction only of their earnings, on the most unworthy pretences.[36]

Stuart supported these allegations with detailed analysis of the reasons why the plantation economy was in jeopardy. To some extent the crucial alienation of the labor force had been the result of the "crazy and criminal apprenticeship system," which had frustrated "immediate and thorough emancipation" in 1834. The "ferocious and insane abuses" that had char-

35. *British Emancipator*, June 12, 1839, p. 255; June 26, 1839, p. 260.
36. Minutes of BFASS, S. 20, E2/6, August 30, September 27, 1839, RHL; *British Emancipator*, July 24, 1839, p. 305.

acterized the apprenticeship period had done much to alienate the blacks. Even then, he felt sure, "had they been wisely, firmly, and kindly governed, according to the emancipation law, little or no difficulty would have been found with them." But the planters had immediately revealed their vindictive, grasping attitudes by demanding rent for the initial three-month period of freedom in which the abolition law had guaranteed the blacks occupancy of their former slave cottages and provision grounds. These demands had been legally upheld by the island attorney general, and bitter disputes had followed on some estates with strikes, destruction of provision grounds, litigation against defaulting tenants, and the use of armed constabulary to suppress riots.[37]

Stuart did not condone violent protests, but he provided detailed calculations to show that in general throughout the island inadequate wages and exorbitant rents made the flight from the plantations inevitable. The freedmen were paying annual rents greater than the freehold value of their cottages and provision grounds. And yet when they understandably found alternatives "in the most harmless, lawful, industrious and manly manner, as they usually do, then they are blamed for ingratitude and idleness; the destitution of continuous labour is proclaimed, and the cry of ruin is thundered through the land."[38]

Very soon Stuart decided that these critical conditions demanded much more sustained investigation. On July 30 he wrote from Kingston to Weld that because of the conditions he had found, he now proposed staying in Jamaica until late November and then returning directly to England instead of going by way of New York. The main problem, he told Weld—as he had told British abolitionists—lay in the "blind and selfish attempts" of the "slave spirit" to exploit the emancipated blacks. He did not add—what he knew only too well—that the "slave spirit" was a dangerous adversary for known abolitionists. His friend A. L. Palmer had been imprisoned for twenty-one days by the House of Assembly for a breach of its privileges, which in essence consisted of giving publicity in the island to critical comments that had appeared in the *British Emancipator*.[39]

Undeterred by the planters' hostility, Stuart proceeded to pursue his investigations with painstaking thoroughness and to report fearlessly the truth as he perceived it. He interviewed a proprietor who had been obliged to close his estate because he could not get labor and concluded that the man's arbitrary treatment of freedmen explained this situation and belied

---

37. *British Emancipator*, July 24, 1839, p. 305.
38. *Ibid.*
39. Stuart to Weld, July 30, 1839, WP; *Anti-Slavery Reporter*, I (1840), 4, 12, 21.

his reputation as "one of the wisest men in the island." He attended court sessions and listened to cases that demonstrated similar white arrogance. And in August he made excursions to two settlements of recently imported white laborers at the eastern extremity of the island. One consisted of thirteen Scottish families brought out by an individual named Patterson. The other, at Altamont in Portland parish, had been sponsored by the local government and had originally contained some eighteen families. In both settlements attractive surroundings masked even more serious problems, in Stuart's eyes, than the unhealthy conditions that had already carried off many people with fever. At Altamont the settlers had no legal title to their dwellings; employment opportunities in the immediate vicinity were poor; there was no market at which they could dispose of any agricultural surplus; and social conditions were morally depraved, with drunkenness rife.[40]

At the second settlement Stuart was assailed by a chorus of despairing parents who bemoaned the lack of employment opportunities for their children and of educational and medical facilities. He could "scarcely stand the scene, as they thronged round me in the little cottage room in which we attended worship together, and while they bent upon me their eager gaze." But despite his compassion he felt some rough justice had prevailed. The settlement might have succeeded with better planning and leadership and with a good schoolmaster in attendance. But this in itself would have been unjust, for the underlying motive of its planners was the "proud, insane, and cruel object" of "crushing" the native laborers down to meager wages by introducing foreign laborers.[41]

While Stuart was thus preoccupied, his failure to arrive in the United States in July, as originally planned, caused some concern among his American friends until his letter of July 30 reached Weld in mid-September. Both Grimké sisters wrote expressing their anxiety and the belief, in Sarah's words, that "if his life and health have been preserved" he must have returned directly to Britain. For Angelina this conclusion was disappointing as well as reassuring: "As the best beloved friend of my Theodore, and as a truly Christian philanthropist, I have greatly desired to see him under our roof, and to know him, for as yet I have had a very slight acquaintance with him; but he is doing a great work and I desire not that he should come down from it. I am willing to wait the Lord's time."[42]

    40. Stuart, "The 'General System,'" *British Emancipator*, July 24, 1839, p. 303; Stuart, "White Labourers in Jamaica," *ibid*.
    41. Stuart, "White Labourers in Jamaica," p. 303.
    42. Angelina Grimké Weld to Elizabeth Pease, August 14, 1839, Sarah Grimké to E. Pease, August 25, 1839, in Taylor, *British and American Abolitionists*, 78–83.

The Lord's time, Stuart soon decided, involved a still longer stay in Jamaica. On October 10 he again wrote to Weld, saying that he now expected to remain until March but would then, after all, return to Britain via New York. This letter demonstrated once again that Weld was indeed Stuart's own "best beloved friend" but that such friendship had to be secondary to the quest for "impartial truth":

> Why have I not written to you again & again—Because I am the abortive thing which is called Charles Stuart—Have I loved you the less?—You know that I have not; and the reason, is the same, except that in this, there is no abortion—O, how sweet & rich it is, a gift of God.
>
> My delay in this island has thwarted all my temporal plans; and some of them very bitterly—yet even that bitterness is sweet—I am convinced that it is dutiful; and this, you know, is our soul's delight and shall be through him that loveth & strengtheneth us, however it may crucify our infernal desires.

He had always felt that truth was the great object of every benevolent association and above all of the antislavery societies: "I am staying here in order to explore it." His inquiries were still circumscribed, but he felt it best to write at once with his interim conclusions.[43]

These ideas proved to be very detailed, and, as he wrote substantially the same letter two weeks later to Joseph Sturge, they amounted to a copious report to both British and American abolitionists. Although his tone was often optimistic, his report could only have confirmed the misgivings of his antislavery colleagues in Britain. The "Blessings of Jamaica" lay mainly in the "general character and conduct of the labourers" and the "happy & generous influence of the local executive & of the home Government." His British readers knew only too well that the home government, in recalling the local executive, Sir Lionel Smith, had abandoned its attempts to exercise a restraining influence on the Jamaican planters. The bulk of Stuart's report was a chilling appraisal of the power and attitudes of that traditional ruling class: "The elective franchise, is miserably circumscribed, and the elected form a malcontent, selfish & dangerous oligarchy." When apprenticeship had ended, the planters had indulged "insane notions" about maintaining a virtual slavery: "They still felt *like* slave holders—Even yet, I scarcely find a trace of *real repentance* amongst them for their enormous crime, in having framed & perpetrated the slave system. They dreamt (the waking and monstrous dream!) that they had

---

43. Stuart to Weld, October 10, 1839, WP; Stuart to Sturge, October 23, 24, 1839, S. 22, G. 61, RHL.

nothing to do, but to devise amongst themselves, what wages they would give, and what terms they would propose, and that then, the labourers would have nothing to do, but servilely to follow their devisings." He gave detailed examples of the terms concocted by two of the most respectable planters. And he pointed out that much of the "wild clamour" that had arisen against the blacks resulted from their "manly aversion" to such procedures and also to the attempts by masters to bind them to a form of "villeinage" through control of cottage rents and tenures.[44]

The Negroes, too, he conceded, had exhibited certain "grievous errors" on securing freedom. One, still not fully eradicated, was the belief that "'Missus Queen,' as they call her, had given their cottages, grounds & fruit trees to them, and that their masters were guilty of fraud in keeping them back." This misconception, however, was understandable, morally if not legally justified, because, in most cases, they had built their cottages themselves, planted and maintained the fruit trees, and used as provision grounds mainly "mountain lands, used for no other purpose by their masters." The freedmen had also understandably objected to the notion that they should work nine hours per day because even under apprenticeship—"that crazy & criminal system of expiring despotism"—they had, in theory, been required to labor only seven or eight hours (although in practice usually *"much more"* was exacted). The blacks indeed emerged as heroes in Stuart's report: "Emancipation was yielded with so slow a hand—and when yielded, was clogged in its operation, by attempts at legislation, so flagrantly unjust, and by measures so repulsive, that I know of no people but the Negroes, who could have borne so much evil, with so little return in kind." But planters' attitudes made continuing supervision essential: "Every new inquiry demonstrates to me more and more, the importance of an observer on the spot—and satisfies me, more and more, with my decision to remain."[45]

Over the next four months Stuart continued to observe, inquire, and report back extensively, via Joseph Sturge and the new *Anti-Slavery Reporter*, to British abolitionists. He visited plantations, courts, and jails. He interviewed planters, magistrates, clerics, black laborers, and additional groups of white immigrants. His reports revealed much continuing abuse. White immigrant communities had been decimated by disease, and most were in desperate economic and psychological situations. Visiting the jail at Savanna la Mar, he was repelled by the "nauseous smell" and outraged by the inadequate separation of the sexes. But what he found

44. Stuart to Weld, October 10, 1839, WP.
45. *Ibid.*

most "grievous" were the charges on which two young women and one man had been convicted. Their cases, which involved failure to meet demands for rent, were particular examples of what he discovered to be a general trend. There were many cases before the courts involving failure to pay arbitrarily doubled rents and as many others in which landlords were claiming separate rentals from each member of a family occupying the same dwelling.[46]

Such cases, he felt, were central to the most basic problems of Jamaica. Blacks were being victimized by their former owners and being tried by local magistrates drawn from the same elite. Moreover, irregular sittings were leading to heavy arrears of court business, which, in turn, were impoverishing the blacks and paralyzing the plantation economy because those charged were sometimes compelled to wait for days in the vicinity of the courtroom until their cases could be heard.[47]

Stuart did what he could to overcome the evils he identified. But action could rarely be as effective as when he insisted, through a special magistrate, that lime be supplied to combat the unsanitary conditions at the Savanna jail. He threw himself wholeheartedly into the movement to establish free villages and thus liberate blacks from the planters' control of living quarters and family provision grounds. This strategy was already having some effect, but it was to be some time before events would prove that the blacks who became freeholders would be reluctant to work for wages on the plantations. Stuart can thus be partly excused for failing to see that the development of free villages might jeopardize the plantation economy which he was insisting could and should be revitalized. But on other questions he well knew that the most he could do was demand and recommend action. He suggested that a parliamentary commission be established to inquire into white immigration since 1833. And, overall, he reminded his abolitionist friends that hopes of freedom in the West Indies depended on constant pressure on "the home government to make and keep it right if possible."[48]

Probably few of his friends and acquaintances remained optimistic when they read those words in the *Anti-Slavery Reporter* among continuing criticisms of the abdication of authority by the home government. Stuart's catalog of Jamaican ills seemed so full and reform so dependent on nonexistent British controls that optimism was an unlikely reaction to the grim conditions he had observed. And yet he himself remained sublimely op-

---

46. Extracts from letters by Stuart to Sturge, January 11, 25, February 4, 1840, *Anti-Slavery Reporter*, I (1840), 61, 70–71.
47. Ibid., 70–71.
48. Ibid.

timistic: "Many of the estates are gloomily standing still, determined to flourish, as of old, by oppression, or to perish. I cannot fear, indeed, that they will go on to perish, neither can I hope that oppression will altogether cease; but pride knows how to bow to necessity; and God has given to youthful freedom in Jamaica a growth so vigorous, that the weeds seek in vain to overpower her. She is rising beautifully above them all." Overtly his optimism rested on sustained faith in the potential of the black population. Amid all their problems they displayed "patient manliness": "They are too strong in the law, in the churches, in the wants of the estates, in their own ready industry, and in the supervision of Great Britain, to be crushed. They are steadily, peaceably, and irresistibly rising above the lawless freaks of oppression which dash over one another."[49]

His conclusions may have been in part a result of his isolation from British antislavery opinion. He looked forward to the arrival of Sir Charles Metcalfe with "bright hopes" that were certainly not shared by his friends who had lobbied so hard against the recall of Sir Lionel Smith. But Jamaica's future economic stagnation and racial turmoil seem so clearly foreshadowed in his descriptions that this isolation alone cannot explain an optimism that seems almost ludicrously naive.[50]

Wishful thinking in relation to some of his own long-cherished antislavery principles provides part of the explanation. In particular, he was reluctant to repudiate the faith in the economic superiority of free over slave labor which he had asserted so trenchantly in *The West India Question*. Sugar production, though diminished, was flourishing remarkably considering the problems of the months since the end of apprenticeship; he was confident that it would improve in the future. Increased cultivation costs were only temporary, and time would prove that, with the end of the destructive slave system, some sugar estates would be run more economically than formerly. And he also hoped cultivation of other crops, such as coffee and cotton, would greatly increase. Throughout his antislavery career he had been almost a figure of fun in his determination to boycott all slave-grown produce; now he eagerly foresaw the day when Jamaica might produce cotton in such quantities that people everywhere could dress themselves "in clean raiment, and not, as now, in habiliments steeped in the blood of the guiltless poor."[51]

His optimism, however, went beyond a desire to see particular points in his antislavery creed vindicated. Optimism was psychologically essen-

49. *Ibid.*, 70.
50. Stuart to Sturge, October 23, 24, 1839, S. 22, G. 61, RHL.
51. *Ibid.*

tial to maintain the momentum of his activity. He was too honest not to report in detail all the ills and abuses he discovered in Jamaica. But without the tenacious faith that virtue would eventually triumph, he would never have completed investigations that were almost prodigious in their scope for a man of his age. At the beginning of his letter to Weld in early October he had written wistfully of his desire to see again old friends and relatives and added: "How my soul craves rest!" He had sustained his resolve to remain in Jamaica by recalling how the two of them had walked near Cincinnati some five years before at the outset of the great American antislavery crusade and his young friend had sighed: "Oh where shall rest be found"? Ceaseless activity had been the response of both men to that rhetorical question, and it was still Stuart's answer to the temptations of withdrawal from the campaign. He disclosed how he had recently traversed the parish of St. Mary, attending the petty court of sessions in each of three districts and accumulating much detailed information about rents and wages and about a recent civil disturbance in one area. "I sometimes get tired indeed," he had concluded that letter, "but I am quickly ashamed of it—and then, Oh, how much sweeter will rest be, when I can dutifully take it."[52]

The dutiful moment had still not arrived two months later. Nothing can so well convey the frenetic dedication of this sixty-year-old "half a man" than an extensive extract from a letter he wrote to Joseph Sturge in January, 1840:

> On Wednesday, 1st of January, I reached Hampden, Blyth's station, and that evening addressed a large meeting in his church, after laying the corner stone of a new free village, close by his dwelling. On Thursday, I visited with him Mr. George Gordon . . . distance several miles. On Friday visited Dundee estate, called at Orange Valley, laid the foundation of another new free village, about four or five miles distant. Both of these villages are founded on the tee-total temperance principle, and on both occasions we had very large and interesting companies. On Saturday, I went by Bethlephel to Salter's-hill, Dendy's, about twelve or fifteen miles, and on Sunday preached to his congregation, of about 2000 people, and spoke particularly afterwards to the church. On Monday returned from Salter's Hill to Hampden, distant about twelve miles, and attended an exceedingly interesting meeting in the evening in Blyth's church. On Tuesday, went to Bethlephel, and presided in the evening at an anti-slavery meeting in Dendy's church. On Wednesday, rode to breakfast at Montego Bay, distant about fourteen miles; and in the evening visited Burchell at Mount Carey, distant about nine miles. On Thursday, re-

52. Stuart to Weld, October 10, 1839, WP.

turned to Montego Bay to breakfast, and hurried over a few indispensable arrangements and inquiries and snatched the first time-fraction for this letter. I am now writing on Thursday evening, the 9th; tomorrow (Friday the 10th) I purpose attending the petty sessions at Adelphi, about eleven miles distant. On Saturday, the petty sessions, and the Mico school here, with personal inquiries from people attending market. On Sunday, 12th preaching in Burchell's church, &c; and on Monday, 13th, going to Mr. Hunter's for statistics. . . .

Sabbath, 12th January, 1840—It is now about 4 p.m. This is the first daylight hour in which I have had anything like rest since I left Dexter's. I have just returned from preaching as intended, and from partaking of the memorials of the dying love of our blessed Love. My subject was John v. 30. "My judgment is just, because I seek not my own will, but the will of my Father who sent me." The church, which is symmetrical and spacious, was filled; it seats 2000, there were probably 2500 present—a most decorous and solemn company. . . .

But I must hasten to snatch a fact or two before the light fails. I could give you many particulars that would refresh you, and some that would pain you, in relation to the condition of the negro population, but, admitting every exception, as a body it is well with them.[53]

Stuart's letter also revealed that a new aspect of the cause had engaged his attention. In early December more than five hundred Africans, recaptured by the Royal Navy from slaving vessels, had been landed in Jamaica. They were in good health and had been generally well treated except that insufficient regard was being paid to the character of those to whom they had been indentured for a period of one year. And in particular he objected to the enlistment of the physically strongest recaptives in Her Majesty's military forces. Stuart was neither the first nor the last to publicize the problem of such recaptives. But he was influential in persuading the British and Foreign Anti-Slavery Society to take up the issue. Extracts from two letters he wrote in early February were discussed in April by the society's committee, which decided that "they should be transmitted to the Colonial Office and the particular attention of Government solicited to this subject."[54]

Diligent though he was in thus exploring every aspect of the island situation, what was most striking about his activities was the way Jamaica became the scene for yet another Stuart antislavery campaign. The antislavery meeting referred to in his January letter to Sturge was not an

53. *Anti-Slavery Reporter*, I (1840), 61.
54. *Ibid.*; BFASS, April 30, 1840.

isolated incident. Improbable though it may seem in the circumstances, he was now in the midst of an attempt to do in Jamaica what he had done in Ireland in 1830 and 1831, in England in 1832 and 1833, in the United States from 1834 to 1837, and in the British Isles again in 1837 and 1838: he was preaching the abolition gospel as widely as possible in an endeavor to create a formal network of local antislavery societies. Not even Jamaica, with all its postslavery problems, should be allowed to ignore the wider problem of global slavery. On the recent Christmas Day he had chaired a public meeting at Falmouth at which resolutions were passed deploring especially the slave trade and slavery in the United States and calling for a general antislavery convention to be held in Spanish Town the following March. He followed up this meeting with a circular reporting it and inviting delegates to come from all over Jamaica to the planned convention. The main purpose of this gathering, he wrote, would be to select delegates to attend the next conventions of the American and British national societies in the following May and June.[55]

Others—both residents and visitors—played conspicuous parts in the March convention. A principal speaker was the English Quaker J. J. Gurney, who several times paused in his survey of West Indian conditions to seek the corroboration of "his friend Captain Stuart." But in view of his extensive speaking tours and his printed circular it seems reasonable to accept the assessment of the normally modest Stuart that he himself had been the "chief means" of calling the convention together. Along with W. W. Anderson, he was selected as a Jamaican delegate to attend the British and American conventions. A few days later the Kingston Anti-Slavery Society resolved that the same two men should be among its own delegates to the forthcoming conventions. The two other resolutions passed by that Kingston meeting neatly sum up Stuart's own attitudes at this stage of his career. The first asserted simply—and in a manner typical of a thousand such gatherings—that since slavery was opposed to the command of God and subversive of natural rights it was the duty of every individual to attempt its abolition. Just as no one had surpassed Stuart in acting on that principle over the previous decade, there were probably few abolitionists who would have so fully endorsed the conviction of the second resolution: "That the transition from slavery to freedom in this colony, has fully realized the reasonable expectations of its advocates, while it affords a practical demonstration of the fitness of the negro population to receive the boon."[56]

55. *Anti-Slavery Reporter*, I (1840), 60–61.
56. Ibid., 107–108; Stuart to John Morgan, June 3, 1840, S. 18, C22/26, RHL.

The attempt to link the infant Jamaican antislavery movement with both American and British abolitionism was, of course, equally typical of Stuart's international perspectives. But although he was uniquely well traveled in the cause, many others at this period were making serious attempts to foster international antislavery cooperation. His own close associates in the British movement—both before and after the transformation of the Central Negro Emancipation Committee into the British and Foreign Anti-Slavery Society—had for some months been urging his American associates to attend the 1840 British convention. The American response had been favorable, and by the time he was ready at last to leave Jamaica, plans were already well developed to make the June convention in London effectively a world antislavery gathering.[57]

Almost certainly Stuart knew of these plans. Although there is no direct record of his receiving letters from Britain, his receipt of correspondence earlier in his West Indian tour from such men as Sturge and Blair makes it improbable that he would be totally starved of antislavery news during his several months in Jamaica. Almost certainly, too, his contacts with America made him aware of the crisis developing within the American abolition movement. During the recent years of his absence from America the disputes among American abolitionists over the role of women, the question of seeking political solutions, and attitudes to the Sabbath and other religious issues had come into the open. William Lloyd Garrison had become an increasingly controversial figure, opposed even in his own state by critics who, in 1839, launched the rival Massachusetts Abolition Society. Although his opponents remained a minority in New England, in that same year they held sway at the national convention, advocating their political abolitionism to an extent that made decisive conflict with the Garrisonians almost inevitable.[58]

In the event, for reasons which surviving letters do not make clear, Stuart's visit to North America in late April and early May, 1840, was too brief for him to become directly embroiled in the controversy. He must have been fully informed about the anti-Garrisonian position when he spent a day with Lewis Tappan early in May. But most of his short stay was spent visiting his relatives in Toronto. He was unable to find time to visit Gerrit Smith or even Theodore and Angelina, who had recently done him the honor of naming their first child Charles Stuart. His only antislavery activity was the delivery of "a liberal donation for the Anti-Slavery treasury from the freedmen of Jamaica." It was a sign of his detach-

57. Temperley, *British Antislavery*, 85.
58. Filler, *Crusade Against Slavery*, 133–35.

ment from the controversy that his arrival and this donation should be warmly greeted by the organs of each side, the *Emancipator* and the *Liberator*. Perhaps at this stage the activities of his British colleagues—both in organizing antislavery auxiliaries at home and in preparing to stage the world convention—were more appealing to him than rancorous debate among old friends in America. At all events he quickly determined to sail from England in the *Great Western,* knowing that its May 9 departure date would mean he would miss the convention of the American society, which he had diligently attended on four previous occasions and to which he had recently been accredited by Jamaican abolitionists.[59]

The convention met three days after his departure. The Garrisonians had made great efforts to mobilize a large attendance of their supporters. Their opponents, sensing the probability of losing control of the national society, took the defensive measure of handing over the society's newspaper, the *Emancipator,* to the New York Anti-Slavery Society and the society's books to Lewis Tappan and S. W. Benedict. The threatened schism finally occurred when a woman, Abby Kelley, was elected by a substantial majority to the society's business committee. Led by Stuart's old associates, Lewis Tappan and Amos Phelps, large numbers of anti-Garrisonians promptly withdrew from the convention and effectively handed over the national society to the Garrisonians.[60]

Charles Stuart may have sailed away from this fateful confrontation expecting its result. But the imminence of the London convention, to which Americans of both factions had been invited, meant that neither he nor the British antislavery movement would remain untouched by the American controversies for much longer.

---

59. Lewis Tappan to Weld, May 4, 1840, Letterbooks, Vol. 2, p. 391, Lewis Tappan Papers; *Liberator,* May 1, 1840, p. 69; *Emancipator's* announcement in *ibid.*; Stuart to Smith, May 8, 1840, SP; Lewis Tappan to E. A. Walbridge, May 9, 1840, Letterbooks, Vol. 2, p. 405, Lewis Tappan Papers.

60. Filler, *Crusade Against Slavery,* 135–36.

8 WORLD CONVENTION

THE GENERAL—or "World"—Anti-Slavery Convention in June, 1840, marked a distinctive stage in the abolitionist career of Charles Stuart. In different circumstances it might have been a happy climax to his first decade of antislavery activity. No one had worked harder for international cooperation on behalf of the slave; no one had so intimate a knowledge of the antislavery scene in the two major participating countries, Britain and the United States. But the occasion turned out not to be a fulfillment of the past but a harbinger of a discordant future. The recent American split introduced controversies that came close to wrecking the convention. In these circumstances it would have been difficult for any abolitionist to continue to enjoy universal popularity. But Stuart's problems were deeper. Even in its more harmonious deliberations the convention showed that abolitionism was developing in new directions that would not be to the taste of one who remained rigidly committed to traditional goals and methods.

STUART'S JOURNEY to Britain can only have confirmed for him the depth of the divisions within the American abolition movement. His companions on the *Great Western* included the Reverends Nathaniel Colver and Elon Galusha, who were to press for the exclusion of women from the forthcoming convention, and Professor William Adam, an Englishman at Harvard, and Colonel Jonathan Miller from Vermont, who were to be vocal in support of female participation. Although this group embarked before the final split had taken place, the divisions had become so clear that they were already well understood in Britain. Even as Stuart crossed the Atlantic, the committee of the British and Foreign Anti-Slavery Society (which is generally referred to as "Broad Street" from its London address) was preparing for embarrassments at the convention. Meeting on May 15, it attempted to clarify its original invitation to American "delegates" by resolving that the intention had always been to accept only men, with women welcome as nonparticipating visitors. On May 23 Joseph Sturge, John Scoble, and William Bevan were appointed as a subcommittee to welcome delegates and inform any women among them of this resolution.[1]

In its concern to find out how disruptive the issue was likely to be, the committee sought the opinions of Stuart soon after his arrival. At the beginning of June he wrote from Bath, where he was staying as usual with the Blairs, that he was unable precisely to predict the relative sizes of the delegations from the two American factions. Nominations in the United States had been "scattered," with churches and antislavery societies appointing delegates as they pleased: as a result "no central, general account exists." But his letter offered no comfort to the Broad Street committee even as it made clear where his own loyalties lay. He had discovered while in New York that there would be a large number of delegates from Massachusetts, "some of them of the most troublesome description, particularly on the points of intruding women into public life, and of denying the rightfulness of human governments." Within days both this prediction and the committee's prejudices were confirmed when the main body of American delegates arrived with several women in its ranks. Reaffirming its determination to exclude women, the committee now delegated to four more of its members the task of meeting and explaining its position to them. They did so decorously but inconclusively. The committee was soon confronted with a letter from some of the women delegates, offering thanks for the "kind attentions received by them since their arrival in London" but expressing deep regret at their rejection as delegates. The committee responded by sending "a Lady's or visitor's ticket" to each of the American women.[2]

Even though the most notable and vigorous champion of the women, Garrison, had not yet arrived, these exchanges made conflict on the issue inevitable when the convention began on Friday, June 12. For the moment, however, there was a more general excitement in the air, as more

1. Liberator, July 3, 1840, p. 106; BFASS, May 15, 23, 1840.
2. Stuart to John Morgan, June 3, 1840, S. 18, C22/26, RHL; BFASS, May 29, June 9, 11, 1840.

than four hundred delegates and scores of visitors and observers assembled. Many experienced the pleasure of reunion. Many others who knew each other by correspondence met for the first time. And, particularly for younger devotees to the cause, there was the satisfaction of meeting individuals of repute. Above all, even for the most distinguished delegates, there was the enticing prospect of seeing the legendary father-figure of the antislavery movement, Thomas Clarkson, who, though frail and nearly blind, had agreed to accept a largely symbolic role as chairman of the convention. One young observer, Maria Waring, a member of the tight-knit circle of Quakers who were a significant group in the small Irish antislavery milieu that Stuart knew so well, commented: "We went to the Freemason's Hall at ten o'clock; there we saw Charles Stewart [sic], George Thompson, Edward Baldwin, James Birney, James Haughton, Billy Martin, R. R. Moore, Lucretia Mott, and a great many others that we had not known of before. They stood or sat about for a long time, talking to and recognizing each other. After some time it was announced that Clarkson was coming in, and they were requested not to clap, but to stand up instead. It was extremely beautiful and refined to receive him in this manner."[3]

Quiet refinement persisted, as Stuart's friends Blair, Sturge, and Birney were elected vice-presidents of the convention in anticipation of Clarkson's inability to attend regularly. And harmony prevailed as the movement's greatest orator, George Thompson, delivered a eulogy of the venerable president. Maria Waring found Thompson "eloquent and fascinating, and he has a kind of bewitching gracefulness about him." But soon she and the other female spectators in the gallery saw unanimity evaporate as the Garrisonian Wendell Phillips urged the convention to accept women delegates. He was opposed by spokesmen of the British and Foreign Anti-Slavery Society and of the anti-Garrisonian Americans, who had quickly formed their own American and Foreign Anti-Slavery Society after the final split a month before. Stuart's recent traveling companions joined the argument on both sides. Colver pointed out to his British hosts that Phillips spoke for only some American abolitionists, whereas Colonel Miller, in supporting female participation, hoped that the issue could be settled quickly before it destroyed the convention.[4] If most of these arguments were repetitions of confrontations that had already taken place in America, for the first time British abolitionists openly disagreed

3. Maria Waring's comments in Ms. A.1.2. vol. 9, p. 60, BPL.
4. *Proceedings of the General Anti-Slavery Convention, 1840*, 4, 10, 23–28.

on the issue. In particular, there was a sharp exchange between the British veterans of American campaigning, Stuart and Thompson.

Stuart said that he was happy to let the convention adjudicate the dispute between the Broad Street committee and "our friends from Massachusetts and Pennsylvania" about whether the original invitation to Americans had implied acceptance of women. But he was convinced from his firsthand knowledge of abolitionists in those two states "that some of the noblest and most uncompromising friends of liberty and of the slave there, are against the reception of lady delegates, and in favour of the British view. I am satisfied that there is a vast amount of that feeling." Thompson promptly challenged this assertion. But though he spoke at length in favor of the Garrisonian branch of the movement, he ultimately urged a withdrawal of the motion to seat women, and he asked the women delegates to cooperate to "promote the peace of the convention."[5]

Not everyone was so conciliatory. British spokesmen such as the Reverend John Burnet called for calmness while demanding that Americans conform to the practices of their hosts. And, on the American side, George Bradburn attacked the dominance of the British and Foreign Anti-Slavery Society, complaining, "What a misnomer to call this a World's Convention of abolitionists." Yet despite these tensions, and despite Stuart's outspoken partisanship, there is no evidence to support the subsequent charges of his Garrisonian adversary, John A. Collins (who was not present), that "the behaviour of Mr. Stuart in the London Convention was, at times, turbulent, wild, and disorderly." Even allowing for the restraint of the reporting that eventually found its way into the official *Proceedings* of the convention, it is hard to believe in this portrait of an unbalanced zealot. At every stage of his career Stuart's enthusiasms and eccentricities provided ammunition for his opponents. But all available evidence suggests that these characteristics were still attractive to many others. To a reporter of the Dublin *Weekly Herald*, who strove to add color to his account with pen portraits of some half-dozen convention notables, the "dark-browed military-looking" Stuart was "one of the most pure minded, distinguished, and courageous living philanthropists." And Maria Waring, despite becoming an ardent admirer of Garrison during the convention, enthused: "Stuart is delightful. . . . He is full of love, it even overflows and seems to pour into one, and makes one almost feel as if they were full of love too. He is very amusing. He screeches out in the meetings and says 'Dear brother' and 'Dear sister' out of the meetings." He was an unmistakable eccentric in his dress, with "a leathern pouch sus-

---

5. Ibid., 32–35.

pended to a strap, which is fastened around his shoulder." Asked whether such a device was necessary, he had replied, "not necessary but useful," and had promptly emptied it to reveal its contents to his amused audience of Irish Quaker women.[6]

The bitter atmosphere in which Collins made his allegations several months later has meant that posterity, too, has remembered the 1840 convention almost exclusively for the controversies over the woman question. These were severe enough. The danger of disintegration on the first day had been real. Subsequently, Garrison, arriving late, refused to take his seat as a delegate and joined the women as a spectator in the gallery for the duration of the convention. Even so, it would be wrong to see these issues as dominant. After the initial disagreements, most delegates threw themselves with enthusiasm into discussion and debate of far more than the American divisions over the remaining nine days. The arrival of a small French delegation on the second day could not prevent it from being overwhelmingly an Anglo-American gathering. And yet in their deliberations the delegates did much to justify the popular label of a "world" convention. Some delegates arrived with papers that were read and debated. On some issues subcommittees were formed to produce reports that were, in turn, debated; and on others, extempore speeches introduced resolutions for further debate. Overall, by these various devices the delegates addressed themselves to an impressively wide range of topics relating to the global problem of slavery. There were reports on slavery in the colonies of France, Denmark, Holland, and Sweden and in Latin America and the Moslem world, as well as discussion of the situation in the United States, the British West Indies, and India. There was analysis of thorny political issues such as slavery in the still independent republic of Texas and investigations into more insidious problems, including the question of British capital investment in the Atlantic slave trade.[7]

On some issues there were heated exchanges, but these did not reflect the divisions of the opening day. T. F. Buxton was pressed hard by James Birney to state unequivocally that the formation of the new African Civilization Society did not imply support for the American Colonization Society. And Americans from both warring factions bluntly attacked the record of British antislavery visitors to the United States. George Brad-

---

6. *Ibid.*, 25–29; *Liberator*, May 21, 1841, p. 82; Dublin *Weekly* quoted in Leeds *Mercury*, July 4, 1840, p. 7; Ms.A.1.2. vol. 9, p. 60, BPL.

7. The various issues were reported most fully in the 592 pages of the official *Proceedings of the General Anti-Slavery Convention, 1840*. There were also extensive reports in the *Anti-Slavery Reporter*, I (1840), 132–224; and, during the convention, in the London *Times*, June 19, 22, 24, 1840.

burn and Henry B. Stanton both suggested that British abolitionists, especially clergy, were armchair philanthropists unwilling to confront the harsh conditions of American campaigning. "To be an abolitionist in England and in America," said Stanton, "are very different things; and, if I may be permitted to say so, but few of your abolitionists have stood fire on our side of the Atlantic." Stuart supported these remarks with typical vehemence, insisting that "the ministers from England, who visit the United States, are among the most powerful supporters of the slave system in that land." This remark provoked an indignant response from the Reverend Dr. F. A. Cox, who felt himself maligned. And some months later it involved Stuart in a flurry of newspaper correspondence with one Dr. James Matheson, who had not been at the convention and who was under the impression that Stuart was an American. Those who were present well knew that Stuart and Thompson were major exceptions to the Americans' charges. Stanton pointed to Thompson as one "who did stand fire—who stood fire bravely." And the Reverend C. E. Lester recalled Stuart's presence during the Utica riot of 1835 and affirmed that "from that day to this" he had "proved that rotten eggs and brickbats cannot overthrow principle."[8]

Almost inevitably, however, in such a large and varied assembly, Stuart's oft-praised purity of principle was more than once displayed in brusque confrontations with fellow abolitionists. On the convention's second day he had prepared the way for his subsequent denunciation of English clerical visitors to America by attacking more generally the responsibility of organized religion for the continuing crime of slavery. A paper by an Oxford cleric on the sinfulness of slavery had prompted long discussion about biblical justifications of slavery and about differences between the slavery of early Christian times and that of the modern era. Eventually—shortly after Thomas Clarkson had been helped from the hall, "apparently overcome by fatigue"—Stuart intervened to say that he would "feel he had come here in vain unless their common God was vindicated from the aspersions that had been uttered against him. They ought to go into the matter like brethren, and fully, fairly, and freely declare to the world what they thought the mind of the God of love to be, about slavery." He was impatient with debate about the existence of slavery in early Christian times. He was prepared to admit that there had been slaveholders in the primitive church "just as there were incestuous persons in

8. *Anti-Slavery Reporter*, I (1840), 173; *Proceedings of the General Anti-Slavery Convention, 1840*, 126, 135–37, 317; Matheson's complaints in *Anti-Slavery Reporter*, I (1840), 318; Stuart to editor, January 7, 1841, *ibid.*, II (1841), 7.

the primitive church—drunkards and persons who went to the table of the Lord in the way they read of in the Corinthians." Those who thought this an important defense of modern slaveholders, he scornfully suggested, "should take what courage they could." He reminded the audience that the real lesson to be drawn from such historical reflections was that primitive Christians had been merely subjects, whereas modern Christians were rulers and legislators: "The primitive Christians submitted to slavery, while the Christians of the present day created it." These sentiments naturally elicited many cries of "hear, hear!" in such a forum. But they were nonetheless altogether too simple and direct for many others, who agonized over the question of whether the convention could morally and practically urge the many different churches represented there to exclude slaveholders from their congregations.[9]

Stuart's comments on this issue did not lead to confrontations with any of his friends. In asserting the sinfulness of slavery he was reiterating the fundamental principle of his own abolitionism and that of virtually all those—British and American—who had embraced immediatism with him a decade earlier. But on another issue—that of boycotting slave-grown produce—his views and practice had always been an extreme version of attitudes shared only by the tight circle of British and Irish abolitionists among whom he had entered the movement. His refusal knowingly to use any slave products, in either food or clothing, had been widely known and tolerantly, even affectionately, regarded. But as his published debate with Elizur Wright had shown, his principles had not been shared by any of the leading American abolitionists. By 1840, there was at last some wider interest in the notion of a broad economic boycott, if not in the rigorous personal regimen followed by Stuart. In British circles there had been increasing advocacy of East Indian sugar, which had been promoted since the early 1820s and intermittently before that as a preferable alternative to the slave-produced commodity. And now that British West Indian sugar, too, was a product of free labor, other abolitionists joined Stuart in hoping for the survival of the plantation system for the same reasons, as well as to vindicate old predictions about the economic superiority of free labor. At the same time American delegates reacted enthusiastically to a new campaign, launched under the auspices of the British India Society by George Thompson and others, to promote Indian cotton as an alternative to the slave-grown staple of the American South. These wider implications meant a livelier interest than might have been expected some years before, when Stuart, on the eighth day of the convention, moved

9. *Liberator*, August 14, 1840, p. 130; *Anti-Slavery Reporter*, I (1840), 139–40.

the resolution that "this association earnestly recommends to the friends of humanity and religion, everywhere, to disuse slave-labour produce, as far as is practicable." But lively interest meant lively disagreement, and a surprisingly contentious debate followed.[10]

Stuart introduced his motion with what were for him standard arguments. Using slave produce strengthened slavery: those who did so "mingled their superfluities with the blood of the slave." Using free labor instead would help the "industrious poor." But he stressed that these two measures should be undertaken only "as far as practicable" because he was persuaded that "duty in this matter required only what was practicable without sacrificing either life or health." He may have expected this qualification to appease those who had regarded his own practice as quixotically extreme. But in fact it helped to make his resolution more controversial. From one side he was assailed by those who felt that the qualifying phrase weakened the resolution to the point of blandness; and from the other he met the more familiar criticism that the goals of the boycott were impracticable.[11]

All critics stressed their admiration for Stuart. "I know the purity of Captain Stuart's views," said Nathaniel Colver, "I love the purity of his mind, but in this resolution there is no standard." Richard Allen, the Dublin Quaker, insisted: "No one has a higher opinion of Captain Stuart's anti-slavery principles than I have; but I think the words, 'as far as practicable', savour too much of compromise." From the other extreme of criticism the Reverend J. T. Price, who had known Stuart since Agency Committee days, said that the resolution "could not be brought forward by a more consistent man than Captain Stuart." He knew very well that Stuart himself was not clothed in cotton and would never take sugar. But he could have supported the resolution only if he could be persuaded that all members of the convention were equally consistent and "would carry out in practice that which they recommended." The Reverend James Carlile of Belfast was virtually a solitary voice in offering such reassurance. He had abstained from slave produce for some years, having been persuaded by Stuart that "it was my duty to abstain."[12]

In the face of these obvious conflicts of opinion some delegates asked Stuart to withdraw the motion. Others were in favor of amendment. George Thompson reported recent communications he had had from the Free Produce Association of Philadelphia as evidence of great American

10. Temperley, *British Anti-Slavery*, 101–102; *Proceedings of the General Anti-Slavery Convention, 1840*, 348 n., 349–50, 384–410, 417–18, 428–30, 437.
11. *Proceedings of the General Anti-Slavery Convention, 1840*, 437–47.
12. Ibid.

interest in the question. If the resolution could not pass as it stood, it should be modified at least to declare abstention "a principle worthy of being observed." The Reverend J. Kennedy suggested an amended resolution calling on the British and Foreign Anti-Slavery Society to provide lists of products of slave and free labor.[13]

Stuart rejected these criticisms and suggestions with his usual bluntness: "I should like to speak against all the amendments. I have not for several years past used any article of slave-grown produce, and I have never found any difficulty in it. On all occasions, from my youth upwards, I have had reason to bless God that my conscience has been my own and not another's. I see that you are not prepared for the discussion of this question; but I cannot withdraw the resolution. I therefore leave it in your hands, to do with it what you please." At this point Kennedy's amendment was put and carried "almost unanimously."[14]

It would be wrong to conclude from these various issues that Stuart was either a dominant figure or a focus of major controversy at the convention. As the debate over abstinence from slave produce had shown, his individuality and sincerity were widely respected. His prestige was indicated by the way engravings, taken from a portrait of this "highly esteemed philanthropist" owned by William Blair, were advertised for sale in the *Anti-Slavery Reporter* to coincide with the convention: "We feel sure many of our friends will be glad to avail themselves of the opportunity of possessing a portrait of so zealous and indefatigable an advocate of the rights of the oppressed." At this period, too, some influential members of the antislavery elite succeeded in having his pension raised to that of major in recognition of his services to the cause. Although he would remain known as "Captain Stuart" to virtually all, this was effectively a promotion, which was remarkable in view of the disgraceful circumstances in which his military service had ended. In the convention Stuart spoke at length and with authority on the conditions he had recently observed in the West Indies; he was appointed a member of the subcommittee to prepare a report on the postapprenticeship situation; and the published *Proceedings* of the convention included further material on the subject by him in a footnote. He was also a member of other subcommittees, including one examining slavery in British India. But despite all this industry and recognition, others, such as Thompson, Stanton, and Birney, were much more consistently in the limelight as speakers. His forthrightness led him into minor arguments, as, for instance, when he

13. Ibid.
14. Ibid.

accused John Scoble of giving a distorted version of events in Saint Domingue at the turn of the century—an allegation that forced Scoble hastily to agree that Toussaint L'Ouverture was "one of the noblest spirits that ever graced the world." But the conference saw lively debate and often outspoken clashes on many other issues in which Stuart remained a silent spectator.[15]

With the benefit of hindsight, it is possible to see the convention as a watershed in Stuart's career; the period when he virtually personified the main characteristics of abolitionism had come to an end. Although few abolitionists had been more truly international in outlook and activity than Stuart, his abolitionism had always focused exclusively on Negro slavery, despite a genuine concern for the plight of other non-European peoples such as American Indians. Now the convention revealed that many former friends and associates were looking at other forms of oppression, particularly in British India. His uncompromising immediatism had made him appear radical in many ways, but his determination to achieve his ends through existing political systems was the hallmark of a reformer with basically conservative social and political attitudes. Already that conservatism was in evidence in the opposition he had voiced to the "woman-intruding," antigovernment Garrisonians. Eventually it would involve a stubborn defense of British imperialism in India such as he had always displayed in relation to Ireland.

For the moment, conflicts were latent on these issues. When the question was raised as to whether East Indian sugar was the produce of slave labor, he backed up the denials of William Adam and George Thompson; "all his experience" plus recent examination of parliamentary inquiries convinced him that such sugar was "not obtained by agrestic slavery, but by free labor." But this discussion had been stimulated by a paper by Adam titled "Slavery in British India," which was evidence of a new interest by abolitionists in human rights on the subcontinent. In serving on the subcommittee that was established to examine this question, Stuart almost certainly—to judge from his later activities—found it less easy to reconcile his Indian experience and antislavery priorities with fellow abolitionists' attitudes to India.[16]

Moreover, he remained true not only to time-honored goals but also to methods. The closing stages of the convention saw him as confident as

15. *Anti-Slavery Reporter*, I (1840), 144; Barnes and Dumond (eds.), *Weld-Grimké Letters*, II, 701 n. 3; *Anti-Slavery Reporter*, I (1840), 89, 348–50 n.; *Proceedings of the General Anti-Slavery Convention, 1840,* 179.
16. *Anti-Slavery Reporter*, I (1840), 140–41; *Proceedings of the General Anti-Slavery Convention, 1840,* 77–86.

ever that agitation through the established political system was the only way to proceed. Not even his return to the realities of Westminster and Whitehall had shaken the optimism he had shown in Jamaica that planter dictatorship could be overcome by continued political pressure in Britain. It was not solely the fault of the British government that bad laws had been passed and planter authority strengthened: "The fault was with the British people.... The government had endeavoured to correct the evils in Jamaica but they were foiled in the attempt." At the next election they ought to "beat up for anti-slavery men, and then Lord John Russell would be glad to do his duty."[17]

Such agitation was, of course, the very antithesis of the radical policies now espoused within the American context by Garrison and his supporters, who believed that any involvement in electoral politics was a culpable compromise with a slave-supporting Constitution. Over the next year Stuart's main preoccupation would be to combat the Garrisonian heresy throughout the British Isles.

ALTHOUGH the controversies that had nearly wrecked the convention at its outset had been quickly stilled, the foundations of future British conflict over the American split were laid during those two weeks in June and consolidated in the following months as American delegates from both sides visited antislavery societies in many parts of the country. The principal spokesmen of the so-called "New Organization" American and Foreign Anti-Slavery Society, Birney and Stanton, developed their friendships with the Broad Street committee, which had organized the convention, and one of that body's leading figures, John Scoble, accompanied them on an extensive provincial lecturing tour. Since Broad Street had recently been organizing its network of provincial auxiliaries, this tour helped to spread fairly widely the notion that New Organization was the true version of American abolitionism. But they did not have the field to themselves. Charles Lenox Remond, a black abolitionist, who had opted out of the London convention along with Garrison, was a popular "Old Organization" spokesman who toured Britain extensively. And, more important, many Irish and Scottish abolitionists, never keen to acknowledge leadership from London, had responded eagerly to Garrison's magnetism during the convention. Although their hero returned to America early in August, he found time to visit both Glasgow and Dublin. His visit to Scotland strengthened the commitment to Old Organization of two stalwarts of the Glasgow Emancipation Society, William Smeal and John

17. *Anti-Slavery Reporter*, I (1840), 223.

Murray. But it also prompted the first stirrings of hostility from the equally prominent abolitionist Congregational minister, Dr. Ralph Wardlaw, on the woman question. In Dublin, however, Garrison received a rapturous welcome from the small antislavery coterie led by Richard Webb. Although Garrison decided firmly that he liked the Scots and Irish "better than I do the people of England," he also developed a most important English friendship with the Darlington Quaker Elizabeth Pease, and he quickly forgave George Thompson's prevarications at the convention. Thompson's speech had been "unfortunate and incoherent," but he was soon "ashamed" of it and by August was unequivocally "with us, through evil report and through good report—for better, for worse—on the woman question—on the side of non-resistance, old organization, etc."[18]

Garrison ended his brief visit convinced that it had been "one of the most important movements of my life." His mission, he reported on his return to America, had been greatly assisted by the controversies at the convention: nothing could have so speedily publicized the question of women's rights as the exclusion of the female delegates and his own refusal to take his seat. And in his subsequent tour he and his companions had diligently "'sifted into' the minds of those with whom we came in contact, all sorts of 'heresies' and 'extraneous topics', in relation to Temperance, Non-Resistance, Moral Reform, Human Rights, Holiness, &c &c."[19]

Despite Garrison's determination to further his own radical objectives, controversies among British abolitionists over the American split remained muted. Birney and Stanton pushed the opposition line with sufficient restraint to retain at least guarded respect from those like Webb who were firmly Garrisonian. And two of Garrison's main supporters, George Thompson and Elizabeth Pease, were heavily preoccupied with their own "extraneous topic," the British India Society's campaign to develop Indian cotton in opposition to the American slave-produced commodity. It was a sign of the dormancy of the American issues that Charles Stuart, in Ireland a short time after Garrison, spent his public time discussing the West Indian situation rather than the woman question. At a

---

18. BFASS, July 9, 26, December 27, 1839. The activities of Birney, Stanton, Scoble, and Remond are discussed in the following chapter. William Smeal to Garrison, August 1, 1840, in Taylor, *British and American Abolitionists*, 105; Garrison to Henry C. Wright, August, 1840, *ibid.*, 110; Garrison to S. J. May, September 6, 1840, *ibid.*, 114; Thompson to R. D. Webb, August 9, 1840, *ibid.*, 109.

19. Garrison to Wright, August 1840, in Taylor, *British and American Abolitionists*, 110.

public meeting of the Belfast Anti-Slavery Society, he spoke for nearly three hours about his recent Caribbean tour.[20]

No doubt Stuart and others voiced privately the opposition they had already expressed to the Garrisonian cause at the London convention. But it is a moot point whether such criticisms would have become a major source of dispute in British antislavery circles if John A. Collins had not paid a controversial visit to the British Isles between October, 1840, and July, 1841. This dispute would enable Stuart to move back briefly to the center of British antislavery politics but in a way that would again reveal his fundamental indifference to British society.

---

20. Webb to Elizabeth Pease, November 4, 1840, in *ibid.*, 119; *Anti-Slavery Reporter*, I (1840), 248.

9 THE WRATH OF CAPTAIN STUART

JOHN ANDERSON COLLINS, the general agent of the Garrisonian Massachusetts Anti-Slavery Society, crossed the Atlantic to seek British financial support for the American Anti-Slavery Society and in particular for its newspaper, the *National Standard*, which was intended to counter the *Emancipator*, now in the hands of the opposition American and Foreign Anti-Slavery Society. According to covering letters to Elizabeth Pease from Garrison and others in Boston, only extreme financial hardship had persuaded the Old Organizationists to make this plea for British assistance. But they were also well aware that the visit was likely to polarize British antislavery opinion. "I have told my friend Collins," wrote Garrison, "of the difficulties that will lie in his path, especially in consequence of the introduction of the new organized spirit among you in England." The appeal was going out, wrote Boston Quaker William Bassett, to the "true friends of freedom in Britain," who were *"misrepresented* by the committee of [the] British & Foreign A.S. Society."[1]

On arrival in England, Collins was careful to avoid immediate contact with Broad Street. In London he consulted only some members of the British India Society sympathetic to Garrison, and he quickly moved north in late October to confer with Elizabeth Pease in Darlington and George Thompson in Edinburgh. Thompson, in particular, was clearly disconcerted by the mission. Because the Garrisonians were "despised, disparaged, and everywhere spoken against," he suggested that Collins should

---

1. William Bassett to E. Pease, September 23, 1840; Garrison to E. Pease, September 30, 1840, in Taylor, *British and American Abolitionists*, 115–16.

join forces with Charles Remond in a tour "in those districts where there is the greatest, present probability of a favourable reception." He felt that the tactics should be those already adopted by Remond, "a line of conduct as would preclude an open warfare upon the disputes between the American societies." On October 27 Thompson wrote to Elizabeth Pease pointing out that, to his knowledge, the New Organizationists had not publicly broached the American issues since the London convention: "Is it then necessary or likely to promote success for Collins to do so.... Suppose for the present he feels his way, and meets objections as they come up, and does not come forth publicly, till a good excuse is given him, *by some overt act of the other party?*" Unknown to Thompson, his advice was already redundant. On October 24 Charles Stuart had written from Liverpool to Birney, Scoble, and Stanton in Dublin telling them that he was on his way to Edinburgh. Although the letter mentioned no details, it marked the start of the conflicts Thompson had feared.[2]

Stuart and Collins reached Edinburgh almost simultaneously in late October, 1840, at the same time Scoble, Stanton, and Birney arrived in the Garrisonian stronghold of Dublin. On November 4 Richard Webb wrote a long letter to Elizabeth Pease, complaining bitterly of Scoble's conduct. He had made serious but vaguely defined charges of "shocking things he could reveal about the non-resistants... he would not tell— something obscene or abominable which he had documents to confirm in his possession." On that same day in Edinburgh Collins was complaining no less bitterly about Charles Stuart's opposition to his mission.[3] For the next eight months Collins was to be hounded as relentlessly as the colonizationist Elliott Cresson had been by Stuart and his associates almost a decade earlier. Collins and Stuart could scarcely have been more different. After a few weeks in Britain the American was appalled by the harshness of the British class system and social problems to which Stuart remained supremely indifferent. Yet although Stuart launched the attack, he was never taken seriously by his new American opponent. Close analysis of his role shows that he was as independent as ever and that he significantly influenced events. But to place that analysis in some perspective, it must first be emphasized that to Collins he was no more than a minor figure in a plot organized with venom and finesse by Broad Street.

George Thompson's worst fears were quickly confirmed, as Collins and

2. Collins to Maria Weston Chapman, December 3, 1840, *ibid.*, 126–28; Thompson to E. Pease, October 24, 27, 1840, JR; Thompson to Webb, November 2, 1840, in Taylor, *British and American Abolitionists*, 118; Stuart to Birney, October 24, 1840, WP.

3. Webb to E. Pease, November 4, 1840, BPL; draft letter by Collins to Stuart, Ms. A. 1.2. vol. 10, p. 35, BPL.

Stuart debated the American schism before both male and female committees of the Edinburgh Emancipation Society. On November 7 he wrote to Elizabeth Pease: "I have already been made ill by what has transpired. I cannot see altercations amongst friends, and be myself brought into hostile colision [sic] with those with whom I have hitherto been cordial without much suffering. So strong is the prejudice excited against Garrison and his friends that any who venture to say a good word in his behalf are set down as his disciples, and tabooed accordingly."[4]

Collins, who quickly developed a deep contempt for almost all British abolitionists, was coldly indifferent to the consternation his presence was causing. He was much more optimistic than Thompson that his skirmishes with Stuart were winning support for Old Organization. But he was acute enough to realize that Thompson was almost demoralized by encountering opposition in his adoptive city of Edinburgh, where "his influence has been, previously almost omnipotent." This perception convinced him only that Thompson was "not the man I once considered him." He did not doubt that his "heart, soul and sympathy is entirely with us." In common with all contemporaries, he acknowledged that "his eloquence is captivating." But, "though bold, free and enlarged in his mind . . . he is in my estimation, emphatically a *creature* of circumstances. With the bold and daring, in a cause his conscience approves, Geo. Thompson would be bold & daring. . . . He is not prepared or qualified to lead a cause through the assaults of its enemies & the treachery of its friends."[5]

The American had no such public reservations about his own ability. Depicting his jousts with Stuart as easy victories over a ludicrous opponent, he left Edinburgh convinced that he had won significant support. Contacts with British Garrisonians, notably Elizabeth Pease, however, left him under no illusions that he would be well received when, in early December, he wrote to the Broad Street committee, presenting his credentials and formally requesting financial assistance and official endorsement of his mission. As he explained soon afterward to Garrison, this was merely a tactic "to make them show their colours." They had already done "infinite evil to our cause" while pretending to be neutral in the American dispute. But although he expected his requests to be rejected, he hoped he might succeed in dividing the committee. He intended to follow up the expected initial rebuff with a demand for a personal hearing, whereupon he would win some sympathy—probably from among Quaker commit-

4. Thompson to E. Pease, November 7, 1840, JR.
5. Collins to M. W. Chapman, December 3, 1840, in Taylor, *British and American Abolitionists*, 129.

tee members—"& then old organization will soon assume a tangible appearance."⁶

In the event the opposition to Collins was even stronger than he foresaw. When the committee met on January 1, 1841, it considered not only Collins' letter but four others, including one from Stuart, opposing his request for British support for the American Anti-Slavery Society. Of the four, the most significant was one from the Reverend Nathaniel Colver in Boston. Colver's letter had been written on November 30, apparently to Joseph Sturge, and extracts were already circulating before the Broad Street committee met, for Collins himself received them from Elizabeth Pease at almost exactly the same time. On January 2 he sent copies of them back to America with the comment: "I find that the opposition is increasing in consequence of these letters to an almost inconceivable length."⁷

Colver's letter claimed that Garrison's influence was "on the wane": "He so identifies himself with every infidel fanaticism, which floats, as to have lost his *hold* on the *good.*" He had recently "headed an infidel convention, gathered from different states to call in question the validity of the Sabbath, the Church, and the ministry." Identifying himself with those who were "against the Bible as our Standard of faith," he and his followers had become "a source of great reproach, & embarrassment" to the antislavery cause. And now, said Colver, J. A. Collins had left for England "under suspicious circumstances." His objectives were unknown, "but we fear to practice some imposition upon British sympathy for our cause. I hope you will beware of him—*he is not entitled to your confidence.*"⁸

In the six months after Broad Street's predictable rejection of Collins' requests for moral and financial aid, the Colver allegations were at the center of the British dispute over the American divisions. The charges were probably mild and vague compared with accusations that were bandied about verbally. Richard Allen and James Haughton of the Hibernian Anti-Slavery Society were soon to complain of "those stabs in the dark, with which the character of our honored friend William Lloyd Garrison has been assailed in 'social meetings' by professed abolitionists both English and American." But for the Irish and other provincial Garrisonians, the

6. *Ibid.*; E. Pease to Collins, November 16, 1840, BPL; Collins to J. H. Tredgold, December 10, 1840, and to Garrison, December 27, 1840, in Taylor, *British and American Abolitionists*, 132, 135.

7. BFASS, January 1, 1841; Collins to Henry Grafton Chapman, January 2, 1841, in Taylor, *British and American Abolitionists*, 138–39.

8. Colver's letter, dated November 30, 1840, quoted in Collins to H. G. Chapman, January 2, 1841, in Taylor, *British and American Abolitionists*, 138–39.

real issue was that Colver's letters were widely circulated by Broad Street. Scoble's eventual denial that the committee had done this may have been strictly true. But it could only have confirmed his reputation for deviousness in the eyes of Irish critics who claimed that various committee members had sent out the "cruel and unwarrantable" charges on official stationery and under the society's seal. In these circumstances, not only did Scoble's denial seem disingenuous but also the committee's earlier insistence that, in rejecting Collins, it had brought no charges against the American Anti-Slavery Society but merely felt that the American and Foreign Anti-Slavery Society was now a more fitting representative of American antislavery.[9]

Although Colver's allegations caused the most controversy, the same questions about Broad Street's role in endorsing anti-Garrisonian material were raised by the circulation of charges by Amos Phelps. Implying that Collins was of doubtful honesty, this attack was perhaps even more defamatory than Colver's. It had less impact because it was less widely circulated and, more particularly, because, by the time it became an issue in February and March, the divisions were already irreparably wide.[10]

By the end of January even George Thompson, who had been so reluctant to fall out with old associates in London, was complaining to Elizabeth Pease about the way the "*affected* neutrality of Broad Street" masked aggression, "stabbing in the dark," and character assassination "by means the most clandestine and mean." For others the situation seemed, rather, a welcome opportunity to renounce metropolitan influence. Richard Webb showed every sign of enjoying the increasingly acerbic correspondence he conducted with Broad Street on behalf of the Hibernian Anti-Slavery Society. After complaining to the London abolitionists about the circulation of Colver's letter, he told William Smeal in Glasgow that he intended to "send them an answer to their answer which I think they will like less than our first epistle." Smeal, too, engaged in a spirited exchange with Joseph Sturge. Conceding that he and some Glasgow colleagues had been critical of some American abolitionists, he stressed that "our cause has been open and manly—bespeaking our motives to be at once honest and independent, (for we *are* indepen-

---

9. Allen to Tredgold, n.d., C4/46–47; BFASS, January 15, February 12, 1841; C. Lenox Remond to Allen, January 7, 1841, S. 18, C15, 4/202; James Haughton, Richard Allen, Hibernian Anti-Slavery Society, to Tredgold, March 31, 1841, S. 18, C4/50; Scoble to Pease, April 25, 1841, S. 18, C9/72, RHL.

10. Garrison to E. Pease, June 1, 1841, in Taylor, *British and American Abolitionists*, 153; Webb to Collins, March 30, 1841, BPL.

dent, as a *Society*) whereas, the policy of others has been secret; may I not say, mean and dastardly."[11]

As the controversy developed, the scattered pro-Garrison forces cooperated by correspondence. Letters passed between Glasgow and Dublin and between both those centers and Darlington, from where Elizabeth Pease kept in regular contact with Thompson. Yet despite these efforts, British Garrisonians were by early 1841 a beleaguered minority. Only Dublin among the centers where they flourished was solidly committed to Old Organization. Although Elizabeth Pease had earned unstinting praise from Collins since their first meeting, she was, he discovered, virtually a lone voice in Darlington. In late January he attempted to win support from the local antislavery committee for his protests against Broad Street's circulation of the Colver extracts. But as Elizabeth Pease herself reported, most members of the committee objected to being placed in a position that might force them to choose between Broad Street and Collins. They refused to convene formally as a committee, allowing Collins to meet them merely as a visitor in an informal social gathering. Even then, though he spoke "very movingly" against Broad Street, only Pease and one other member of the committee were sympathetic; the other eight advised him to go home. Collins reacted angrily to this rebuff: "I have seen but five as yet genuine abolitionists in all the kindgom," he wrote to Richard Webb. Even John and Joseph Pease had given only lukewarm support to his endeavors in Darlington.[12]

To some extent Collins' difficulties were of his own making. He had an undiplomatic manner, which offended many even among his supporters and may have estranged him from Remond early in 1841. His lack of "tact & talent as a public speaker & debater" persuaded George Thompson to support the publication of a pamphlet by Collins as a preferable alternative to "viva voce explanations." Even Richard Webb, in finding Collins less "rash and intemperate" than he expected, had to concede that "his mode of procedure may not be the best for the collection of golden opinions, or for the lightening of purses." Certainly if Collins gave any signs

11. Thompson to E. Pease, January 25, 1841, JR; Webb to Smeal, March 24, 1841, BPL; Smeal to Sturge, Glasgow, February 4, 1841, in Glasgow Emancipation Society, *Resolutions of Public Meetings of the Members and Friends of the Glasgow Emancipation Society; Correspondence of the Secretaries; and Minutes of the Committee of Said Society, Since the Arrival in Glasgow, of Mr. John A. Collins, the Representative of the American Anti-Slavery Society, in Reference to the Divisions Among American Abolitionists* (Glasgow, 1841), 77.

12. Collins to M. W. Chapman, December 3, 1840, in Taylor, *British and American Abolitionists*, 128; E. Pease to Tredgold, January 29, 1841, S. 18, C9/74, RHL; Collins to Webb, January 28, 1841, BPL.

in public of the contempt for Britain he revealed in his letters to Garrison, he could only have made enemies. A radical who was soon to abandon abolitionism, repudiate religion, and opt out of the mainstream of American life in pursuit of a utopian communal experiment, he regarded the British political system as "a vast and complicated system of slavery.... It gives to the poor subject the ostensible appearance of freedom the more successfully to grind him to powder." Since Collins' social criticisms involved him in a minor dispute with Elizabeth Pease, who was a tentative supporter of Chartism, it is not hard to surmise that he antagonized many others who were less committed to his mission than the Darlington Quaker.[13]

But although Collins' arrogance made him inclined to dismiss all opposition as treachery, he was partly correct in attributing his problems to determined and, at times, unscrupulous opponents. And, superficially, he was also correct in not seeing Charles Stuart as his most important enemy. It was not Stuart but John Scoble who was most consistently seen by British Garrisonians as the evil genius mobilizing the resources and prestige of Broad Street in support of New Organization. In early November, Richard Webb was already warning of Scoble's "unsleeping hostility, his watchful malignity against the old organizationists in general & Garrison in particular": he was "a self-willed, tyrannically minded, narrow souled, clever bigot." Commenting at this early juncture on the prospects for Collins and Remond, Webb added: "I fear that Scoble has poisoned the way for them in wealthy England and that they would meet but a cold reception from most of the friends of the Antislavery cause." Some months later Webb was to insist that the British and Foreign Anti-Slavery Society had been "altogether led astray by Scoble . . . who hates Garrison more than he hates the devil." Webb particularly regretted Scoble's pernicious influence on Joseph Sturge, "a truly noble hearted man." Collins, however, was more inclined to see Sturge as his main enemy. He told Webb that he was "sorry to express such an opinion of Joseph Sturge," but he must judge people by their actions, not their reputations: "The Broad St. committee is the establishment of J.S. and John Scoble is the overseer. In Joseph it lives, moves, and has its being."[14]

There is no evidence that Stuart was the prime intermediary between his old associates, Nathaniel Colver and Amos Phelps, and the British and

13. Thompson to E. Pease, February 6, 1841, JR; Thompson to Webb, February 8, 1841; Webb to Garrison, May 30, 1841, BPL; Collins to Garrison, December 27, 1840, in Taylor, *British and American Abolitionists*, 133; E. Pease to Collins, December 10, 1840, BPL.

14. Webb to E. Pease, November 4, 1840, in Taylor, *British and American Abolitionists*, 120; Webb to Smeal, March 24, 1841; Collins to Webb, April 4, 1841, BPL.

Foreign Anti-Slavery Society. And it is clear that others, notably Scoble, Sturge, and the society's secretary, J. H. Tredgold, did most to exploit the divisive polemics of these two American clerics. Moreover, Stuart did not meet Collins again after their early debates in Edinburgh.

Nevertheless, Stuart did play an important and distinctive role in the campaign against Collins. And the American's failure to understand that role is a further sign of his own limitations, not least his inability to perceive that he was being opposed by more than a sordid conspiracy orchestrated by Broad Street.

FROM THE TIME of their first and only encounter in Edinburgh in November, 1840, Collins affected deep disdain for Stuart even in private letters: "On the subject of new and old organization I think him the greatest ignoramus I ever met with." To an extent, his disparaging comments were the result of genuine ignorance of Stuart's significance. Had he known of his adversary's numerous American connections and wide American experience, he would have been less likely to sneer: "He knows just as much about the Am. controversy, as *it* knows about him." Still only thirty years old, he evidently knew nothing of the anticolonization campaigns that had made Stuart a hero of early American immediatists, for he ridiculed the older man's claims, in one early argument, that others such as Gerrit Smith and Beriah Green "had done as much as Garrison to put down Colonization, insinuating at the same time a compliment to Chas. Stuart."[15] But such comments were contained in letters that attempted to put a favorable gloss on Collins' own progress in his British mission. They were often belied by other evidence suggesting a more significant role for Stuart. And even Collins himself was probably more clearly aware that he was dealing with a formidable opponent than he was prepared to admit to third parties.

Writing to Maria Weston Chapman about his first confrontation with Stuart a month after the event, Collins described how George Thompson had worked to counter statements made on a recent visit to Edinburgh by Stanton, Birney, and Scoble. He had succeeded in arranging a meeting of the Edinburgh Emancipation Society to hear from Collins when "a day previous to the meeting who should present himself, but that ignorant tool of Joseph Sturge, Chas. Stuart." At the time, however, in early November, Collins had been more alarmed than this dismissive comment implies. He reacted angrily when Stuart requested an interview "to take

15. Collins to M. W. Chapman, December 3, 1840, in Taylor, *British and American Abolitionists*, 128–30.

down my own views in my own words" so he could make further inquiries in America about the schism "to sustain the charges you have been and are still resolved to retail over Great Britain." In a draft note of November 4 the American went on: "My brother, ponder well, I beseech you, the course you are persuing [sic]. Examine this subject in the light of eternity. . . . How much better could the energies of your disinterested and active mind be devoted to enlisting the energies of the indolent than to paralyse the enthusiasm and chill the zeal and sympathies of those consecrated to mans redemption."[16]

Although Collins declared his willingness to meet Stuart's request, he claimed that he was too busy for anything but a very brief meeting. This draft note was evidently not rewritten and dispatched, for Collins discovered that he could not so lightly brush Stuart aside. Two days later, in a very different letter to Stuart, he was suggesting ground rules for a meeting of the committee that had been called to hear statements from the two of them about the American divisions.[17]

In his subsequent description of that debate before the Edinburgh committee, Collins again tried hard to disparage and distort Stuart's role. He had suggested that they should speak alternately "for 20 or 30 minutes until the subject should be used up." But he later claimed that Stuart had refused to do this, wanting "me to close my speech & then let him have the entire field." In fact, although Stuart had written to him that he would prefer "you to complete your address and then for me to answer it," he had gone on: "If however you would prefer it, I am quite willing to proceed at once with my reply, together with such other matter as may occur to me, and then, when I have done, to leave you to proceed, without interruption. In either case, after each of us shall . . . have concluded our views without interruption, should occasion appear I shall have no objection to prolong the discussion ad libitum."[18]

More importantly misleading than his distorted version of the preliminaries was Collins' purported confidence about the course and outcome of the debate. The committee had refused to accept his suggestion that it should act as a quasi-judicial body and decide formally whether Stuart had proved his case against the American Anti-Slavery Society. Instead, it had given Stuart three-quarters of an hour to make his speech, "whereupon he pulled from his bosom a small book, from which he read for about 35

16. *Ibid.*; Collins' unposted draft, November 4, 1840, is in Ms. A.1.2. vol. 10, p. 35, BPL.
17. Collins to Stuart, November 6, 1840, BPL.
18. Collins to M. W. Chapman, December 30, 1840, in Taylor, *British and American Abolitionists*, 130; Stuart to Collins, November 7, 1840, BPL.

minutes, a most indifferent & prosy essay, reiterating the same things previously stated, such as that the Am. Socty. was a woman's rights intrusion society, that Garrison was an apostate . . . [and] entertained sentiments which his soul abhorred & &c." Although the committee had been strongly pro-Stuart, "being entirely composed of evangelicals," after this performance, claimed Collins, "I found a change. Invitations began to flock in, to breakfast here, dine there & sup somewhere else, and I was resolved not to leave the place until I had broken down that prejudice." He described Stuart's discomfiture by saying that "a goodly number of those who gave him at first a most cordial greeting" had become Collins' own "warmest friends."[19]

A very different impression had been given by George Thompson in letters to Elizabeth Pease immediately after the event in early November. Describing the debate with Stuart as "sharp," he stopped far short of seeing the progress claimed by Collins. The attitude of most committee members was still in effect: "Ought we not to rely upon such men as Birney, the Tappans, Judge Jay, Sturge, Stuart. . . . Surely these men know better than we do, and would not for any light cause withdraw themselves from W.L.G. and his associates." Far from seeing Stuart as disheartened and discredited, Thompson had gloomily pointed out that the older man was shortly to meet the Ladies Committee of the Edinburgh society, when "he will have the ladies all to himself and make, I am afraid, the worse appear the better reason, as he will have the prejudices of his audience on his side." Ultimately, Collins, too, met the Ladies Committee. Again he subsequently described an inept performance by Stuart, "who thrust himself in & reiterated the old stereotyped objections." But even Collins substantially confirmed Thompson's assessment of the women's attitudes. Remond and Thompson had joined him in debating with Stuart for more than three hours. In contrast to some other recent vacillating performances, Thompson had acquitted himself "manfully," talking "like an old organized abolitionist." But the women were still much more willing to hear "Garrison & his coadjutors traduced by Stuart" than to listen to Collins' attacks on the "new organizers." At much the same time as he wrote these words, a month after the event, Collins was receiving confirmation of the attitudes of the Edinburgh women from one of his supporters there, Mrs. Harriet Gairdner. One of her colleagues on the Ladies Committee had been impressed by Collins on his recent visit but still retained "a strong bias to the other side": her conviction that Garrison must

19. Collins to M. W. Chapman, December 3, 1840, in Taylor, *British and American Abolitionists*, 130.

be in the wrong in the American dispute had apparently been sealed when "Capt. Stuart said he was so disgusted with the Liberator now, he could not read it."[20]

Undoubtedly, in introducing the American issues to Edinburgh Collins had caused dissension in the ranks of the city's abolitionists. But notwithstanding his claims that Stuart had left the city "greatly disheartened" and with his influence dispelled, by the time he was writing a month later Collins must have known he was faced with a determined opponent. Elizabeth Pease had written to him in mid-November, commenting on his "adventures" in Scotland. Though fully sympathizing with his plight, she had made it clear that he had taken on a dogged adversary: "We are almost hourly expecting to see Stuart marching in. A letter has arrived at my brother's from him." Some ten days later Pease reported to Collins the outcome of Stuart's visit to Darlington. He had spent only part of a day with the Pease family, quickly realizing that Elizabeth's opposition made it pointless to meet the local Ladies Committee. She had bluntly told him of her disappointment at his opposition and complained particularly about his "meanness" in writing an anti-Garrison letter recently published in the *Irish Friend*: "He was equally honest with me—and we parted excellent friends—*agreeing, cordially to differ*."[21]

In subsequent letters to Collins in December Pease was less cordially indignant about Stuart, "who ought and [is] in duty bound to know better." She was scathing in her denunciation, seeing him as "a pigmy gazing upon an eminence he cannot reach" in relation to Garrison: "We must be merciful upon the poor man. I believe he has persuaded himself that he is doing a real service to mankind!!" Although such comments may have reinforced Collins' contempt for Stuart as an "ignoramus," even now Pease made it clear that Stuart was a relentless and influential opponent. Her ire had been aroused by another of his "snarling attacks" in the *Irish Friend*. Despite her Quaker connections, she was by no means certain, she warned Collins, that she could persuade its editor to include a counter to Stuart's anti-Garrison polemics.[22]

Before the end of 1840, Collins had further evidence of Stuart's mobility and determination. He received a letter from John Murray, joint secretary with Smeal of the Glasgow Emancipation Society, commenting on the not unexpected obstructions he had so far faced: a chance meeting

20. Thompson to E. Pease, November 5, 7, 1840, JR; Collins to M. W. Chapman, in Taylor, *British and American Abolitionists*, 130; Harriet Gairdner to Collins, December 3, 1840, BPL.
21. E. Pease to Collins, November 16, 28, 1840, BPL.
22. E. Pease to Collins, December 6, 10, 17, 1840, BPL.

at Smeal's house had shown him "a specimen of the wrath of Capt. Stuart against your project." Murray took Stuart's opposition seriously enough to follow up that encounter by writing to ask him to explain his opposition to Garrison "& the cause of his great change of mind in regard to him." Stuart's detailed reply to that question (which will be discussed in the following chapter) was written from Newcastle-upon-Tyne on November 15. And before the end of that month Collins was aware of Stuart's presence in London when he had his own first encounter with some members of the Broad Street committee some weeks before he formally applied to that body for support. He attributed the "cold and distant" attitude of Sturge to Stuart's presence in his home. Perhaps Collins saw in this circumstance evidence merely that Stuart was reporting faithfully the results of his recent mission to Scotland, rather than pressing his own views on Sturge. Certainly it was after this that he depicted Stuart as the ignorant "tool" of the Birmingham Quaker in his letter to Maria Weston Chapman. And he soon developed this interpretation of Stuart's role when he wrote to Garrison about "a crafty and subtle plan for taking revenge upon yourself" devised by Broad Street. The plan had involved "securing Birney, Stanton & Stuart to travel the country ostensibly to create an antislavery feeling, but really to sow discord & retail falsehood & calumny." Wherever he had followed these three, Collins found "people possessing the most distorted views about Garrison and old organisation."[23]

Collins was doubtless correct in seeing the neutrality still affected by Broad Street at this stage as a camouflage for deep hostility to Old Organization. But he was probably wrong in believing Sturge had devised an elaborate plan to commit British abolitionists to an anti-Garrison line out of "revenge" for Garrison's disruptive posture at the London convention. And he was certainly wrong to see Stuart as a mere agent of Sturge. The relationship between the two men is typified by a comment Stuart made to Weld in a letter written in March, 1841. Sturge was about to visit the United States, and Stuart had promised him "a true brother's heart & home" should he visit Weld: "As from you," he told Theodore, "I differ from him utterly on some points—but to the moral and religious grandeur & beauty which characterize him, I cannot be insensible."[24]

Because the leading abolitionists had many opportunities to meet and discuss attitudes and tactics, there is a dearth of documentary evidence

23. Murray to Collins, December 23, 1840; Collins to E. Pease, November 26, 1840, BPL; Collins to Garrison, December 27, 1840, in Taylor, *British and American Abolitionists*, 134. In fact it was Scoble, not Stuart, who accompanied the two Americans, but Collins' slip of the pen may indicate how much Stuart was on his mind.
24. Stuart to Weld, March, 1841, WP.

that could prove conclusively the primary importance of particular individuals in organizing opposition to Collins. It seems most likely that there was no single "guiding hand" and that discussions among like-minded individuals produced broad plans for cooperative action. And the indirect evidence relating to this action combines with the logic of personality, past activities, and private comments such as that to Weld to insist that Charles Stuart was very much his own man.

It would always have been completely out of character for him to serve simply as a spokesman for others. Over the past decade he had found emotional satisfaction in cooperative ventures. But he had always found like-minded individuals or associations through which to press his own uncompromising views. When he had found no such endorsement, he had doggedly pursued his own course, notably in relation to boycotts of slave-grown produce. Therein lay some of the reasons for his reputation for individuality verging on eccentricity. His independence, which had recently been displayed publicly on that issue at the London convention, was being asserted privately in disputes with Broad Street on other questions even as Collins crossed the Atlantic. In late September the nationwide lecturing tour of Stanton, Birney, and Scoble had reached Stuart's West Country base, and he joined his three old friends at meetings on successive nights in Bristol and Bath. If the four were presumably able to agree about the American issue, Stuart remained forcefully hostile to some new major preoccupations of Broad Street. Scoble wrote to his London colleagues that he had criticized "our views on the subject of East Indian slavery" and had also pained Scoble by talking favorably about Buxton's African Civilization Society. Indeed, he was so enthusiastic about Buxton's scheme that he and William Blair were talking of forming a local auxiliary society during the winter. This, wrote Scoble, would be "a mischievous precedent" that should be prevented if possible.[25]

In the months ahead, Indian slavery, in particular, continued to be discussed at length by the Broad Street committee. And events would prove that Stuart's opposition to its views remained complete. But for the time being, these differences were submerged because he found once again an American issue that he could press in Britain. The pull of America was very great when he bade a reluctant farewell to Henry and Elizabeth Stanton on December 3. As he wrote to Theodore Weld, "The associations which arise hurry me across the Atlantic. I almost dream and then in a moment I awaken, & find myself far from you and my beloved sisters & friends in America, and my heart beats and questions, when oh when

25. Scoble to Tredgold, October 29, 1840, S. 18, C10/27, RHL.

shall I again embrace them?" What held him back, as always, was "all the bustle of antislavery travelling"; the arrival of Collins had fortuitously made it possible for the time being to make common cause with fellow abolitionists whose paths were otherwise diverging from his own.[26]

One assessment of the way Stuart's activities complemented, rather than merely executed, Broad Street policies was provided by one of Collins' English supporters, Thomas Sturge. A cousin of Joseph, but from the outset a supporter of Old Organization, Thomas wrote to mutual American friends explaining Collins' difficulties. By the time he had arrived in Britain many members of the national society had made a premature commitment to the American and Foreign Anti-Slavery Society without fully understanding the woman question. Collins had played into the hands of rumormongers by not bringing with him properly signed credentials to present to Broad Street. Moreover, continued Sturge, Collins had found himself in a "distressing" situation "in as much as being in poor health when he arrived, he met with a very unkind & uncalled for opposition from a violent man, a Captain Stewart . . . I have heard his conduct condemned but this did not prevent your friend Collins being greatly hurt by it, & I do not wonder that this, and the improper conduct of the British and Foreign Anti-Slavery Society Committee made him almost despair of obtaining justice from the latter body."[27]

Stuart may not have been averse to private gossip and character assassination, but his overall contribution was distinctive for the openness of his hostility to Collins. At a time when all the pro-Garrison British abolitionists were complaining of sinister, clandestine maneuvers, Stuart had characteristically proclaimed his opposition in print. In January, 1841, he published a two-page pamphlet that was soon circulating as widely as the alleged slanders and slurs propagated by Broad Street. The publication took the form of a heavily biased historical summary of American antislavery trends followed by a demand that Collins and Remond be rejected by British philanthropists. The American schism was the result of the "insane innovation" that had insisted that "women ought to be intruded, as delegates, debaters, and managers, into mixed Societies of men and women." Collins and Remond had come "to beg our money" to aid the "pernicious" "*American*—or *woman*-intruding—Anti-Slavery Society." To give that organization money would "impede rather than aid the general progress of Abolition," and "the sacred and powerful influence

26. Stuart to Weld, December 3, 1840, WP.
27. Thomas Sturge to the Chapmans, April 5, 1841, in Taylor, *British and American Abolitionists*, 146.

exercised so nobly and so beneficially by the late London Convention, in decidedly and at once rejecting the woman-intruding delusion, would be paralysed or lost." Abolition in America was a "cause *worthy of all support*," for American slavery was the "most desperately corrupt and ferocious" system in existence. But those with money to spare should send it to Lewis Tappan in New York rather than help those who, "after making the most injurious discord in their own Country, did their best to distract our Meeting in June" and now solicited money "as if the American Anti-Slavery Society represented the great body of the Abolitionists of the United States, instead of a minor and evil part of them, which is full of dogmatism and contention."[28]

Stuart's pamphlet was widely read by his opponents. Elizabeth Pease sent a copy to Harriet Martineau, who returned it with the wry comment: "I am edified by Stuart's complaint of *dogmatism*." In common with other Collins sympathizers, Martineau was less indignant about Stuart's blunt polemics than about the "vague insinuations" propagated by Broad Street. It was a "prodigious breach of the plainest rules of morality" to suggest that Collins was disreputable or dishonest "without explaining what they mean!"[29] Nevertheless, Stuart's attack was taken seriously by Collins and his supporters as the controversies surrounding the fund-raising mission reached a climax in Glasgow.

EVEN BEFORE Collins arrived in the city in February, 1841, the Glasgow Emancipation Society was convulsed by disputes over the American issues. And for a number of reasons those controversies were to assume a prominent place in the public life of the city. As C. Duncan Rice has explained in some detail, antislavery in Scotland had developed both more recently and more vigorously than in many other areas. In the later eighteenth century Scottish philosophers had provided some of the strongest intellectual arguments against slavery without developing a comparably strong organization to attack an institution with which Glasgow had major economic connections. Some abolitionists had appeared in the early nineteenth century, but even in 1833 the Scots had played no more than an ancillary role in the campaign that had led the British government to outlaw slavery. That decision, however, freed them of their inhibitions. Glasgow no longer had an economic involvement in slavery. And by focusing on American slavery, which was beyond the direct influence of the

---

28. The broadsheet, printed by George Wood and Sons, Bath, has no title. It is reprinted verbatim in Barnes and Dumond (eds.), *Weld-Grimké Letters*, II, 858–60, and in *Liberator*, May 7, 1841, p. 74.
29. Harriet Martineau to E. Pease, February 27, 1841, BPL.

British government, the Scots embraced a cause that did not require them to acknowledge the privileged position of an antislavery society based in London. In addition to this regional pride, the links with George Thompson pushed many abolitionists into a pro-Garrison position. Thompson had been a major force in Scottish abolitionism in 1833 and 1838. And it was under Scottish patronage that he had visited America and consolidated his friendship with Garrison.[30]

Nevertheless, these trends did not make Scottish support for Old Organization monolithic. In Rice's words, antislavery disagreements developed to an "extraordinary level of vehemence" because they were used as a means of furthering existing religious feuds. Scottish religious politics may have been unusually intense because, in this nation without a government of its own, there were inadequate outlets for the energies and talents that might have found expression in a national parliament. This does not mean that the Scots were insincere in attacking American slavery. On the contrary, Scottish evangelicals, no less than their English counterparts, were convinced that slavery was the embodiment of sin. But their religious politics encouraged partisan views about the connections between religion and American slavery. The general context was a conflict between the established Church of Scotland and various voluntary denominations—the old Presbyterian Secession churches, the Congregationalists, and the Baptists—which were gaining strength, particularly in Glasgow. Since there was no established church in the United States, members of the established Scottish church could make capital out of the flourishing of slavery in a society dominated by voluntarism. It thus became urgent for Scottish voluntarists to combat American slavery to vindicate the voluntarist principle. Even so, Scottish divisions over the American antislavery split were not simply a matter of established church against voluntary denominations. The Scottish denominations tended to have strong links with their American counterparts. With so many American clerical abolitionists supporting New Organization, such links in some cases may have helped influence Scottish decisions about taking sides. At the same time, the voluntary denominations, in their competition for ascendancy at home, were not averse to making capital out of the links between rival denominations and American churches tainted by slaveholding connections.[31]

Despite these distinctive local influences, Scottish abolitionists were also typically British. As affluent members of the middle class they were as

---

30. C. Duncan Rice, *The Scots Abolitionists, 1833–61* (Baton Rouge, 1981), 19–29.
31. *Ibid.*, 49–58, 197–98.

likely as Englishmen to feel threatened by more radical domestic political agitation. In the climax of Collins' visit, local manifestations of Chartism were to play a vital role. The same middle-class conservatism was potentially—if more remotely—at odds with the radical implications of Garrisonism. Individual decisions about the American issue could easily be influenced by personal responses to the implications of women's equality. In these circumstances the role of an interpreter of the American scene could be very important. Such was to be Stuart's contribution.

The immediate cause of the contentious atmosphere that greeted Collins in Glasgow was an appendix to the Glasgow Emancipation Society's sixth annual report published in late 1840 in which the secretaries, Smeal and Murray, had effectively endorsed the Garrisonian position. This stand enraged other committee members, led by the Reverend Ralph Wardlaw, who claimed that such a commitment had not been discussed by the society and was an unauthorized reversal of the position its delegates had taken at the London convention, when they had voted to exclude female delegates. The dispute had spread beyond Glasgow in late January, when Joseph Sturge had asked for his name to be withdrawn from the Glasgow society's list of honorary corresponding members in protest against the offending appendix.[32]

When Collins met the Glasgow Emancipation Society committee on February 11, two of his three most prominent opponents, Wardlaw and the Reverend Dr. Hugh Heugh, stayed away. The third, the Reverend Dr. David King, was in the chair and questioned Collins closely about the American divisions. Although King presented the Garrisonian case "at some length," the committee decided to postpone consideration of his requests for "sympathy and pecuniary support" pending publication by his supporters of a pamphlet explaining the American divisions which he had mainly written while in Darlington.[33]

In the eyes of Smeal and Murray, the hostility of the three clerics was not attributable primarily to Joseph Sturge, even though they knew he had recently corresponded with Wardlaw. It was the work of Stuart: "About this time it was *discovered*, that Captain Stuart had sent to Dr. Wardlaw a printed letter, containing charges against the Original American Anti-Slavery Society, and against Messrs COLLINS and REMOND, its representatives in this country; which letter found its way to Dr. Heugh and also to Dr. King, whilst no copy was sent by the Captain to the official organs of the Society, the Secretaries. . . . The Captain *knew*, that *that*

---

32. *Resolutions of the Glasgow Emancipation Society*, 5–7.
33. Ibid., 14.

was not the quarter for his purpose."[34] Collins himself at last had to admit that Stuart's opposition was important. He was soon referring to Stuart's publication as "a most defamatory printed circular" and complaining that from the time it was received "certain members of the Committee began to exhibit hostile feelings towards the American society, and coldness towards its representatives." Smeal and Murray decided that the best response would be to invite Stuart to Glasgow to debate his charges with Collins before the committee and later at a public meeting. In a letter to vice-presidents of the society, including Wardlaw and Heugh, they pointed out that the emancipation of American slaves, which was "now the main object of the Friends of Freedom," was imperiled by the American divisions. In the United States the disputes were "paralysing the efforts of both parties." In Britain they would "tend to damp the energies of Abolitionists . . . and perhaps be laid hold of, as an excuse for refusing co-operation in the great work of advancing human liberty." The only remedy seemed to be a "full and free examination into the differences which separate our American friends." And Stuart was the obvious man to invite to represent New Organization against the Old Organization advocacy of Collins: "Charles Stuart—or Captain Stuart as he is often termed—has been the most assiduous in spreading information regarding the state of matters in the United States; and is, we believe, the best acquainted with the circumstances of any man in this country."[35]

The invitation to Stuart intensified the conflict in the Glasgow Emancipation Society, partly as a result of his contemptuous response. In a letter from Bath dated March 8 he rejected the invitation out of hand. He was not aware that his charges needed any defense. They were simple matters of fact, which could be proved or disproved "quite irrespective of me." He was "not of opinion that *truth* becomes *more true* by mere repetition." Nonetheless, he did "most unequivocally, solemnly, and fully, re-affirm their entire truthfulness." With a thrust reminiscent of his counterattacks against superior officers in India thirty years before, he continued: "I may add, my dear Smeal, with all candour and kindness, that *if* I am to judge of the Glasgow Emancipation Committee, by the sentiments and positions advanced by you and dear John Murray, *on this subject*, when I last met you in Glasgow, I should be insane in submitting myself to you as judges, knowing the total and deplorable derangement of your views, *in this matter*, both as to facts and principles." He went

34. Ibid., 11.
35. *Liberator*, May 21, 1841, p. 82; also letter from Collins to Glasgow *Argus*, reprinted in *Liberator*, June 25, 1841, p. 102; *Resolutions of the Glasgow Emancipation Society*, 11–12.

on to dismiss Collins with the same contempt the American had displayed toward him. He had offered months before in Edinburgh to debate the issues with Collins around the kingdom. But since then he had satisfied himself that he had "at that time greatly over-rated his power of mischief in the Abolition cause amongst us, so that I do not feel at all warranted at present, in duty, to turn any portion of my time and means from the direct service of God and of my fellow-men, to the indulgence of irrelevant, captious, and pernicious questions."[36]

Stuart concluded by pointing out that he was shortly "to make a trip of a few months to America." He would there explore the question further and, on his return, "probably make a pretty extensive Anti-Slavery tour" to report his findings. This reply left Smeal and Murray with no alternative but to abandon the proposed Collins-Stuart debate. But their invitation to Stuart had already precipitated a crisis. His allies on the Glasgow Emancipation Society committee responded as indignantly as he had to the joint secretaries' plans for a debate. Wardlaw promptly resigned from the society. Heugh told Smeal and Murray that a debate would "bring upon us the merited derision of the public in Glasgow." He remained in the society for two further committee meetings before resigning on March 16. These resignations—and all the turmoil they caused when Smeal and Murray made sincere attempts to have them withdrawn—were not, of course, the result of Stuart's influence alone. In both cases the overt issue was the commitment to Old Organization and women's rights allegedly made in the appendix to the sixth annual report of the society. But Stuart's "printed letter" can only have powerfully reinforced the misgivings that both Wardlaw and Heugh already felt on this question. Heugh, in rejecting the proposal for a Stuart-Collins debate, wrote exclusively of the woman question of America and the inappropriateness of advocating women's rights in Britain. Smeal and Murray affected astonishment at "so irrelevant a reply." They were not surprised that Heugh should disapprove of a public discussion, but they claimed to regard it as inexplicable that he believed "the discussion was to be upon a question never once in the most distant manner referred to in our letter." The argument of Smeal and Murray here was disingenuous polemics. They must have known quite well why Heugh had associated the invitation to Stuart with the woman question. Stuart's circular, which had prompted the committee to nominate him as the most suitable British advocate for New Organization, had attributed the American schism exclusively to the woman question. It had argued that those who supported

36. Reprinted in *Resolutions of the Glasgow Emancipation Society*, 24–25.

Collins would be demonstrating that they "value the intrusion of women into the debates and management of mixed Societies more highly than the cause of liberty and love." This allegation can only have hardened the resolve of Heugh and Wardlaw against committing the Glasgow society to Old Organization, for both had equally conservative views about the role of women. As Wardlaw put it in his resignation correspondence, such a commitment placed "Woman's misnamed *rights* in opposition to Woman's appropriate *character*." And Heugh was no less confident that he knew what "British Ladies" needed and desired: "They would thank no man to advocate imaginary rights, from the exercise of which, were they conceded, they would shrink with becoming sensitiveness."[37]

Collins was to spend nine weeks in Glasgow. Amid a flurry of private lobbying, extraordinary committee meetings, and, eventually, public meetings attended by thousands, fortunes fluctuated between the two contending factions. The resignations of Wardlaw and Heugh seemed to leave the committee leaning to the pro-Garrison side. But the more conservative—largely clerical—opposition, led by King, was regularly able to muster sufficient support to frustrate open commitment of the society to Collins' mission. In early March the secretaries circularized their own membership "and all the leading Anti-Slavery Friends in the United Kingdom" soliciting financial support for Collins' pamphlet on the American split, *Right and Wrong Among the Abolitionists of the United States*. But soon opposition within the committee compelled a second edition of the circular in which Smeal and Murray accepted responsibility as individuals, expressly denying any official commitment by the society. Similarly, a committee meeting on March 29 approved a pro-Collins circular, addressed to "the abolitionists of the United Kingdom," only to see the decision overturned at the next meeting on April 13. A series of resolutions was passed declaring the neutrality of the Glasgow Emancipation Society in the American dispute and expressly refusing to endorse "any publication or agent" of either American society "till the most ample opportunity has been afforded of investigating their differences."[38]

By this stage Collins was deeply pessimistic about his prospects in Glasgow. The March 29 decision, he told Richard Webb, had been produced by the regular committee, which was strongly in favor of the American Anti-Slavery Society. The subsequent reversal had been achieved when "the clergy" had packed the April 13 meeting with nominal but usually inactive members of the committee. His conviction that

37. Ibid., 25, 12–13, 18–23.
38. Ibid., 30–36.

the committee had been "sacrificed to New organization" was unshaken by a public meeting attended by twenty-five hundred people. The meeting had lasted six hours, and there had been evidence of considerable public support for his position. But nothing had been settled. And although there was to be another meeting, he was dispirited because the first one had been disrupted by a Chartist demonstration and then reported in a biased fashion by a conservative press. But though he wrote despondently to Webb of the difficulties of contending with "a great body of Chartists on the one hand and a large body of the tools of clergymen on the other hand," there was no question which of these extremes Collins preferred.[39]

For Scottish evangelical reformers it may have been a major departure to seek alliance with the Chartists. For Collins it was not only a necessary tactic but also a logical development of the radical distaste he had already expressed for the iniquities of the British class system. On April 27 a public meeting of four to five thousand included an unusually large working-class component. By accepting pro-Chartist resolutions the antislavery organizers were at last able to resolve their own issue in Collins' favor. Resolutions were passed condemning the committee's treatment of the American, expressing no confidence in the British and Foreign Anti-Slavery Society, and pledging "sympathy and support" to "the *original* American Anti-Slavery Society." By resolving to add seventeen new members to the committee of the Glasgow Emancipation Society the meeting ensured that its pro-Garrisonian posture would be virtually permanent. Collins' reaction was smugly arrogant: "By plotting and packaging on the part of the clergy & [sleepy?] & most foolish credulity on the part of my friends, the Glasgow Em. Com. became new organized. I then told them that I would leave unless they would put themselves under my direction and do according to my commandments, which if they would, I would again restore the com. to them. They agreed to it. . . . They have got the society back into their own hands, where they do not again foolishly mean to lose it."[40]

Nevertheless, it was close to a Pyrrhic victory for Collins. His protracted stay in Glasgow prevented him from any extensive fund-raising or campaigning elsewhere, and it caused constant modifications of his plans to visit Dublin, until eventually he was able to spend only a few days there

39. Collins to Webb, April 25, 1841, BPL.
40. *Resolutions of the Glasgow Emancipation Society*, 3–5; Collins to Garrison, May 2, 1841, in Taylor, *British and American Abolitionists*, 150; Webb to Garrison, May 30, 1841, ibid., 152; Rice, *Scots Abolitionists*, 108–13.

before returning to the United States in mid-1841. Charles Stuart's condescending conclusions about the American's limited "power of mischief" had been largely vindicated, despite the eventual Old Organization victory in Glasgow.

10 THE SENSE OF BETRAYAL

STUART'S OPPOSITION to Old Organization in 1841 was not confined to his attacks on the mission of John A. Collins. Indeed, he pursued his vendetta against the Garrisonians with a thoroughness that puzzled and sorrowed many who had been his friends. For some the eccentricity he had always displayed now seemed the only explanation for a cruel betrayal. In his only detailed explanation of his attitudes, Stuart plausibly argued that he was being more consistent than his opponents. Yet though this explanation was intellectually honest as well as coherent, it remained incomplete. To an extent he himself perhaps did not appreciate, his opponents were correct in drawing attention to the emotional intensity that now made him an implacable opponent of Garrison.

STUART'S ASSERTION in early March, 1841, that he had more important things to do than travel to Glasgow to meet Collins may have sounded evasive and provocative, with its accompanying claim that "my circular has produced, in a good measure, the healing and purifying effect, for which it was solemnly and kindly intended." But it was very far from being an empty excuse. Exactly a week before writing to the Glasgow committee he had written to Weld of his impending return to the United States. As usual, he exuded intense commitment to both their friendship and the antislavery cause. Recent correspondence had evidently revealed, not for the first time, wide divergence in their religious views—"but we differ, as of old, in love." Delighted to hear of the birth of a second son to Angelina, he added: "Dearest Theodore, I beg you, I require you, by our love, to call your younger boy, *Theodore*—I want our names to go together. Were it possible indeed, I should call the elder Theodore, & the younger Charles." But although he looked forward to a reunion in New York in May, he made it clear that he was drawn principally by "the cause of our dear down trodden brother." The American and Foreign Anti-Slavery Society was "more than ever an object of solemn tenderness" to him, and he wanted to attend its anniversary meeting. He enclosed a copy of the circular that had caused such a stir in Glasgow to show Weld how he had been preoccupied by "the intrusive pertinacity of Mr. Collins in this country." He was now confident that, though Collins had "succeeded in alienating a few of our noblest minds," the "evil" was very limited.[1]

More than simply the chores of travel, however, preoccupied him in early March. For a moment there was a strange echo from the past with the news that his old adversary, Elliott Cresson, was once again in Britain, this time accompanied by R. R. Gurley. Two days before rejecting the Glasgow invitation, Stuart had written to Broad Street asking for news of a discussion between Scoble and the two colonizationists.[2] But knowing that Scoble and others in the national society were hostile even to Buxton's Civilization Society, he doubtless felt that there was little need on this occasion for a further anti-ACS campaign. His preoccupation with the struggle against Old Organization made him unwilling to spend time in Glasgow.

In the long term, British sympathy for the Garrisonians was centered not only in Dublin and Glasgow but also in Bristol. There Dr. J. B. Estlin, a Unitarian eye specialist, and his daughter Mary emerged in the late 1840s as strong supporters and diligent correspondents, particularly after a visit by Garrison in 1846. But it was some years after that before their fellow abolitionists in the neighborhood became wholeheartedly committed to Old Organization. A major reason for the delay, as the Estlins eventually made clear, was the strong influence Stuart had exerted, particularly on women abolitionists, in 1841. A decade afterward Mary Estlin wrote proudly to Anne Warren Weston in Boston about Fanny Tribe, a recent convert to pro-Garrison convictions: "I feel particularly proud of her as a pupil because she received her early anti-slavery lessons from Capt. Chas. Stuart & was long under Scoble's tutorship." Mrs. Tribe herself soon confirmed this. She wrote to Maria Weston Chapman that she had recently met some of the Bath antislavery women, who exhibited strong

1. Stuart to Smeal, March 8, 1841, in *Resolutions of the Glasgow Emancipation Society*, 24; Stuart to Weld, March 1, 1841, WP.
2. Stuart to Tredgold, March 6, 1841, S. 18, C10/89, RHL.

prejudice against Garrison and his friends: "I can fully sympathise with them, having myself had all the feelings and prejudices under which they labour: for I, like them, learnt much of my A.S. from Capt. Chas. Stuart & Mr. Scoble."[3]

Fanny Tribe had been no isolated disciple. On March 4, 1841, at the very time he was being invited to debate with Collins in Glasgow, Stuart met the committee of the Bristol and Clifton Auxiliary Ladies Anti-Slavery Society. The minutes of the committee reveal only that he "laid down some interesting statements before them" and that, at a subsequent meeting, "it was resolved to devote £2 to Captain Stuart's mission." The full extent of the activities represented by these terse entries was revealed only in 1852, when the Bristol group published its reasons for renouncing its affiliations with the British and Foreign Anti-Slavery Society. The society had been "established under the auspices of Captain Charles Stuart," who had advised cooperation with the American and Foreign Anti-Slavery Society, claiming that this organization had been formed in 1833 but changed its name in 1840, when others had intruded "new and injurious views" and appropriated "the original name of the society":

> He represented the American and Foreign Anti-Slavery Society as embracing the Christian abolitionists of the United States; and the American Anti-Slavery Society, from which it had separated, as composed chiefly of persons who were infidel in their sentiments, opposed to all that is deemed Christian, and unfaithful to the cause of the slave; making it subsidiary to the promotion of their infidel views, and introducing for discussion on the anti-slavery platform the questions of "woman's rights", "anti-sabbath", "no human government", and such like.
>
> Fully relying on this information, we carefully avoided any intercourse with the members of the American Anti-Slavery Society; and, at the recommendation of Captain Stuart, entered into correspondence with Miss Martha V. Ball, of Boston, secretary of the Massachusetts Abolition Society, requesting to be informed of any way in which we could aid the cause we had so much at heart.[4]

---

3. Mary Estlin to Anne Warren Weston, October 11, 1851; Fanny Tribe to M. W. Chapman, June 11, 1852, BPL.

4. Minutes of Bristol and Clifton Auxiliary Ladies Anti-Slavery Society, March 4, 1841, Estlin Papers, microfilm reel 3, Australian National Library, Canberra; Bristol and Clifton Ladies Anti-Slavery Society, *Special Report of the Bristol and Clifton Ladies Anti-Slavery Society; During Eighteen Months, from January 1851 to June 1852 with a Statement of the Reasons for its Separation from the British and Foreign Anti-Slavery Society* (London, 1852), 6.

At the same time as he was working directly on local opinion in the West Country Stuart was preparing yet another pamphlet for the press. Published on April 1, 1841, *Oneida and Oberlin* contained brief histories of those two antislavery educational institutions and an account of the martyrdom of Elijah Lovejoy. But it was essentially a plea for British financial support for the "noble band of upright and impartial spirits" who were fighting for abolition amid "danger and contumely." He stressed that this noble band was *"not they*, who hold the intrusion, as delegates, debators, and governors, of women into mixed societies of men and women, so dear, that they trample upon all harmony in their effort to impose it upon others: not they, who affirm we owe no allegiance to human governments: not they, who would destroy the christian sabbath, &c.: but they, who, rejecting all these destructive dogmas, confine themselves to their proper object; viz., the emancipation of the slave, on christian principles, in a lawful, peaceable, and christian manner."[5]

The last thing Stuart did in Liverpool immediately before going on board ship for New York on April 15 was to scribble a hasty note to the assistant secretary of the Broad Street committee, asking that he circulate "my 'Oneida and Oberlin' as extensively as you can." The pamphlet was soon advertised for sale in Bristol, London, Edinburgh, and Glasgow in the society's organ, the *Anti-Slavery Reporter*. Editorial comment in the same paper summarized its contents—without mentioning its polemical nature—and concluded: "It is full of interesting matter, of very small cost, and highly deserving of general circulation."[6]

STUART'S 1841 visit to America proved to be short. He spent much of his time visiting his relatives in Canada. He also had brief reunions with the Weld family, including one with Cornelia, which produced no recorded flickers of emotion or regret. By September, when the *Liberator* was reporting the details of Collins' belated success in Glasgow, Stuart was already preparing to return to Britain. On September 25 he was saying farewell to Theodore in characteristic style. He hoped to return to America within two years: "If earlier called home, do not unduly mourn that your poor, tottering, struggling friend, was the sooner called from battle to victory—Then oh then our Meeting!!"[7]

As in the past, these by now almost ritual references to physical disintegration were not to be taken too seriously. In June Lewis Tappan had

5. Stuart, *Oneida and Oberlin*, 4.
6. Stuart to Joseph Soul, April 15, 1841, C115/56, RHL; *Anti-Slavery Reporter*, II (1841), 81, 112.
7. *Liberator*, September 10, 1841, p. 145; Stuart to Weld, September 25, 1841, WP.

commented on Stuart's arrival in New York "in good health." He had brought with him "a pamphlet from John A. Collins, which I can not but look upon as a vile production—full of misrepresentation and calumny." During the rest of his short stay he had continued to pursue his antislavery commitments with typical dedication. He traveled extensively among fugitive blacks and sought answers, through a published letter, to fifteen questions about their numbers and condition. And he sent out two circulars, from Toronto and New York, asking abolitionists to supply him, "as *briefly* & as *lucidly* as may be in their power, with *their* views, as to the causes of *division* in the Anti-Slavery Associations of the United States." In the absence of any list of addressees it is hard to know whether this was a serious attempt to understand a range of opinion or merely a device to acquire further ammunition against Old Organization. Sarah Grimké—like her sister uncomfortably neutral in the great American quarrel—eventually wrote to Elizabeth Pease that "Charles Stuart took much pains to ascertain the real cause of the dissention [sic] in our ranks." But Pease was unlikely to be convinced by these words, for Stuart's activities on his return to Britain had seemed to her a mere continuation of his previous campaign. The first she knew of his return was when her mother received from him a copy of a pamphlet put out by the anti-Garrisonian Massachusetts Abolition Society. "Poor fellow," she wrote to Collins in October, 1841, "he seems resolved on not allowing the subject to rest."[8]

Any latent Garrisonians in Bristol would have reached the same conclusions as Elizabeth Pease. In late October Stuart addressed a meeting of his protégées in the Bristol and Clifton Ladies Anti-Slavery Society. He reported on his recent observations among the colored people of Canada, mentioning the great opportunity that existed for British educational projects among the one-thousand-strong black population of Toronto. And he also stressed that a main reason for his recent transatlantic journey had been to try to ascertain "the cause of divisions existing there" among abolitionists. He had discovered, as he had been willing to assert before this fact-finding mission, that the problem "proceeds from mistaken zeal on

8. Lewis Tappan to Tredgold, June 18, 1841, in Annie Heloise Abel and Frank J. Klingberg (eds.), *A Side-Light on Anglo-American Relations 1839–58 Furnished by the Correspondence of Lewis Tappan and Others with the British and Foreign Anti-Slavery Society* (New York, 1927), 81; Sandwich, Upper Canada (Ontario) *Western Herald*, July 16, 1841, p. 2, cols. 4–5; handwritten circular from Stuart, June 11, 1841, Ms. A.21,12, p. 39, BPL; and, soliciting replies to a New York City address, similar circular, June 5, 1841, SP; Sarah Grimké to E. Pease, February 11, 1842, in Taylor, *British and American Abolitionists*, 163; to Collins, October 15, 1841, BPL.

the part of individuals obnoxiously intruding extraneous and distracting questions."⁹

This activity was to be far from the end of Stuart's opposition to Old Organization. And in the phrase "extraneous and distracting questions" lies the basic explanation for the hostility that both annoyed and puzzled his former abolitionist friends.

"*Et tu, Brute?*" ran the heading in the *Liberator* in May, 1841, when it reproduced in full Stuart's pamphlet attack on Collins and Remond. The Shakespearean cliché hinted at the seriousness and the sorrow with which his hostility was viewed. But in implying bewilderment at the treachery of an old friend it was also representative of a widespread misunderstanding of Stuart's position by both American and British supporters of Old Organization.¹⁰

The *Liberator* initially affected indifference to Stuart's campaign with a curt introduction: "The following is a circular from the pen of C. STUART of England, which he has widely distributed in that country. To the friends of primitive abolitionism in the United States its spirit and design will be obvious, and render all comments unnecessary." But the sense of betrayal was deeply felt. Privately Garrison was soon to complain to Elizabeth Pease of rumors that Stuart had recently circulated widely in England copies of *Knapp's Liberator*, a paper produced once only by Garrison's estranged former publishing partner, Isaac Knapp, and designed to prove "that I am no better than a swindler or knave!" "Et tu, Brute!," he repeated to Pease. "Is it possible that my old friend Stuart can be guilty of this mean and wicked conduct? Have I indeed fallen so low in his estimation, that he regards me as a villain in practice, as well as a heathen in speculation?"¹¹

Stuart's attack was resented not just because he was a man whom Garrison numbered "once amongst my most ardent friends" but because he had seemed one of the very few British abolitionists in tune with the American antislavery temperament. The two men had drifted apart since the early days when the *Liberator* had exuberantly reproduced Stuart's anticolonization tracts. But as recently as October, 1840, the paper had recalled Stuart's distinctive qualities. In a contemptuous editorial on the London convention it had referred to British abolitionism as "cowardly, heartless, and corrupt." The British movement was an upper-class affec-

9. Minutes of Bristol and Clifton Auxiliary Ladies Anti-Slavery Society, October 27, 1841, Estlin Papers, reel 3.
10. *Liberator*, May 7, 1841, p. 74.
11. *Ibid.*; Garrison to E. Pease, May 15, 1842, BPL.

tation. Its exponents liked to "bask in the sunshine of royalty, and to be applauded to the echo in Exeter Hall, with a royal duke in the chair." But "as soon as any portion of it is imported into this country," it shunned American abolitionists and stood aloof from all contact with black Americans. Only Stuart, George Thompson, and Harriet Martineau had remained "faithful and true" in America.[12]

Two weeks after declaring any comment on Stuart's pamphlet to be "unnecessary," the *Liberator* reproduced extensive extracts from the appendix to Collins' pamphlet, *Right and Wrong*, about Stuart's "defamatory printed circular" and about their direct confrontation in Edinburgh the previous November. Also reproduced was a comment on Stuart's circular from Charles Remond. From Stuart's condemnation of him as a delegate of the American Anti-Slavery Society and a member of the "Garrison party" it would appear, wrote Remond, that "what was great, and good, and noble, and christian, and philanthropic, and *anti-slavery*—in 1835, has become small, and evil, and mean, and infidel and slavish, and pro-slavery—in 1841! Indeed may we not exclaim, 'How have the mighty fallen!'" A week later the next edition of the *Liberator* carried a detailed account of the way Stuart's circular had ruined Collins' reception in Glasgow. From the time it was received "certain members of the Committee began to exhibit hostile feelings towards the American Society, and coldness towards its representative."[13]

To several of his new opponents there was a simple explanation for Stuart's hostility: he was mentally unbalanced. Garrison concluded his complaint to Elizabeth Pease about Stuart's vendetta in Britain: "For this and for other acts of unkindness, on his part, toward myself, I make all possible allowance on account of his peculiar temperament, and most cheerfully forgive him." Far less forgiving was John A. Collins in his allegations about Stuart's "turbulent, wild, and disorderly" conduct at the London convention: "The epithet *frantic* is the only one that exactly defines the temper of his mind, in relation to old organized anti-slavery in the United States." And Thomas Sturge explained Collins' predicament as stemming from almost schizoid behavior by Stuart, "a most sincere & zealous abolitionist, capable of great pleasantness of manner & patience & persuasive power—but from some weakness capable of a degree of inveteracy more befitting those bereft of reason than a peaceable Christian."[14]

12. *Liberator*, October 23, 1840, p. 170.
13. *Ibid.*, May 21, 28, 1841, pp. 82–83, 85.
14. Garrison to E. Pease, May 15, 1842, BPL; Collins quoted in *Liberator*, May 21, 1841, p. 82; Thomas Sturge to H. G. and M. W. Chapman, April 5, 1841, in Taylor, *British and American Abolitionists*, 146.

Such explanations no doubt appealed to many Garrisonians because Stuart's earlier work made his hostility now seem a betrayal. The "Et tu, Brute" theme was in other minds long before Garrison published it in May, 1841. The previous November Elizabeth Pease had depicted Stuart, in a letter to Collins, as one of those Garrison associates "who seemed to have drunk so largely into his spirit. . . . Alas! how might the dear Garrison exclaim 'twas not an Enemy that did it, else I could have borne it, but my familiar friend." It was no doubt also from Pease that Collins heard some of the "many anecdotes" which, he claimed, could be cited about Stuart's "various efforts, to bring women forward in the anti-slavery cause." She had presumably been very much in Stuart's mind when, according to Collins, he had attempted to secure a female delegate from Darlington to the antiapprenticeship convention in London in 1837.[15] As Stuart developed his polemics against the woman-intruding Garrisonians, none of his opponents stressed that as an elderly bachelor he might be expected to conform to the orthodoxies of the period about the place of women in society. Failing to see that his previous advocacy of female abolitionism had always stressed separate roles, they chose to cite his antifeminism as further evidence of the way he had changed.

Yet not all Stuart's opponents saw his hostility as a wild *volte-face*. Both Richard Webb and John Murray recognized that American trends had introduced new issues, and they believed that Stuart's background and training, rather than an irrational temperament, dictated his attitudes to them. Webb found Garrison's now crucial nonresistant and anticlerical views compatible with his own Quakerism. Indeed, he was "utterly amazed at the hostility" shown by his fellow Quaker, Joseph Sturge. Far less surprising to him was the position of Scoble, "who is a priest to the back bone," or Stuart, "who altho' a man of good impulses is a priest & a soldier too!"[16] Stuart's military background seemed to Murray, too, to be the most obvious reason for his "inveterate opposition" to Garrison. He put it to Stuart that, if Garrison's "views on the Peace question" became general, "they would overthrow all the paraphernalia of war and make it incumbent on him and all conscientious men who held anything like peace principles to abandon an income derived from such a source."[17]

Murray put this hypothesis forward when he wrote to Stuart "asking him to state his objections to Garrison & the cause of his great change of mind in regard to him." In reply, Stuart insisted that it was Garrison and

15. E. Pease to Collins, November 16, 1840, BPL; *Liberator*, May 21, 1841, p. 82.
16. Webb to Collins, January 7, 1841, BPL.
17. Murray described his interrogation of Stuart and reproduced a copy of Stuart's reply, dated November 15, 1840, in Murray to Collins, December 23, 1840, BPL.

not himself who had apparently changed. "I judged of Mr. Garrison *formerly*, as he *then* appeared—I judge of him *now*, as he *now* appears." Formerly he had seemed a "thorough and zealous friend of the slave":

> He is *now* just as much of an Abolitionist, as *other new* dogmas which he has since brought out will permit: He is an abolitionist, when he can get others to adopt his *womans-right notions*: but until then the rights as he conscientiously deems them of women, drown in his ear, the cry of the Slave. . . . He is an Abolitionist; but he does all that he can to discredit & destroy, one of the most dutiful and powerful means for the deliverance of the Slave i.e. faithfulness to duty at the Elections, thereby giving over the government completely, to the hands of the slave party.

It was now that Stuart recalled his willingness to subordinate his belief in a boycott of slave produce to the interests of antislavery unity.[18] This was an accurate reflection of his disagreements in 1835 with Garrison, Elizur Wright, Gerrit Smith, and others, when he had articulated his principle of "a wise division of labour" in the reform movement. He had maintained his personal boycott but agreed that it would be as inappropriate for the American Anti-Slavery Society to become an anti-slave-produce society as it would be for temperance societies corporately to pursue abolition. This was the principle that was violated by the Garrisonian tendency to pursue other reform causes under the antislavery banner.

It is probably true, as the historian Aileen Kraditor has argued, that before the American split had finally occurred, the Garrisonians had not in fact infringed this principle: they had largely kept their other reform goals off the antislavery platform. Stuart had entered the controversy late, when the split had released the Garrisonians from the need for self-denial in the interests of antislavery unity. In these circumstances the changes he perceived in Garrison may have stood out particularly starkly. But there is every reason to suppose that, had he remained in the United States through the period of growing dissension, he would have seen the tendencies of Garrisonian policies in the same hostile terms. The issues he defined as central—the woman question and the question of political action—were much more than matters of tactical disagreement. Stuart inevitably would have opposed Garrison on these issues because they related to fundamental questions about the nature of society and government.[19]

18. *Ibid.*
19. Aileen S. Kraditor, "An Interpretation of Factionalism in the Abolitionist Movement," in Curry (ed.), *Abolitionists*, 76–88; the themes of this article are fully developed in Kraditor's *Means and Ends in American Abolitionism: William Lloyd Garrison and His Critics, 1834–50* (New York, 1969).

In the terminology applied particularly to this question by Aileen Kraditor, Stuart was a "reformer" to whom slavery was a blemish on a basically satisfactory society. He might be well aware of other blemishes such as drunkenness, but he was horrified by the attitude of "radical" abolitionists that slavery was merely "the worst example of the nation's reliance on force rather than love" and that abolition was therefore only one measure toward a total reorganization of American society, which would eliminate inequalities between the sexes, economic competition, and ultimately the system of government itself. Without doubt many British supporters of Garrison were far less radical than this. Murray felt, after reading Stuart's letter, that the only "tangible and tenable" objection he had to Garrison was the woman's rights question. But, wrote Murray to Collins, abolitionists had "nothing to do with this question" except when it was directly connected to the participation of women "in abolition societies and committees in equality with men." Collins may well have smiled at the naivete of this view. He and Garrison and others were certainly by now committed to a wider view of women's rights. Yet even so, Murray evidently failed to perceive that his own simple desire that women should be allowed to join antislavery societies raised in Stuart's mind the wider question of women's rights. As his anti-Collins circular had stressed, the crux of his opposition was that the intrusion of women "as delegates, debaters, and managers, into mixed societies of men and women" was an assertion of the principle that "whatever is morally right for a *man* to do is morally right for a woman to do." And to Stuart this principle was unacceptably disruptive of society. It placed the "Abolition effort as at war with the most sacred and fundamental of human relations—even with those relations, by which God has given to men and women their respective spheres, and by sacredly regarding which alone, the vast moral power of women with all its purifying influences, can be preserved to society."[20]

That the Garrisonian refusal to work through the established political system was at odds with Stuart's own constant preference for political agitation requires little further emphasis. Even though the lobbying methods he had been identified with since 1830 had been most effectively applied in Britain, his lecturing agency in New York, and particularly his organization of petitions to Congress, had demonstrated his commitment to orthodox political action in America, too. And as recently as the Lon-

20. Kraditor, "Interpretation of Factionalism," 76–88; Murray to Collins, December 23, 1840, BPL; Stuart's circular in Barnes and Dumond (eds.), *Weld-Grimké Letters*, II, 858–60.

don convention in June, 1840, the antislavery fraternity had heard him reiterate his faith in such methods. But as his letter to Murray made clear, this faith reflected something much more fundamental than a preference for time-honored tactics. The tactics themselves resulted from his commitment to government and order. To "beat up" for antislavery election candidates, as he had recommended to the convention, was in his eyes an effective way of achieving abolitionist goals. But even if the Garrisonian method of opting out of the political process had seemed more effective, he would have rejected it. An orderly government pursuing the wrong policies was preferable to anarchy. And in the same way—as he showed in answering Murray's direct question about his own military affiliations—he saw strong sanctions as the best guarantee of peace.

This orthodox political philosophy was related to equally orthodox religious beliefs. Stressing to Murray his belief "that there is a hell as well as heaven—that there is a force at hand, to restrain or cancel as well as exuberant kindness to cherish & to bless," he went on to suggest that "the streams of blood which have hitherto crimsoned the earth, would be but rills to the torrents which would deluge it should Mr. Garrison's principles prevail." He agreed with Murray that "the principles of Christianity are very sweeping . . . but it is equally true that under the idea of making for peace & order they do not sweep away either force or government—Anarchy & War, the inevitable results of 'no government' are what they sweep away."[21]

Stuart was correct in stressing the consistency of his views—in contrast to the changes in Garrison's—over the past decade of antislavery activity. His innovative work in the Agency Committee days may have seemed radical, but he had been merely exploiting new opportunities within the political system. He may have openly proclaimed that those opportunities were enhanced by the "agitation of the public mind" in Britain in late 1831. But he had stressed that this was, "of course, only as far as is consistent with good order and the public peace." And he had condemned "the outrages on the public safety which have so disgraced one or two places." In the United States the same commitment to government authority as he now proclaimed to Murray had been shown in his letters to James Birney: "God invests civil governments, with corrective powers, without limit, for the support of good, & for the punishment of evil doers." Moreover, there had been no inconsistencies in his related views on military force. Although he may have appeared to fellow abolitionists as a most unlikely military pensioner, he had never been an un-

21. Murray to Collins, December 23, 1840, BPL.

qualified pacifist. He had not, for instance, repudiated the views he had published as long before as 1820 carefully defining the circumstances in which war was justified. He had on that occasion expressed his "most affectionate admiration" for the papers published by peace societies. In the Scriptures he had found "the most lucid and undeniable condemnation of the whole spirit of contention." And this reinforced his emotional abhorrence of the cruelties of warfare. But he had also found compelling scriptural authority in support of "defensive war," and in certain circumstances he would go further. For instance, the war against "the gigantic and horrible power of Bonaparte, was an exception, and, generally speaking, fully warranted all the measures, of which I am aware, that were taken against him."[22]

Yet though this consistency makes Stuart's explanation of his position both honest and more accurate than those of his critics, even he had not told the full story of his opposition to Garrison. His critics might have been wrong in seeing his behavior as insane or even erratic. They were not wrong in identifying an underlying emotional intensity. To Stuart the antislavery cause was a substitute for almost all other emotional outlets. The dogmatic views about female decorum and modesty which he had developed in India and Canada can be linked directly to his attitudes to the woman question: "Women were made to be our protectors, by their delicacy, and modesty, and sweetness; by attracting us to all gentleness, and holiness, and truth." These words, written in 1820, were echoed by his polemical insistence, in 1841, on "the vast moral power of women, with all its purifying influences." But more important than the conventional social attitude expressed was the accompanying intensity of feeling. It was a sensitive Stuart who had experienced "real distress" on seeing women exposed to "profaneness, levity, and noise" in frontier societies. It was a passionate man, attracted but discomfited by women, who had pleaded for modesty "by all that is lovely in yourselves" on the part of those "whose glance is so capable of filling us with despair, or firing us with unconquerable resolution!"[23] Following the failure of his courtship of Cornelia Weld, the antislavery cause had provided a lasting focus for passion. It had become more important to him emotionally even than his enduring friendship with Theodore. Although he was still writing to the younger man with the words of love, again and again his most fervent protestations of affection told of a preeminent commitment to the anti-

22. *Report of the Agency Committee*, 14; Stuart to Birney, September 30, 1836, WP; Stuart, *Emigrant's Guide*, 189–92.
23. Stuart, *Emigrant's Guide*, 125–27, 162–63.

slavery movement, as he apologized for hurried notes or long silences, or broke news of reunions deferred yet again as some new aspect of the great cause monopolized his attention. Intellectually consistent though Stuart's attitudes to Old Organization may have been, Garrison's real crime was to have diluted and diverted the movement that had offered him this fulfillment.

Even after reading Stuart's letter, John Murray was not impressed by his consistency. "Do all those with whom he acts so cordially hold the same views?" he asked John Collins rhetorically, on such questions as the Sabbath, peace and war, and human government: "Let him ask the Friends—& friend Sturge at the head."[24] For the moment, however, "friend Sturge," though a Quaker pacifist, was not seriously retarding the antislavery drive. Events would soon show that he and other British abolitionists would also earn Stuart's wrath for allowing their abolitionism to develop in new directions.

---

24. Murray to Collins, December 23, 1840, BPL.

11 FOR AND AGAINST BROAD STREET

For over a year since the world convention in June, 1840, the campaign against Old Organization had consumed Stuart's energies to the exclusion even of his relationship with Theodore Weld. In October, 1841, he wrote to "My Theodore, most dearly beloved & longed for," apologizing for the brevity of his recent stay in America. Weld had been unwell when he left: "How could I go! but I went—What good could I have done by staying? It will not always be so, my Theodore: There *is* a land of promise; and I know, when the long Sabbath of the tomb is come, we two shall meet in Christ to part no more." These were not yet the words of one weary with the world, for he showed a lively interest in the American political scene and went on to demand a few lines to "tell me, how you are—how you all are—how the cause of the Slave is doing—how is dear little Charley & how smiling Theodore [Jun.]."[1] But events would prove this to be almost the last time he would contemplate eternity with the old buoyant enthusiasm for the challenges of the present life.

For the past few years occasional references to advancing age and declining vigor had appeared in his letters. It would no doubt have become increasingly difficult for him to maintain his activities with the energy he had shown two years before in the West Indies. But the real reason for the onset of pessimism and bitterness in his private correspondence over the next two years was emotional rather than physical. American divisions had isolated him from his most likely British allies: from George Thompson, whose search for alternatives to slave-grown produce should

---

1. Stuart to Weld, October 21, 1841, WP.

236

have appealed to a hard-line boycotter, and from the Irish and Scottish abolitionists who alone shared his single-minded interest in American slavery.

In the early 1840s severe economic depression gave impetus to demands for fundamental political reform within Britain and also to the movement for free trade. These preoccupations were not directly inimical to the antislavery movement. Many free-traders proclaimed themselves abolitionists. And Joseph Sturge demonstrated, in his support for the more moderate wing of Chartism, that it was not only the supporters of Old Organization such as Elizabeth Pease and George Thompson who were politically radical. But domestic problems may have made the antislavery movement more attractive to some members of the middle class who sought the fulfillment of good works while shying away from the uncertainties of radical domestic reforms. But undoubtedly for many abolitionists it was less clear than it had been a decade earlier exactly what their priorities should be now that the Negro was free everywhere in the British Empire.

Charles Stuart was one who had no such doubts. He was as committed as ever to widespread grass-roots provincial agitation. He was equally certain that the overthrow of American Negro slavery should be the main objective. But in 1841 it was much harder for him to marry the old methods with this objective. His formative influence on the Bristol and Cifton women's auxiliary had shown again the ability to influence middle-class provincials which he had demonstrated in his Agency Committee days a decade earlier. But once Collins had departed, the American feuds could not indefinitely be used to inspire actual and potential rank-and-file abolitionists with a sense of purpose. Thirteen years of almost manic antislavery energy were giving way to the depression of frustration and old age.

ONE OF probably many groups of provincial women with an ill-defined yearning to embrace the antislavery cause was in Evesham, Worcestershire. Early in 1841, Anne Mann had written to Broad Street reporting the foundation of the Evesham Ladies Anti-Slavery Society and requesting affiliation as an auxiliary of the British and Foreign Anti-Slavery Society. Further desultory correspondence through the year involved requests for pamphlets and for stationery headed with the well-known picture of a kneeling, manacled slave. But by the end of the year the group was at a loss as to what to do with these paper resources. On December 30 Mrs. Mann wrote to London asking if there was any chance of a visit from an agent of the society: "We have heard of Captain Stuart and should be glad if he were near to engage him to visit us, hoping thereby to excite a more general interest in the cause."[2]

Stuart was normally eager to respond to such a request. But at this precise time he was at loggerheads with Broad Street over the question of slavery in British India. His preoccupation with the campaign against Collins had blinded him temporarily to the growing commitment of the national society to the Indian issue. After his initial disagreement with John Scoble at Bath in September, 1840, he had made no further protest in the ensuing year, when the Broad Street committee passed strong resolutions against slavery in British India and Scoble published a series of papers on the question in pamphlet form and in the *Morning Chronicle*.[3] But as the controversies over the American split faded into the background in the autumn of 1841, he quickly came to see the "grossly exagerated [sic] statements, as I deem them, of the B. & F.A.S. Society in relation to British India" as a major obstruction to his antislavery activities.[4] He believed the way forward for the movement lay in the creation of a large infrastructure of provincial groups auxiliary to the national society. But he refused to work for this goal until Broad Street agreed to publish his dissenting views on the issue.

On December 31, accompanied by William Blair, he attended a meeting of the Broad Street committee convened to discuss his criticisms of the society's stance. After he and Scoble had presented very different views about the nature of slavery in India, it was agreed that Stuart should be given space to make his case in the *Anti-Slavery Reporter*.[5] Within a week he had dispatched a letter that occupied three closely printed columns of the paper's January 12, 1842, edition.

Stuart stressed that he did not object to the society's attack on Indian slavery in itself: his goal was "the immediate and thorough extirpation of every vestige of slavery from the whole dominions which God has given us." With his usual honesty, he admitted that "*some* features of slavery" existed in India; that "unspeakable atrocities are sometimes perpetrated under shelter of those features"; and that "these facts are disgraceful to our government, implicate us all in guilt, and ought to be attacked and extirpated immediately, by every right means in our power." He even

2. Anne Mann to Tredgold, February 19, 26, May 25, December 30, 1841, S. 18, C8/102–105, RHL.
3. BFASS, April 16, June 11, 1841; Broad Street's commitment was reflected in a vast number of articles and comments on British India in the *Anti-Slavery Reporter* in 1841 and beyond.
4. Stuart to Weld, February 21, 1842, WP.
5. BFASS, December 31, 1841.

expressed a sense of urgency because current schemes to increase investment in Indian sugar and cotton threatened to aggravate the bondage that did exist. The crux of his complaint was that, despite these important qualifications, "the bondage yet existing in Hindostan" was much less of a problem than the society's spokesmen were suggesting:

> With local exceptions as to *agrestic* bondage, especially excepting Malabar, and with *occasional* exceptions, as to domestic servitude, especially in the Mohammedan Zenandahs, the *actual condition* of those under bondage in our territories, generally speaking, *is so free* from *suffering* by their bond-condition, that, properly speaking, it cannot be *fairly* called *slavery* at all, when we mean by slavery a thing which involves not only the grossest legal wrong, but, generally speaking, severe actual oppression.[6]

Stuart argued that the contrary exaggerations of his opponents were an obstacle to reform of actual wrongs "because facts alone can permanently sustain assertions." He found their crude generalizations an affront to his "personal knowledge of India, from a residence of thirteen years," and he accordingly prefaced his arguments with a lucid account of the various legal codes in India—Hindu, Moslem, and British—and their interaction, especially with reference to slavery. But above all, his opposition was clearly founded on the unspoken assumption that the national society's exaggeration of the Indian problem diverted resources and energies away from the abolition of Negro plantation slavery. For this reason his account of Indian slavery consisted of an implicit but detailed comparison with all the most grievous faults of the Negro system.[7]

Indian slaves could hold property "as securely as other men." They were rarely sold against their will, and "very extensively their bondage is not inherited by their children." A large proportion of them had been sold into slavery as children by their parents "during famines or seasons of extreme distress, in order to save their lives." They then often came to be treated as part of the extended family with duties "not infrequently lighter than that of hired servants." When engaged in agriculture they were "very rarely driven," and much of their time was their own. Marriages among slaves were "sacredly performed" and in general "as sacredly regarded as any others." Underlying all these redeeming features were the comparative mildness of both Hindu and Moslem slave codes and the enlightened controls of British administrators, who were themselves forbidden to hold slaves. Finally, to put the question in perspective, he

6. *Anti-Slavery Reporter*, III (1842), 6–7.
7. Ibid.

insisted that slaves formed at most one-twentieth of the population of 80 to 100 million and that, "judging as fairly as I can from all the evidence before me, less than one twentieth of these, that is less than one four hundredth of the whole population, are suffering any actual infringement of their wills." The evidence before him, he stressed, was not only his own extensive knowledge of India but also various official publications, including "nearly 1000 pages" of the parliamentary papers, *Slavery in India*, published in 1828.[8]

Although Stuart's letter had begun by expressing his "love" for the British and Foreign Anti-Slavery Society and his desire to help establish auxiliary societies, its publication did not immediately smooth the path for the tour he wanted to undertake for that purpose. Late in January, 1842, he wrote from Bath to Broad Street asking for a supply of printed sheets containing instructions for the formation of auxiliaries and also "an equal number of Scoble's little tract . . . provided the reference to my views respecting E.I. slavery as published in the Reporter, be inserted in them." His request was evidently ignored, for soon he wrote back: "I regret that I am so poorly able to get my friends to understand me." It was a matter of "common honesty" to insert the reference. He could not distribute the tract in question "without *so far at least* recording my extreme dissent from it, on the subject of East Indian slavery." He refused to give tacit approval to "a monstrously erroneous opinion." He was also unable to use copies of a printed card he had been sent "without drawing my pen across the calculation which they contain of the numbers of slaves in B. India." The dispute was resolved by Stuart's returning the offending material to Broad Street and agreeing to ignore the issue of Indian slavery on his forthcoming tour: "It is better," he wrote, "to avoid every point of collision, which sacred duty permits us to avoid."[9]

Despite this conciliatory note, the weeks of argument combined with other events and trends to induce a growing feeling of despondency, which became conspicuous in a long letter to Weld from Bath dated February 21, 1842. He referred to his recent difficulties over the Indian slavery question but devoted most space to hostile appraisals of the political atmosphere on both sides of the Atlantic. He was most scathing about the "disgusting and ridiculous" spectacle of the United States:

> Applauding liberty, yet keeping slaves!—calling the slave trade piracy if practised in Africa, but ready to wade thro' blood to honor & sustain it in

8. *Ibid.*
9. Stuart to John Beaumont, January 31, February 5, 1842, also n.d., and April 13, 19, 1842, S. 18, C11/111–15, RHL.

America! Boasting of freedom, yet trampling upon free & generous discussion! Pretending to be brave, yet skulking like cowards from the light of truth! Professing religion, yet grasping as tenaciously as the idolater of India, clasps its Juggernaut, its gross idolatry of a white, & its atrocious ahborrence of a colored skin! The spires of its churches, pointing heavenward thro' the land; and the interior arrangements of its churches, proclaiming not only without shame, but boastfully, the dominion of Satan within. . . . What a loathsome and portentous spectacle!—What a jest to demons! What a grief to Angels, if angels can mourn.

Stuart's hostility to the American system was not new, but this level of scorn was. His disenchantment with American democracy was reinforced by growing distaste for new democratic tendencies within Britain. He recognized the existence of "old abuses yet cherished" as well as "providential disadvantages"; but the main problem in Britain was the "abuse of liberty." Government would have rectified the abuses "but for the insane measures which have been adopted to precipitate a change; and the bold pursuit of which threatens national convulsion."[10] Yet the main reason for this concern lay in his fervent commitment to abolition, which for a long time had made him largely indifferent to domestic turmoil. In late 1841 and early 1842 the same commitment made it impossible for him to ignore the turmoil.

During 1837 and 1838 he had been too preoccupied with the campaign against apprenticeship to give much attention to the proliferation of radical societies petitioning for the "six points" of fundamental electoral reform that were soon adopted as the "People's Charter." In July, 1838, in a letter to Weld, he had seen the government as unduly repressive toward would-be domestic reformers. But the main inspiration for his hostility had seemed to be that "the ministry of the day, of course, supports the abomination of slavery." And he had shown his distaste for the mounting radicalism by concluding that "the cause of reform (I mean social and political reform) has been rolled back, in great measure, by the extravagances of many of its votaries, as much, by the rousing & banding together & concentration of the forces of its enemies." Even more revealing of his attitudes was that these comments were a tiny interpolation in a long account of the imminent success of the fight against apprenticeship, with the climax due within a few days on August 1. It was that distant event, rather than the formal launching of the Chartist movement in Birmingham on August 6, which had monopolized his attention as he

10. Stuart to Weld, February 21, 1842, WP.

worked in London as acting editor of the *British Emancipator* and prepared for his extensive tour to the West Indies.[11]

Stuart, of course, had been in the West Indies throughout 1839, while the Chartist agitation gathered momentum and the Anti–Corn Law League held its first national conferences. The Chartist riots in Birmingham and the rejection by Parliament of the first Chartist petition in July, 1839, coincided with his arrival in Jamaica and the start of the most intensive phase of his Caribbean tour. He was still totally preoccupied with the Jamaican situation as Chartism moved closer to open insurrection, in particular in South Wales and Yorkshire in November, 1839. That first phase of the agitation was long past—with many of its leaders jailed or transported—by the time he had returned to Britain in May, 1840. For the next year he could hardly have been unaware of reform agitation, not least because Chartist interruptions of antislavery meetings became a common tactic. Making few platform appearances and finding his anti-Garrison attitudes endorsed by Joseph Sturge and other leading abolitionist friends, however, he had been able largely to ignore Chartism until after his five-month visit to the United States ending in September, 1841.[12]

The Chartists disrupted antislavery meetings because they felt abolitionists were concentrating on distant evils to the detriment of more immediate domestic reform priorities. That charge has long since been severely qualified by historians who have examined the wider reform goals of many leading abolitionists. Stuart's old friend Joseph Sturge stands out in particular as one with a most comprehensive social conscience. In late 1841 he made an imaginative attempt to reconcile Chartism with the anti–Corn Law agitation which most Chartists had regarded as an employers' movement indifferent or hostile to working-class problems. Sturge's *Reconciliation Between the Middle and Labouring Classes* urged the formation of "Complete Suffrage Associations," which would press both for repeal of the Corn Laws and suffrage reform. By early 1842 the plan had won over large numbers of less revolutionary Chartists.[13]

In contrast to Sturge, Charles Stuart embodied the old stereotype of an abolitionist blind to the domestic scene. His attitudes to reform were the direct antithesis of the Chartists'. By early 1842 he could no longer ignore domestic upheaval because he felt it was obstructing his own goals. He did not name Sturge in his letter to Weld, but there can be no doubt that the Birmingham Quaker was in his mind when he remarked: "The zeal

11. Stuart to Weld, July 18, 1838, WP.
12. Cole and Postgate, *Common People*, 279–91.
13. *Ibid*; Temperley, *British Antislavery*, 140–41.

with which some of our leading friends enter into other questions, will I apprehend, much impede the Anti-Slavery cause."[14]

Stuart was affected deeply by these trends. The British political ferment prompted him to confide to Weld that "were we not assured by evidence which we cannot doubt, that the Lord reigneth, we might well despair." And in a postscript to the same letter, addressed to Angelina and Sarah Grimké, the comments on his own frailties, which had crept into some previous letters, took on a more serious tone: "I begin to realize forcibly the truth that 'age is dark & unlovely'—it seems to be chilling my soul, and I often feel, as if the only suitable place for me, would be some chimney corner, away from human bustle, where I might quietly fade away, without notice." Even now Stuart had no intention of fading into retirement: "I do not despair, for He bids me rejoice, and while He helps me, I will rejoice. . . . I pray that whatever work my Father may have for me to do, He will keep me diligently and cheerfully about it." He pointed out that in the near future this work involved a visit to an antislavery convention in Paris as well as the projected provincial tour.[15] Nevertheless, he must have sensed already that the mood of the country was far from accepting the urgency of his antislavery message.

THE CONVENTION in Paris in March, 1842, seems to have been an episode of minor importance in Stuart's career. His surviving private correspondence virtually ignores the event, and the published account in the *Anti-Slavery Reporter* and a box of uncataloged papers in the British antislavery societies' archives simply record his presence as a delegate from Bath among a total of twenty from Britain and Ireland. There were small delegations from as far afield as Sweden and Russia, and one can easily imagine Stuart's reaction to the attempt to broaden the antislavery impulse to include the emancipation of Russian serfs. Overall, the convention was a subdued event reduced to private sessions when the French government intervened at the eleventh hour to prohibit public meetings. With Daniel O'Connell unable to take his place as a delegate from Dublin, the majority of British and Irish delegates were men who had been Stuart's close associates in the various British antislavery societies over the past decade. The occasion must have given him the chance to discuss recent disagreements with the official representatives of Broad Street, for both Joseph Sturge and John Scoble took prominent parts in the proceedings.[16]

14. Stuart to Weld, February 21, 1842, WP.
15. Ibid.
16. *Anti-Slavery Reporter*, III (1842), 41; Conferences and Congresses, Paris, 1842, S. 22, G. 115, RHL.

It was perhaps as a result of these renewed personal contacts that on his return to Britain Stuart was quickly drawn into consultation with the national society over an emerging issue of concern to abolitionists. A parliamentary inquiry was about to consider the question of meeting the labor problems of the West Indies with voluntary immigration from Africa. Stuart was among thirteen men with experience of the West Indies who were approached on April 1 by the Broad Street committee as potential witnesses before the parliamentary inquiry. He replied five days later, pointing out that he was about to leave Bath for an antislavery tour of the West Country. But he was willing to appear before the committee of inquiry: William Blair would forward to him any such request, and he would "at once turn off to London." Although he did not have to do this, his concern about the threat of a virtual slave trade operating under the guise of African emigration was deeply felt. It was a logical development of his general attitudes to the postslavery situation and the particular attention he had given in Jamaica to the question of the treatment of "recaptive" Africans released after intervention by the Royal Navy in the Atlantic slave trade. His opposition on the related question of the importation of Indian labor to the West Indies and Mauritius was equally consistent. The direct action he and Scoble had taken in British Guiana three years earlier reflected the same concerns that in April, 1842, made him the instigator of a petition to local MPs by Bath abolitionists protesting the exploitation of "Hill coolies."[17]

Over the next six months, as he visited every significant town in Somerset, Devon, and Cornwall, Stuart remained closely in touch with Broad Street on these issues. In September, after eventually greeting the report of the parliamentary committee on Africa as "particularly contemptible and hateful," he drew attention to a further abuse of the West Indian labor problem. The latest number of the *Anti-Slavery Reporter* had included a copy of a letter from a certain Peter Gallego to Dr. Thomas Rolph, government emigration agent for Canada. Gallego, who was black, had cited numerous examples of color prejudice in Canada in an endeavor to sustain his argument that fugitive blacks would be better off emigrating to Jamaica. Stuart conceded that there was "horrible prejudice" in some parts of Canada, particularly the Western District, and that its exposure might do good. But on the whole he was sorry that Gallego's article had been published. He had met the man, "an emigration agent of the West

17. BFASS, April 1, 8, 1842; Stuart to Beaumont, April 6, 1842, S. 18, C10/93, RHL; Stuart to Beaumont, April 19, 1842, S. 18, C11/115, RHL.

Indian planters," the previous year in Toronto and found that he was not trusted by the majority of blacks in Canada.[18]

Later that month the same transatlantic knowledge and interests made him the instigator of a new Broad Street policy initiative. In a letter of September 26, commenting on the "mighty strides" that were being taken toward renewal of the slave trade through West Indian immigration schemes, he went on to identify a still more sinister threat to the black man—the tenth article of the newly concluded Webster-Ashburton Treaty between Britain and the United States. Ostensibly concerned with the extradition of criminals, the article, said Stuart, "contains plainly a horrible pledge from us, to make ourselves runaway slave catchers for the United States." It was a mark of his enthusiasm and knowledge that from the distant vantage point of Penzance he should see before any other abolitionist that the extradition clause could be applied to fugitive slaves in Canada. It would be easy, he pointed out, for slaveholders to invent crimes to justify extradition. It was also typical that his letter was vibrant with emotion. He railed against American hypocrisy—"boasting of liberty" yet supporting the "vilest system" of slavery—and against Britain, "with her eyes open, and the pretence of horror and virtue on her lips, binding herself to be their blood-hounds." It would be "a pity—a burning bleeding pity, if thus, the last secure asylum on earth of the outraged slave should be demolished." He implored his London colleagues: "If anything, which christian men could devise or do, can be done, do it, and do it speedily."[19]

Those colleagues did react speedily. Three days after his letter was written it was being formally discussed in Broad Street. The committee at once requested an interview with the antislavery MP Dr. Stephen Lushington to ascertain whether "by a forced construction or otherwise" the clause could be applied to fugitive slaves in Canada. Stuart's letter was reprinted verbatim in the next edition of the *Anti-Slavery Reporter* on October 5. This somewhat surprised him for he wrote back pointing out that his letter had been hastily written and not intended for publication. He enclosed a more considered letter, which he insisted should be published. In it he explained that the offending treaty seemed "more and more horrible" to him because in all slave states, and in Ohio at least of the free states, blacks, whether slave or free, were banned from giving evidence in the courts. If Britain returned a black accused of being a criminal, it would

---

18. Stuart to Beaumont, September 17, 1842, S. 18, C11/123, RHL; *Anti-Slavery Reporter*, III (1842), 143–44.

19. Stuart to Beaumont, September 26, 1842, S. 18, C11/124, RHL.

accordingly be sending him to a trial where he had no chance of proving his innocence. He was unwilling to believe that Lord Ashburton knew this or that the British government would approve the article without guarding against these dangerous contingencies.[20]

This second letter was published in the *Anti-Slavery Reporter* on October 19. In the same period John Scoble and another Broad Street committee member took up the issues it raised with Dr. Lushington. The MP believed that the tenth article could be applied to fugitive slaves only by "the most forced and treasonable construction." Nonetheless, he advised the committee to memorialize the British government urging that no black charged with any offense whatsoever should be given up by the Canadian authorities: such extradition should be agreed to only by the "authorities at home deciding after the case had been fully submitted to them."[21]

The issue Stuart had opened up became significant in antislavery circles for months to come. Letters and resolutions on the question soon flowed in to London from many provincial antislavery groups. Broad Street followed up Lushington's advice with a memorial and subsequent deputations to Ashburton and Lord Aberdeen, the foreign secretary. Stuart himself retained a close interest in the matter throughout this period. He pleaded the "poverty of my talent" in refusing an invitation to join the deputation to Ashburton in November. But he used the same letter to argue again in detail about the vulnerability of blacks to the "ferociously cruel & iniquitous judgments, which the state of Society in the United States, renders all but inevitable." Later he predicted "murderous collisions" in Canada if the article was invoked against fugitive blacks.[22]

Yet although his influence on this issue was significant, and although it kept him in touch with the leaders of British abolitionism, his most immediate concern throughout these months was to win much greater public support for the antislavery cause. And this was proving a most difficult task. Stuart may have been dubbed the "antislavery Quixote" by friend and foe in the early 1830s. But then at least the assault on colonial slavery had been a major political concern. It was far more quixotic in 1842 to be attempting to revive political antislavery sentiment to the levels that had sent floods of petitions to Westminster twice during the 1830s. On May 3, just as his tour was beginning, Parliament was receiving the second

20. BFASS, September 30, 1842; *Anti-Slavery Reporter*, III (1842), 159, 167–68; Stuart to Beaumont, October 5, 1842, S. 18, C11/125, RHL.

21. BFASS, October 28, 1842.

22. *Ibid.*, October 28, November 4, December 30, 1842, January 27, February 13, 24, 1843; Stuart to Beaumont, November 13, November [?], 1842, February 20, 1843, S. 18, C11/127, 133, RHL.

Chartist petition—six miles long and with more than three million signatures. Soon Stuart was reporting a public meeting in Newton Abbott, where all had been harmonious "except for a few who wished all our energies to be confined to England, till we got all right at home." He was not unduly worried by such opposition, as long as it was "moderate and civil," because it seemed to increase interest in a flagging cause. But he well knew that the cause was flagging not least because domestic problems seemed much more urgent than Negro slavery to many more people than a handful of hecklers in Devonshire.[23]

He faced this issue directly in a broadsheet published to coincide with his tour, *The Anti-Slavery Cause in 1842*:

> Is not slavery abolished in the British territories? Do not the heathens and the Jews demand all our sympathies? Or, if we could multiply ourselves a hundredfold, would not the ignorance, the crime, and the misery at our own doors; the consuming poverty which is around us, pressing upon multitudes of the worthiest of our land; and the political strifes, which threaten our very existence; would not—*ought* not—these to engage our every energy?
>
> Yes; Slavery is abolished in the British territories, except some scattered dregs in Hindostan. The wants of the Heathen, especially of the female part, and of the Jews, are indeed heart-rending; and our domestic condition calls in thunder upon every heart.

But after conceding all this, he asked, "What misery equals the misery of the slave?" He described in detail the oppression of "about 6,000,000 of our immortal fellow men" and gave an equally detailed breakdown of the numbers of slaves in different parts of the America.[24]

In answering his own rhetorical question—"what can we do about all this?"—he discussed and rejected the possibility of physical force. The only acceptable method was moral force: "by conversation; by corresponding; by removing the ignorance and misconceptions" that surrounded slavery. And this in turn could best be done "by anti-slavery associations auxiliary to the British and Foreign Anti-Slavery society; because that Society is upright in its principles, energetic in its zeal, and loyal and peaceable in its measures."[25]

Superficially, Stuart was successful in pursuing his goal. He was thorough and persistent. Repeated letters back to Broad Street demanded cop-

---

23. Cole and Postgate, *Common People*, 289; Stuart to Beaumont, June 8, 1842, S. 18, C11/118, RHL.

24. Charles Stuart, *The Anti-Slavery Cause in 1842* (N.p., 1842), 1–2: copy attached to letter cited in note 23.

25. *Ibid*.

ies of the society's publications for local distribution. They also reported public meetings he had held and the formation of male and female auxiliaries in virtually every town he visited. He arranged for these new societies to be kept in touch with national policies and events by opening subscriptions to the *Anti-Slavery Reporter*: "If they do not pay it, put it to my account," he wrote from Torquay. And he arranged for most local officials to write directly to antislavery societies, churches, and individual abolitionists in the United States. This dedication impressed people in the way it always had—especially dissenting clergy, middle-class women, and people like himself with backgrounds in colonial or military service. They were people with leisure and reforming instincts but sharing his distaste for the more radical agitation of the day. In Taunton he stayed for a week with spinster sisters, Sarah and Elizabeth Dymond. "His sweet spirit & christian conversation has been quite delightful to us," wrote Sarah. In Penzance he struck up a warm friendship with a retired navy surgeon, Mitchell Thompson, and Captain Philip Jackson, a retired officer of the Bengal artillery, whom he described as "a singularly lovely man." The Reverend John Orange of Torquay described Stuart as "indefatigable," "enlightened," and "benevolent."[26]

Some of these new acquaintances became almost euphoric about his successes. Orange twice wrote to Broad Street saying that Stuart had been "instrumental in kindling a flame" in South Devon, "which he cannot quench if he were to try." Sarah Dymond reported to Angelina Weld in America that Stuart's "eloquence & solemn appeal" had revitalized a moribund female antislavery group in Taunton. And from America Martha Ball of the Massachusetts Female Emancipation Society wrote to Broad Street commenting on the "most beneficial results" of Stuart's tour, which had been described to her by Mary Garland of Redruth.[27]

But Stuart himself was under no such illusions. He reported glumly from Plymouth on the formation of small auxiliaries in Totnes and Dartmouth in the South Devon region, which the Reverend Orange believed to be aflame with abolitionist fervor. He had found the established church "aloof," despite some notable exceptions among its laity. And in Plymouth itself the men's committee merely "*exists*"; he was unsure whether the women's was "alive or dead." He felt it would be difficult or impos-

26. Stuart to Beaumont, May 9, 1842, S. 18, C11/116, RHL; Stuart to Beaumont, September 26, 1842, S. 18, C11/124; Sarah Dymond to Angelina Weld, November 4, 1842, WP; Rev. John Orange to Beaumont, July 13, October 8, 1842, S. 18, C11/89, 90, RHL.

27. Orange to Beaumont, July 13, October 8, 1842, S. 18, C11/89, 90; S. Dymond to A. Weld, November 4, 1842, WP; Martha V. Ball to Beaumont, March 1, 1843, S. 18, C11/21, RHL.

sible to revive the work there, "but my business is not to anticipate, or hope or fear, but to try." Accompanying this fatalism was a realistic appraisal of the reasons for apathy. There was the distraction of economic distress. And there was an ignorance, "supposing that all is done," and an indolence, "wearied with past labors." He appended a sober postscript to Sarah Dymond's letter to Angelina. The cause needed "persevering, affectionate & faithful advocacy—The heart of England is open to it— but there is still immense ignorance on that heart—and the horrible parties, which distract us, politically, ecclesiastically, & even religiously, sadly keep its ignorance from light." He quickly acknowledged that the major issues that dominated his own correspondence with Broad Street were not likely to grip the public imagination. The very letter in which he first drew attention to the flaw in the Webster-Ashburton Treaty contained an account of local reaction in Penzance, which was to prove typical. His attempt to form a gentleman's auxiliary had been disappointing: some in the audience approved of the new schemes for African emigration, and some approved of Ashburton's treaty, despite his explanation of the ominous implications of the tenth article. "And these," he went on, "were the leaders—in their way, all good men . . . but certainly either they or I must be enormously mistaken." Those meeting had agreed to form only a "vague association," and he had even less enthusiasm for the signs of female interest in the cause. Although there were many benevolent women there, he had visited scarcely any place "where women seemed so dead to action in behalf of the Slave."[28]

His pessimism was reinforced when, with typical thoroughness, he began to revisit many of the auxiliaries he had established at the start of his tour. He wrote from Exeter in mid-October that he had recently retraced his steps through Truro, Liskeard, and Tavistock and found that "the new auxiliaries existed but wanted nourishment." He was due to meet the Exeter committee the following day but feared that it was in a very "dull" state. On his tour, he added, he had faced one recurring question: "'But what can we do? What can a few of us here, in *this* place, do, to get Slavery abolished in America?'"[29]

His reactions were confirmed by some of his new acquaintances. Philip Jackson wrote to Broad Street at the end of October about the formation of the Penzance committee. It was still "without strength" and needed continuing help in finding a sense of direction: "We are ignorant of the

28. S. Dymond to A. Weld, November 4, 1842, WP; Stuart to Beaumont, July 4, 1842, S. 18, C11/119, RHL; Stuart to Beaumont, September 26, 1842, S. 18, C11/124, RHL.
29. Stuart to Beaumont, October 14, 1842, S. 18, C11/126, RHL.

modus operandi." He added: "Many of us feel truly sorry that we could not do more justice to the noble philanthropy of Captain Stuart and we all hope to see a livelier feeling excited ere long amongst us." Sarah Dymond twice wrote to Broad Street in early November requesting publications illustrating the Hill coolie, African emigration, and Ashburton treaty questions, adding a note of urgency on the second occasion: "I fear the effects of Capt. Stuart's lecture will be worn off."[30]

The apathy he encountered in the West Country must have been dispiriting enough to Stuart. But over the next few months further public and personal disappointments combined to increase his frustration. He discovered first of all that many of his oldest antislavery colleagues did not share his enthusiasm for grass-roots campaigning. In his October letter commenting on the general perplexity about the efficacy of local abolitionist pressure on a distant, foreign slave system, he had implored his London colleagues: "Get some of your clearest heads, & kindest hearts, & plainest writers to answer this, in an affectionate and solemn manner, in the Reporter." In the January 11, 1843, edition of that journal he made his own contribution by describing the total insecurity which, at best, was the lot of the American slave. There were more than six million blacks in that condition in the Americas, and "the vast influence, which God has given to Great Britain with all these nations, is a glorious talent, which cannot be abused without guilt, nor neglected without danger."[31] But at this same period he was making it plain that for him such literary exhortations were secondary in importance to more direct campaigning.

His experiences in the West Country convinced him that the founding of auxiliaries was not enough: what was needed was a revival of the old Agency Committee system of itinerant professional lecturers. In mid-December, 1842, he persuaded the male and female antislavery committees in Bath to send circulars to their counterparts throughout the country stressing the need for public education about the horrors of slavery and for a concerted effort to persuade the national society "to engage and send forth properly qualified lecturers." From the start Broad Street was left in no doubt about his intentions, for he had requested a list of names and addresses of all secretaries of female auxiliaries; he wanted them to join the Bath ladies in "stirring up the London Committee," he told the secretary of that same committee.[32]

Over the next two months, while he retained his usual wide interest in

30. Jackson to Beaumont, October 29, 1842, S. 18, C11/74; Dymond to Beaumont, November 4, 14, 1842, S. 18, C11/53, 54, RHL.
31. Stuart to Beaumont, October 14, 1842, S. 18, C11/126, RHL.
32. Stuart to Beaumont, December 16, 19, 1842, S. 18, C11/129, 130, RHL.

all antislavery issues, this project dominated his activities. He continued to press Broad Street about the major problems of West Indian immigration and the Webster-Ashburton Treaty in a letter in February attacking what he deemed "a very corrupt influence" in the colonial secretary's department. But although this corruption "makes me shudder, and calls up all that is left, of the soldier in me," the main purpose of his writing was to explain an accompanying parcel of letters that had been received from around the country in answer to the recent circular.[33]

He may have sounded confident when he told Broad Street that these replies revealed "the mind of the country," but it was a confidence that he did not truly feel. Almost certainly he knew that the Broad Street committee more than a year previously had rejected a much more modest proposal to employ a single antislavery lecturer because of the "state of the country and of the funds of the Society." That proposal had been put forward by the society's treasurer, G. W. Alexander, who had been in Paris with Stuart soon afterward and whom Stuart met in Bath within days of this February letter to London. And in the weeks before the dispatch of that letter and the parcel, Stuart had received a much more mixed response to the circular than his comments implied. From Evesham Ann Mann had replied that her committee was unwilling to act except in accord with the views of the national society. It felt, moreover, that with the expense of a second world convention planned for the following June, the British and Foreign Anti-Slavery Society probably could not afford to support traveling lecturers. Nothing, however, could have more poignantly conveyed to Stuart that times had changed than the guarded reply he received from Mary S. Lloyd of Wednesbury, Staffordshire, on behalf of the female abolitionists who had pointed the way for the Agency Committee by employing him and Edward Baldwin as agents in the spring of 1831. She had shown the circular to Sophia Sturge, who had commented sympathetically on the apparent lack of success of his recent West Country tour: "We are both of the opinion that all we can do is to lay thy letter before our next Ann. Meeting which is usually held in the Spring and if it be the judgment of that meeting to urge the Brit. & Foreign A.S. Society to send forth Agents, it will be done accordingly—Thou wilt recollect that our Ladies Antislavery Association was I believe the first to propose and to assist in procuring an Agency of this sort."[34]

It was as usual in his correspondence with Theodore Weld that Stuart

33. Stuart to Beaumont, February 20, 1843, S. 18, C11/133, RHL.
34. *Ibid.*; BFASS, October 29, 1841; Stuart and William Blair to Beaumont, February 23, 1843, S. 18, C11/22, RHL; A. Mann to Stuart, January 31, 1843, S. 18, C159/46; Mary S. Lloyd to Stuart, January 18, 1843, S. 18, C158/239, RHL.

revealed most clearly the pessimism he had hidden in his public endeavors to revive the techniques of a decade earlier. On January 31, 1843, some days after he had received that noncommittal reply from Staffordshire, he wrote to Weld:

> The present Anti-Slavery posture of this country, I regard as decidedly worse than it has been for several years. Our ministry (I mean, our Colonial Secretary's Office) seems to me clearly pro-slavery & compromising. The anti-slavery heart of the nation wants re-rousing, and we can obtain no adequate means of re-rousing it. Several of the oldest & staunchest friends of the slave are departed—and some of the noblest & most energetic now existing, have greatly lost their Anti-Slavery influence by plunging into political strifes.[35]

At the same time he remained bitter about the American divisions. Weld's recent letter had conveyed an invitation for him to represent the New Jersey State Anti-Slavery Society at the second world convention in London later that year. He would be "delighted" to accept if the New Jersey society was free from "the Garrisonian dogmas." Despite all his other preoccupations, he had clearly kept in touch with the American scene, for he went on to say that the accounts he had lately read, especially in the American *Anti-Slavery Standard*, made him regard the Garrisonian society "as more destructively hostile to emancipation, than even the corruptions, loathsome & dreadful as they are, of the church." He hoped that no Garrisonians would come to the convention, "except they come merely as Anti-Slavery men (not women), and leave their peculiarities, so destructive of love, so hostile to liberty, so fatal to harmony & so discordant with truth, behind them."[36]

His letter was suffused with fervent affection, not only for "Dearest friend & brother of my soul, my Theodore" but also for Angelina, who had recently written "kind Baby talk" about the Weld children. "Thank you a thousand times," he wrote to her in a postscript, "for the generous love which thus leads you to bring up your precious children, to love your absent friend, so little worthy of any love—and yet thro' Grace the object of love so surpassing." Yet underlying this characteristically fulsome style was a growing emotional tension that reflected more than the frustrations of his antislavery efforts. Although he wrote wistfully of a possible visit to England by the Welds—and rather more firmly of his own hopes to recross the Atlantic the following summer—recent correspondence from Weld had pained him. He referred to "a wide difference between our views

35. Stuart to Weld, January 31, 1843, WP.
36. Ibid.

of christian character," and he deplored Weld's refusal to join the American and Foreign Anti-Slavery Society. He claimed that "these things would have given me, much more pain, some years ago: but I have learnt to judge others, less by [my] own standard, than I used to do, and to leave those whom I love, without anxiety in the hands of their own master."[37]

This was not a hollow claim, for in the same letter he wrote warmly of their old mentor, Charles Grandison Finney, who had offended them and most abolitionists in the 1830s by advocating racial segregation. He welcomed the news that his sister Anne had joined Finney's congregation in New York. Although the revivalist had "sinned so enormously in relation to colour," Stuart had found such inspiration in Finney's teaching that "I should prefer his ministry, were it within my reach, to any other which I have ever heard."[38]

Yet these genuine expressions of tolerance did not mean that Stuart was any more relaxed or had a less fanatical commitment to his evangelical faith. He would have accepted Finney's ministry only "could I be left unshackled by his views, in judging by myself, of the scriptures. . . . My own devotion to the Truth, as I deem it in Jesus," he told Weld, "is at least as decided as ever." And this same letter made it plainer than ever that this faith was becoming as much consolation as inspiration. As he had done almost exactly a year previously, he concluded his account of antislavery frustrations by mentioning that only his certainty that "the Lord reigns" kept him from despair. He went on: "Oh what a new treasure does my Bible appear to me, & with what awakened gratitude & admiration do I clasp it to my heart, when I think of the desolation of spirit that would shroud me, had I not God's own sure word to resort to, from human doctrines or opinions." He was more conscious than ever of physical decline and death, telling Angelina that it was "most probable that human nature's term will cease with me" before her "children's characters are fixed." And his anticipation of reunion after death with Theodore was both less jaunty and less theoretical than in previous letters: "Ask your heart, & let it speak of your Charles; yet it will speak too favourably—believe but half—the remainder we shall realise, when this corruptible puts on incorruption & we shall rise *complete* in *Him*, against whom while yet in the body *the old man in us*, yet struggles."[39]

Although Stuart explicitly saw the Bible as his great consolation, he still strongly craved personal friendship. As always he spoke longingly of fu-

37. Ibid.
38. Ibid.
39. Ibid.

ture reunions with the Welds. Some months before he had persuaded Sarah Dymond to write from Taunton urging them to make an antislavery visit to Britain. With Angelina's domestic commitments and with Weld now in Washington providing research and advice to antislavery congressmen, he must have always known that this was a forlorn hope. And yet in this letter of January 31, 1843, he enclosed a note from William Blair pressing a similar invitation. He himself would "greatly rejoice" if Weld could accept: "*Do*, my soul's Theodore, *do*, if at all possible to duty."[40]

Blair, however, had provided the more regular human consolation. In November, at the end of his West Country tour, Stuart had looked forward eagerly to being "at home at my William's." As so often in the past, the Blair household remained his home for the following six months. Together the two men consulted G. W. Alexander in February about the need for still more representations against the Webster-Ashburton Treaty. And they wrote a joint letter to Broad Street urging the committee "to call upon all their auxiliaries, to address their representatives in Parliament, earnestly on this behalf." At the same time Mary Blair was active, no doubt at Stuart's behest, in persuading the Bath antislavery women to discuss the question and suggest that the national society petition the queen. Broad Street's decision to petition both houses of Parliament on the subject was probably prompted more by an inconclusive meeting with the colonial secretary than by this pressure from Bath.[41] But for Stuart this collaboration with the Blairs was one of the few bright aspects in a gloomy antislavery scene.

Broad Street had no intention of accepting his plan to engage professional lecturers. Instead, he was offered the consolation of being asked to repeat his recent tour in order to arrange delegations to the forthcoming convention. He agreed to do his best but doubted whether the exercise "will be worth the expence." In the first half of May he visited some of the centers relatively near to Bath and arranged delegations. But he merely wrote to Exeter, Truro, Helston, Penzance, and Redruth, urging them to appoint delegates because for him to visit was not worth the expense of a long journey. And he decided that there was no other place "where a visit from me might probably be useful."[42]

THE 1843 London convention provided some temporary relief from frus-

40. *Ibid.*; S. Dymond to Angelina Weld, November 4, 1842, WP.
41. Stuart to Angelina Weld, appended to Sarah Dymond's letter cited in note 40; Stuart and Blair to Beaumont, February 23, 1843, S. 18, C11/22; M. P. Blair to Scoble, February 27, 1843, S. 18, C13/130; BFASS, February 24, 1843.
42. Stuart to Scoble, April 10, May 2, 5, 14, 1843, S. 18, C22/33–35, RHL.

tration for Stuart. After months of laboring to overcome provincial apathy he found it invigorating to be among committed abolitionists. The imminent abolition of slavery in British India had removed a source of tension with some of his British colleagues. And it was particularly satisfying that the presence of a large delegation from the American and Foreign Anti-Slavery Society gave American issues the prominence he felt they deserved but now rarely received in Britain. Outside the formal sessions of the convention he joined with Amos Phelps in soliciting financial support for the ailing Oneida Institute, writing a glowing testimonial to the character and ability of Beriah Green. He took seriously his role as delegate from New Jersey, producing a memorandum, presumably for circulation among his fellow delegates, which described in detail the unfavorable position of New Jersey blacks: "Of all the nominal free states, New Jersey is fastest wedded to Slavery. It has still, six hundred real slaves—Prejudice & Colonization have done their worst, there." A state law passed in 1798 allowed people to move into New Jersey with slaves and retain them. The same act prohibited blacks from traveling without certificates from two justices of the peace. And the law of 1820, apparently ending slavery, had in fact said that all children born of slave parents after July 4, 1804, should be free, yet "*servants* of the owners of their mothers, until 25 years of age, if males, and 21, if females."[43]

His speeches in the convention reflected the same American priorities. As he had done so often at antislavery gatherings on both sides of the Atlantic in the past, he declared that "the American churches, with but few honourable and increasing exceptions, were the great bulwarks of slavery." And he made equally typical contributions to discussions about the plight of fugitive slaves. When William Johnston from the American and Foreign Anti-Slavery Society said that many abolitionists had doubted the legality of assisting fugitives to reach Canada, Stuart interjected promptly: "I never doubted it!" In later speeches he made it clear that his attitudes were based not on legal niceties but on his loathing of slavery and his knowledge of black refugee communities in Canada. The same perceptions made him reiterate his recent warnings that the tenth article of the Webster-Ashburton Treaty threatened to make British subjects "Kidnappers for American slaves." And he gave eager support to a resolution calling for a subcommittee to inquire into the *Creole* case, a cause célèbre involving the capture of a United States ship by its cargo of American slaves

43. Ms. A.21.13 p. 50, BPL; memorandum signed by C. Stuart, June 19, 1843, S. 18, C22/38, RHL.

and the subsequent demand by the American authorities that the British return the ringleaders from the port of Nassau.[44]

Stuart's knowledge, experience, and commitment were so completely focused on North America that to his fellow delegates he scarcely seemed to be British. This became clear when Henry C. Howells from Pennsylvania—himself English by birth—mounted the now familiar American attack on British abolitionism as comfortable and fashionable and unwilling to "stand in the face of danger" in the United States. When he mentioned "the good done by the delegation of George Thompson and Joseph Sturge," a voice called out, "Charles Stuart!" whereupon Howells retorted: "He is half an American," before adding John Scoble's name to the brief list of British abolitionists who had maintained their reputations in the United States.[45]

Stuart was probably not displeased by this exchange (though he later commented to Weld that Howells "*would* speak too much"). The absence of the Garrisonians meant that there was "greater brotherly love and greater regard to our brother in bondage" than in 1840. Indeed, the main threat to harmony, he discovered, now came not from American frictions but from the activities of those British delegates who made "a hobby of free commerce, as the Garrisonites in the preceding Convention, did of women's rights." In an extensive debate, the leading advocate of free trade, Richard Cobden, led the way in demanding the removal of sugar duties even from the produce of the slave economies of Brazil and Cuba. Most ominous from Stuart's point of view was that the committed abolitionists who spoke in support of this policy included his closest British friend, William Blair. Stuart made no contribution to that debate, but the issue emerged again in the course of discussion over the conditions of slaves in Latin America. William Ewart, MP, expounded a typical free-trade abolitionist philosophy: "You may ask me on what principle I have advocated the extinction of slavery in the British senate. I am a free trader. I have always held this doctrine,—that although I would, by the combination of a nation, put down, even coercively, the system of slavery and the slave-trade, yet our great pervading and animating principle must be, an extension of the commerce of the world. Commerce I believe to be the great emancipator." This view was anathema to Stuart, who interjected: "I trust that while I have a soul that can appreciate justice, liberty, and

---

44. *Anti-Slavery Reporter*, IV (1843), 99, 103; British and Foreign Anti-Slavery Society, *Proceedings of the General Anti-Slavery Convention, Called by the Committee of the British and Foreign Anti-Slavery Society, and Held in London from Tues. June 13 to Tues. June 20, 1843* (London, 1843), 72, 275, 321.

45. *Proceedings of the General Convention, 1843*, 67–68.

humanity I shall never be found uniting in any free trade which is supported by robbery and murder."[46]

Despite these controversies, Stuart's overall reactions to the convention were favorable: "Our harmony was unbroken, tho' not undisturbed," he told Weld. To Gerrit Smith he attributed the disagreements to "a bold, tho' feeble effort . . . to set the duty of free trade, above duty to the slave." To both men he described the meetings as "exceedingly interesting," and he concluded that the final session had been "one of the sweetest, the best, and the finest, which I have anywhere seen." Yet these same letters to his two closest American friends made it clear that he did not really believe his own extravagant conclusion that the convention would "exercise an important influence on the liberties of the world." Rather, they demonstrated that nothing fundamental had occurred to arrest his growing pessimism about antislavery prospects on both sides of the Atlantic.[47]

His exchange of letters with Smith may have reassured him that the Peterboro philanthropist was not a Garrison supporter. The convention itself may have convinced him that the free-trade wing of abolitionism had "nothing left it, but to growl." But whether he looked at Britain or the United States, he saw a fatal inability to come to grips with slavery. "England's eyes," he told Weld, "are but feebly opened, and her heart but faintly moved." America suffered from the proximity, Britain from the remoteness of the problem: "Its contact spreads corruption fearfully through your body, as a nation—Its distance leaves us ignorant of the horrible features of its reality." In these letters of July and August, 1843, all the doubts of the past eighteen months returned to overshadow his warm recollections of the recent convention. Two opposing evils sat "like an incubus" upon the British antislavery movement: "the *anti-reform*, and the *democratic* reform parties—the former, resisting change proudly, the latter proudly & madly urging it." In these circumstances the means could not be found "so to spread & to press home knowledge, as to stir extensively the nation's heart." Against this background he was preparing to recross the Atlantic yet again, but this time permanently: "I am preparing for my expatriation; for such I consider it; not expecting ever to see Britain again, in the body." A decade earlier he had prepared for the transatlantic journey with a sense of achievement in Britain and eager anticipation for the coming surge of immediatist agitation in America. Now he was being drawn across the Atlantic not by the attractions of the

46. *Ibid.*, 137–39, 192–93; Stuart to Weld, July 10, 1843, WP.
47. Stuart to Weld, July 10, August 14, 1843, WP; Stuart to Smith, July 10, 1843, SP.

American antislavery atmosphere but by the call of family duty. His sister Harriet had recently died in New York, and he felt "solemnly called . . . to provide an humble, frugal home, for my remaining sisters, should they need it." America, indeed, was politically more and more repellent to him, an awful warning of the dangers represented by one of those opposing evils that threatened Britain: "Our government indeed has its faults, but compared with other human powers, I cannot sufficiently thank God for its excellencies. . . . With more executive power, we should be what Austria or Prussia, is—With more democratic power, we should be what the United States are—In one case the monarch would make & unmake right at his discretion—In the other, the sovereign people, would do the same, as arrogantly and as outrageously."[48]

The return to America would, of course, bring reunion with Theodore. But now, perhaps because of the widening gap between their religious views, even that prospect seemed little comfort. His references to it were heavily overlaid with the preoccupation with death that had emerged in his correspondence over the past two years: "My soul ever thirsts after thee my Theodore—but it thirsts after thee as a mate for eternity, not for time—When, Oh when, shall we awake and be with God, to weep & to tremble, and to part no more—no more, for ever!" The same preoccupation was lurking in a new conviction that his active antislavery career was at last coming to an end. The prospect of leaving Britain forever was "mournful" to him but also "sweetly pleasing" for it seemed the path of duty: "God, with years, is distinctly giving me a furlough, from the bustle in which I have been engaged. That furlough is becoming more & more legible to me, in every fibre of my body & soul, both evidently waning."[49]

---

48. Stuart to Weld, July 10, August 14, 1843, WP.
49. *Ibid.*

12 ANTISLAVERY ALIENATION AND FAMINE RELIEF

IN ONE SENSE Stuart had accurately forshadowed his future in mid-1843. After one final controversy in 1844, he was henceforth no more than an interested spectator of antislavery issues in both Britain and the United States. This withdrawal from public activity leaves a dearth of newspaper and institutional records, which makes the next seven years one of the hardest periods of his life to assess. Yet in another sense his intimations of approaching retirement proved to be premature. It was to be 1850 before his "expatriation" from Britain was complete. And a further reason for the relative obscurity of these years was that they were marked by a continuing "bustle" that took him in turn to Ireland, the United States, Canada, Britain, the Channel Islands, Ireland again, and finally permanently to Canada. This mobility may not have interrupted his flow of correspondence, and the gaps, sometimes of months, are probably as much the result of letters lost as letters unwritten. But in the absence of continuing commitment to the one great cause, Stuart was more than ever a transient figure in the lives of his myriad acquaintances and friends. Occasionally those networks of friendship might mesh unexpectedly, as in May, 1844, when Elizur Wright, the friend of his American agency days a decade earlier, encountered him in the midst of earnest controversy with his English friends, Blair and Sturge. But how could any of those three be expected to keep in close contact with a man who less than three months later would be on the shores of Lake St. Clair, near Detroit, arranging the transportation of a dozen Canadian Indians to Liverpool?[1]

Although one would like to know much more about this and other incidents, it is clear that Stuart had not slumped into the physical incapacity he had for so long been predicting. Elizur Wright found him "just the same as ever." And in 1847 John Bigsby, who had last seen him twenty-six years earlier at Amherstburg, met him by chance in Bristol: "I knew him instantly; there was the same carelessness about the outer man, the same restless zeal for the old object." A month later, restlessness had carried him to the island of Jersey, and the zeal was being expressed in a letter to John Scoble, offering five pounds to the British and Foreign Anti-Slavery Society and inquiring whether he could be "locally serviceable."[2] Despite this offer—and although the visit to Jersey is another of the enigmas of this period of his life—the overall trend is clear. Stuart was still fit enough, still free enough from family responsibilities, to be an active abolitionist. He still cared passionately about slavery. But he had not overcome the feeling of frustration that had grown in 1842 and 1843, when he had found neither the public nor fellow abolitionists sympathetic to his antislavery methods and goals. An even more personal alienation was involved also, as his friendship with Theodore Weld continued to wither away.

Ironically, there was a moment in 1848 when his views and those of the British and Foreign Anti-Slavery Society were closer than they had been for years. But before this situation could lead to renewed antislavery involvement, he became caught up with a new philanthropic venture in Ireland. There can be no question about his sincere concern for Irish suffering. Yet the irony of his months of work for famine relief was that, for all his compassion and his willingness to share discomfort and even danger with the Irish peasantry, this period revealed again the intensity of his religious and political biases.

INSTEAD OF returning to America in late 1843, as he had predicted, Stuart spent a month in Ireland and then the early part of 1844 embroiled in his last British antislavery controversy. Potentially it was the most bitter, for his main adversary was William Blair and throughout its course he remained Blair's guest in Bath. When Blair had spoken at the 1843 convention in support of the abolition of duties on the slave-grown sugar of

1. Stuart to Weld, August 2, 1844, WP; Elizur Wright to Beriah Green, May 17, 1844, BPL.
2. Wright to Green, May 17, 1844, BPL; Bigsby, *Shoe and Canoe*, 264 n.; Stuart to Scoble, October 14, 1847, S. 18, C22/37, RHL.

Brazil and Cuba, Stuart had listened in silence, though, he claimed later, "with all the energy and kindness of which my soul is capable." He had no doubt been appalled when Blair and another old friend, George Anstie of Devizes, had joined with Thomas Spencer in attempting immediately after the convention to form a new antislavery organization based on free-trade principles. Certainly in the ensuing months he had discussed the matter repeatedly with Blair and Anstie. They were initially unimpressed by his argument that this particular form of free trade would entrench slavery. And they brought matters to a head by joining with Spencer in a letter, published in the *Anti-Slavery Reporter* on April 3, 1844, criticizing the opposition of the national society to the reduction of sugar duties and in effect urging its auxiliaries to repudiate Broad Street leadership.[3]

Joseph Sturge made an immediate reply to these criticisms by pointing out that the national society was committed by its constitution to recommend the use of free-grown produce as far as practicable in preference to slave-grown "and to promote the adoption of fiscal regulations in favor of free labour." Sturge also insisted that this position was morally as well as constitutionally correct, a claim that was widely endorsed by numerous letters published in the next edition of the *Reporter*. Prominent among these was one by Stuart. He wrote of the "devotion" of Blair and Anstie to the antislavery cause and of the "personal affection" he felt for them. If any men could have shaken his "independent convictions" it would be these two. But his conscience owed a greater duty to God, and when he believed his friends wrong in the sight of God, "then does wrong become doubly detestable to me." The question, he insisted, was simple, but he nevertheless contrived to express it in five different variations on the theme, "Ought we to urge our Government to give the same countenance to slavery as to freedom?" Slave sugar was the "bank and mint, and nerve and heart, of slavery, in the case in question."[4]

Whether as a result of this and the other published letters or of the "fervent discussions" that went on in his household, Blair some ten days later wrote to John Scoble reporting that he had changed his mind. His letter was deemed sufficiently important to be published as a separate leaflet, rather than awaiting inclusion in the next edition of the *Reporter*. His explanation made it clear that he had been no less convinced than Stuart that his attitudes were rooted in the basic principles of their com-

3. Temperley, *British Antislavery*, 157; *Anti-Slavery Reporter*, V (1844), 50–52, 54, 56, 67, 68, 77.
4. *Anti-Slavery Reporter*, V (1844), 54, 56, 67, 68, 77.

mon antislavery background. Whereas Stuart's position seemed to follow naturally from his long personal repudiation of slave produce, Blair's free-trade principles had been based on assumptions about the economic superiority of free labor which had never been more boldly stated than in Stuart's own *West India Question*. Even in his recantation Blair insisted that "in the long run, and not a very long run neither [sic], the labour of the free man will displace and abolish the labour of the slave." But he had become convinced that "while the principles of free labour are working their way," the slaveholder, knowing time was short, would make a "convulsive effort" to "reap a double harvest."[5]

Although his long friendship with Blair must have made this change of heart particularly satisfying to Stuart, it could have done little to overturn his conviction that the antislavery movement had lost its sense of direction. On the sugar question he had found himself in alliance with Broad Street and its most notable spokesman, Sturge. Yet only weeks after the climax of his conflict with Blair, Elizur Wright found him at odds with Sturge over suffrage reform. Pleasant though the encounter with Wright was on a personal level, it could only serve to reinforce Stuart's sense of isolation, for the American's attitudes showed again how the unity of the 1830s had dispersed in numerous directions. Impressed by Sturge's commitment to suffrage reform, Wright was nevertheless convinced that his attitudes on the sugar question were "a perfect absurdity." As for Stuart, who both shared those "absurd" attitudes and opposed suffrage reform, Wright could only say, "What a mystery is man!"[6]

There was in fact nothing mysterious about Stuart's attitudes. It was simply that he found it much easier than most of his colleagues to arrange his reform priorities. Seeing domestic problems mainly as a distraction from abolitionism, he had none of the deep social concern that explained Sturge's support of suffrage reform, of Chartism, and of the Anti–Corn Law League. The sugar issue, in particular, presented many reformers with a real dilemma, for the major impulse behind free-trade attitudes was a desire to lower prices for impoverished domestic consumers. Eventually Sturge had decided that the sugar duties could be separated from the corn laws because the plight of the slave was more desperate than that of the British working classes.

It would be too simple to categorize Stuart's relative indifference to domestic reform as mere conservatism. Underlying conservatism was his

5. *Ibid.*, 68; William T. Blair, *On the Introduction of Slave-Grown Produce into the British Markets* (London, 1844).
6. Wright to Green, May 17, 1844, BPL.

rootless background and the compensation he had found for it in an ever more outspoken patriotism and in his evangelical religion. His patriotism had little to do with the real Britain. Overseas birth and a lifetime of mobility left him with none of the normal enthusiasms for cities or scenery, culture or people, boyhood memories or family connections. His numerous letters are bereft of such affinities: in his only description of an English region he was an outsider seeing Yorkshire as "the Connecticut of England."[7] His loyalty was to British authority and institutions, whether in Westminster or the various outposts of the empire—from India to Canada—where it had offered his frequent moves a shred of continuity. Loyalty, in short, was to an imperialism that did little to link him emotionally to the plight of ordinary English people.

Stuart himself would no doubt have strenuously denied that the Bible was another form of compensation for his restless loneliness. But by 1844 he was more and more often citing it as his consolation while the unity and dynamism of the antislavery movement disintegrated around him. At the climax of his dispute with Blair and Anstie he wrote: "My heart sinks within me when I find such views can be urged by such minds; and, had I not God's bible, with free access to it, for my own solemn and prayerful judgment of what God's own truth is, I should be saddened into the conviction that no such thing as truth or falsehood, as right or wrong, as benevolence or malignity, exist; but that all . . . are matters of opinion."[8] Neither patriotism nor religion made him indifferent to human suffering. But in the years after 1844 they had a decisive influence on his relations with other abolitionists and on his own reform activities.

STUART FINALLY made his delayed crossing of the Atlantic in June, 1844. It is not clear why he was so soon negotiating the passage to England of an unnamed lady and gentleman and their entourage of one servant, two children, and "twelve, or 13, or 14 Indians of Walpole Island." But though the large gaps in his correspondence may conceal other philanthropic activities, it is evident that for the next three years, as he had predicted, most of his time was spent in Toronto with his sister, Mary Rankin, and her daughters. It is also evident that he remained detached from the major antislavery trends. Although he subscribed regularly to Broad Street publications and wrote occasionally to Scoble, he showed no desire to involve himself in activities, not even in the British protests against the admission of Texas as a slave state in 1845.[9]

7. Stuart to Weld, March 26, 1831, WP.
8. *Anti-Slavery Reporter*, V (1844), 68.
9. Stuart to Weld, August 2, 1844, WP; Stuart to Scoble, October 9, 1845, S. 18, C22/39, RHL; Stuart to Weld, November 2, 1845, WP.

It is hard to imagine he was totally indifferent to that development. Yet the available evidence indicates that he ignored the chance to voice criticisms of an event that marked a major stage in the development of American antislavery attitudes. After the initial split of the early 1840s, the two rival national societies had fairly soon receded into the background as vehicles for conflicting antislavery philosophies. Many New Organizationists had concentrated on political action through the Liberty party, which nominated Stuart's old friend James G. Birney for president in 1844. The Garrisonians, meanwhile, had moved still further away from electoral politics. But the procedure of "coming out" from churches and political parties that compromised with slavery had not led to a truly revolutionary rhetoric by the mid-1840s. Many radicals who denounced the Constitution as a proslavery document had still been willing to advocate the orthodox procedure of an amending convention to remove its most obnoxious feature, the Fugitive Slave Law. This approach was made to seem much less central to the basic problem now that the admission of Texas had brought a major extension of slavery. The response of the radicals was still uneven. Not many were yet prepared to embrace the extreme "disunionism" of the New Englander Stephen Foster, who urged repudiation of personal allegiance to the Constitution and Union. But the fact that such views were being put forward might have been expected to enrage the Stuart of old. And the emerging argument that the annexation of Texas was unconstitutional and had therefore destroyed the legitimacy of the Union might equally have been expected to engage his attention.[10] Yet despite the uncertainties of the record at this stage of his life, it seems clear that for the moment his interest in the American antislavery scene was narrowly personal and confined to his concern at Theodore Weld's waning involvement.

On his return from his research position in Washington, Weld had opened a boarding school in his home at Belleville, New Jersey, where he, Angelina, and Sarah had been farming since 1839. Stuart's letters in 1845 and 1846 asked, with mounting urgency, whether his friend remained active in the antislavery and temperance causes. In the process he revealed the essence of his own ideological commitment to reform: "The Anti-Slavery, and Teetotal causes, seem to me, eminently of God—not as necessarily involving the regeneration of the being; but as removing barriers to that regeneration which render it next to impossible."[11]

10. Jane H. Pease and William H. Pease, "Confrontation and Abolition in the 1850s," *Journal of American History*, LVIII (1971–72), 923–37.
11. Stuart to Weld, November 2, 1845, April 11, 1846, WP.

For this reason his concern about Weld's withdrawal was secondary to misgivings about his retreat from scriptural orthodoxy. In November, 1845, Stuart wrote regretfully about "Pecuniary embarrassments," which had made it impossible for him to make a planned visit to Weld the previous summer. He had strongly desired the meeting, not only to "refresh" their friendship but because he feared that Weld was "declining from that noble walk of glorious usefulness" with which God had endowed him. His fears were still too vague for him to engage in argument. But a recent reference by Weld to "Scriptural religion" made him anxious for a clear exposition of his friend's views. Although he expressed confidence that the Scriptures remained "the great foundation of your faith and practice," doubts were clearly at the back of his mind: "I could not love you, as I do, without believing this fully."[12]

A quick exchange of letters before the end of the year brought renewed protestations of confidence from Stuart: "Yes, thou knowest my heart,—Yes, we are far from each other; and yet are not the bonds which unite us, as imperishable as He, whom we believe to be, the Author of our mutual love." But he went on, no less anxiously than before: "I shall be awaiting thy letters—but shall probably not attempt to reply to them, until they are concluded; for I shall wish to have thy *profession* all before me, ere I judge of its real character."[13]

Four months later his fears were being confirmed. The old passionate tone was still there as he began: "I thank thee, my Theodore, long dearly beloved of my soul, I tenderly thank thee for thy letter just received." It "still breathes the living love, for which I have always loved you, towards God as you know him, and the amazing love which I have always experienced from you." But he did not understand most of Weld's recent "profession," and what he did understand he did not approve. For all its tenderness it threw a dense, impenetrable cloud around his friend: "I want to see through it—not that I may love you the less—but that I may love *you*, not a *fiction*."[14]

When the cloud dispersed in the future Stuart would prove unable to continue loving the real, freethinking Weld who emerged. The scriptural orthodoxy to which he now referred would then be reiterated in detail and ad nauseam as a barrier to affection between himself and others as well as Weld. But even as his letters of 1845 and 1846 showed the inevitability of such conflicts with all who rejected his faith, they also revealed again

12. Stuart to Weld, November 2, 1845, WP.
13. Stuart to Weld, December 26, 1845, WP.
14. Stuart to Weld, April 11, 1846, WP.

another Stuart—deeply emotional, craving human warmth—who would be the worst casualty of such schisms. Letters that began with effusions of love for Theodore commonly ended with affectionate references to Cornelia and other family members and a special word for the children: "Return for me most cordially Charles' hugs and kisses—and still teach him to love me, & tell him I love him—and give Theodore (the younger) a big, big hug for me & to each of them, a kiss for me and a blessing, by morn and eve, daily."[15]

In the same manner he bade farewell to Gerrit Smith and his wife on the eve of his return to Britain in August, 1847. Although he had seen something of the Smiths in recent years, he had been "grieved and disappointed" to find them absent from home on a recent journey between New York and Toronto. Reminding them of his "constant affection" and requesting them to kiss their son Green for him, he marked his departure with a typically fervent antislavery rallying call: his "soul's constant prayer" for them both was that they would show redoubled concern for the plight of the "poor and ignorant." In particular, the "most thrilling features" of the "great cause of Holy and everlasting love" involved the slave—"crushed with sufferings beyond what other men endure." It was a course he prayed would "burn more and more in your hearts" with "a sacred fire from heaven."[16]

Despite this call and despite his immediate return to his old antislavery haunts in the West Country and, within a month, offering his services to Broad Street from the unlikely direction of the Channel Islands, there was still no major antislavery role for him in Britain. His next serious reminder to Americans such as Weld and Smith of their duty to the "poor and ignorant" would concern, not black slaves but the starving peasants of southern Ireland.

His visit to Ireland ironically tore him away from a situation that seemed to put him on the verge of reestablishing a working relationship with Broad Street. The committee of the national society had suffered years of uncertainty over priorities and outright conflict on some issues, notably the relationship between free trade and abolition. But in the later 1840s two issues were emerging on which virtually all British abolitionists could agree. And inasmuch as they demanded decisions by government, they had potential for the old methods dear to Stuart's heart. The continuing labor problems of the West Indian planters had long involved demands for immigrant labor. Indentured Indian coolies had continued to be im-

15. *Ibid.*
16. Stuart to Smith, August 1, 1847, SP.

ported since Stuart's controversial intervention in one of the earliest stages of the traffic in British Guiana in 1839. And now in 1847 the British government had relaxed a long-standing opposition to the recruitment of West African labor. Although the new policy was restricted to the Kroo Coast, which was said to be free from slavery, and although the numbers thus recruited proved to be small, abolitionists saw it as a covert reintroduction of the slave trade, which had been banned by Britain in 1807. In their eyes—and they were aware of foreign criticisms on the issue—the measure was particularly hypocritical in view of Britain's controversial maritime activity designed to suppress the traditional slave trade.[17]

Controversies over the suppression policy formed the second issue behind which antislavery forces were reuniting in the late 1840s. For several years the free-trade lobby had been outspokenly critical of this continuing role of artificial interference in international commerce. For all its amorality, this attitude had not been without support in antislavery circles, even to the extent of some qualified endorsement of the free-trade MP William Hutt, who produced a controversial proposal for a legalized slave trade. By 1848, however, that support was fading, as Hutt's proposals became more radical, and abolitionists were moving toward a policy of attacking the slave trade less by maritime police action than by the introduction of economic sanctions against the slave-importing nations of Brazil and Cuba.[18]

In these circumstances of emerging antislavery consensus Stuart's demand for the resurrection of old methods of agitation was less of a cry in the wilderness than it had been some five years earlier. At the beginning of May he wrote to Broad Street about the restoration of slavery and the slave trade, "which are so portentously involved in the immigration schemes & Legislative enactments lately sanctioned by our Government." These measures "call upon us, in a voice of thunder, to be up and to be doing on behalf of our brother in bondage." And what should this entail? "My answer is—Rouse the British heart again, by suitable lecturers—by men of George Thompson's talents, but of noble spirit—So might we hope that our Government, urged and supported by the people, would resort to those righteous measures which are beyond its power without such urgency and support." Without such a measure he saw no hope for the antislavery cause, despite the unceasing exertions of the London committee and local associations. "And *if* this be done," he went on, "on a somewhat commensurate scale—say *at least* six liberally sal-

17. Temperley, *British Antislavery*, 132–35.
18. Ibid., 176–81.

aried and regular lecturers of the requisite endowments; I hereby pledge myself to subscribe annually one fourth of my income, or nearly fifty pounds sterling, for that purpose."[19]

There is no evidence that Stuart ever fulfilled this promise, even though later that year Broad Street did embark on an extended campaign using lecturers as well as other old methods of agitation and persuasion.[20] It is impossible to believe his offer was not sincere. The reason he did not honor it was that, immediately after it was made, he went to Ireland, was distracted by the conditions he found there, and discovered a new philanthropic use for his income.

It is not possible to explain in any detail the processes that took Stuart to Ireland. His Irish antislavery activities had been considerable in the past and given him knowledge of virtually every part of the island. But almost certainly those activities had been partly motivated and facilitated by more personal associations probably dating from his boyhood years in Belfast. Unfortunately, his surviving letters and the record of his antislavery activity give no real information. Only his later marriage to a distant relation, whom he had known "upwards of thirty years," would give a hint of the depth and range of his Irish connections.[21] He may have gone to Ireland in 1848 primarily for personal reasons. But if so, the situation was too grim to be ignored by anyone with personal affiliations or even a shred of Stuart's humanitarian impulse.

IN 1830–31, when Stuart had begun his antislavery career in Ireland, the burning political question there had been neither the abolition of West Indian slavery nor the imminent reform of Parliament, which promised to make abolition possible, but repeal of the Act of Union between Britain and Ireland. Stuart had not then been indifferent to Irish poverty, but he had refused to join either Irish nationalists or American critics in attributing it to the English connection. Despite his close antislavery links with Ireland, he had always been cool toward the leading Irish politician of the age, Daniel O'Connell, who, though an abolitionist, had advocated repeal of the Act of Union. In the 1840s O'Connell had begun to urge repeal with more force but had nonetheless found himself at odds with a more militant Irish nationalism, which was still less to Stuart's taste. As a modest landlord, O'Connell could not go all the way with those who insisted that a full solution of Irish problems demanded fundamental land reform as

19. Stuart, "To the friends, in deed of the Slave," Bath, May 9, 1848, S. 18, C22/40, RHL.
20. Temperley, *British Antislavery*, 181.
21. Stuart to Weld, April 22, 1852, WP.

well as the severing of the English connection. As a parliamentary politician he could go none of the way with those who saw revolutionary violence as the essential means to reform.

More radical views had gained coherence in 1842 with the foundation of a Dublin newspaper, the *Nation*, by a group who became known as the Young Irelanders. O'Connell had seen the group as valuable allies on some issues but had tended to recoil from their extremism even before the onset of the great potato famine in the autumn of 1845 had acutely intensified the endemic Irish problems. O'Connell had died in 1847. He had seen various ineffectual British government responses to the Irish famine: the repeal of the Corn Laws, the organization, initially in secret, of emergency food supplies, the belated institution of an inadequate system of poor relief in Ireland, all of which had failed to avert disaster. O'Connell had lived long enough to see widespread distress and death. He did not live long enough to see the climax of a nationalist agitation, which in 1848 threatened to add Ireland to the list of European countries shaken by revolution.

With a population of eight million, Ireland was one of the most densely populated countries in Europe. Because half that population was totally dependent on the potato for subsistence, there had long been potential for disaster. Every year large numbers of people had been destitute for short periods. Periodically there had been longer-term local famines. Now since 1845 the nationwide and repeated failure of the crop had exposed the Irish to the catastrophic effects of famine and fever. To the Young Irelanders the situation was the result not only of the mysterious root-rotting fungus nor of inadequate, almost punitive, British relief measures but of a land tenure system in which predominantly Protestant landlords had exploited a wretched peasantry. Under the leadership of John Mitchel, who had joined the movement as recently as 1845—and inspired by the outbreak of revolution in France—the Young Irelanders advocated armed resistance against Britain, repeal of the union, and popular sovereignty over the land.[22]

Charles Stuart was in Ireland at the climax of these events. He was far from insensitive to Irish suffering and had long ago commented critically on the absence of an Irish poor law. In 1843 he had even been prepared to list among the "wrongs" of the Irish the "legal tenures of their lands." But these had been grudging qualifications of an attitude that consistently saw Catholicism as the major blight of Ireland and took British rule for

22. R. Dudley Edwards, *A New History of Ireland* (Dublin, 1972), 158–75; J. C. Beckett, *The Making of Modern Ireland* (London, 1966), 306–50.

granted. From some mutual acquaintances he received a favorable impression of Mitchel, scarcely a "gigantic mind" but "valuably endowed" in many respects. Mitchel's advocacy of rebellion, however, violated both Stuart's belief in orderly, constitutional political action and his underlying assumptions about the benign role of British imperialism in Ireland. It was "insane" for Mitchel to have attempted "to substitute a mobocratic rule, for an enlightened, benevolent and peaceful sway," and it was fitting that he had been arrested promptly. Observing his conviction in May, 1848, by a packed jury, Stuart was pleased that British benevolence recognized the man's redeeming features by sentencing him to fourteen years' transportation rather than to the "death I believe he deserved."[23]

The rebellion that Mitchel had predicted would follow his arrest did not occur. With the Catholic clergy hostile and the mass of the population too devastated by famine to rise, the remaining rebels were quickly isolated and suppressed by the government.[24] Though totally approving of these trends, Stuart nevertheless saw the imposition of authority as an opportunity for his own response to Irish distress. For the next nine months the Irish famine was to be the focus of his last sustained personal humanitarian enterprise.

From mid-1848 he devoted himself to "an exploring journey of three months, from north to south." As a man of private means, he was scarcely exposing himself to the same dangers as the masses, who faced starvation not only because they had no potatoes but because they had no money to buy alternatives. As the guest of Protestant landlords, he moved among the exploiters as much as the exploited. Indeed, his one letter to Weld from this "exploring" period revealed only the rediscovery, after more than thirty years, of an old East India Company acquaintance, Theophilus Bolton Jones. There was no hint of Irish distress when he wrote of a pleasant stay on Jones's "fine hereditary estate" at Mohill, County Leitrim. Modern studies were to place Mohill in one of the areas of Ireland most heavily depopulated in the 1840s. Yet Stuart's letter to Weld did not refer to mass emigration; it merely requested Weld's help and hospitality for a nephew of Jones, "a gentleman in a fair and natural sense," who was emigrating to New York "in pursuit of those honorable prospects, which animate the ambition of most young men."[25]

23. *Liberator*, November 26, 1836, p. 190; Stuart to Weld, August 14, 1843, WP; Stuart to editor, March 21, 1854 (1853 printed in error), *Frederick Douglass' Paper*, April 7, 1854.
24. Edwards, *New History of Ireland*, 175.
25. Stuart to Weld, July 3, 1848, WP; see map showing percentage decline in population, 1841–51, in R. Dudley Edwards and T. Desmond Williams, *The Great Famine: Studies in Irish History 1845–52* (Dublin, 1962), 260.

When he eventually ended his explorations with a firm commitment to share the sufferings of the people of Cape Clear Island, Stuart threw in his lot with Protestant clergy, and his choice of this region was at least partly because the people were "more than usually free from the popish influence which so deeply blights the western and southern population of Ireland." He was active in organizing a Sunday school and regular religious meetings during the week "from house to house." As the winter wore on, he continued to regard "Popery" as "our greatest external curse," though he had hopes that it was "totering [sic] to its fall." Yet though such activities and comments reveal Stuart's fundamental prejudices about Ireland unshaken by the famine, his decision to spend the winter in this community was much more than an easy sectarian gesture.[26]

Cape Clear Island was the most extreme southern inhabited point of Ireland. It was about three miles long and one to two miles wide, with a rugged, mountainous surface, half of it naked slate, the other half only poorly cultivated and totally without trees. On this small outcrop lived some thirteen hundred people, with a good water supply but depending entirely on fuel imported from the mainland six miles away at its nearest point, Baltimore. When Stuart arrived, the potato crop had failed utterly, "not a *green* leaf or stalk remaining." Famine loomed "on the darkened horizon of the coming winter," and "again it threatens, with its accompaniment, fever, to waste the perishing people around them." The people, he wrote to Weld, were "some of the most desolate, physically speaking of our fellow men—I tremble at times in view of the enterprise which I have undertaken for the winter, in thus throwing myself among them."[27]

By December the situation seemed even more desperate: "Their wretched habitations, filthy and furniture-less; the tattered rags of their clothing; the almost total want of means to employ them; and their consequent want of even half a sufficiency of the coarsest food; fill me at times with feelings of impatient despair; and seeing how utterly unable I am to relieve their terrible wants, I am prompted to fly, and get out of sight of their wretchedness." His faith would not let him fly. He had committed himself to the winter's stay with foreboding but also with a feeling of "precious privilege to have the opportunity, of thus far seeking to follow the Master, whom we love." He was still there at the end of February, reporting on a winter of "dangerous and severe" distress which had yet

26. Printed letter signed C. Stuart, Cape Clear Island, Care of Rev. Edward Spring, Baltimore, County Cork (WP), with added handwritten comments addressed to Weld. The letter is undated, but the date "Ca. 1846" penciled at the top, presumably by an archivist, is clearly wrong, for Stuart was in Canada in 1846.
27. Ibid.

been not quite "so pitifully consuming" as he had expected. An alarming fever was prevalent, but it was "by no means general." His plans were uncertain, but, as always, he was prepared for "God's leadings, *wherever they may lead or keep me.*"[28]

His winter on the island, however, had been an exercise in practical philanthropy rather than religious masochism. The eccentric figure who had arrived from nowhere to take board and lodging in a local farmhouse had not been content to organize Sunday schools and prayer meetings for the islanders. He had arrived to share their distress and to invite them to share his income. And he had done his best to supplement his regular income with donations from his antislavery friends. His communications with the outside world took the form of appeals to such as Gerrit Smith and the Welds. Although letters only to these two individuals have been seen, it is plain that he cast his net much wider, for his first appeal took the form of a printed leaflet describing conditions on the island and asking "for aid, that the poor, fed, comforted, and instructed in the scripture by your aid, may bless you; and that the God of the poor, whom you love, may acknowledge it." On the copy he sent to Weld he scribbled a request that the appeal be brought to the notice of their mutual friends.[29]

It is impossible to say how successful the appeal was, but Stuart was persistent. When Gerrit Smith sent a mere four pounds, he immediately replied, stressing the "perishing wants" of his neighbors and asking for a further fifty pounds. Although he wrote tactfully of the continual demands made on Smith's benevolence, he artfully tried to shame him into sending more. Fully understanding that even Smith's "great resources" were heavily in demand, he asked that the fifty pounds should be sent as a gift, if possible, but otherwise as a loan. If Smith chose the latter alternative, Stuart would, "as soon as the winter is over, if preserved so long," seek out "some cheap spot of Britain or America, and scrupulously husband my means" in order to repay it within a year. The tactic was only partly successful. Stuart eventually sent his thanks for an unspecified donation with the comment that "I cannot wonder at your inability to help *this little* spot, to the amount solicitted [sic]."[30]

By this time, however, the worst crisis of winter was over. Although he would go wherever God led him, he now expected to remain no longer than early May. His letter to Smith showed a new stirring of interest in the antislavery cause. Yet it also showed that his stay in Ireland had not

28. Stuart to Smith, December 12, 1848, February 21, 1849, SP.
29. See note 26.
30. Stuart to Smith, December 12, 1848, February 21, 1849, SP.

only taken him away from British antislavery activity but also accentuated his emotional and intellectual isolation from the American scene. Were the leading principles of the main American antislavery associations "scriptural" as they had been in the days when they first met in New York, "or do they compromise like some and boast and bluster like others?" The questions showed that his attitudes to Garrisonism had not mellowed or kept pace with American developments. Increasingly the issues between Old and New Organization were of less concern to American abolitionists than the emergence of slavery as the central political problem in the United States. Stuart showed that he was aware that the recent war with Mexico had given the United States vast territories threatening the sectional equilibrium between North and South. But rather than probing the political complexities, his response was a cynical generalization about American democracy, "a plague spot leering with hypocrisy and crimsoned with blood."[31]

Whether he knew it or not, the final "expatriation" he had predicted six years before was about to take place. His contempt both for American democracy and for many American abolitionists would help to make his retirement in Canada the least tranquil phase of a restless life. And this last, Irish, stage of his public life had revealed once again the strength of his religious dogmatism and the stiffness of his British imperialism—traits that would make it harder than ever for him to find common ground with his American friends in retirement.

31. Ibid.

13 RETIREMENT, MARRIAGE, AND ISOLATION

STUART BEGAN what proved to be a fifteen-year retirement when he returned to Canada in 1850. Writing separately to Weld and Smith from his sister's home in Toronto, he showed continuing interest in the American antislavery scene. But he was never again to be a part of that scene. He was already planning to move north at the end of winter to a family property. And from there mounting bitterness toward America and his former American friends would be a conspicuous feature of his declining years. Before he left Toronto he did seem briefly to be seeking a new path to his long-cherished goal of international antislavery cooperation. In February, 1851, he attended the inaugural meeting of the Canadian Anti-Slavery Society and was elected to the potentially influential position of corresponding secretary. George Thompson, visiting the United States at the time, was quick to react to the implications for "old organization" of the appointment of such "a great Garrison-hater."[1]

Thompson need not have worried about Stuart's influence. Although letter-writing was to be a major activity of his retirement, there is no evidence that he seriously pursued his official duties with the Canadian society. He did not attend the annual meeting a year later and was never again an officeholder.[2] His only future antislavery activities would be local speaking engagements.

   1. Stuart to Weld, November 5, 1850, WP; to Smith, n.d. 1850, SP; *Anti-Slavery Reporter*, VI (1851), 65–66; Thompson to Anne Warren Weston, March 17, 1851, in Taylor, *British and American Abolitionists*, 375.
   2. *Anti-Slavery Reporter*, VII (1852), 74–75.

Such a withdrawal from public activity might seem entirely normal for a man seventy years old in 1851. For more than a decade he had referred to his waning physical powers, and for the rest of his life his correspondence would return regularly to the theme that "age is dark & unlovely." But when he depicted himself as "encrusted with age" in 1853, when he referred to "crushing infirmities" in 1855, and even when he mentioned his "incompetency to be publicly useful" in 1858, he was prematurely declaring an incapacity that was real only in the last three to four years of his life.[3] Only from 1862 onward was he too feeble to contemplate travel. His withdrawal was influenced by his growing distaste for America and many American abolitionists. But the most concrete reason for it was that he began his retirement by getting married in 1852.

His wife was Rebecca Watt, whom he had known for more than thirty years in Ireland. He had, he told Weld, always loved her "as a pure and noble woman," but it was only in the last six months that his heart had been "conjugally drawn" to her. She was twenty-six years younger than he, yet marriage was not in this case simply a means of providing for his own comforts in old age. Instead it involved an abrupt assumption of wider family responsibilities, for he acquired, as well as a wife, two dependent sisters-in-law and a father-in-law some fourteen years older than himself.[4]

This unusual extended family, with a servant, Charles Grant, took up residence on a property at Lora Bay, an inlet on Georgian Bay and near the village of Thornbury in the Collingwood township. They lived in an extensive log house with several large rooms, each with a stone fireplace, and various added wings, including one that housed Stuart's study. The house was surrounded by neat shrubs and flowers and by a "good estate" for growing crops and raising cattle. "Our advantages here," wrote Stuart in 1857, "are great." It was "healthy country," and the scenery was beautiful: as he wrote to distant friends he could look straight out on the lake "rolling in ceaseless commotion."[5]

But it was nevertheless a frontier existence to which he was never completely reconciled. He had acquired the Lora property from his

3. Stuart to Smith, September 30, 1853, November 27, 1855, March 14, 1857, February 6, 1858, SP.

4. Stuart to Weld, April 22, 1852, WP. The 1851 census shows that Rebecca, her father, John, and sisters, Isabelle and Margaret, were already living at Stuart's house some months before the marriage in 1852 (1851 Census, Canada West; Grey County, Collingwood Township: Personal Census, microfilm reel C11723, PAC).

5. Stuart to Smith, September 26, 1857, SP; *Frederick Douglass' Paper*, April 7, 1854; Landon, "Captain Charles Stuart," 17–18.

brother-in-law, Charles Rankin, who had surveyed this part of the Canadian wilderness for the government and had been the first settler in the Collingwood township. In the early 1850s complicated instructions for finding the property still had to be offered to potential visitors from Toronto and beyond. Public transport stopped at Barrie some seventy miles away. There were "tolerably convenient halting and lodging places" on the route through the woods to Collingwood. But even between there and Lora it was necessary to hire a guide. The healthy environment could also be inhospitable. Even at the end of March the "northern blast of yet lingering winter" sent lumps of ice crashing among the waves on the lake. In the summer of 1856 a forest fire "rushed like a whirlwind thro' the adjoining woods, to the very verge of leaving us homeless."[6]

Superficially there was rapid progress. The *Canada Directory* for 1857 described an area passing beyond the frontier stage. The Ontario, Simcoe, and Huron Railroad had recently been pushed through to Collingwood from where steamer services provided links to most parts of the Great Lakes farther west. But Stuart's emotional links with the United States were not to such places as Chicago and Milwaukee but southeast to New York. With the rail terminus at Collingwood some fourteen miles away, not even the journey to visit his relatives in Toronto was easy: "Our roads," he told Gerrit Smith in 1858, "continue all but impassable except for vigorous frames." And in an indirect sense these modern developments had made things even harder for less vigorous frames. As early as 1854, he had complained that railroad projects had raised wage levels so much that servants were almost unobtainable. By 1857 the lack of servants was making it almost impossible to keep the estate properly productive, "as we are all too old to do the work."[7]

Family responsibility and physical isolation regularly frustrated his desire for more contact with American abolitionists. "Imperious duty alone" prevented his attendance at the New York antislavery convention in 1852. A year later he was forced to cancel another visit at the last minute because of "the sudden and aggravated sickness of my wife, together with wildly tempestuous weather." No doubt the same problems confined him to a local role in Canadian antislavery circles, for he clearly would have liked to do more: "Here we are in a measure out of the world; exerting

    6. Landon, "Captain Charles Stuart,"17; Stuart to Weld, April 17, 1853, July 20, 1856, WP; Stuart to Smith, May 26, September 26, 1857, April 31 [sic], 1858, SP; *Frederick Douglass' Paper*, April 7, 1854.
    7. *The Canada Directory for 1857–58* (Montreal, 1857), see entries for Collingwood and Thornbury; Stuart to Weld, June 30, 1854, WP; to Smith, September 26, 1857, April 31 [sic], 1858, SP.

but feebly, the feeble power (the only power which we have) in the holy cause of God and humanity."[8]

He soon came to regard his situation as an "exile" from more congenial company. "The people around us," he told Weld in 1853, "are generally loyal, orderly & sober; but have little to develope [sic] in themselves, or in me, any of the nobler powers of the mind." It was an exile he long sought to escape by permanent removal, sometimes to Britain or Ireland, most persistently to upstate New York. Gerrit Smith and his wife regularly urged a move to Peterboro. Stuart was drawn to the idea; he outlined his requirements in great detail; and he even inspected properties and came to the verge of making offers to purchase. But the move was never made. The reasons were complex, and Stuart's reasoning often focused on his latest disagreement with individual Americans or his disenchantment with American society. The most consistent factor, however, was his desire to provide permanently for his wife and her sisters. This priority made it necessary, he told Smith, to "abstain from many of the sweetest privileges of personal friendship." The Lora property and his own pension provided "a healthful and frugal competency" as long as he lived. But because he also wished to provide for them after his death, his hopes rested on a steady improvement in the value of his land. To sell and remove to Peterboro would jeopardize these carefully calculated prospects. If God willed that they should be poor, he was of course ready to accept it; "but to make ourselves poor for present gratification, however pure & sweet, would be sin." And eventually a temporary fall in land prices was a major factor that "crushed the hopes" he had of settling in Peterboro.[9]

Stuart's devotion to his wife and her relatives could not transform Lora into a rustic paradise. His father-in-law regularly threatened to return to Ireland and finally did so at the age of ninety-five. He was accompanied by his younger daughter, Margaret, who marked their departure with a secret letter to Gerrit Smith about Stuart's suffocating zeal for the family welfare. The other sister, Isabelle, appears in Stuart's letters only in a dismissive reference to "Rebecca's feeble elder sister."[10] Although all this only hints at a baleful Stuart influence, it is clear how much Rebecca herself bore the brunt of her husband's personality.

For Stuart to marry at all so late in life may seem surprising, and the

---

8. Stuart to Smith, [May ?], 1852, September 30, 1853, SP; Stuart to Weld, October 31, 1853, WP.

9. Stuart to Weld, October 31, 1853, WP.; Stuart to Smith, April 10, 1856, August 15, September 26, 1857, February 6, 1858, January 1, 1859, SP.

10. Stuart to Smith, April 19, 1859, May 22, 1861, January 18, April 19, August [?], 1862; Margaret Watt to Smith, August 25, 1862, SP.

record does not make clear the motives of either party. Yet it is possible to see in the fragmentary clues of his earlier infatuation with Cornelia Weld and his published comments about feminine fragility long-frustrated yearnings for an emotional relationship with a woman. Marrying at seventy-one, he is unlikely to have developed a sexual relationship after a lifetime of evident abstinence. Indeed, he came as close to referring to sex as he was ever likely to when he told Weld that his union with Rebecca was "almost entirely a union of souls." But even without sex, after decades of exaggerated respect for ideal womanhood, marriage proved something of a shock to him. Six months after the wedding he confided to Weld that Rebecca "is not all that either you or I could wish," though he hurriedly added that Weld knew only too well "how far I am from being such." Although he wrote tolerantly of the "varieties of taste & habit & principle which exist every where in independent minds," adjustment had been traumatic: "Our differences when fully revealed to us after marriage, were full of deep agony to both of us." He was perhaps able to write in this manner in October, 1852, because he felt some of the necessary adjustment had been made. Despite her faults, Rebecca had a "pure and holy soul"; "taken altogether," he concluded, "she has a glorious heart."[11]

It probably demanded such a heart to take on Stuart in his old age. If he had always placed woman on a pedestal, he was now surrounding it more emphatically than ever with a moat of male domination. "Man," he told the readers of *Frederick Douglass' Paper*, "is the divinely constituted head of woman; and is so constituted, that he may be the protector, and friend, and servant thro' love, of the woman; to revere her, as his best earthly gift of God; to cherish and honor her, as his sister and companion; and to seek, in all his intercourse with her, her highest and holiest interests and happiness."[12] It is clear that the modus vivendi he and his wife devised after the "agony" of mutual discovery was not only in keeping with this philosophy but also involved capitulation by Rebecca to an opinionated eccentric.

Stuart's long-established personal regimen of abstinence from slave produce became the household rule at Lora, and his wife and her relatives were forced to find substitutes for cotton, sugar, and coffee.[13] How irksome Rebecca found this or other particulars of their lives is hard to say. No doubt she had known Stuart well enough to expect this arrangement, and she can hardly have been surprised at the dominant role played by

11. Stuart to Weld, October 15, 1852, WP.
12. *Frederick Douglass' Paper*, April 28, 1854.
13. Landon, "Captain Charles Stuart," 18.

Bible reading in their daily routine. But whether it was the difficulty of coping with Stuart's ideas or more generally with his personality, there are hints from early in their marriage of the stress Rebecca was experiencing. Plans for the couple to visit the Smiths in upstate New York were always overshadowed by doubts about her robustness for the journey. After a visit was achieved in 1855, Stuart's letter of thanks to Smith remarked on the "temporary relief so sweetly & wonderfully experienced by Rebecca" during the visit. Since their return to Lora, however, "her *tic* pains have severely returned." Escape from Lora was not always so therapeutic. In 1857 a similar visit to Smith was aborted at Toronto when Rebecca became "alarmingly ill." Back at Lora she returned to "her usual state of health, always poor."[14]

STRANDED IN the frontier environment he had so warmly recommended to would-be emigrants decades before, enmeshed by domestic ties for the first time in his life, Stuart subjected the outside world to an intense and increasingly belligerent scrutiny. He was an avid newspaper reader. The Canadian papers he found too parochial, but he read them anyway along with equally local American ones. He subscribed to the London *Times*, the British *Anti-Slavery Reporter*, the *American Missionary*, and most of the American antislavery papers, of which *Frederick Douglass' Paper* became his favorite.[15] It was thus not lack of information that alienated him from American abolitionists as the crisis of slavery unfolded.

His return to North America coincided with the Compromise of 1850, a major attempt to reconcile the differences between free and slave states, which had become a threat to the survival of the Union because of the speed of westward expansion and especially the recent acquisition of huge territories through war with Mexico. The compromise admitted California as a free state but left the issue of slavery in the other new territories of Utah and New Mexico to be settled by the natural process of "popular sovereignty." It abolished the slave trade in Washington, D.C., but balanced this by revitalizing the Fugitive Slave Law.

By the middle of the decade the hollowness of the popular sovereignty doctrine was being revealed in Kansas, as pro- and antislavery forces battled to ensure that nothing like a natural process took place. Stuart observed this battle with "pain" but not with impartiality. According to the

14. Stuart to Smith, August 31, 1855, July 11, 1857, SP.
15. Stuart to Smith, March 14, 1857, SP; to George Whipple, October 17, 1857, AMA; to Lewis Tappan, February 13, 1858, AMA; "Receipts," *Frederick Douglass' Paper*, January 6, 1854.

Recollections of abolitionist Frank Sanborn, Stuart met the eventually notorious John Brown at Gerrit Smith's in the summer of 1855 and gave him five dollars toward "arming the Brown family in Kansas." An inaccurate reminiscence concerning a later meeting between the two makes Sanborn's recollection suspect. But Stuart did stay with Smith at this period, and in other ways he left no doubt about his reactions to the Kansas situation. When the proabolition Senator Charles Sumner delivered a two-day tirade in Congress on the "Crime against Kansas" in 1856 and was savagely assaulted by Representative Preston S. Brooks, wielding a walking stick, Stuart wrote a private letter to the victim. He expressed "earnest admiration for your Senatorial course" and said his soul burned at this "dastardly, assassin-like abuse."[16]

Stuart offered his thanks to Sumner "in behalf of your country, which on many solemn accounts I love; & which such conduct as yours, rescues in a measure, from the contempt & execration of mankind." But by this time his love for the United States was rarely evident, and he was more and more consciously a foreign critic joining in the general contempt and execration. In late 1855 he told Smith that the Fugitive Slave Law was a major reason for his reluctance to move to the United States. He honored the efforts of Americans such as Smith who were resisting the execution of the law: as American citizens they had no option if they wanted to be true to God. As a foreigner, on the other hand, he saw the law as the natural product of a "base" and "hypocritical" system. He heard no call from God and could see no personal "pleasure or benefit" in challenging "a satanic power by rushing unguarded into his fangs."[17]

Although this same letter acknowledged financial and family obligations that also kept him in Canada, his estrangement from the United States was now profound. Friendships might occasionally lure him there, but an alien political and moral climate repelled him. His revulsion was in striking contrast to the near-euphoria he had displayed twenty years earlier as the itinerant antislavery agent who carried with him a miniature edition of the Constitution and publicly and privately extolled the virtues of American agrarian democracy. Now he showed extreme nostalgia for those pioneer days when the antislavery cause had flourished "amidst, slander & persecutions, & mobbings."[18]

This was the nostalgia of a zealot who had ignored the practical obsta-

---

16. Frank B. Sanborn, *Recollections of Seventy Years* (Boston, 1909), 144–45; Stuart to Smith, August 31, 1855, SP; Stuart to Sumner, June 1, 1856, Houghton Library, Harvard University.

17. Stuart to Sumner, June 1, 1856; to Smith, November 27, 1855, SP.

18. Stuart to editor, *Frederick Douglass' Paper*, January 20, 1854.

cles to American abolition in the 1830s. Then he had frequently lauded the virtues of the American Declaration of Independence and Constitution. As written, he had argued, they embodied the highest and holiest principles of morality. All that was needed was to arouse the moral indignation of the people against slavery and make the practice of American democracy conform to those principles. Events in the 1830s should have made it plain that the attempt to stir the conscience of the nation was politically counterproductive. While the South had closed ranks in defense of slavery, public opinion in the North had been violently hostile to abolition. Stuart had not accepted this sectionalism at the time. He had found mob opposition almost exhilarating and had left the United States optimistic. But since the 1830s the chances of political solutions had become immeasurably complicated. The South's insistence on sharing in the massive territorial expansion of the nation had led to more northerners opposing the extension of slavery than had ever supported the abolitionists of the 1830s. But a great deal of that opposition was a racist determination to exclude black competition from jobs and land; as such it was the antithesis of the morality embraced by Stuart.

In the 1850s Stuart was still occasionally willing to praise the principles embodied in the Declaration of Independence and the Constitution. But his belief that men would willingly conform to those principles had evaporated. Whether writing privately to a southern racist congressman, publicly to Frederick Douglass, or intimately to Weld and Smith, he expressed constant disillusionment with American democracy. The Declaration of Independence, he told his southern adversary, proclaimed principles incompatible with slavery, unless the ludicrous proposition that blacks were not men could be sustained. He yearned for Weld "amidst the degradation of your country, under the atrociously hypocritical & tyrant government of your slave-holding, slave-hunting, and slave-destroying democracy." "The democratic principle in *human action*," he told Gerrit Smith, "is a hydra-headed monster, full of the grossest hypocrisy, the most grasping ambition, the most lawless, impure & ferocious tyrany [sic]."[19]

This scorn did not make him any more sympathetic toward those abolitionists who, long before himself, had denounced the American system. Indeed, in his nostalgia for the idealism of the 1830s he betrayed a continuing obsession with the divisions that had ended the decade. In a series of articles published in *Frederick Douglass' Paper* in 1854 and 1855

19. Stuart to Smith, with copy of his letter to Congressman William Preston, January 27, 1854; to Smith, April 16, August 31, November 27, 1855, November 18, December 9, 1856, April 18, 1857, SP; to Weld, April 22, 1852, WP.

he made impassioned pleas for a recovery of unity, reiterating his hard-line attitude to the central issue in the 1840s split. Eventually Elizabeth Cady Stanton and Betsy D. Hawks responded indignantly to his emphasis on the "simple facts, that God created man and woman spiritually and morally, the same; physically and socially different, each for its own peculiar and sacred sphere." Yet despite this feminist reaction, Stuart's tirade was strikingly irrelevant to the 1850s. Now the slavery extension issue compelled many erstwhile New Organizationists to ponder whether the goal of abolition justified the means of cooperation with essentially racist free soil politicians who were bringing into being the new Republican party. The same issue had fragmented Old Organizationists. Some still clung to "disunionism" and effectively opted out of the political struggle. But for others the incorporation of Texas had prompted the argument that a new constitutional convention was necessary. Subsequently, war with Mexico had led to calls for noncooperation with the federal government and for state conventions to form a new free Union. And the new Fugitive Slave Law had prompted some in the 1850s to adopt various tactics of confrontation. Even here individual attitudes varied greatly. The defiance of authority in a handful of dramatic rescue incidents in northern cities was for some no more than a necessary means of helping fugitive blacks. Others hoped that mob action might lead to a more basic disruption of society. Although some would confine violence to what was necessary to secure a rescue, other abolitionists were willing to contemplate killing kidnappers, and still others hoped that the example of violence in the North would be a stimulus to slave revolt in the South.[20]

Those opposing the Fugitive Slave Law in these various ways included Garrisonians Wendell Phillips and Abby Kelley Foster; Frederick Douglass, who had long since split from Garrison; and even Gerrit Smith, who remained otherwise committed to electoral politics but who hoped to win greater publicity by being brought before the courts for defiance of the law. In these circumstances Stuart's obsession with the divisions of 1840 was not only irrelevant but personally constricting, since his own letters revealed intense concern about the fugitive law.[21] His failure to make common cause on the issue with other abolitionists was, however, inevitable. Underlying all his political attitudes was faith in the Bible as divine revelation. This conviction led him into criticisms of even the abolition-

20. *Frederick Douglass' Paper*, January 20, March 17, April 7, 28, May 26, June 16, 1854, March 2, 13, April 20, 1855; Pease and Pease, "Confrontation and Abolition," 923–37.

21. Pease and Pease, "Confrontation and Abolition," 923–37; Stuart to Weld, November 5, 1850, WP; to Smith, n.d., 1850, SP.

ists of whom he approved.[22] It was futile, he told Gerrit Smith in 1855, to argue that the fugitive law had no existence. It was in fact one of numerous "bad laws" violating God's commandments and should be opposed on those terms. Smith should not be demanding its rejection "because you refuse it the title of law"; rather, he should be "calling upon me as a Subject of God, to trample upon an outrageously sinful law of man." He accused Frederick Douglass of failing to condemn the notion of women's rights because he did not give due attention to "the Scriptures as a divine and perfect rule of all human life."[23]

If these evangelical beliefs loomed in the background of every argument he had with Americans and the American system, they dominated the agonizing withdrawal symptons that accompanied the end of his spiritual love affair with Theodore Weld. And the severing of that emotional bond was probably the biggest single factor in the alienation from America that marked his retirement.

THE HISTORIAN Robin Winks has suggested that Stuart's religious dogmatism was a mask for religious doubts. The only source he cites in support of this claim, however, is Edward Talbot, the critic of Stuart's Canadian emigration tract of the 1820s.[24] In that period Stuart had indeed undergone a religious crisis. But by the time of his retirement his correspondence and publications had revealed decades of theological consistency to support his claim that his doubts had been resolved when he came to accept a divinely inspired Bible. It is possible that the increasing outspokenness of the 1850s was an outward sign of inner anxieties at the approach of death. But it is at least as plausible—and far more demonstrable—to stress that the bitterness of these latter years was primarily the result of profound changes in the views of his friends, notably Weld. That he could oppose those changes when opposition meant a massive emotional blow suggests that Stuart's overriding religious convictions were very strong indeed.

Since the antislavery campaigns of the 1830s Stuart and Weld had met scarcely at all. Stuart had always been quick to explain the frequent missed opportunities for reunions as owing to prior duty to the antislavery cause

---

22. In 1854 these included "such men as Sumner, Chase, Giddings, Wade, Seward, Gerrit Smith, De Witt, H. W. Beecher, A. and L. Tappan, B. Green, Wm. Goodell, J. McCune Smith, Frederick Douglass, etc. and such women as Mrs. H. B. Stowe, Mrs. Douglass, etc." (*Frederick Douglass' Paper*, April 7, 1854).

23. Stuart to Smith, January 8, 1853, November 27, 1855, SP; to Frederick Douglass, March 3, 1854, *Frederick Douglass' Paper*, March 17, 1854.

24. Winks, *Blacks in Canada*, 264.

or even to family responsibilities to his sisters. But the rarity of their contact is in such marked contrast to the continuing fervor of Stuart's letters to his "own most dearly beloved Theodore" that it seems he was at least half aware that their spiritually passionate friendship was now mainly an idealized memory. Even when they had been close in the 1820s and 1830s they had differed widely over religious issues. In the 1840s Stuart had claimed to believe that increasingly freethinking views were obscuring the real Weld. It was only now in the 1850s that he at last came to acknowledge that the real Weld repudiated completely his own unchanging scriptural orthodoxy.

The decisive moment of recognition came in an exchange of letters early in 1853. Although Weld's letter has not survived, it is clear from Stuart's reply that he had, more firmly than ever before, rejected the notion that the Bible was "a divine revelation, the only recorded & authoritative standard, of His Being, His Character, and His Law; as well as of man's character & conditions; of man's duties & prospects." Much previous correspondence over the past decade had prepared Stuart for this rejection. Yet he now acknowledged it with an even more emotionally tortured greeting than usual:

> My long & dearly, dearly beloved Theodore; long the most intimate brother of my heart; earnest companion with me, in the cause of the slave; the fervent enemy of tyrannical & impure power; the lover & preacher & practicer of God's pure & unadulterated truth, as revealed by God himself, remote alike from the atrocious hypocrisy, of the great body of the outward churches in your country; and from the Christ crucifying atheism, of what is called or deemed, rational christianity; your letter of March 20th now before me, realises my worst fears; for, while it warms my heart by its loving kindness to me, it smites my soul, with the fearful conviction, of the desperate aberration from God's truth of your present mind!

He went on to indicate with stark clarity how much more than religious differences were at stake. Weld—especially perhaps the idealized Weld of their long separation—had assumed an importance in Stuart's emotional life that dwarfed the significance of the real personal relationships of his everyday life: "Such are my feelings towards you, that could I, as God's minister, bring you back, to what you were, according to every appearance, for some time, after your change of life, under Finney's ministry in Utica & elsewhere, greatly as God has blessed me, in my present situation, & sacredly dear to me, as are my wife & her sisters, I could cheerfully consent to instant death, & glory in dying, for your recovery."[25]

25. Stuart to Weld, April 17, 1853, WP.

Such feelings could not be simply discarded, even though subsequent letters confirmed that there was no hope of turning Weld back to his previous views. Soon Stuart was writing that a recent letter from Weld precluded all further religious discussion between them. He could not resist "one or two parting thoughts," which occupied two pages on the usual theme that the Bible was the only acceptable indicator of God's will. And over the next few years he was periodically to resume the argument. But from mid-1853 on he was conspicuously fighting to convince himself and his "dearly, *dearly* beloved brother" that religious differences could not mar their mutual love "for that love is irrespective of creeds or opinions or principles."[26]

There was, however, less and less to keep that love alive. In October, 1853, Stuart sent condolences on the death of Weld's mother: "I feel a blight upon my spirit, for she was ever sweetly precious, & sacredly dear to my soul." He wanted to know what Weld was doing for the antislavery and temperance causes and wrote expectantly of a planned visit to the Welds the following summer. But almost seven months later a very brief letter was much less effusive: "Leaving out of the question, our differences of conscientious belief respecting religion, I wish to know, why you have not replied to my last letter, & what you are doing in the Anti-Slavery and T.T. causes." Although even now his plans for a reunion were still alive, within a few weeks he was writing that the journey was out of the question that year. He complained about expense and social unrest in Canada. But it was evident that a bigger factor had been a belated letter from Weld revealing implicitly that the antislavery and temperance causes now played little part in his life. He and Angelina and Sarah were on the point of leaving their Belleville farm to settle in the Raritan Bay community at Perth Amboy, where Weld was to head the community's Eagleswood School. Stuart might greet him as "my ceaselessly precious Theodore!" But Weld's new commitment underlined that their principles were "as opposite as the Poles." "I mourn for you," he wrote: "Your Raritan Bay plan, wanting the Scriptures for its basis and its rule, wants all that could be fundamentally agreeable to me."[27]

The following year Stuart made contact with James Birney after many years and confided in him the extremes of his admiration and despair for Weld: "I thank God for such a man, & only wonder how such an one, can love as he does such as I am. I look up to him with admiration & with affection as deep as I believe it to be deathless. Yet, as far as I can judge

26. Stuart to Weld, July 31, 1853, WP.
27. Stuart to Weld, October 31, 1853, May 26, June 30, 1854, WP.

of him, on any grounds within my reach, Theodore is one of the most melancholy & anomalous objects that could be presented to me." He was now clearly sensing that whatever he might say about his own "deathless affection," Weld was much less preoccupied with their friendship. Some letters in these middle years of the 1850s made it plain, in their pleas for news of Weld and his family, how one-sided the correspondence had become. When a reply eventually came in early 1856, it was "sweetly refreshing" to Stuart. Yet his relief indicated how much their friendship had withered: "I began to fear . . . that the wide & deep jarring of our souls, in relation to God's revealed truth, had wearied you of me." Regretting that he had not followed through with a plan to visit Weld the previous summer, he asked for full details of the Eagleswood enterprise "so that I may be able to see you, as it were, hour after hour, & day after day." And he asked that one or other of the Weld children be encouraged to write to him unless Weld thought that such a correspondence "might hurt them."[28]

Stuart was hurt by the reply to this letter. It was "exceedingly sweet" to receive a reply, but the accompanying school prospectus "pained" him because of its lack of emphasis on the Bible.[29] By now Weld was evidently growing tired of the argument, for Stuart's long reiteration of his commitment to the Bible marked the start of a three-year break in their correspondence. When it resumed in August, 1859, the final breach would be imminent.

28. Stuart to Birney, March 6, 1855; to Weld, April 12, 1856, WP.
29. Stuart to Weld, July 20, 1856, WP.

14 TERRIBLE ORTHODOXY

By 1857 Stuart's estrangement from the United States had many ingredients: his doomed relationship with Weld; physical isolation, accentuated by the reduced mobility of old age and the burden of family responsibility; contempt for the differences among American abolitionists; and scorn for a political system that proclaimed liberty and condoned slavery. The deepening slavery crisis can only have confirmed this revulsion. In 1857 the Supreme Court's long-awaited and eventually infamous decision in the Dred Scott case had declared that blacks were not citizens, that Congress had no power to exclude slavery from federal territories, and that therefore the Missouri Compromise of 1820, which had defined a boundary between freedom and slavery, was unconstitutional. In the following year the nationally reported Illinois debates between the rising Republican, Abraham Lincoln, and the prominent Democrat, Stephen Douglas, would make it clear how completely politicians of the two major parties were forced to pander to a crude northern racism. Yet though these trends were vindicating his cynicism about America, it was paradoxically an event on the far side of the world that most clearly deepened his alienation. The Indian Mutiny stirred him to a defense of British imperialism as outspoken as his attacks on American democracy, and the accompanying controversies saw him more completely than ever in the role of a foreign critic of the United States.

His chief adversaries were officers of the American Missionary Association, notably his old friend Lewis Tappan and another abolitionist acquaintance, George Whipple. Stuart had joined the American Missionary

Association at the end of 1854. He admired its general antislavery posture, its assistance to fugitive slaves, and its policy of rooting out proslavery influences from the churches. This admiration was threatened in October, 1857, when he found in the *American Missionary* an article ascribing the recent Indian Mutiny to British tyranny. The allegation was so painful to him that he at once wrote to Whipple, stressing his personal knowledge of India and outlining the "simple facts" in three closely written pages of invective. He was fully prepared to admit the mutiny was partly the fault of the British: they had "insanely fostered the system of Hindoo castes & of Mahomedan fanaticism" among their native troops. But only the "grossest slanders" could justify the "most atrocious crimes of the mutineers" as a response to British tyranny. The mutiny had plunged Bengal into the "most loathsome anarchy." If the mutineers prevailed, millions of Indians would be restored to "Mahomedan & Brahminic sway; always careering from one excess of licentious impurity & blood to another."[1]

The argument might have ended quickly if Whipple had agreed to publish this letter accompanied by any comments he chose to make. If that were done, Stuart promised to drop the matter. But his letter was not published, and the next issue of the *American Missionary* gave space to views that linked India with the other area dear to his imperialism: "Sweeter than the voice of love, is the news of British discomfiture in India, to the breasts of the Irish people." This moved Stuart to such "deep loathing" that even he was unable to find a vocabulary of abuse that would do justice to the "multitude of abhorrent observations which swell in my heart." Instead, he merely lamented the apparent desire to foster enmity between the abolitionists of Britain and the United States. And in a page-long postscript, he made his own equations between India and Ireland. Britain's "enormous guilt" in "fostering popery" as well as Islam and Hinduism did not alter the truth that both countries had been more benevolently governed by Britain than by "any prior power."[2]

Soon Lewis Tappan entered the controversy with an allegation that Stuart's views on the mutiny were conditioned by his military profession. In insisting that it was, rather, his "christian profession" that moved him, Stuart displayed the authoritarian side of the political philosophy that had recently denounced American democracy. Without strong government, society disintegrated into anarchy: "Every wise & virtuous gov-

1. L. Tappan to Stuart, December 31, 1854, Letterbooks, vol. 8, p. 90, Lewis Tappan Papers; Stuart to S. S. Jocelyn, n.d., to Whipple, November 28, October 17, 1857, AMA.
2. Stuart to Whipple, November 28, 1857, AMA.

ernment, of which we have any record, commensurate with the occasion, has had vigorously to blend violence in its stewardship, with benevolence & Justice."[3]

This conservative emphasis in his political views had grown much stronger over the past decade, as he observed popular agitation on both sides of the Atlantic. In Britain, however, popular agitation was against the system of government; in America it was characteristic of the system. The Indian Mutiny, in focusing Stuart's mind more closely than ever on this contrast, decisively reinforced his British patriotism and his growing anti-Americanism. In a letter to Gerrit Smith he commented on the threats faced by both Britain and the United States in late 1857. The threat of the Indian Mutiny was "more immediately fraught with unutterable horrors" than the "slavery-dangers" facing the United States. Yet he felt that British problems would be more easily overcome "by the restoration of order" in Bengal than American problems would be "by your abolition of chattel slavery."[4]

This was the most extreme criticism of the United States he had ever expressed. Hitherto American democracy had been contemptible because of its hypocrisy in countenancing slavery. Now American democracy would still evidently be contemptible even without slavery. These views were made clear as he explained to Smith his continuing hesitations about the mooted removal to Peterboro. He gave a new emphasis to the financial considerations involved: "My income depends mainly upon my country, and the idea of spending it in a foreign land, especially in view of recent events, is very repulsive to me." And he stressed anew the "democratical-demagogical character of your country." It was "more & more, a serious question to me, whether, I could wisely subject my wife & myself, to the liabilities of such a state of society."[5]

Even now Stuart's disillusionment with the United States was not complete because his personal friendship with a few abolitionists survived. To a great extent this was a tribute to the forbearance of these often savagely mauled individuals. Gerrit Smith not only constantly urged Stuart to move permanently to Peterboro but had also become in effect financial manager to the Lora household, arranging mortgages on the property in Rebecca's name and transfers of money between the United States and Canada. He coped with a torrent of letters from Stuart which must have often seemed irritatingly petty distractions from his extensive

3. Stuart to Tappan, December 26, 1857, AMA.
4. Stuart to Smith, September 26, 1857, SP.
5. *Ibid.*

business and philanthropic interests and political duties. Stuart was always suitably appreciative, but the same letters that offered thanks for financial advice were often scathing about Smith's crumbling prospects of eternal salvation and almost abusive about the evils of the American political system. Although he regularly depicted himself as a financial simpleton, he was always ready to challenge Smith's advice and even his arithmetic. In these circumstances Smith's continuing good humor and solicitude are a tribute to his benevolence and the strength of his regard for Stuart.[6]

Lewis Tappan also occasionally helped in what Stuart persistently called his "little pecuniary concerns." And the climax of their argument over the Indian Mutiny suggests that he regarded Stuart's apoplectic abuse with amused affection. Stuart had canceled his subscription to the *American Missionary* after the offending articles had appeared. And yet the *American Missionary* continued to arrive at Lora. No doubt the reason was an administrative error, but early in 1858 Tappan himself sent a copy and, under separate cover, a letter asking Stuart to comment on a particular article. Before that letter arrived, Stuart returned the paper unread and "with indignation." Tappan evidently poked fun at Stuart's unwillingness to read even a single column of the offending paper, for Stuart acknowledged his second letter "notwithstanding the levity which disgraces it." He explained that he had returned the paper before receiving Tappan's earlier letter, "thereby supplying you with a new *curiosity* for your cabinet of wonders."[7]

These friendships had survived, however, because Stuart had always been at pains to separate policies from personalities when it seemed important to do so. To Smith he wrote: "I love you anew for your affectionate tolerance of my earnest remonstrances on topics on which we differ . . . we must bear with each other, and I believe so many vital sympathies to exist in our mutual hearts that the task is not difficult." "And why do I not equally reject you?" he asked Tappan, on canceling his subscription to the *American Missionary*: "because, I cannot reject, one of the noblest advocates of God & man, equally with a human peri-

---

6. Stuart to Smith, November 27, 1855, April 10, September 4, November 18, December 9, 30, 1856; January 20, 26, February 9, March 14, April 18, July 11, August 15, September 26, 1857; February 6, 1858; March 26, April 9, 26, May 28, June 1, 10, 1859; February 21, March 9, April 20, May 22, September 28, 1861, SP; some of these letters include mortgage agreements, contracts, affidavits, and other documents signed by Stuart and his wife and Smith.

7. Stuart to Smith, November 18, December 9, 30, 1856; Tappan to Smith, March 28, 1857, SP; Stuart to Tappan, February 13, 1858, AMA.

odical." He even took complicated steps to continue subscribing to the American Missionary Association because he admired its antislavery activities, even though he rejected its journal.[8]

It was easier for him to separate issues from personalities in this way because he was for most of the time so physically remote. Perhaps if he had remained completely in isolation in Canada, his last years after 1857 might have been slightly less bitter (if no less uncomfortable for his wife). But in 1858 and 1859 he managed two final journeys to New York and New Jersey, and the personal contact was sufficient to end his relationship with Weld and put severe strains on that with Gerrit Smith.

In June, 1858, he and Rebecca made an oft-postponed visit to upstate New York. Gerrit Smith's home was their base, but they also made a sentimental visit to Utica. Outwardly to those who met him casually, it was a frailer but no less endearing Stuart than the eccentric schoolmaster of thirty-five years before. He was helped hobbling into the office of one Erastus Clark, who had been very young in the 1820s and who remembered Stuart mainly as a family friend and the teacher of his sisters:

> As I stepped down from my desk and went towards him, I thought that I had never seen a finer face than his. There was no lack of force in it, but in combination with the force, and dominating it, was a rare gentleness and love.
>
> His manner was very affectionate; he blessed me, and called on God to bless me; he spoke of my mother who had gone, and of my sister in the South, expressed the hope that my sister and I were doing what we could for Christ and for the poor and oppressed whom Christ loved. The impression his face made on me was very strong; his presence brightened the room. . . .
>
> There is no absurdity in all this . . . it surely is no marvel that great natural humanity, that a life of self-sacrifice for others' good, that fifty years of earnest work for what he deemed to be the glory of God, and the welfare of his race, should have given to Captain Stuart a presence of loveliness scarcely human.[9]

Yet even in the 1820s his "thunderous volcanic" moods had shown the people of Utica another side of his character. And now in the summer of 1858 his host, Gerrit Smith, saw that side apparently for the first time. The two old friends had a monumental argument that was to overshadow their correspondence for the next year. It centered on their religious dif-

---

8. Stuart to Smith, November 27, 1855, SP; to Tappan, 1858; to Whipple, January, 1859, AMA.

9. *Memorial of the Semi-Centennial*, 213–14. Clark was, presumably, the son of the Erastus Clark who had supported his nephew, Theodore Weld, in the early 1820s before Stuart took over the responsibility.

ferences but became bitter because of Smith's outrage at the way Stuart treated Rebecca. When she showed interest in the freethinking religious views Smith was developing in this period, Stuart reacted with harsh words and violent temper. In Smith's view, this was the outburst of a man who had used religious orthodoxy as the rationale for a domestic dictatorship: "You are intollerant [sic] and abusive: in a word you are a tyrant, a tyrant even towards your wife, towards her who is so beautiful & heavenly in her temper, & whose husband you have shown yourself entirely unworthy to be. Deeply & frequently do dear Nancy & I, lament the life of this lovely woman, should be embittered by her connection with a tyrant." Smith epitomized his own behavior in ways that made this indictment more specific: "I do not oppress my wife. I accord to her the right of her own religion. I am not jealous of her. I do not claim her for my servant. I go to bed & leave her to sit up as long as she chuses, & to enjoy life with whom she chuses!!"[10]

Stuart denied "utterly" that he was selfish or jealous or made unjust claims on his wife's time. But in doing so he implicitly confirmed much of Smith's allegation of tyranny: "My words are sometimes severely harsh; but the holiest love is most severe, when harshness is necessary to do it justice; and I am fully persuaded, that a sacred regard for her rectitude, as a worshipper of Christ, has invariably been my heart-loving motive, for any harsh words rendered by me towards her." Moreover, he made no attempt to deny aspects of Smith's criticism that suggest the strains under which Rebecca was forced to live: "Violent *bursts* of temper, have been all my life, one of my besetting sins, & this is yet far from being eradicated."[11]

It had evidently come as a shock to Smith to discover this aspect of Stuart's character. Stuart was glad the discovery had been made because he wished "to be truly known for what I am." Only Smith's tolerance—and no doubt his sympathy for Rebecca's plight—prevented the dispute from ending the friendship, as Stuart made even his admission of faults the occasion for counter-attack. He trusted that the revelation that he had a bad side might help Smith to "saner views of human nature & human reason." No less provocative was the way he began this particular letter. His usual "My beloved Gerrit" was replaced by the slightly cooler "My dear Gerrit," which was in turn crossed out in favor of a blunt "Sir." Smith replied no less pointedly: "My dear Charles,—for such you will always be, notwithstanding my letter has so deeply offended you." And he con-

10. Smith to Stuart, August 15, 1858, SP.
11. Stuart to Smith, August 10, 1858, SP.

cluded a long appraisal of their religious differences: "You are a precious man in spite of your violent temper & terrible orthodoxy."[12]

This exchange set the tone for a prolonged argument that would be temporarily ended by Smith's mental breakdown in late 1859. Until then Stuart bombarded him with even more letters than hitherto. From August, 1858, to August, 1859, at least a dozen long and detailed letters mixed requests and thanks for financial advice with endless reiteration of Stuart's religious principles. In this correspondence Stuart continued to condemn his friend's views forcefully, and early in 1859 he took him into the public arena, as Smith's rejection of "scriptural orthodoxy" gained publicity in the press. In March Stuart's relentless scrutiny of every accessible newspaper uncovered a disturbing item in the *Free Press* of Glens Falls—a report of a sermon in which Smith had asserted the supremacy of human reason over the Bible as a source of religious truth. He immediately decided to publish his own "heart-burning views" on the sermon and "all its horrors."[13]

Stuart's four-page *Remarks upon the "Religion of Reason,"* which appeared in June, 1859, proved to be his last publication. It began by insisting that the controversy between the two old friends, "heartful and uncompromising as it is, is not in enmity but in love, for they love each other." In a sense this was true. Stuart had gone to great lengths to consult Smith at every stage of the publication process and to give him the chance to proofread his pamphlet in case published versions of Smith's sermon had been distortions. But it was a love that imposed great strains on Smith's tolerance. He had already been asked by Stuart to pass on to the Peterboro Methodist minister a letter denouncing his own views. Now he was expected to distribute fifty copies of Stuart's pamphlet among their mutual friends, correcting a printing error in each one as he did so. At the same time he was being pressed for ever more detailed reassurances about the investments he was handling on behalf of the Stuart household. In an April letter Stuart asked for another copy of Smith's sermon, spoke of his forthcoming critique, and used two pages of detailed accounting to question sarcastically a recent financial explanation by Smith: "Now, being a skilful man of business, as you are, this want of understanding in me, may amuse you, as ridiculous, or offend you, as troublesome: but I prefer being quite frank with you." And, frankly, the explanation Smith found satisfying "to me . . . is double-darkness." Frankness was no less evident in Stuart's published attack, as he denounced Smith's "endeavour to set up

12. *Ibid.*; Smith to Stuart, August 15, 1858, SP.
13. Stuart to Smith, March 26, 1859, SP.

a new sect, and thus to substitute his own anarchical dogmas for revealed religion."[14]

Stuart might write publicly of their mutual love, but in private he was steadily qualifying his own feelings. Already he had told Smith: "I love you with less sympathy." And, as he discussed the publication of the pamphlet with Smith, he kept asking rhetorically how he could continue feeling any love for an enemy of Christ. Soon it became clear that residual love rested on the hope that Smith would abandon his rationalist views and return completely to Christ.[15]

Smith evidently expressed bewilderment at Stuart's warning that he now loved him with less sympathy. There were two kinds of love, replied Stuart: the "love of sympathy which is natural to all animals human or brute" and *"the love of* Benevolence, which is perfect in God alone, & which real Christians alone can feel or understand." He no longer felt the "love of sympathy" for Smith, and although he expected always to cultivate the "love of benevolence" toward him, this was no more than he felt for "all men."[16]

Yet this same correspondence in the year after their great quarrel reveals that this intellectual conclusion had been reached at great emotional cost. It shows a man moved by all the common human feelings of nostalgia, gregariousness, gratitude, and memories of shared experiences. In January, 1859, in finally abandoning all thoughts of moving to Peterboro, he wrote with warmth of the many attractions the possibility had offered: the "almost unwearied kindness" of Smith and his family, the "beauty of the place itself," and all its associations with the momentous antislavery gathering in 1835 in the aftermath of the Utica mob.[17] The near tragedy of Stuart's declining years lies in his ruthless subordination of such feelings to the priority of commitment to Christ as revealed in the Bible.

He sounded confident as he saw the attractions of upstate New York pall "before other motives, as far superior to them, as Eternity is to time." He set up a particularly extreme contrast between spiritual "love of benevolence" and the merely animal "love of sympathy," which could encompass not only the "purest virtue possible to mere humanity" but also "the most brutal lusts." And yet there was much more than merely benevolent love for all men when he told Smith: "I am distressed about you

14. Stuart to Smith, February 5, 1859, SP; Charles Stuart, *Remarks upon the 'Religion of Reason', Sermon, of Hon. Gerrit Smith, of Peterboro, N.Y., as Reported in the "Free Press" of Glen's Falls, March 5, 1859* (Lora, Canada, 1859).
15. Stuart to Smith, February 5, April 9, June 1, 10, 1859, SP.
16. Stuart to Smith, August 6, 1859, SP.
17. Stuart to Smith, January 1, 1859, SP.

". . . I cannot but regard you, as in the broad path, which leads to everlasting death." A special regard for Smith was obvious in August, 1859, when he reflected bitterly on their quarrel a year previously and asked: "Say, shall we further correspond or not?" It was particularly evident in his relief when this harsh question prompted a "fond & flattering letter" from Smith and a "sweet *forget-me-not* posy" from Mrs. Smith.[18]

Although Smith's conciliatory gestures kept the friendship alive, this same month marked a further deterioration in Stuart's relationship with Weld. And here the emotional cost was still greater. That he should finally visit Weld after a three-year break in their correspondence is an indication of the desperation with which he clung to the hope of renewed friendship. But he quickly found that Weld was less willing than Smith to humor his relentless dogmatism. According to Stuart, the two friends managed only a hasty conversation because, he accused Weld, "your more important duties as you deemed them" made haste unavoidable. This had been sufficient to convince him that Weld's views were "most incorrect & dangerous to all within your influence." Still unwilling to accept that conclusion, he proceeded to ask eleven questions about Weld's fundamental religious beliefs and to demand that these should be answered also by every member of Weld's extended family circle, including his children, his brother Charles, and his sister Cornelia.[19]

Stuart knew well enough that it was virtually a forlorn hope for him to be "still lingering after the delights of our former sweet & sacred sympathy in the Scriptures." But the rest of his letter revealed again the emotional intensity with which he had discovered Christ and discovered Weld and hence the agony he felt in having to choose between them. He wrote of the desperate uncertainties of his childhood, of the self-destroying pride of his early manhood, and of his wavering until "I found more & more in the Bible, what my soul wanted, a *Perfect God*, a *Perfect Law*, a *Perfect Standard* of morality & religion, with a *Perfect Example*." And he tried to recapture the essence of their mutual love as it had evolved thirty-five years earlier: "It was you Theodore, as you were, or as I believed you to be in my soul; that I loved as I did; and not, a young man named T. D. Weld, adorned tho' you were, with the eminent qualifications which distinguished you—neither an older man named Chs. Stuart, unadorned as he was, whom you loved so ardently; but the character which you believed me to be—and oh, how gratefully & with what delight my heart

18. Stuart to Smith, January 1, June [?], August 6, September 3, 1859, SP.
19. Stuart to Weld, August [?], 1859, WP.

would glow, could I now find in you, the same grounds for equal ardor of affection as formerly."[20]

Before Weld could respond to this letter, Stuart was distracted by an unexpected turn in his relationship with Gerrit Smith. On October 16, 1859, John Brown, with a small band of white and Negro volunteers, made his quixotic raid on the government arsenal in Harpers Ferry in Virginia. The absurdity of this attempt to provoke a black insurrection in the South did not prevent it from having a profound effect on American sectional tensions. The raid stirred the South into more fervent defense of slavery, with tightened discipline of the black population and violent proscription of the few remaining white dissidents. And the eventual hanging of Brown made him a martyr in the eyes of many northerners. But more immediately, news of the failure of the raid plunged Gerrit Smith into temporary insanity.

Smith was always to deny that he was implicated in the planning of Brown's raid. Although it may be true that he did not have precise foreknowledge of its details, there seems little doubt that he was conspicuous among a considerable number of abolitionists who were well aware of Brown's general plans to foment insurrection in the South. It is generally accepted that Brown had discussed his plans with Smith and sought moral and financial support on two visits to Peterboro in February and April, 1859. According to the *Recollections* of Frank Sanborn, "Captain Charles Stewart" was also present at the February meeting when Brown unfolded his "amazing proposition" for a campaign into slave territory. Sanborn's memory seems to be at fault here. Error is suggested not mainly by his belief that the captain was "an old officer of Wellington's army in Spain." There is something familiar about Sanborn's "Stewart," as he sat by the fire "discussing points of theology" with Brown, while Sanborn and Smith walked for an hour in the nearby woods and fields and resolved to support Brown's enterprise. But if Sanborn did see Brown "enjoying the society" of Stuart at Gerrit Smith's, it must have been on some earlier occasion.[21] In those early months of 1859 Stuart was writing regularly from Lora to Smith about finances and about the imminent publication of his hostile pamphlet. Stuart's habitual references to their respective families made no mention of recent or impending visits, and the detail of his letters would scarcely have been necessary if direct discussions had taken place. More-

20. *Ibid.*
21. Filler, *Crusade Against Slavery*, 244, 269–72; Tyler, *Freedom's Ferment*, 541–42; Sanborn, *Recollections*, 144–45.

over, Stuart's response to the news of Smith's affliction in November made no mention of shared knowledge about the Brown enterprise.

Stuart's isolation from American events was reflected in his learning of Smith's illness only through the "public papers." His response was a typical mixture of religious pedantry and emotional warmth. Two-thirds of his letter to Smith's wife, offering sympathy and seeking information, was taken up by corrections to a biblical reference he had misquoted in his previous letter. Yet his concluding words belied his recent claims that he no longer regarded Smith with any special affection: "In your prosperity, I loved you & Gerrit, deeply & warmly—In your adversity, if indeed you be afflicted as I fear, my soul glows towards you both, with yet deeper & warmer love." Only a conviction that his presence could not help prevented him and Rebecca from hastening to Peterboro. Soon he was writing to the superintendent of the Utica Asylum seeking information about Smith. Having "long loved" Smith, he was moved by his "deep affliction," wanted to know of his chances of recovery, and wished Smith to be assured of his "constant love."[22]

This winter of 1859–60 was an emotional time for Stuart. On the same day that Stuart wrote to the asylum superintendent about Smith, Theodore Weld was replying to the religious interrogation of his family in terms that dashed any lingering hopes of a revival of their friendship. Weld had evidently still written with affection but had suggested that he had never deserved Stuart's intense regard. In accepting that criticism Stuart revealed again an aching nostalgia for the earliest days of their friendship:

> Yes, Theodore, in your natural state, delighted with the talents with which God had so eminently adorned you, I thought too highly of your moral state—But, oh, how I was charmed with the blaze of beauty which enveloped you, when, apparently broken-hearted and penitent, you came forth as a believer in Jesus, a fervent preacher & liver, of the gospel of Christ, encountering labor & braving death—Your track was a stream of glory! God visibly led you, and you followed Him apparently with all your heart.[23]

Now at last, however, Stuart gave up the struggle to reclaim Weld. This letter of January 14, 1860, was the last he wrote to his "former friend, my friend intentionally still, T. D. Weld." The question between them was whether there were any man "so wise and holy" that he could "sanely & safely depend upon himself" for knowledge of God's will without a di-

22. Stuart to Nancy Smith, November 21, 1859; to Dr. Gray, superintendent of Utica Asylum, December 17, 1859, SP.
23. Stuart to Weld, January 14, 1860, WP.

vine revelation. If there were, then "might I choose, T. D. Weld, the assumed oracle of Eagleswood, for my God, because he is so eminently adorned with the loveliness of natural talent & virtue & because he so loves me." But because his faith was firmly based on the Bible, all that remained to him was "bitter disappointment."[24]

He loved Weld still but no longer as his friend, "for with the principles which you embrace, & holding the course which you pursue, you know that I do not & cannot as an honest man, believe you to be my friend, or the friend of mankind." He bade farewell with the hope that somehow Weld might escape perdition and they might be reunited "at the feet of Jesus." But his parting shot was a postscript comment on the Eagleswood curriculum, which he saw as hostile to the interests of all who came under Weld's influence: "I pity them & you."[25]

AS THE United States moved closer to civil war, Stuart's comments on public events were overshadowed by his conflicts with Weld and Smith. Only bitter generalizations about the American system greeted the start of southern secession when Abraham Lincoln, candidate of the purely northern Republican party, captured the presidency at the end of 1860. If there was one issue that bridged the chasm separating him from the American crisis, it was the movement of black fugitives into Canada. He had, after all, been associated with some of the earliest fugitives in Amherstburg. Later he had been the first abolitionist to see the implications for such people of the extradition clause of the Webster-Ashburton Treaty. And it was fitting that the last of all his public antislavery activities, as late as January, 1861, concerned probably the major test case involving that clause. A black, John Anderson, was arrested in Canada in the autumn of 1860 on a charge of murder committed in effecting his escape from slavery in Missouri. The case aroused intense interest in Canada in the press and at several mass meetings, in the British antislavery press, and in the United States, from where Gerrit Smith twice visited Canada to address meetings on behalf of Anderson. In view of all this pressure and because Anderson's appeal against extradition succeeded on a technicality in February, 1861, Stuart's intervention in the case can hardly be seen as decisive. But it was revealing of his personal commitment that the case should rouse him to activity at the age of eighty. He wrote to Smith that his age and a "fading heart" had persuaded him he would never again make the journey to Toronto. But a recent letter from his Peterboro friend,

24. *Ibid.*
25. *Ibid.*

suggesting a meeting there, had combined with his deep concern for Anderson to persuade him to make one last effort. He made arrangements to stay with his nieces and to meet Smith: "We shall then," he wrote with a touch of his old enthusiasm for his favorite methods, "I trust be able to collect a public meeting." Smith's address would be "importantly useful" whether Anderson had by then been freed or not, "for this is a subject, on which the Canadian mind, needs to be well-informed, & to which the Canadian heart, greatly wants to be effectively awakened."[26]

By this period he had long since given up hope that American hearts and minds might be similarly awakened. In February, 1861, after the first six seceding states of the lower South had organized the Confederate States of America, he wrote to Gerrit Smith with entirely personal fears about the coming war. He was worried about the fate of Rebecca and her sisters if certain "probable events," including his own death and "aggravated convulsions in the United States," occurred to jeopardize the mortgages Smith had arranged in New York State. Smith must have understood this concern, but he can hardly have been pleased that among the events Stuart considered "probable" was a recurrence of the "physical & mental prostration" that had seized Smith with "tyger-grasp" at the time of John Brown's raid. Nevertheless, he made a sufficiently reassuring reply for Stuart in early March to express a flicker of hope that the United States might still avoid the "pro-slavery abyss of hypocrisy & blood."[27]

That hope proved short-lived and, as the Civil War began a few weeks later, Stuart continued to stress the "deep pro-slavery corruption of the national mind (northern as well as southern)." This pessimism is understandable given the circumstances and his own impatience with compromise. In the Republican party genuine antislavery sentiment was outweighed by "free soil" attitudes epitomized by the president himself. Opposed to the extension of slavery but committed not to interfere with it where it stood, Lincoln most consistently responded to the race problem by advocating colonization of blacks outside the United States. Although such policies were slightly less provocative than they had been thirty years before because some black leaders had become interested in various emigration projects in the 1850s, they can have done little to arouse the sympathy of a mind as inflexible as Stuart's, which had devised some of the most complete and compelling anticolonization arguments. Certainly in the contempt he expressed for Lincoln in a score of letters to Smith over the next two years there was no sympathy for the complexity of the pres-

26. Stuart to Smith, January 7, 1861, SP; Winks, *Blacks in Canada*, 175–76.
27. Stuart to Smith, February 21, March 9, 1861, SP.

ident's political problems, which were also contributing to his failure to turn the war into a crusade against slavery: "In thus doing, he might succeed or fail—but in either case, alike; he would be serving the cause of God and his country; of liberty & impartial right, with God's own weapons, instead of resorting to human policies & arts to help him."[28]

The artful policies of Lincoln that Stuart detested involved not only balancing many conflicting attitudes within Washington but also ensuring that crucial slaveholding border states were not driven to secede. His indifference to such considerations was revealed in his detestation of General John Frémont's proclamation of August 31, freeing the slaves of rebels in the border state of Missouri but allowing loyal slaveowners to keep theirs: "Who are slave-holders, loyal or disloyal? Are they not, as a body, the most iniquitous, impure & ferocious of any other class on earth? What is it to conciliate them, but to conciliate crime, of the grossest, most selfish, proud & ferocious description." Even as Stuart was thus berating this "limping step" toward emancipation, Lincoln was moving to rescind it as too provocative in a delicate military and political situation. As a result, on this and other occasions Stuart saw the differences between Lincoln and his southern counterpart, Jefferson Davis, as a question only of degree. Both were defenders of the slave system he had spent half a lifetime attacking.[29]

Stuart probably wrote other letters during these first two years of the war which either have not survived or have eluded discovery. Yet there can be little doubt that Smith was his main correspondent. A solitary letter to Charles and Cornelia Weld, prompted by anxiety about the war situation in September, 1861, showed that there was no prospect of renewed friendship with Theodore, who "has entirely separated himself from me—except indeed I would prefer him to Christ." It is unlikely that a man as unbending as Stuart made any attempt to reestablish his now long-severed connections with British abolitionists. There is no recorded contact between Stuart and John Scoble, who now also lived in Canada. And although the Civil War at last fulfilled his desire to see American slavery in the center of British antislavery attention, the new Emancipation Society that emerged to express this interest was dominated by British supporters of Garrison. None of this means that Smith's views earned Stuart's approval. It was rather that he found in Smith an ideal outlet for the frustrations of his exile. He was lucky, of course, that Smith was willing to sustain a detailed, repetitive debate even while being warned that the

28. Stuart to Smith, September 28, October [?], 1861, January 1, March 6, 1862, SP; Jane H. Pease and William H. Pease, *They Who Would Be Free: Blacks' Search for Freedom, 1830–1861* (New York, 1974), 251–77.

29. Stuart to Smith, September 28, 1861, January 1, March 6, 1862, SP.

quality of his arguments suggested that a return to the asylum was imminent.[30] Yet the reasons why Smith occupied this central position in Stuart's thoughts went beyond his tolerance and his continuing financial advice. Not only was Smith, like Weld, consolidating and refining the rationalist religious views that enraged Stuart. Unlike Weld, he remained an active abolitionist and politician: he was becoming an admirer of Lincoln and moving steadily toward formal allegiance to the Republican party. As he read Smith's letters and printed reports of his public activities and speeches and as he clung tenaciously to the evangelical fervor that had shaped his entire antislavery career, Stuart saw the New York philanthropist as the embodiment of all the forces that had left him as isolated emotionally and intellectually as he was physically in the Canadian backwoods.

The wartime letters to Smith were divided fairly evenly between political comments and the continuing religious debate. But in Stuart's mind there was no real division. "The principal cause . . . of the horrid troubles of your country," he told Smith, "is the rebellion of your people against God." And Smith himself, with his new rationalist views, was an extreme example of culpable rejection of God's revealed word. Such assertions were airily indifferent to the details of a complex political and military situation. And even when he addressed himself to actual problems, Stuart displayed what can only be described as an equally impractical political fundamentalism. Repeatedly he told Smith—as he had told antislavery audiences a quarter-century before—that the Constitution did not sanction slavery. It was as near perfection as anything man-made could be: "Adherence to it is all that is wanted for the practical safety & happiness of the United States."[31] It required a severely blinkered view and a baldly literal interpretation to sustain this argument. Stuart could not have been unaware of the sectional compromises over slavery that had accompanied the drafting of the Constitution in 1787. And he must have known that though the document made no direct reference to slavery, the institution was recognized by skillful euphemism in three separate provisions.[32] Even if his own knowledge and intelligence had not told him these things the

30. Stuart to Charles and Cornelia Weld, September 9, 1861, WP; Taylor, *British and American Abolitionists*, 14; Stuart to Smith, March 30, April 20, 1861, SP.

31. Stuart to Smith, August 18, 1862, March 27, 1863, March 30, April 20, May 22, September 28, 1861, SP.

32. These were Article I, Section 2, apportioning taxes and representatives to the House of Representatives according to the numbers of "free Persons" and "three fifths of all other Persons"; Article I, Section 9, prohibiting Congress from interfering, before 1808, with the right to import "such Persons as any of the States . . . shall think proper to admit"; and Article IV, Section 2, imposing the need to return any "Person held to Service or Labour in one State" from any other state.

arguments of William Lloyd Garrison and other abolitionists had done so since the mid-1830s. And in that circumstance probably lies the main reason for his stubborn refusal to admit to Smith that "your real constitution" was anything but ideal. Again and again in this final correspondence the name of the Boston editor emerged as a symbol of the immoral wrongheadedness that was destroying the United States. Garrison, "distinguished tho' he be by talents and unbending will," had done most to propagate the "gross & senseless" interpretation of the Constitution.[33]

In late 1861 he saw the "prophet Garrison" as somehow responsible for Smith's misguided views on the *Trent* affair. A Union naval captain had stopped the *Trent*, a British merchant ship, off Cuba and arrested two southern envoys on their way to represent the Confederacy in Paris and London. This action, in violation of international law, seemed to raise a real possibility of British intervention in the war on the side of the Confederacy before Lincoln decided on Christmas Day to release the southerners. Smith's public support for the original Union action triggered a patriotic reflex from Stuart. If England had retaliated, the "subsequent horrors" would have been entirely the fault of the United States. But England's "beautiful & magnanimous forbearance" had saved the Americans from involvement in a foreign war that would have been both "insane & criminal." Smith's anti-British views were painful to Stuart but only what he would have expected from a *"pro-Garrison,* anti-Constitution, and anti-Bible mind." In the same period he inveighed against the *"Garrisonian constitution falsification mania,"* in response to a letter in which Smith had devoted twenty-two paragraphs to what Stuart deemed "groundless flattery" of Lincoln.[34]

Tolerance for the irascibility of old age no doubt explained Smith's willingness to correspond at such length with one who condemned his views as "ridiculously absurd" and dismissed Lincoln as "a disgrace to human nature." Certainly by 1862 there were many reminders in Stuart's letters that he was now in his eighties. His commentaries on the Civil War and his continuing solicitude for the financial security of his dependents revealed a still alert, if rigid, mind. His references to death revealed no apparent wavering of faith. But increasingly spidery handwriting told in more ways than one of physical decline. In April he expressed a wish to visit Peterboro again in the summer, but by July he was declaring that "my travelling days are gone, without any prospect of returning."[35]

33. Stuart to Smith, March 27, 1863, SP.
34. Stuart to Smith, January 1, 10, 1862, SP.
35. Stuart to Smith, January 10, April 19, July 30, 1862, SP.

Soon a debilitating illness gave his female dependents the chance to indicate, through furtive letters to Smith, their own difficulties in sharing what Rebecca called this "very *solitary place*" with Stuart. In August, Rebecca's sister, Margaret, prepared to embark on the return journey to Ireland with their ninety-five-year-old father. She wrote to Smith apologizing for the "precipitance" of Stuart's constant queries on their behalf. She hoped that Smith would ignore any future provocations, would keep secret her own letter to him, and would continue to offer the guidance on which her sisters would remain totally dependent. In December Rebecca was forced to decline an invitation to visit Peterboro. Because of religious differences, "Charles would by no means approve of my visiting you," she wrote, but then added, before posting the letter, "I would." In a secretive postscript she told how very disagreeable it had been for her to write this refusal "dictated by Charles." It was an "abomination" to her to deceive him with these secret comments, but she had no alternative. "I will say of him," she added, "what I frequently said of Father, he was 95, C. is 81, & you bear with him."[36]

Rebecca's letter made it clear that Stuart had been very ill, was much changed since Smith last saw him, and was "very feeble when walking." Smith probably did not notice much change when Stuart resumed writing to him the following month and, after thanking him for his "unwearied kindness," returned to the attack. Lincoln's recently announced Emancipation Proclamation was still "sinfully compromising" and offered no prospects for a "righteous" abolition. In March a more detailed sixteen-paragraph letter reiterated his despair with Smith and his compatriots. The principal cause of the American chaos was "the rebellion of your people against God," but the principal symptom was still the Garrisonian misinterpretation of the Constitution. Although he had recently read that Garrison had "repented," "the poison still deeply rankles, & you my beloved Gerrit, have, I think, shared largely . . . in the disasters which it has produced & is producing."[37]

On June 8, 1863, Stuart wrote to Smith what proved to be his last traceable letter, even though he was to live a further two years. There was nothing valedictory about its contents, as he mixed detailed references to his financial concerns with despair about the American scene. He was more willing than usual to find common ground with Smith, conceding that the atrocious chattel slave system had been aggravated by the "Brazen-faced

36. Margaret Watt to Smith, August 25, 1862; Rebecca Stuart to Nancy Smith, December [?], 1862, SP.
37. Stuart to Smith, January 8, March 27, 1863, SP.

devilism of the Secession movement." Nevertheless, he concluded, "I cannot avoid regarding your nation's rejection of God, as revealed by Himself, in the Bible, your master crime."[38]

In the same letter he wrote of the unexpected need to make a short visit to Toronto, a distance which only "sacred duty" would induce him to attempt. Perhaps the rigors of that journey hastened his physical decline. A year later a letter from Lewis Tappan to Rebecca referred to reports that Stuart was "very low." Tappan asked her to tell him that the Civil War had altered his own views about the morality of sustaining government, "if need be by force of arms." Whether such a message—or indeed any of the developments of the last two years of the war—made any impression on Stuart is impossible to say. It is at least possible that in these last years the religious intensity that had shaped his abolitionism was now focused almost exclusively on his own prospects of salvation. According to Rebecca, he had emerged from his illness of late 1862 "cheerful and happy, looking forward with a good hope and, as we think, on a good foundation . . . for an entrance into that house, not made with hands, eternal in the heavens."[39] Stuart lived to see the end of the Civil War confirm the abolition of slavery. He lived to see the president whose leadership had made abolition possible assassinated. It is a moot point whether he was exultant at the attainment of his life's goal, or still hostile to the devious expediency of Lincoln's antislavery policies, or, at last, indifferent to the realities of the American scene which had so long offended his religious convictions.

He died on May 16, 1865. A death notice appeared in the Toronto *Globe* some weeks later, but there was no obituary either there or anywhere else. His contribution to the antislavery cause was already largely forgotten.[40]

Much of this enveloping obscurity was inevitable. The unrivaled geographical scope of his activities—in all parts of the British Isles, in the United States, and in the West Indies—meant that probably few fellow abolitionists had been aware of the full range of his international contribution even in the 1830s. And the group that had known of his creative role in Britain was long since dispersed. James Cropper, probably as important as any individual in the Anglo-Irish network that was Stuart's first antislavery milieu, had died in 1840. William Blair, who had known Stuart

38. Stuart to Smith, June 8, 1863, SP.
39. *Ibid.*; Tappan to Rebecca Stuart, July 23, 1864, Letterbooks, Vol. 8, p. 90, Lewis Tappan Papers; Rebecca Stuart to Nancy Smith, December [?], 1862, SP.
40. "Died: At his residence, Zora [sic], Township of Collingwood, on 16th May, in his 84th year, Major Charles Stuart, H.E.I.C.S., Madras establishment. Extensively known for his ardent Anti-slavery principles" (Toronto *Globe*, June 9, 1865).

perhaps longer than any abolitionist, was also gone. Joseph Sturge's death—marked by a flood of British and American eulogies—had come in 1859. Charles Orpen, who had praised Stuart's pamphleteering and his itinerant lecturing in Ireland in 1830, had faded from the antislavery movement and eventually retired to South Africa. George Stephen, knighted for his leadership of the Agency Committee, had joined a son in Australia, taking with him not only memories but, it is presumed, all the manuscript records of that radical body.[41]

There were also those who had perhaps not forgotten Stuart but who had no wish to recall his achievements. George Thompson, Stuart's fellow lecturer for the Agency Committee, had been persuaded by him to believe in Garrison's integrity and had shared with him the task of consolidating the early Anglo-American antislavery cooperation. But Thompson had remained Garrison's friend and had visited him on a third transatlantic voyage as recently as 1864. Stuart's emergence as a "great Garrison-hater" in 1840 had no doubt obliterated in Thompson's mind the warm admiration he had expressed for Stuart in the early 1830s. And though Garrison himself cannot have known that his name recurred with obsessive frequency in Stuart's last correspondence, he, too, had long since recoiled from what he deemed the treachery of his once dear friend. John Scoble had been Stuart's ally in working for the repudiation of Garrisonian Old Organization by British abolitionists. But the two had clashed over antislavery policies toward India and Africa. For this reason—or because he was in his own way as abrasive a character as Stuart—Scoble, even though also living in Canada in 1865, ignored the death of his old Agency Committee associate, his companion in the West Indies in 1838 and 1839, the man who had greeted his own appointment as secretary of the British and Foreign Anti-Slavery Society with warm private congratulations and tireless provincial activity on behalf of that national body in the early 1840s.

Most poignant of all, there was no published appreciation from the man who had meant so much to Stuart for the past forty years. Theodore Weld—long withdrawn from antislavery activity—did not choose pub-

41. As a British-born Australian I resent the British (and perhaps American) assumption that anything that has traveled "down under" has "disappeared": for example, Temperley, *British Antislavery*, 15 n. 38 ("The Committee's own minute books have now disappeared, having been taken, so it was later asserted, by Stephen to Australia when he emigrated there in 1855"). Nevertheless, I must admit that attempts to find this material by inquiries to custodians of Stephen family papers in Sydney and Melbourne have so far been unsuccessful. Also unsuccessful have been inquiries about antislavery material in the papers of Charles Orpen and his descendants held by the Cape State Archives, Cape Town, South Africa.

licly to recall the intensity Stuart had brought to their friendship, to their shared involvement in Finney's revival, and to the great cause they had both discovered in the early 1830s.

This alienation was, of course, mainly of Stuart's own making. The absence of obituaries could well have reflected charitable concern to spare criticism of a man whose once inspiring faith and fervor had long since frozen into tedious dogmatism. Nevertheless, the man who thus helped to confine himself to near-oblivion on the margins—and in the footnotes—of antislavery history deserves a better fate.

His involvement in the beginnings of immediatist agitation on both sides of the Atlantic was unmatched by any other single individual. In Britain his pamphlets led the way in insisting that "immediately" meant "now" rather than "as soon as practicable." And his lecturing agencies in Ireland and the English Midlands developed methods of presenting the immediatist case which meant that his role as founder-member and then field agent of the all-important Agency Committee was vital. It is ironic that these positive contributions have been forgotten and Stuart has hitherto been given most recognition as a British abolitionist for his contribution to the lost cause of denying compensation to colonial slaveowners. In fact, *The West India Question*, in which he developed his anti-compensation argument, is most important for its transatlantic impact, which in turn points to his international significance in the late 1830s.

Although much of his contribution to American antislavery was more indirect than in Britain, it was not insignificant. His personal contacts with Weld and the inspiration of his anticolonization arguments on Garrison made him an important early influence on two key American abolitionists. If his own work as an American antislavery agent was less innovative than his comparable role in Britain, it confirmed his stature as a vital exponent of international antislavery cooperation. He had become a hero of the American antislavery press, not because of his private influence on Weld but because of the public and very successful attack he had mounted on the American Colonization Society in Britain. In the United States he survived grueling months of campaigning with a success that eluded George Thompson for all his eloquence. And he did so not by compromising his principles—as Americans accused other British abolitionists of doing—but by painstaking industry in dozens of local meetings, by constant reiteration of his simple creed in state and national gatherings, by private instruction to the fledgling agents of the national society, and by conspicuous nonchalance in the face of public danger in New England and upstate New York.

The late 1830s saw him repeating his influential role in Britain in the final overthrow of Negro apprenticeship. If he remained energetic for years to come, this was the end of his truly positive achievements. In the West Indies in 1839–40 the energy was remarkable but its relevance to antislavery priorities questionable. In the early 1840s in Britain it was a negative force helping to disrupt the international antislavery unity he had done so much to consolidate. And if his quick response to the implications of the Webster-Ashburton Treaty revealed unimpaired perception, it coincided with a growing pessimism about antislavery prospects on either side of the Atlantic which soon hardened into carping alienation.

Stuart's years of achievement were therefore a very small portion of a long life. He had become an abolitionist only in middle age. He was effective in that role for less than a decade. And he spent his last twenty-five years in ineffectual isolation. The long decades of groping for fulfillment and the long period of anticlimax can be understood only in the context of a personality so eccentric that he appeared to some insane. And yet it would be wrong to conclude that such a distinctive life has no wider relevance. Such might be the case if eccentricity had been the product of senility and the anticlimax a question of failing faculties. But Stuart was distinctive, eccentric, or, according to the viewpoint, insane all his adult life. For this reason the way his passionate fervor was in turn compelling, disruptive, and finally irrelevant says much about the antislavery circumstances in which he successively flourished and floundered.

Much of what his career reveals is already broadly familiar. But in one important respect it sheds new light on the overthrow of British colonial slavery between 1829 and 1833 which historians are still striving to explain. The validity of recent emphasis on popular pressure on a massive scale cannot be denied; the petitions that flooded Parliament from every corner of the British Isles in particular point to the breadth of concern with the question. But the populace needed to be informed, petitions organized, and the techniques of extracting pledges from candidates refined and explained. Charles Stuart's involvement in these processes before and after the foundation of the Agency Committee points to the importance of local organizers in the provinces and particularly to the connections between them. Stuart, with his private means and lack of personal ties, was a particularly suitable agent: with his American revivalist experience he had something distinctive to contribute. But there can be no doubt that if he had married Cornelia Weld and remained in the United States in 1829, the well-established network that linked the abolitionists of the West Country, the Midlands, and Ireland would have found other agents for the new task.

That network was held together by predominantly religious motives.

Although in important individual cases religious and East Indian economic interests were conveniently compatible, it would be impossible to contemplate the abolitionism of Stuart—who himself had a vested interest in the East India Company—and subscribe to any theory that diminished the overwhelming importance of a genuine religious impulse among abolitionists. Stuart's own attitudes, however, are a clear reminder that even the most unworldly abolitionists were likely to have economic assumptions and that even the most sophisticated modern assessments of the slave economy will reveal nothing about the motives of those who challenged slavery. It obviously suited Stuart's purposes to insist that slavery was economically less efficient than free labor. But he and others who advanced similar arguments were clearly doing so in an atmosphere in which the decline of West Indian slavery was widely assumed, notwithstanding modern demonstrations of its vigor.

Underlying Stuart's continuing optimism about free labor, in the face of contrary evidence and amid the daunting demands of his West Indian journey, was a large measure of sheer stubbornness. And that stubbornness soon helped to limit his antislavery role. Yet his limitations are as revealing as his achievements. By his rigid refusal to alter or develop any of his attitudes, he demonstrated the inadequacies of the immediatist innovations of the 1830s outside the special circumstances of a British decision about British colonial slavery. His constant calls for a return to proven methods were mostly too simplistic for a British antislavery movement identifying evil in many corners of the world but deprived of a single massive target. And they were always irrelevant to the complexities of the American situation. Although a less intense personality could have continued to find much in common with both British and American abolitionists, Stuart's career does also serve to emphasize that the Atlantic community of reform depended on much more than mobility, a common language, and a common religious impulse. With his Bermudan birth and his Anglo-American background there could be no more international figure. But his views on Ireland and India revealed an arrogant British imperialism distasteful to even conservative American abolitionists. And both his enthusiasm for a "bold and generous peasantry" in the 1830s and his scorn for the "hydra-headed monster" of American democracy in the 1850s revealed a man out of touch with the real America. Yet he had no greater interest in the real Britain. Even his eventual work among the starving Irish peasantry emphasizes his corresponding indifference to British urban poverty, class antagonism, and Chartist agitation. As he crossed and recrossed the Atlantic thirteen times between 1815 and 1850, his ultimate fate was to be irrelevant in both English-speaking countries: a perpetual outsider in Britain, a foreign critic in and on the borders of the United States. It was inevitable but unfortunate that this should obscure the importance of the abolitionist who most completely personified the religious fervor that had challenged slavery head-on and with dramatic suddenness from 1829 onward.

BIBLIOGRAPHY

PRIMARY SOURCES

Manuscript Collections

Australian National Library, Canberra
   American Colonization Society. Papers (microfilm).
   Douglass, Frederick. Papers (microfilm).
   Estlin, John Bishop and Mary. Papers (microfilm).
Boston Public Library, Department of Rare Books and Manuscripts
   American Anti-Slavery Society. Records.
   Estlin, Mary. Papers.
   Garrison, William Lloyd. Papers.
   May, Samuel J. Papers.
   Miscellaneous antislavery letters.
   New England Anti-Slavery Society. Records.
George Arents Research Library, Syracuse University, Syracuse, New York
   Smith, Gerrit. Papers.
Harvard University, Cambridge, Massachusetts.
   Houghton Library
      Stuart, Charles. Correspondence.
   Widener Library
      American Missionary Association, Archives (microfilm).
      Douglass, Frederick. Papers (microfilm).
      Tappan, Benjamin. Papers (microfilm).
Historical Society of Pennsylvania, Philadelphia
   Stuart, Charles. Correspondence.
India Office Library, London
   Court Minutes, East India Company, 1813–15. B/157–60.

Madras Letters Received, 1811–14. E1/127, E/4/341.
Madras Military Consultations, 1806–12. Ranges 255–57.
Personal Records o/6/5, pp. 133–52 (Summary of papers relative to suspension of Captain Charles Stuart.)
Register of Cadets. L/Mil./9/255

John Rylands Library, Manchester
Raymond English Deposit. Antislavery letters.
Thompson, George. Anti-Slavery Scrapbook (5 vols.) and Diary.

Library of Congress, Washington, D.C., Manuscript Division
Tappan, Lewis. Papers (microfilm).

Mitchell Library, Glasgow
Smeal Donation. Glasgow Emancipation Society. Records.

New-York Historical Society, New York City
Clark, Edwin C. Papers.
Stuart, Charles. Correspondence.

Public Archives of Canada, Ottawa
Census, 1851: Collingwood Township, Grey County, Canada West. Microfilm reel C-11723.
Executive Council Minute Books of Land Matters (RG1, L1). Land Books J, K, L (1816–24). Microfilm reel C-103.
Executive Council, Upper Canada Land Petitions (RG1, L3). Microfilm reels C-1615, 1653, 2811, 2813.

Rhodes House Library, Oxford
Manuscripts of British Empire
Series 18, C1–121. Correspondence of officials of Committee on Slavery and of officials and other committee members of British and Foreign Anti-Slavery Society.
———, C154–60. Correspondence of people holding no major office in the antislavery societies.
Series 20, E2/1–7. Minute Books of Committee on Slavery and of British and Foreign Anti-Slavery Society, 1823–43.
Series 22, G.61. Jamaica correspondence.
———, G.84. U.S.A. correspondence, 1833–52.
———, G.114–18. Conferences and congresses on slavery.

William L. Clements Library, University of Michigan, Ann Arbor
Weld-Grimké Papers.
Birney, James G. Papers.

Newspapers and Periodicals

Abolitionist, 1834–35. Published by the British and Foreign Society for the Universal Abolition of Slavery and the Slave Trade.
Abolitionist, January–December, 1833. Published by the New England Anti-Slavery Society.
African Repository, 1830–34. Published by the American Colonization Society.

Amherstburg, Canada, *Echo*, September 3, 1953.
American Anti-Slavery Reporter, 1834–36. Published by the American Anti-Slavery Society, New York.
Anti-Slavery Record, May, 1832—June, 1833. Published by the Anti-Slavery Society, London.
Anti-Slavery Record, 1835. Published for the American Anti-Slavery Society by R. G. Williams.
Anti-Slavery Reporter, 1833. Published by the American Anti-Slavery Society, New York.
Anti-Slavery Reporter, 1826–36. Published by the Anti-Slavery Society, London.
Anti-Slavery Reporter, 1840–65. Published by the British and Foreign Anti-Slavery Society.
Aris's Birmingham Gazette, 1829–32.
British Emancipator, 1837–40. Published by the Central Negro Emancipation Committee, London.
Emancipator, May, 1833–July, 1835 (weekly); August, 1835–April, 1836 (monthly). Published by the American Anti-Slavery Society.
Frederick Douglass' Paper, Rochester, New York, 1854–55.
Genius of Universal Emancipation, 1821–33. Published by Benjamin Lundy in Washington and Baltimore.
Gentleman's Magazine, 1830–43.
Glasgow *Chronicle*, 1840–41.
Leeds *Mercury*, 1830–33, 1840–43.
Liberator, 1831–65.
London *Times*, 1829–33, 1837–38, 1840–43.
Quarterly Anti-Slavery Magazine, 1835–37. Published by the American Anti-Slavery Society.
Sandwich, Upper Canada (Ontario) *Western Herald*, July 16, 1841.
Toronto *Globe*, 1865.
Tourist; or Sketch Book of the Times, 1832–33. Published by the Agency Anti-Slavery Society.
Voice of Freedom, May–June, 1836.
Westminster Review, 1830–33, 1837–38, 1840–43.

Publications by Charles Stuart in Chronological Order

The Emigrant's Guide to Upper Canada or, Sketches of the Present State of That Province, Collected from a Residence Therein During the Years 1817, 1818, 1819 . . . London, 1820.
On the Prospective Emancipation of Slaves' Unborn Children. Dublin, [1830?].
Petitions Respecting Negro Slavery. Bristol, 1830.
Is West Indian Slavery Justifiable by the New Testament? Dublin, n.d. [ca. 1830?]. Authorship not positively identified.

On Sophistical Arguments Against a Conscientious Disuse of Sugar Produced by Slave Labour. Dublin, n.d. [*ca.* 1830?]. Authorship not positively identified.

Appeal of the Negro's Friend Society to the People of Ireland on Behalf of the Slaves in the British Colonies. Dublin, n.d. [*ca.* 1830?]. Authorship not positively identified.

Can West Indian Slavery Be Justified from Scripture? Dublin, 1830.

Have Slave-Holders Any Right to Be Compensated on Being Deprived of Their Power to Continue to Steal Men's Personal Liberty? Dublin, 1830.

Is Slavery Defensible from Scripture? Belfast, 1831.

The West India Question. London, 1832.

A Letter on the American Colonization Society Addressed to the Editor of the "Herald of Peace." Birmingham, 1832.

Remarks on the Colony of Liberia and the American Colonization Society: With Some Account of the Settlement of Coloured People at Wilberforce, Upper Canada. London, 1832.

Prejudice Vincible: Or the Practicality of Conquering Prejudice by Better Means Than by Slavery and Exile, in Relation to the American Colonization Society. London, 1832.

Liberia: Or, the American Colonization Scheme Examined and Exposed. A Full and Authentic Report of a Lecture Delivered by C. Stuart, Esq. at a Public Meeting in Rev. M. Anderson's Chapel, Glasgow, 15th April 1833. Glasgow, 1833.

To the Friends of Religion and Humanity. Bath, 1833.

The American Colonization Scheme Further Unravelled. Bath, n.d. [*ca.* 1833].

Letter Addressed to Elisha Bates, Esq. Minister of the Society of Friends by Captain Stuart. Bath, n.d. [*ca.* 1833?].

Men and Brethren. N.p., n.d. [*ca.* 1834-36].

"On the Abolition of Slavery by Great Britain." *Quarterly Anti-Slavery Magazine,* I, No. 1 (October, 1835), 3-21; I, No. 2 (January, 1836), 107-17.

"On the Colored People of the United States." *Quarterly Anti-Slavery Magazine,* II, No. 1 (October, 1836), 11-22.

"On the Use of Slave Produce." *Quarterly Anti-Slavery Magazine,* II, No. 2 (January, 1837), 153-75.

A Memoir of Granville Sharp, To Which Is Added Sharp's "Laws of Passive Obedience" and an Extract from His "Law of Retribution." New York, 1837.

Immediate Emancipation . . . [American version of *The West India Question*]. Newburyport, 1838.

"White Labourers in Jamaica." *British Emancipator* (1839), 303.

"The 'General System.' " *British Emancipator* (1839), 303.

[Circular on divisions in the American Anti-Slavery movement]. Bath, n.d. [1841?].

Oneida and Oberlin: Or, a Call Addressed to British Christians and Philanthropists, Affectionately Inviting Their Sympathies, Their Prayers, and Their As-

sistance, in Favour of the Christians and Philanthropists of the United States . . . Bristol, 1841.
The Anti-Slavery Cause in 1842. N.p., 1842.
[Circular Letter on Irish Famine]. Cape Clear Island, [1848].
Remarks upon the "Religion of Reason," Sermon, of Hon. Gerrit Smith of Peterboro, N.Y., as Reported in the "Free Press" of Glen's Falls, March 5, 1859. Lora, Canada, 1859.

Other Contemporary Publications and Published Collections of Contemporary Documents

Abel, Annie Heloise, and Frank J. Klingberg, eds. *A Side-Light on Anglo-American Relations 1839–59 Furnished by the Correspondence of Lewis Tappan and Others with the British and Foreign Anti-Slavery Society.* New York, 1927.
Agency Society for the Universal Abolition of Negro Slavery and the Slave Trade Throughout the World. *To the Anti-Slavery Associations and the Friends of Negro Emancipation Throughout the United Kingdom.* London, 1834.
———. [Broadsheet] 18. Aldermanbury, October 14, 1834.
American Anti-Slavery Society. *Second Annual Report, with the Speeches Delivered at the Anniversary Meeting of the American Anti-Slavery Society in the City of New York, 12th May 1835.* New York, 1835.
———. *Third Annual Report, with the Speeches Delivered at the Anniversary Meeting of the American Anti-Slavery Society in the City of New York, 10th May 1836.* New York, 1836.
———. *Fourth Annual Report . . . of the American Anti-Slavery Society. . . .* New York, 1837.
Anti-Slavery Society, London. *Address to the People of Great Britain and Ireland Unanimously Adopted at a General Meeting . . . April 23, 1831.* London, 1831.
———. [Circular]. London, 1833.
———. [Letter from J. Crisp . . .]. Sheffield, 1833.
———. *Negro Apprenticeship in the British Colonies.* London, 1838.
———. *Report of the Agency Sub-Committee of the Anti-Slavery Society, Established in June 1831 for the Purpose of Disseminating Information by Lectures on Colonial Slavery.* London, 1832.
Bagg, Moses Mears. *The Pioneers of Utica: Being Sketches of Its Inhabitants and Its Institutions . . .* Utica, N.Y., 1877.
Bath Ladies Auxiliary British and Foreign Anti-Slavery Society. *Report . . . for the Years 1838, 1839, and 1840.* Bath, 1841.
Bigsby, John J. *The Shoe and Canoe, or Pictures of Travel in the Canadas.* 2 vols. London, 1850.
Birmingham Ladies Negro's Friend Society. *Seventh Report of the Ladies Negro's Friend Society for Birmingham, West Bromwich, Wednesbury, Walsall, and Their Respective Neighbourhoods.* Birmingham, 1832.
Blair, William T. *On the Introduction of Slave-Grown Produce into the British Markets.* London, 1844.

Bristol and Clifton Ladies Anti-Slavery Society. *Special Report of the Bristol and Clifton Ladies Anti-Slavery Society; During Eighteen Months, from January 1851 to June 1852 with a Statement of the Reasons for Its Separation from the British and Foreign Anti-Slavery Society.* London, 1852.

British and Foreign Anti-Slavery Society. *Proceedings of the General Anti-Slavery Convention Called by the Committee of the British and Foreign Anti-Slavery Society and Held in London from Fri. June 12 to Tues. June 23, 1840.* London, 1841.

———. *Proceedings of the General Anti-Slavery Convention, Called by the Committee of the British and Foreign Anti-Slavery Society, and Held in London from Tues. June 13 to Tues. June 20, 1843.* London, 1843.

British Opinions of the American Colonization Society. New York, 1833.

The Canada Directory for 1857–58. Montreal, 1857.

Central Negro Emancipation Committee. *Circular Address and Forms of Petition for the Abolition of the Apprenticeship System in the British Colonies.* London, 1837.

———. *Report of the Proceedings of the Public Meeting Held at Exeter Hall, on Thursday the 23rd of November, 1837, to Take into Consideration the Present Condition of the Negro Apprentices in the British Colonies.* London, 1837.

Collins, John A. *Right and Wrong Among the Abolitionists of the United States: Or, the Objects, Principles, and Measures of the Original American Anti-Slavery Society, Unchanged . . .* Glasgow, 1841.

Conder, Josiah. *Wages or the Whip. An Essay on the Comparative Cost and Productiveness of Free and Slave Labour.* London, 1833.

Cropper, James. *Speeches Delivered at the Anticolonization Meeting in Exeter Hall, London, July 13, 1833.* London, 1833.

Darlington Ladies' Anti-Slavery and British India Society. *Report . . .* Darlington, 1840.

"Defensor." *The Enemies of the Constitution Discovered; Or, an Inquiry into the Origin and Tendency of Popular Violence. Containing a Complete and Circumstantial Account of the Unlawful Proceedings at the City of Utica, October 21st, 1835; the Dispersion of the State Anti-Slavery Convention by the Agitators, the Destruction of a Democratic Press, and of the Causes Which Led Thereto. Together with a Concise Treatment on the Practice of the Court of His Honor Judge Lynch.* Utica, N.Y., 1835.

Dublin Negro's Friend Society. *Objects of the Society.* Dublin, 1829.

Dumond, Dwight L., ed. *Letters of James Gillespie Birney.* New York, 1938.

Dumond, Dwight L., and Gilbert H. Barnes, eds. *Letters of Theodore Dwight Weld, Angelina Grimké Weld, and Sarah Grimké, 1822–1844.* 2 vols. New York, 1934.

Edinburgh Emancipation Society for the Abolition of Slavery Throughout the World. *Report . . .* Edinburgh, 1835.

Finney, Charles Grandison. *Memoirs of Rev. Charles Grandison Finney.* New York, 1876.

Garrison, William Lloyd. *Thoughts on African Colonization: Or, an Impartial Exhibition of the Doctrines, Principles, and Purposes of the American Colonization Society. Together with the Resolutions, Addresses, and Remonstrances of the Free People of Color.* Boston, 1832.

Glasgow Emancipation Society. [Letter to the Editor of the Glasgow *Argus,* from Mr. J. A. Collins and the Emancipation Committee]. Glasgow, 1841.

———. *Resolutions of Public Meetings of the Members and Friends of the Glasgow Emancipation Society; Correspondence of the Secretaries; and Minutes of the Committee of Said Society, Since the Arrival in Glasgow, of Mr. John A. Collins, the Representative of the American Anti-Slavery Society, in Reference to the Divisions Among American Abolitionists.* Glasgow, 1841.

Hibernian Negro's Friend Society. *A Retrospective View of West India Slavery* ... Dublin, 1832.

Hodgkin, Thomas. *An Inquiry into the Merits of the American Colonization Society: And a Reply to the Charges Brought Against It. With an Account of the British African Colonization Society.* London, 1833.

India Registers. London, 1768–1876.

Jones, Pomroy. *Annals of Oneida County.* Rome, N.Y., 1851.

Journals of House of Commons. Vols. LXXXIV (1829), LXXXV (1830), LXXXVI (1831), XCIII (1837–38).

May, Samuel J. *Some Recollections of Our Anti-Slavery Conflict.* Boston, 1869. Facsimile Reprint, Miami, 1969.

A Memorial of the Semi-Centennial Celebration of the Founding of the Sunday School of the First Presbyterian Church, Utica, N.Y. Utica, N.Y., 1867.

Merrill, Walter M., and Louis Ruchames, eds. *The Letters of William Lloyd Garrison.* 5 vols. Cambridge, Mass., 1971–79.

A Narrative of the Revival of Religion in the County of Oneida, Particularly in the Bounds of the Presbytery of Oneida in the Year 1826. Utica, N.Y., 1826.

New England Anti-Slavery Society. *Annual Convention 1834: Proceedings.* Boston, 1834.

———. *Proceedings of the New England Anti-Slavery Society Convention Held in Boston: May 24, 25, 26, 1836.* Boston, 1836.

Orpen, Charles Edward Herbert. *The Principles, Plans, and Objects of the "Hibernian Negro's Friend Society," Contrasted with Those of the Previously Existing "Anti-Slavery Societies"; Being a Circular, Addressed to all Friends of the Negro, and Advocates for the Abolition and Extinction of Slavery; in the Form of a Letter to Thomas Pringle, Esq. Secretary of the London Anti-Slavery Society.* Dublin, 1831.

Perkins, Ephraim. *A "Bunker Hill" Contest, A.D. 1826, Between the "Holy Alliance" for the Establishment of Hierarchy, and Ecclesiastical Domination over the Human Mind, on the One Side, and the Asserters of Free Inquiry, Bible Religion, Christian Freedom and Civil Liberty on the Other* ... N.p., n.d.

Prinsep, Charles C., ed. *Record of Services of Honourable East India Company's Civil Servants in the Madras Presidency, 1741–1858.* London, n.d.

Proceedings of the New York Anti-Slavery Convention Held at Utica, October 21, and the New York State Anti-Slavery Society Held at Peterboro, October 22, 1835. Utica, N.Y., 1835.
Richard, Henry. *Memoirs of Joseph Sturge.* London, 1864.
Sanborn, Frank B. *Recollections of Seventy Years.* Boston, 1909.
Stephen, Sir George. *Anti-Slavery Recollections in a Series of Letters to Mrs. Beecher Stowe.* London, 1854.
Society for the Extinction of the Slave Trade and for the Civilization of Africa. *Prospectus.* N.p., 1840.
Talbot, Edward A. *Five Years Residence in the Canadas.* London, 1824.
Taylor, Clare. *British and American Abolitionists: An Episode in Transatlantic Understanding.* Edinburgh, 1974.
Thompson, George. *An Appeal to the Abolitionists of Great Britain, on Behalf of the Cause of Universal Emancipation.* Edinburgh, 1837.
———. *Discussion on American Slavery, in Dr. Wardlaw's Chapel, Between Mr. George Thompson and the Rev. R. J. Breckenridge . . .* 2d ed. Glasgow, 1846.
———. *A Voice to the United States of America, from the Metropolis of Scotland . . .* Edinburgh, 1836.
Thomson, Andrew. *Substance of the Speech Delivered at the Meeting of the Edingburgh Society for the Abolition of Slavery on October 19th, 1830.* Edinburgh, 1830.
Three Years Female Anti-Slavery Effort. Glasgow, 1837.
Wigham, Hannah Maria. *A Christian Philanthropist of Dublin: A Memoir of Richard Allen.* London, 1886.

SECONDARY SOURCES

Abzug, Robert H. *Passionate Liberator: Theodore Weld and the Dilemma of Reform.* New York, 1980.
Anstey, Roger. *The Atlantic Slave Trade and British Abolition, 1760–1810.* London, 1975.
Barker, Anthony J. *The African Link: British Attitudes to the Negro in the Era of the Atlantic Slave Trade, 1550–1807.* London, 1978.
Barnes, Gilbert H. *The Antislavery Impulse.* New York, 1933.
———. "The Western Revival Origins." In Richard O. Curry, ed., *Abolitionists*, 11–21. Hinsdale, Ill., 1973.
Beckett, J. C. *The Making of Modern Ireland.* London, 1966.
Bolt, Christine. *The Anti-Slavery Movement and Reconstruction: A Study in Anglo-American Co-Operation, 1833–77.* London, 1969.
Bolt, Christine, and Seymour Drescher, eds. *Anti-Slavery, Religion, and Reform: Essays in Memory of Roger Anstey.* Folkestone, 1980.
Cole, G.D.H., and Raymond Postgate. *The Common People, 1746–1946.* London, 1964.

Cross, Whitney R. *The Burned-over District: The Social and Intellectual History of Enthusiastic Religion in Western New York, 1800–1850.* New York, 1965.
Curry, Richard O., ed. *The Abolitionists.* Hinsdale, Ill., 1973.
Davis, David Brion. *The Problem of Slavery in the Age of Revolution, 1770–1823.* Ithaca, N.Y., 1975.
———. *The Problem of Slavery in Western Culture.* Ithaca, N.Y., 1966.
Drescher, Seymour. *Econocide: British Slavery in the Era of Abolition.* Pittsburgh, 1977.
Duberman, Martin, ed. *The Antislavery Vanguard: New Essays on the Abolitionists.* Princeton, 1965.
Dumond, Dwight L. *Antislavery: The Crusade for Freedom in America.* New York, 1966.
Edwards, R. Dudley. *A New History of Ireland.* Dublin, 1972.
———, and T. Desmond Williams. *The Great Famine: Studies in Irish History, 1845–52.* Dublin, 1962.
Eltis, David, and James Walvin, eds. *The Abolition of the Atlantic Slave Trade: Origins and Effects in Europe, Africa, and the Americas.* Madison, 1981.
Filler, Louis. *The Crusade Against Slavery, 1830–1860.* New York, 1963.
Fladeland, Betty. *James Gillespie Birney: Slaveholder to Abolitionist.* New York, 1955.
———. *Men and Brothers: Anglo-American Antislavery Co-operation.* Urbana, 1972.
Garrison, Wendell P., and Francis J. Garrison. *William Lloyd Garrison, 1805–1879: The Story of His Life Told by His Children.* 4 vols. New York, 1885–89.
Green, William A. *British Slave Emancipation: The Sugar Colonies and the Great Experiment.* Oxford, 1976.
Kraditor, Aileen S. *Means and Ends in American Abolitionism: William Lloyd Garrison and His Critics, 1834–50.* New York, 1969.
Landon, Fred. "Captain Charles Stuart, Abolitionist." *Western Ontario History Nuggets,* No. 24 (1956), 1–19.
Litwack, Leon F. *North of Slavery: The Negro in the Free States, 1790–1860.* Chicago, 1961.
Pease, Jane H., and William H. Pease. "Confrontation and Abolition in the 1850s." *Journal of American History,* LVIII (1971–72), 923–37.
———. *They Who Would Be Free: Blacks' Search for Freedom, 1830–61.* New York, 1974.
Perry, Lewis, and Michael Fellman, eds. *Antislavery Reconsidered: New Perspectives on the Abolitionists.* Baton Rouge, 1979.
Ragatz, Lowell Joseph. *The Fall of the Planter Class in the British Caribbean, 1763–1833.* New York, 1928.
Riach, Douglas Cameron. "Ireland and the Campaign Against American Slavery, 1830–60." Ph.D thesis, Edinburgh University, 1975.
Rice, C. Duncan. "The Anti-Slavery Mission of George Thompson to the United States, 1834–35." *Journal of American Studies,* II (1968), 13–31.

———. *The Scots Abolitionists, 1833–1861*. Baton Rouge, 1981.
Richards, Leonard L. *"Gentlemen of Property and Standing": Anti-Abolition Mobs in Jacksonian America*. New York, 1970.
Spear, Percival. *A History of India*. Vol. II. Harmondsworth, Middlesex, 1971.
Temperley, Howard. *British Antislavery, 1833–1870*. Columbia, S.C., 1972.
Thomas, Benjamin P. *Theodore Weld: Crusader for Freedom*. New Brunswick, N.J., 1950.
Tyler, Alice Felt. *Freedom's Ferment: Phases of Social History from the Colonial Period to the Outbreak of the Civil War*. New York, 1962.
Wilberforce, Robert Isaac, and Samuel Wilberforce. *Life of William Wilberforce*. 5 vols. London, 1838.
Williams, Eric. *Capitalism and Slavery*. 2d ed. London, 1964.
Wilson, William John. *History of the Madras Army*. 5 vols. London, 1882–89.
Winks, Robin W. *The Blacks in Canada: A History*. Montreal, 1971.

INDEX

Abolitionism. *See* American antislavery movement; Anglo-American antislavery movement; British antislavery movement; Canadian antislavery movement; Immediatism; Jamaican antislavery movement; Women abolitionists
Adam, William, 188, 197
African Civilization Society, 167–68, 192, 213, 224
African immigration to West Indies. *See* West Indies, conditions after slavery
Agency Committee, 39, 42, 45, 46, 50–63, 74, 76, 78, 80–81, 84–85, 86, 129, 143, 145, 146, 149, 150, 195, 233, 250
Agency Society for the Universal Abolition of Negro Slavery and the Slave Trade, 85. *See also* British and Foreign Society for the Universal Abolition of Slavery and the Slave Trade
Alexander, G. W., 251, 254
Allen, Richard, 147, 154, 155, 195, 204
Allen, Mrs. Richard, 155–56
American and Foreign Anti-Slavery Society, 190, 198, 201, 255. *See also* New Organization
American antislavery movement: origins and growth, 1–2, 64–66, 84, 86–119; division in, 120, 124–34, 161, 186–87, 188–92, 198–200, 201–22, 223–35, 237, 238, 264, 281–82. *See also* Immediatism; New Organization; Old Organization; entries under names of national and local societies
American Anti-Slavery Society, 3, 65–66, 71, 84, 86–120, 129, 140, 157, 187. *See also* Old Organization
American Colonization Society, 2, 40, 66–85, 94, 95, 129, 136, 166, 192, 208
American Colonization Society Further Unravelled, 83, 85
American Missionary Association, 287–88, 290–91
Anglo-American antislavery movement, 2, 4. *See also* Stuart, Captain Charles—as Anglo-American abolitionist
Anstie, George, 261
Antiabolition violence: in United States, 89–90, 92–93, 99–100, 112–13, 115–19, 193, 280–81, 294; in Britain, 46, 86, 174
Antigua, 169, 170, 171
Anti-Slavery Cause in 1842, p. 247
Anti-Slavery Reporter, 38, 39, 40, 97, 180, 181, 226, 238, 243, 245–46, 279
Anti-Slavery Society. *See* London Anti-Slavery Society
Apprenticeship, 74, 140, 143–56, 162, 176–77, 241–42
Atlantic slave trade, 184, 192, 244, 267

Baldwin, Edward, 46, 53, 56, 147, 148, 149–50, 154–55, 190
Ball, Martha V., 225, 248

321

Barbados, 162–65, 167, 171, 174
Bassett, William, 201
Bath, 77, 80, 148, 213, 243, 244, 250, 254, 260
Beardsley, Samuel, 116–17
Beecher, Lyman, 95, 97
Belfast Anti-Slavery Society, 200
Berbice, 167–68
Bigsby, John, 25–26, 260
Birmingham Anti-Slavery Society, 145, 148
Birmingham Female Society for the Relief of Negro Slaves, 47, 52, 80. See also Ladies Negro's Friend Societies of Birmingham, Wednesbury, Walsall, and Their Respective Neighbourhoods
Birney, James G., 94, 95, 97, 101, 103, 105, 106, 108, 121, 122–23, 130–32, 142, 190, 192, 196, 198, 202, 208, 210, 212, 213, 233, 264, 285
Blair, Mary, 40, 146, 172, 254
Blair, William, 40–41, 45, 46, 47, 53, 57, 140, 146–47, 150, 172, 189, 196, 213, 238, 254, 256, 259, 260–63, 304–305
Bourne, George, 65, 87
Boycotts of slave produce, 45, 47, 48–49, 52, 53, 57
Bradburn, George, 191, 192–93
Breckenridge, J., 137–38, 140
Bristol and Clifton Auxiliary Ladies Anti-Slavery Society, 225, 227, 237
Bristol riots (1831), 62
British abolitionists. See British antislavery movement
British and Foreign Anti-Slavery Society, 156, 161, 167, 176, 184, 186, 189–91, 196, 198, 201, 203, 205, 207, 208, 212, 236–58, 260, 263, 266–68, 273
British and Foreign Society for the Universal Abolition of Slavery and the Slave Trade, 84, 143, 144, 145. See also Agency Society for the Universal Abolition of Negro Slavery and the Slave Trade
British antislavery movement, 1, 38–63, 143–58, 201–22, 236–69. See also Agency Committee; Agency Society for the Universal Abolition of Negro Slavery and the Slave Trade; British and Foreign Anti-Slavery Society; Emancipation Society; Immediatism; Irish abolitionists; London Anti-Slavery Society; Midlands abolitionists; Provincial abolitionists; Scottish abolitionists; West Country abolitionists; Women abolitionists
British Emancipator, 149, 153, 156, 161, 163, 175, 176, 242
British Guiana, 159, 167–69, 244, 267
British India Society, 194, 199, 201
British Opinions of the American Colonization Society, 73, 136
Broad Street, 189. See also British and Foreign Anti-Slavery Society
Brougham, Henry (Lord), 41, 42, 152–53, 155, 174
Brown, John, 3, 280, 296, 299
Buffalo, N.Y., 99–100, 114–15
Buxton, Thomas Fowell, 41, 42, 44, 76, 80, 143, 144, 150, 166–67, 192, 213, 224

Canada, 2, 3–4, 20–26, 98–99, 101, 165, 174, 186, 226, 259, 274–305. See also Free blacks
Canadian antislavery movement, 274, 276
Canadian Anti-Slavery Society, 274
Can West Indian Slavery Be Justified From Scripture?, 49
Cape Clear Island, Ireland, 271–72
Carlile, James, 195
Catholic emancipation, 37, 40
Central Negro Emancipation Committee, 145, 149, 150, 153, 155, 156, 159, 161, 175, 186
Chapman, Maria Weston, 208, 212, 224
Chartism, 157, 207, 217–22, 237, 241–43, 246–47
Cincinnati, 95–96, 102–103, 105, 121, 123, 130–32
Civil War, American, 298–304
Clark, Erastus, 291, 291n
Clarkson, Edward, 63
Clarkson, Thomas, 72, 73, 76, 77, 135, 189, 193
Cobden, Richard, 256
Colebrook, Sir William, 171
Collins, John A., 149, 191, 201–22, 223, 224, 226, 227, 229, 230, 232, 235, 237

Colonial Office, 159, 162, 174, 184
Colonization of blacks. *See* American Colonization Society
Colver, Nathaniel, 132, 188, 190, 195, 204, 205, 207
Compensation for slave-holders, 50, 74. *See West India Question*
Conran, Colonel, 14–16
Constitution (U.S.), 86–87, 105, 264, 280, 281, 301–303
Cooper, Emmanuel, 56
Cox, F. A., 109, 193
Crandall, Prudence, 87, 91–92, 128
Creole case, 255–56
Cresson, Elliot, 66–83, 86, 89, 99, 129, 172, 202, 224
Crisp, John, 56, 57
Cropper, Edward, 61
Cropper, James, 47, 57, 69, 72, 73, 82, 146, 304

Darlington Anti-Slavery Society Ladies Committee, 211
Davis, Jefferson, 300
Del Hoyo, Harriet, 7n, 258
Denison, Charles W., 89
Denman, Thomas, 41, 42
Derby riots (1831), 62
District of Columbia, 87, 104, 130, 279
Dominica, 169, 170, 172
Dred Scott case, 287
Douglas, Stephen, 287
Douglass, Frederick, 281, 282, 283. *See also Frederick Douglass' Paper*
Dublin Ladies Anti-Slavery Society, 47
Dublin Negro's Friend Society. *See* Hibernian Negro's Friend Society
Dymond, Elizabeth, 248
Dymond, Sarah, 248–50, 254

East India Company, 9–20, 57–59
East India sugar, 47, 57–58
Edinburgh Anti-Slavery Society, 79, 148
Edinburgh Emancipation Society, 203, 208–11
Emancipation Proclamation, 303
Emancipation Society (Britain), 300
Emancipator, 89, 99, 100, 103, 106, 107, 164, 187, 201

Emigrant's Guide to Upper Canada, 23, 25, 27
Estlin, J. B., 224
Estlin, Mary, 224
Evesham Ladies Anti-Slavery Society, 237

Finney, Charles Grandison, 2, 32–34, 36–37, 95, 253, 284
Foster, Stephen, 264
Frederick Douglass' Paper, 278, 279, 281–82
Free blacks: in United States, 66, 70, 73, 74, 81, 83, 87, 92–93, 95–96, 101, 103, 245–46, 255; in Canada, 26, 227, 244–45, 255, 298. *See also* Fugitive slaves; West Indies, conditions after slavery
Free Produce Association of Philadelphia, 195
Free trade, 237, 256–57, 260–63, 266, 267
French abolitionists, 192, 243, 251. *See also* Paris Anti-Slavery Convention
Frost, John, 89
Fugitive Slave Law, 264, 279–80, 282–83
Fugitive slaves, 2, 26, 37, 48, 83, 103, 245–46, 255, 298–99

Gairdner, Harriet, 210
Galusha, Elon, 188
Garland, Mary, 248
Garrison, William Lloyd, 5–6, 64–75, 77, 78, 83, 84, 87, 88, 90, 92–95, 118–20, 124–30, 146–47, 186–87, 189, 191–92, 198–201, 203, 210–12, 216, 224–25, 228–34, 282, 302, 303, 305
General Anti-Slavery Conventions. *See* World Anti-Slavery Conventions
Genius of Universal Emancipation, 52–53, 73, 82
Gladstone, Sir John, 168
Glasgow Emancipation Society, 138, 148, 153, 155, 199, 211–12, 215–22
Glenelg, Lord, 153, 154
Goodell, William, 65, 99, 100
Grant, Charles, 275
Green, Beriah, 72, 95, 108, 110, 113, 124, 132–34, 208, 255
Grimké, Angelina, 6, 124, 128, 142, 152, 157, 172, 178–79, 223, 227, 243, 248–49, 252, 254, 264, 285

324 INDEX

Grimké, Sarah, 124, 128, 178, 227, 243, 264, 285
Gurley, R. R., 82, 224
Gurney, J. J., 81, 185

Haughton, James, 190, 204
Have Slave-Holders Any Right to be Compensated on Being Deprived of Their Power to Continue to Steal Men's Personal Liberty?, 50
Hawks, Betsy D., 282
Heugh, Hugh, 217–20
Heyrick, Elizabeth, 38, 44, 47, 58
Hibernian Anti-Slavery Society, 147, 204
Hibernian Bible Society, 48
Hibernian Negro's Friend Society, 47–53, 56, 70, 84, 147
Hilhouse, William, 168–69, 176
Hodgkin, Thomas, 83
Howells, Henry C., 256
Hume, William, 56

Immediatism: interpretations, 4; in Britain, 38–63, 136–37, 194; in United States, 64–65, 71, 86–119, 136–37, 194
India. *See* British India Society; East India Company; East India sugar; Indian Mutiny; Slavery; Stuart, Captain Charles—early life; Stuart, Captain Charles—political attitudes
Indian Mutiny, 287–89
Ireland. *See* Irish abolitionists; Irish famine; Stuart, Captain Charles—as British abolitionist; Stuart, Captain Charles—political attitudes
Irish abolitionists, 40, 46–53, 147. *See also* Belfast Anti-Slavery Society; Dublin Ladies Anti-Slavery Society; Hibernian Anti-Slavery Society; Hibernian Negro's Friend Society; O'Connell, Daniel
Irish famine, 269–72
Irish Friend, 211
Is Slavery Defensible from Scripture?, 49

Jackson, Philip, 248, 249–50
Jamaica, 156, 160, 161, 173–87
Jamaican antislavery movement, 185–87
Jones, Theophilus Bolton, 270

Kansas, 279–80

Kelley, Abby, 187, 282
King, David, 217, 220
Kingston Anti-Slavery Society (Jamaica), 185

Ladies Negro's Friend Societies of Birmingham, West Bromwich, Wednesbury, Walsall, and Their Respective Neighbourhoods, 53, 251. *See also* Birmingham Female Society for the Relief of Negro Slaves
Lane Seminary (Cincinnati), 95–97, 102, 113, 123, 124
Lester, C. E., 193
Letter on the American Colonization Society, 67
Liberator, 63, 67, 68–75, 85, 87, 89, 92–93, 126, 135, 157, 164, 187, 211, 228–29
Liberia. *See* American Colonization Society
Liberty party, 132, 264
Lincoln, Abraham, 287, 298–304
Lloyd, Mary S., 251
London Anti-Slavery Society, 38–39, 41, 42, 45, 47, 53–57, 67, 76–77, 143–45, 146, 150
Lora Bay, 275–78
L'Ouverture, Toussaint, 126, 197
Lovejoy, Elijah P., 121–22, 226
Lundy, Benjamin, 73
Lushington, Stephen, 41, 42, 245, 246

Macaulay, Zachary, 57
Maitland, Sir Peregrine, 21, 24, 25
Mann, Anne, 237–38, 251
Martineau, Harriet, 76, 215, 229
Martinique, 171
Massachusetts Abolition Society, 186, 225, 227
Massachusetts Anti-Slavery Society, 201
Massachusetts Female Anti-Slavery Society, 118
Massachusetts Female Emancipation Society, 248
Matheson, James, 193
Mauritius, 138, 144, 244
May, Samuel J., 87, 92, 119, 125
Memoir of Granville Sharp, 136
Metcalfe, Sir Charles, 175, 182

Mexican War, 273, 279, 282
Middletown, Conn., 89
Midlands abolitionists, 46, 79–80. *See also* Birmingham Anti-Slavery Society; Birmingham Female Society for the Relief of Negro Slaves; Ladies Negro's Friend Societies of Birmingham, West Bromwich, Wednesbury, Walsall and Their Respective Neighbourhoods
Miller, Colonel Jonathan, 188, 190
Mitchel, John, 269–70
Mohill, Ireland, 270
Montserrat, 161, 170, 172
Mott, Lucretia, 190
Mountain, Bishop Jacob, 21, 59
Murray, John, 199, 211–12, 217–20, 230, 232, 233, 235

National Standard, 201
Nelson, David, 122
New Brunswick, Canada, 7, 36
New England, 64, 87, 89–91, 113, 132
New England Anti-Slavery Society, 72, 74, 83, 84, 89, 90, 121, 125–26
New Jersey State Anti-Slavery Society, 252
New Organization, 198, 201–22. *See also* American and Foreign Anti-Slavery Society
New York state, 26–28, 64, 94–95, 99–102, 105–109, 113–19, 122–23, 133–34
New York State Anti-Slavery Society, 116–18, 121
Nonconsumption of slave produce. *See* Boycotts of slave produce
Nonresistance, 130–31, 230, 233–34, 288–89
Nottingham riots (1831), 62

O'Connell, Daniel, 40, 41, 74, 150, 243, 268–69
Ohio, 64, 83, 94, 101, 103, 121, 245
Old Organization, 198, 201–23, 227–28, 255. *See also* American Anti-Slavery Society
Oneida and Oberlin, 226
Oneida County Anti-Slavery Association, 108
Oneida Institute, 34, 95, 113, 133–34, 255

On the Prospective Emancipation of Slaves' Unborn Children, 49
Orange, John, 248
Orpen, Charles, 46, 47, 51, 54, 147, 305, 305n

Palmer, A. L., 141, 146, 151, 161, 177
Paris Anti-Slavery Convention (1842), 243, 251
Parliamentary reform, 61–62
Paul, Nathaniel, 70, 74, 83
Pease, Elizabeth, 141, 149, 199, 201, 202, 203, 204, 205, 206, 207, 210, 211, 215, 227, 228, 229, 230, 237
Pease, John, 206
Pease, Joseph, 150, 206
Peterboro Anti-Slavery Society, 102
Petitions against slavery, 39, 40, 41, 43, 51, 53, 54, 130
Petitions Respecting Negro Slavery, 44, 46, 48, 54
Phelps, Amos A., 113–14, 124, 132, 187, 205, 207
Philanthropist, 121
Phillips, Joseph, 69, 84–85, 172
Phillips, Wendell, 190
Plainfield, Conn., 92
Pownall, Henry, 41, 42, 44
Prejudice Vincible, 71–73, 139
Price, J. T., 195
Pringle, Thomas, 67
Provincial abolitionists (Britain), 38, 41–46. *See also* Irish abolitionists; Midlands abolitionists; Scottish abolitionists; West Country abolitionists

Quakers, 46–48, 75, 145, 146, 147, 150, 190, 201, 203–204, 230

Racial prejudice: in the United States, 87, 95–96, 281; in Canada, 244–45. *See also Prejudice Vincible*; Stuart, Captain Charles—racial attitudes
Rankin, Charles, 20, 276
Rankin, George, 20
Rankin, John, 20
Rankin, Mary, 20, 26, 96, 161, 263
Remarks on the Colony of Liberia and the American Colonization Society, 70

Remarks upon the "Religion of Reason," 293
Remond, Charles Lenox, 198, 202, 206, 207, 217, 229
Revivalism, 27–34
Rhode Island State Antislavery Convention (1836), 121, 132
Rochester, N.Y., 114–15, 122
Rolph, Thomas, 244

Saint Domingue, 197
St. Kitts, 169, 170, 171–72, 173
St. Lucia, 159, 169, 170, 171
St. Vincent, 165, 167
Salem Ladies Anti-Slavery Society, 128
Sanborn, Frank, 280, 296
Schimmelpenning, Maria, 80
Scoble, John, 56, 145, 146, 153, 161, 163–64, 167–69, 174, 189, 197, 202, 205, 207, 208, 213, 224, 230, 238, 243, 244, 256, 260, 261, 263, 300, 305
Scottish abolitionists, 84, 92, 147. *See also* Edinburgh Anti-Slavery Society; Edinburgh Emancipation Society; Glasgow Emancipation Society
Shippey, Charlotte, 7n
Slavery: in India, 161, 192, 196, 197, 213, 238–40, 255; in United States, 86–87, 273, 279, 282; in West Indies, 140–41, 144–46, 156
Slave trade. *See* Atlantic slave trade
Smeal, William, 155, 199, 205, 211–12, 217–20
Smith, Gerrit, 7, 94, 97, 103–108, 110, 112–13, 115, 117–18, 121, 127, 132–34, 141–42, 165, 208, 231, 257, 266, 272–73, 276, 279–83, 289–303
Smith, Sir Lionel, 174–76, 179, 182
Spencer, Thomas, 261
Stanton, Elizabeth Cady, 213, 282
Stanton, Henry B., 96, 98, 124, 132, 134, 193, 196, 198, 202, 208, 212, 213
Stephen, George, 54, 55, 56, 60–61, 305
Stephen, James, 42, 54
Stephen, Sir James, 42–43, 174
Stewart, Alvan, 117, 134
Stuart, Anne, 7n, 253
Stuart, Captain Charles
—early life: birth, family, education, 3, 7, 8–9; military service in India, 3, 5, 9, 10–14; dismissal, 14–20
—middle life: magistrate, missionary, patron of fugitive blacks in Canada, 2–4, 20–26; school principal, Utica, 26–30; Finney revivalist, 33–37, 43, 51, 54–55, 89
—as British abolitionist: West Country, Ireland, Midlands initiation, 39–40, 48–53; Agency Committee founder, agent, 52–63; in antiapprenticeship campaign, 143–58; in West Indies, 159–87; at 1840 World Convention, 189–200; in provinces, 1840–43, pp. 201–68
—as American abolitionist: agent of American Anti-Slavery Society, 101–19, 121–25; and mob violence, 89–90, 92–93, 99–100, 112–13, 115–19, 193, 294
—as Anglo-American abolitionist: opposes A.C.S. in Britain, 64–85; encourages transatlantic cooperation, 88–89, 97–98, 100–101, 105, 108, 110, 112, 120, 134–40; reports to British and American abolitionists from West Indies, 160–61, 169, 172, 177, 179, 185, 196, 199–200; opposes Old Organization in Britain, 189, 191, 201–35
—antislavery beliefs and methods: basic philosophy, 44, 48–50, 58–63, 84, 161, 182, 185, 193–94, 197, 238–40, 247, 264; as lecturer, preacher, 3, 39, 51–55, 60–63, 91, 94, 98–99, 100, 104–105, 106, 121, 123; as pamphleteer, 3, 39, 133, 214–15, 219, 226, 293; as political activist, 129–30, 163, 197–98, 231–33, 237, 250–52, 257, 267–68; on boycotts of slave produce, 48–49, 126–27, 194–96, 213, 231, 236, 262; on woman question, 189, 191, 210, 214–15, 218–20, 224–28, 230–32, 252
—political attitudes: British patriotism, imperialism, 7, 138–39, 263, 289; attitudes to British society and domestic politics, 23, 62–63, 139–40, 156–57, 197, 202, 241–43, 249, 257–58, 263, 289; to Ireland, 8, 37, 51–52, 140, 269–72, 288; to India, 12, 17–18, 20, 29, 36, 50, 51, 83, 136, 140, 197, 213, 238–40; to United States, 23, 36, 105–106, 108–

109, 112, 130, 232, 240–41, 245–46, 257–58, 273, 277, 280–81, 289, 299–302
—religious life: basic beliefs, 3, 20, 22, 44, 233, 252–53, 264–66, 271–72, 282–86, 291–98, 300–304; fervor, 8, 14, 20–21, 28–29, 33–34, 156, 263; as Anglican, 8, 20, 21; as Presbyterian, 28, 87–88, 100, 110; anti-Catholicism, 8, 28, 51, 59, 269
—racial attitudes: to Negroes, 3, 12, 67, 99, 110, 125, 136, 139, 165–67, 171, 180; to American Indians, 23, 25, 51, 66, 83, 138, 139, 197, 259, 263
—personality: emotional, psychological intensity, 8–9, 30–31, 34–35, 58–61, 98–99, 102, 112–13, 122–23, 124, 141–42, 152, 160–61, 182–84, 233, 234–35, 237, 243, 245, 252–58, 260, 263–66, 292, 294, 297–99; eccentricity, 19, 24–25, 28–30, 60–61, 74, 92, 100, 117–18, 160–61, 191–92, 213, 229, 278–79; physical intensity, 28–30, 107, 117–18, 123, 151, 160–61, 163, 172–73, 183–84, 226–27, 236, 243, 258, 260, 275, 287, 291, 298–99, 302–304; puritanism, attitudes to women, 11, 14, 23–24, 35–36, 79–80, 128–29, 149, 157, 235
—private life: finances, 18, 20, 58, 100, 113, 265, 267–68, 272, 277, 280, 289–90, 293, 296, 302; relationship with Cornelia Weld, 33–56, 59, 90, 96; retirement, 274–304; marriage, 268, 275–79, 291–92
—friendships. *See* Birney, James G.; Blair, William; Garrison, William Lloyd; Smith, Gerrit; Weld, Theodore
Stuart, Charlotte. *See* Shippey, Charlotte
Stuart, Harriet. *See* Del Hoyo, Harriet
Stuart, Rebecca, 275, 276, 277–79, 289, 291–92, 299, 303, 304
Sturge, Joseph, 42, 47, 140–41, 149–54, 157, 162, 167, 172–73, 179–80, 183, 189, 204, 205, 207, 210, 212, 217, 230, 235, 237, 242–43, 246, 256, 259, 261
Sturge, Sophia, 251
Sturge, Thomas, 214, 229
Sugar duties, 260–63

Talbot, Edward, 23

Tappan, Arthur, 65, 66, 73, 83, 95, 114, 124
Tappan, Lewis, 65, 66, 95, 124, 125, 132, 133, 186, 187, 210, 215, 226–27, 287–90
Temperance, 28, 34, 51–52, 95, 127, 232, 264
Temperley, Howard, 3, 54–55, 144–45, 153, 155
Texas, 139, 192, 263–64
Thompson, George, 56, 60, 74, 76, 78–79, 84, 93–94, 97, 104, 106, 108–13, 118, 125, 135–38, 140–41, 145–57, 190–99, 201–10, 216, 229, 236–37, 256, 268, 274, 305
Thompson, Mitchell, 248
Tobago, 165, 167
Townsend, Lucy, 80
Tredgold, J. H., 208
Trent case, 302
Tribe, Fanny, 224–25
Trinidad, 159, 169, 175

United States. *See* Constitution (U.S.); Free blacks; Slavery
Utica, N.Y., 26–27, 32–33, 103–109, 114, 121–22, 133–34
Utica Academy, 26–30
Utica Anti-Slavery Society, 104–105, 108
Utica *Friend of Man*, 137–38, 157

Wager, David, 134
Wardlaw, Ralph, 138, 199, 217–20
Waring, Maria, 189, 191
Watt, Isabelle, 275n, 277
Watt, John, 275n, 277, 303
Watt, Margaret, 275, 275n, 277, 303
Watt, Rebecca. *See* Stuart, Rebecca
Webb, Richard, 147, 199, 205, 206, 207, 220–21, 230
Webster-Ashburton Treaty, 245–46, 248, 250, 251, 254, 255, 298
Wedgwood, Sarah, 80
Weld, Angelina. *See* Grimké, Angelina
Weld, Charles, 295, 300
Weld, Charles Stuart, 186, 236, 266
Weld, Cornelia, 31, 35–36, 59, 88, 90, 96, 98, 226, 266, 295, 300
Weld, Theodore: Stuart's financial assis-

tance to, 31, 34, 97; influence on Stuart, 66, 88, 105; influenced by Stuart, 2, 4–5, 65–66, 95–98, 106, 123–24, 137; changing relations with Stuart, 6–8, 40, 89, 101–102, 122, 141–42, 151–52, 157, 161, 164–65, 172–73, 177, 178–79, 183, 186, 212, 213–14, 223–26, 236, 240–41, 243, 251–54, 257–60, 264–66, 272, 277, 281, 283–87, 295–98, 300, 305–306; as Finney revivalist, 31–37; as abolitionist, 64–65, 72, 84, 95–98, 121–24, 128, 134
Weld, Theodore, Jr., 223–24, 236
West Country abolitionists, 45, 46, 244, 246–51. *See also* Bath; Blair, William; Bristol and Clifton Auxiliary Ladies Anti-Slavery Society
Western Reserve College, 72, 95, 101
West India interest, 46, 86, 174
West India Question, 50, 58, 71, 72, 76, 135–36, 182, 262
West Indies, conditions after slavery: planter and freedmen's attitudes, 159–87; African immigration to, 244, 249, 250, 251, 267; European immigration to, 160, 178; Indian immigration to, 160, 168, 244, 266–67. *See also* Slavery; entries under names of specific islands
Whipple, George, 287–88
Whittier, John Greenleaf, 83–84, 90

Wilberforce, William, 6, 41, 76, 77, 88, 90, 135
Wilberforce Settlement, Canada, 70
Women abolitionists, 128, 189, 210, 224–25, 249, 250–51, 254. *See also* Birmingham Female Society for the Relief of Negro Slaves; Bristol and Clifton Auxiliary Ladies Anti-Slavery Society; Darlington Anti-Slavery Society Ladies Committee; Dublin Ladies Anti-Slavery Society; Evesham Ladies Anti-Slavery Society; Ladies Negro's Friend Societies of Birmingham, West Bromwich, Wednesbury, Walsall, and Their Respective Neighbourhoods; Massachusetts Female Anti-Slavery Society; Massachusetts Female Emancipation Society; Salem Ladies Anti-Slavery Society; Stuart, Captain Charles—antislavery beliefs and methods: on woman question
World Anti-Slavery Conventions: 1840, pp. 5, 186–87, 188–200, 212–13; 1843, pp. 252, 254–57, 260–61
Wright, Elizur, Jr., 72, 83, 93, 98, 102, 106–107, 127, 136, 194, 231, 259–60
Wright, Henry C., 135

Yerbury, Rebecca, 80